MW01620536

ANNA SUI

THE NINETIES

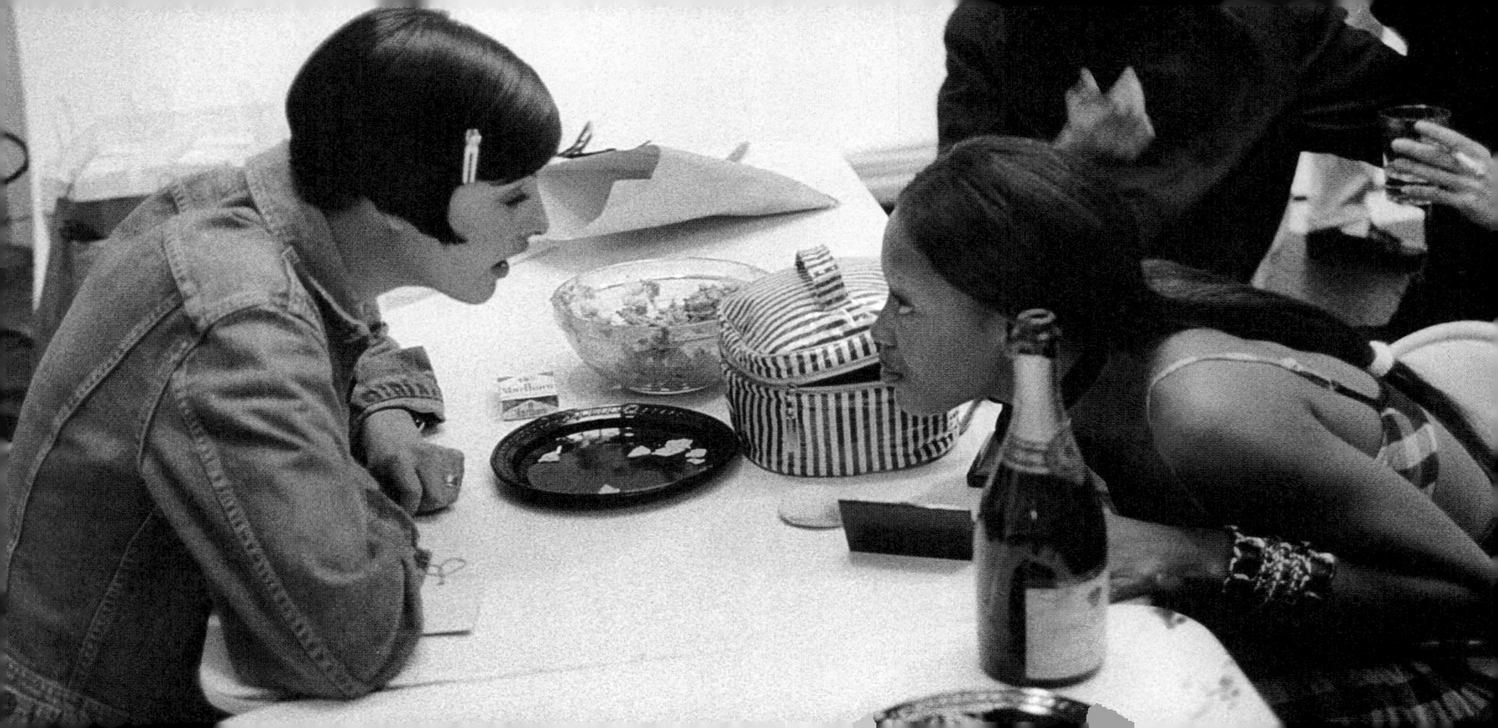

ANNA SUI

THE NINETIES

Edited by
Ileen Gallagher

With commentary by
Christy Turlington Burns
Sofia Coppola
Linda Evangelista
Marc Jacobs
Anna Sui
Steff Yotka

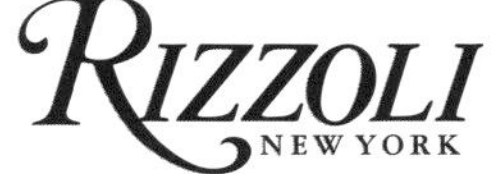

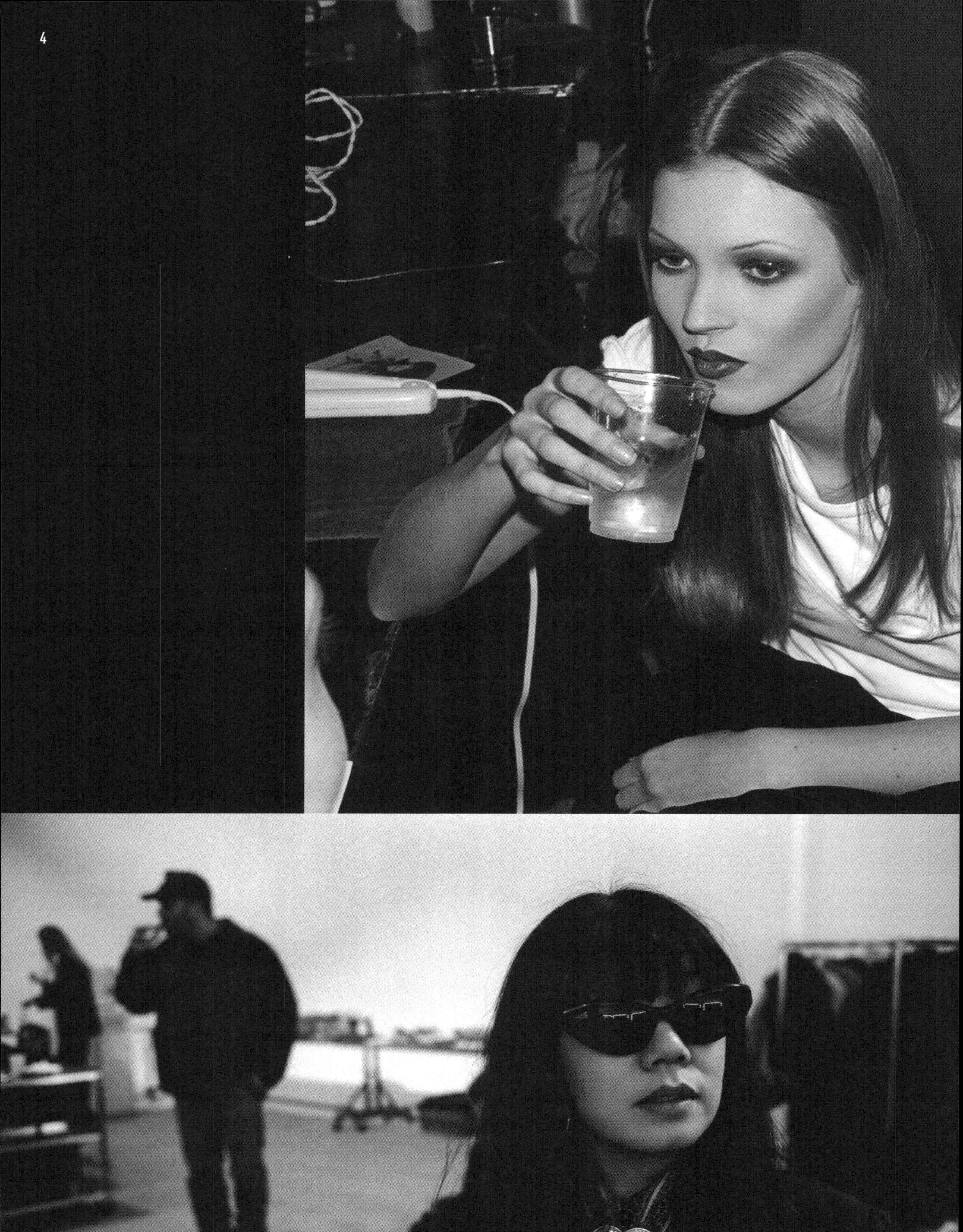

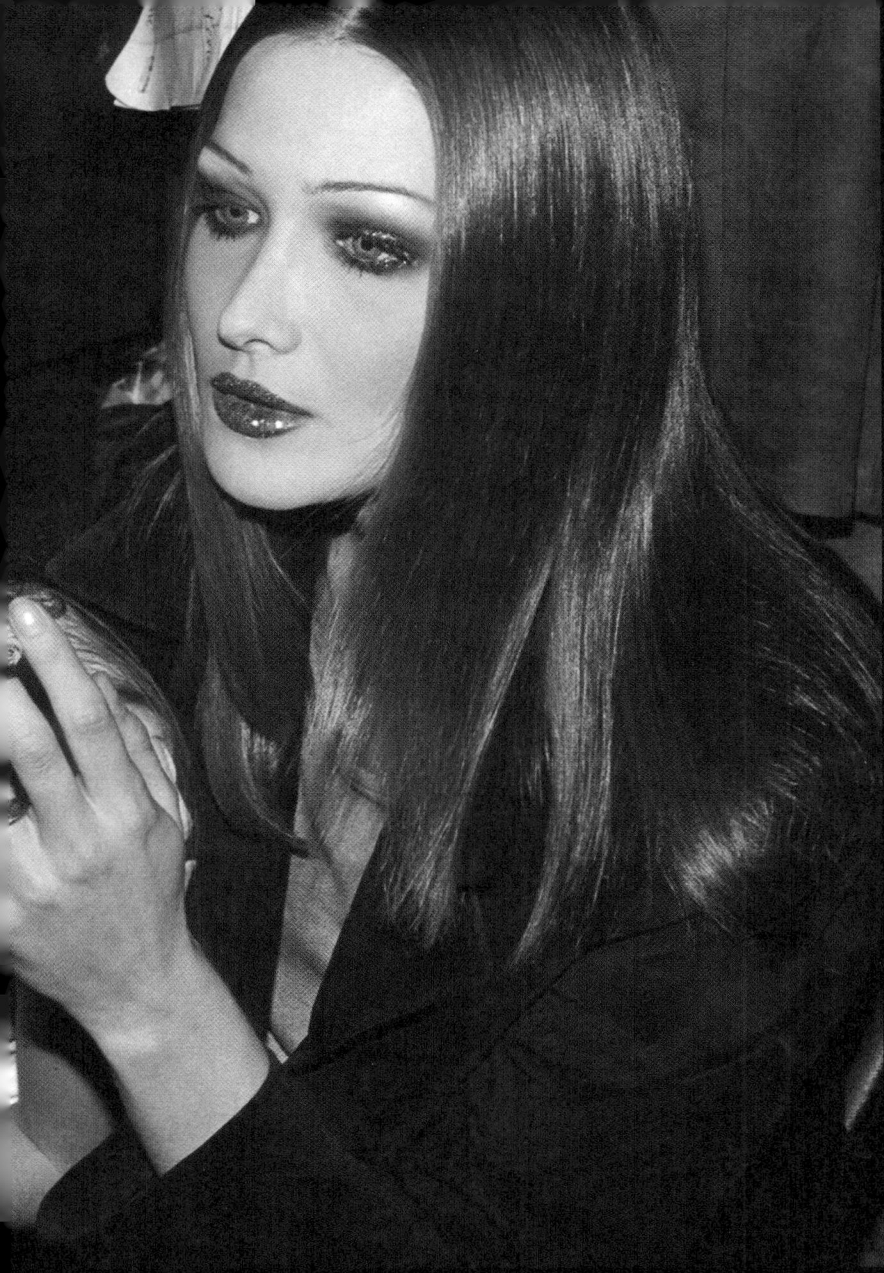

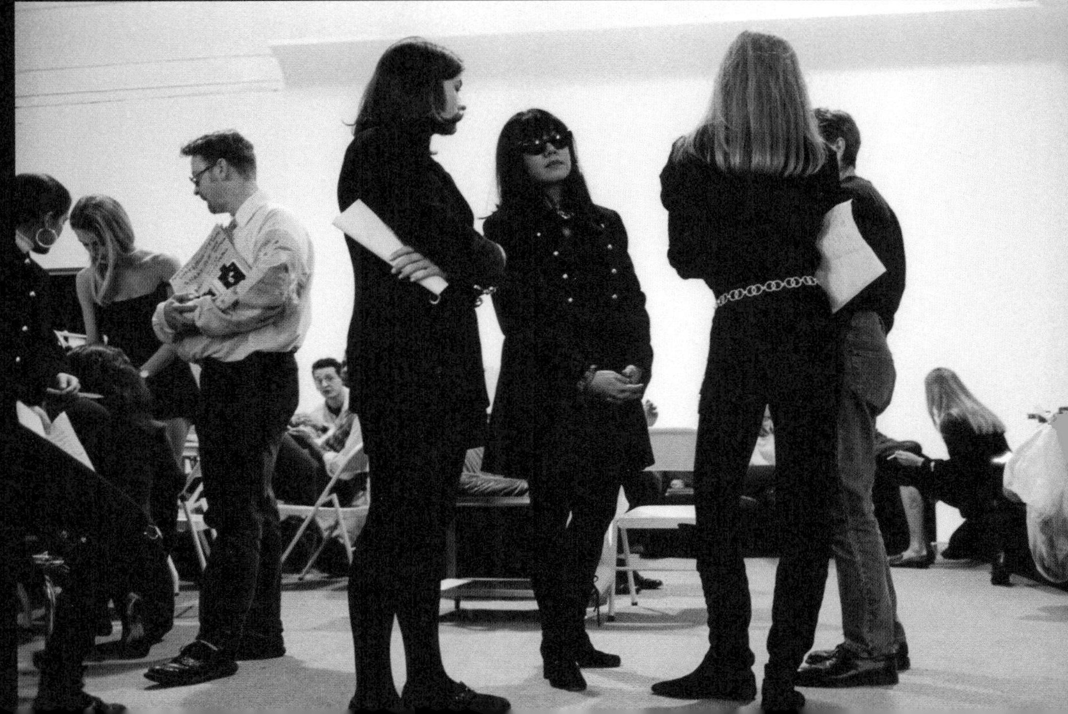

Kate Moss backstage, Fall 1992
Anna Sui backstage, Fall 1992
Carla Bruni backstage, Fall 1992

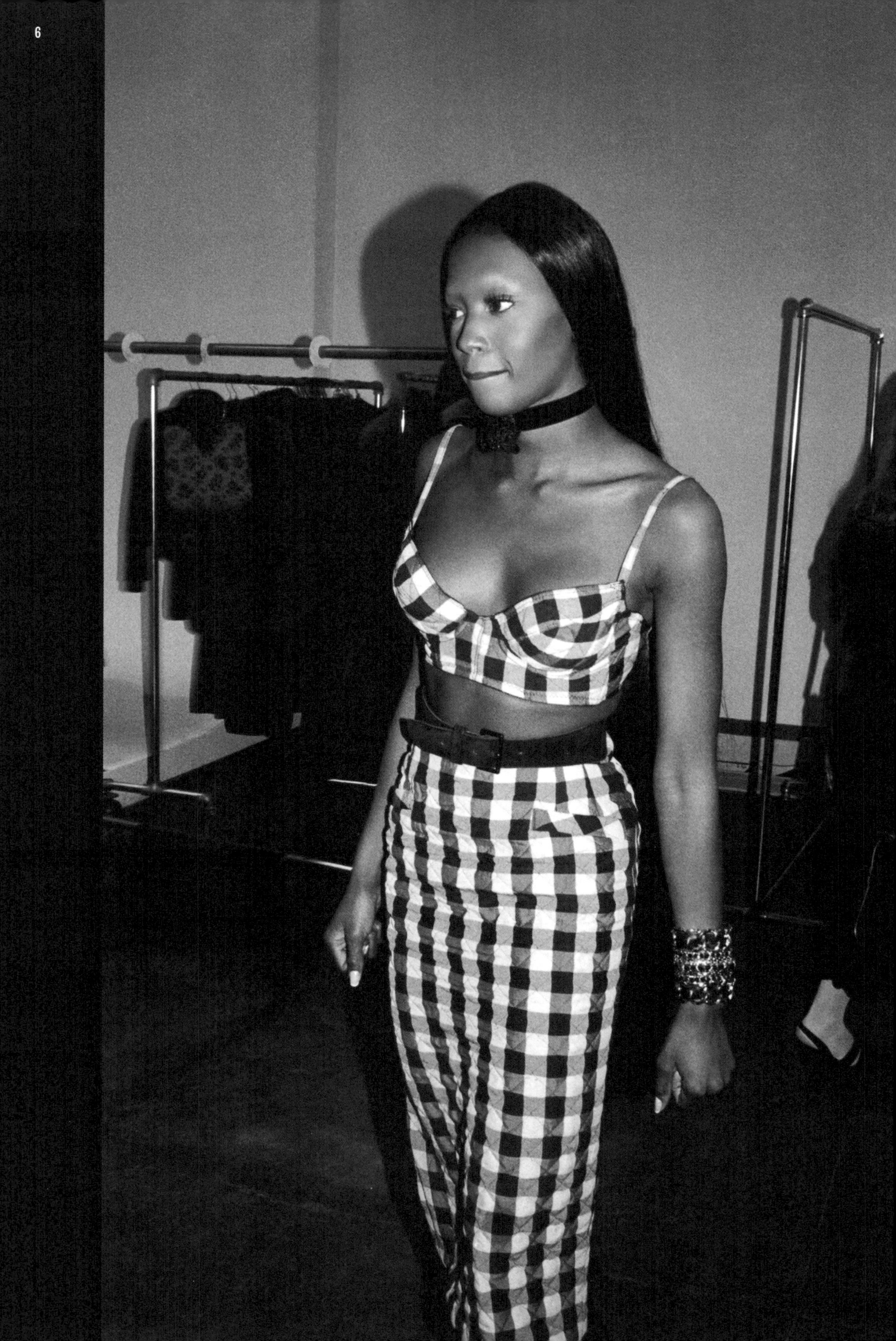

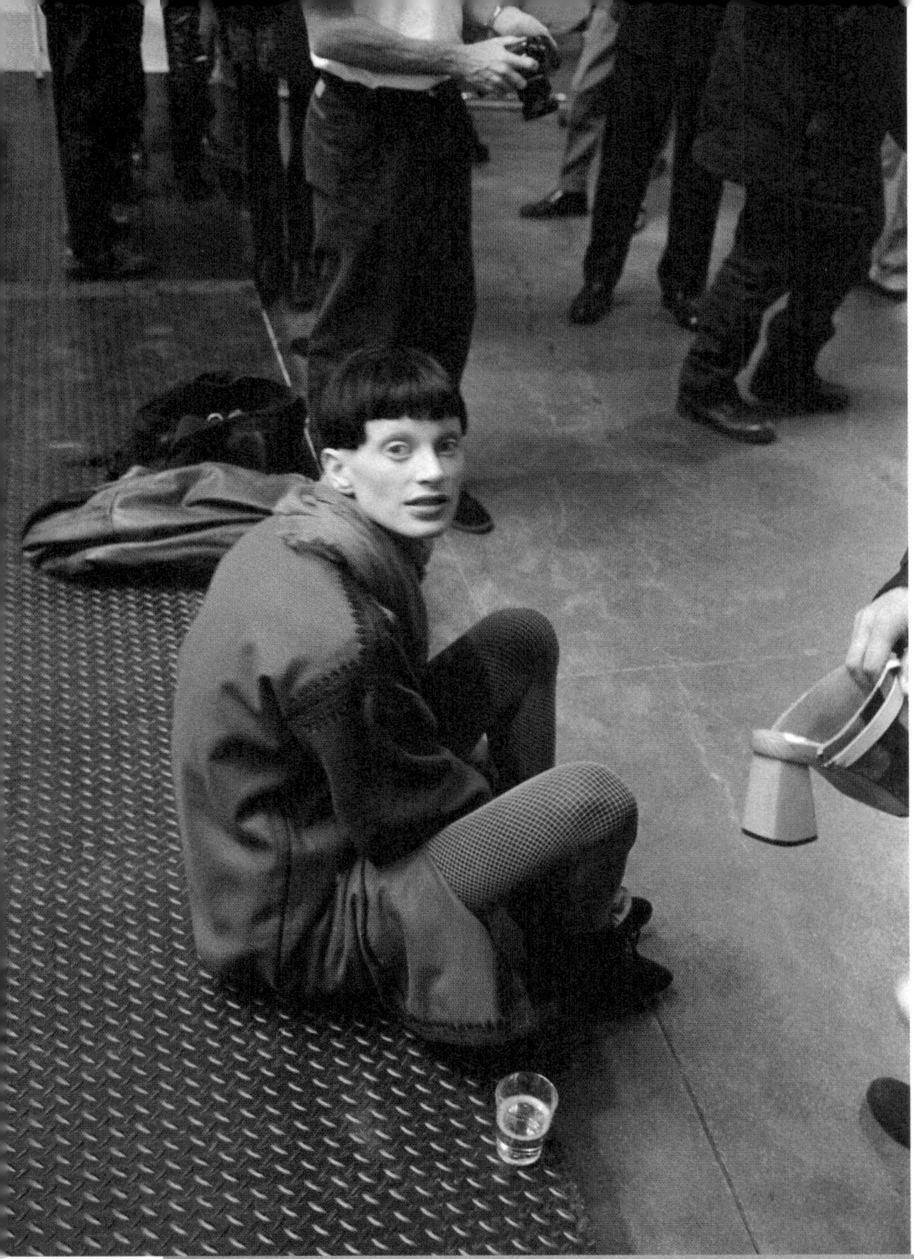

Naomi Campbell wearing Spring 1992 collection backstage, Fall 1992

Kristen McMenamy backstage, Fall 1992

Garren and Gail Elliot backstage, Fall 1992

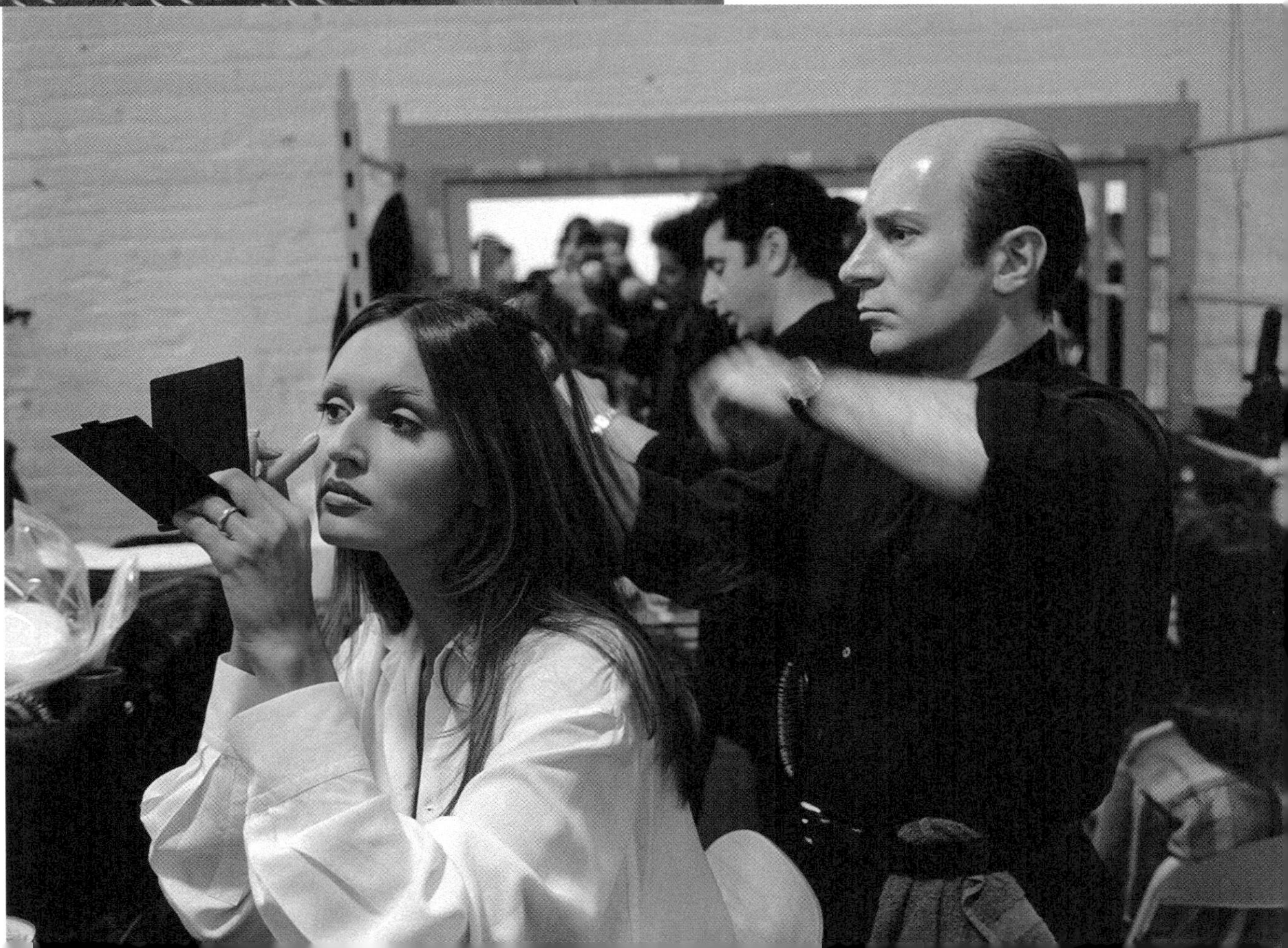

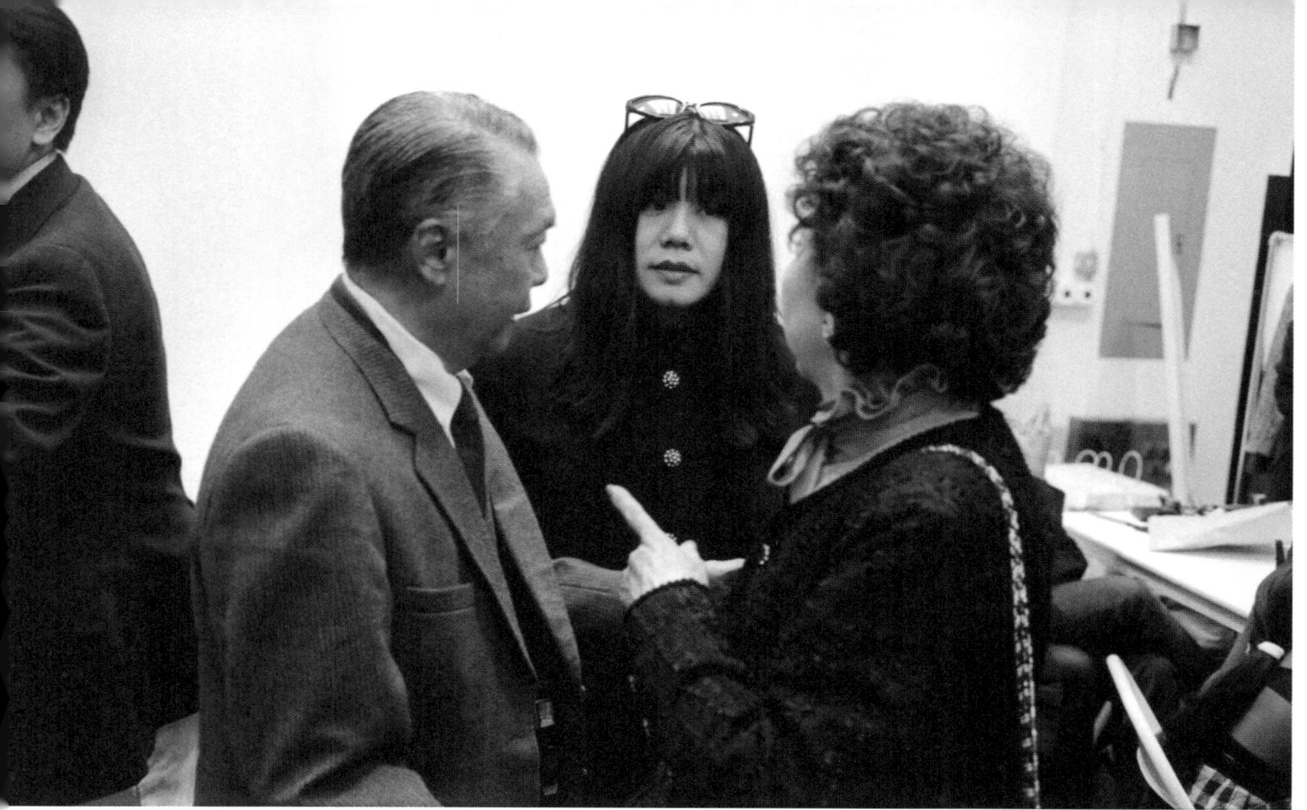

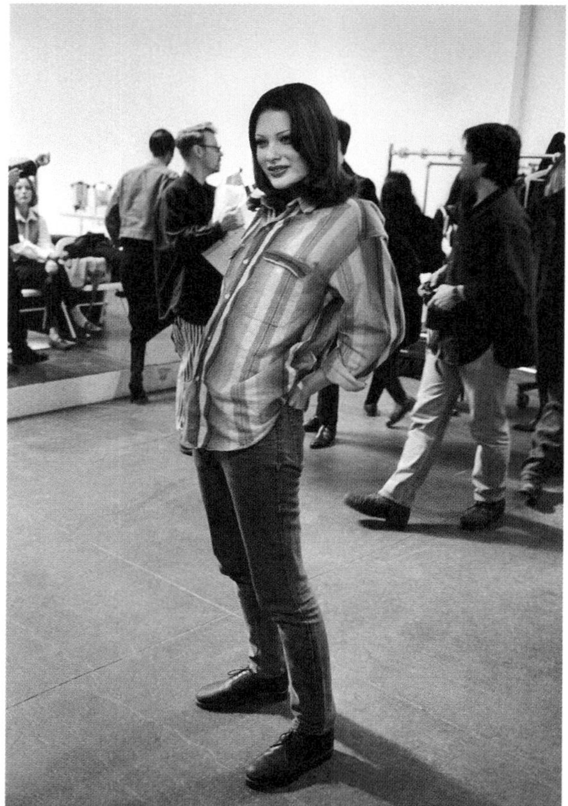

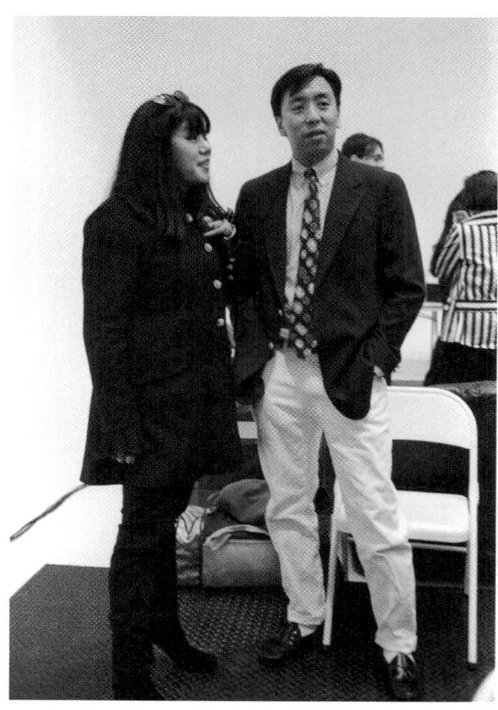

Anna Sui with her parents Grace and Paul Sui backstage, Fall 1992

Shalom Harlow backstage, Fall 1992

Anna and her brother Eddy Sui backstage, Fall 1992

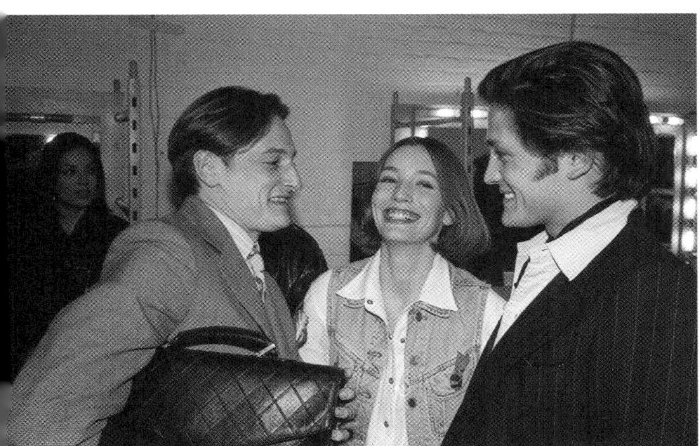

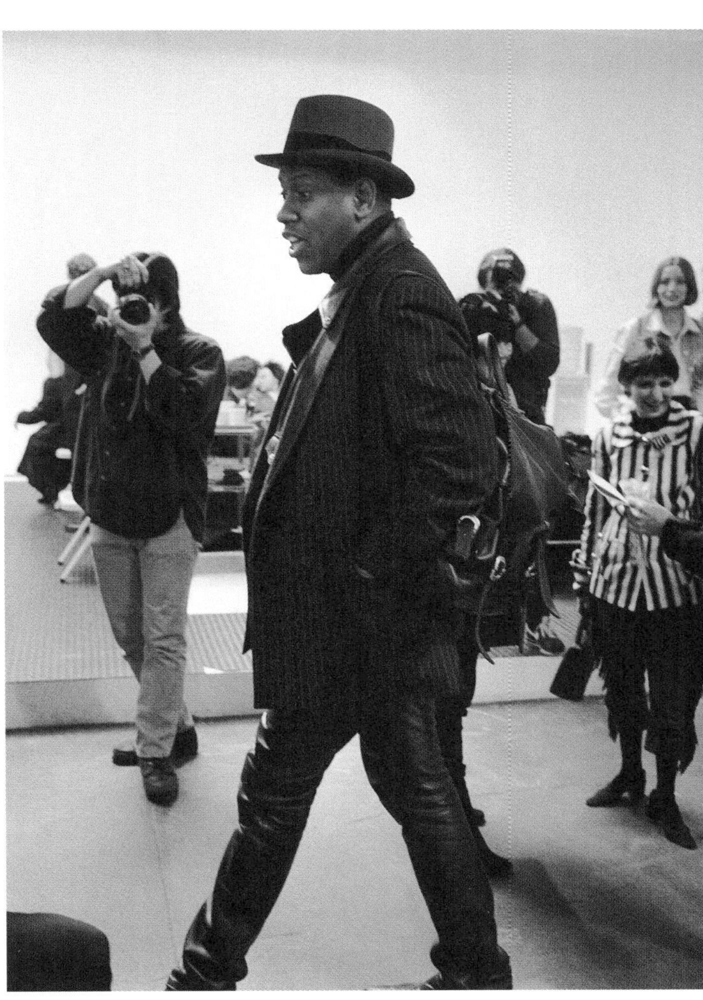

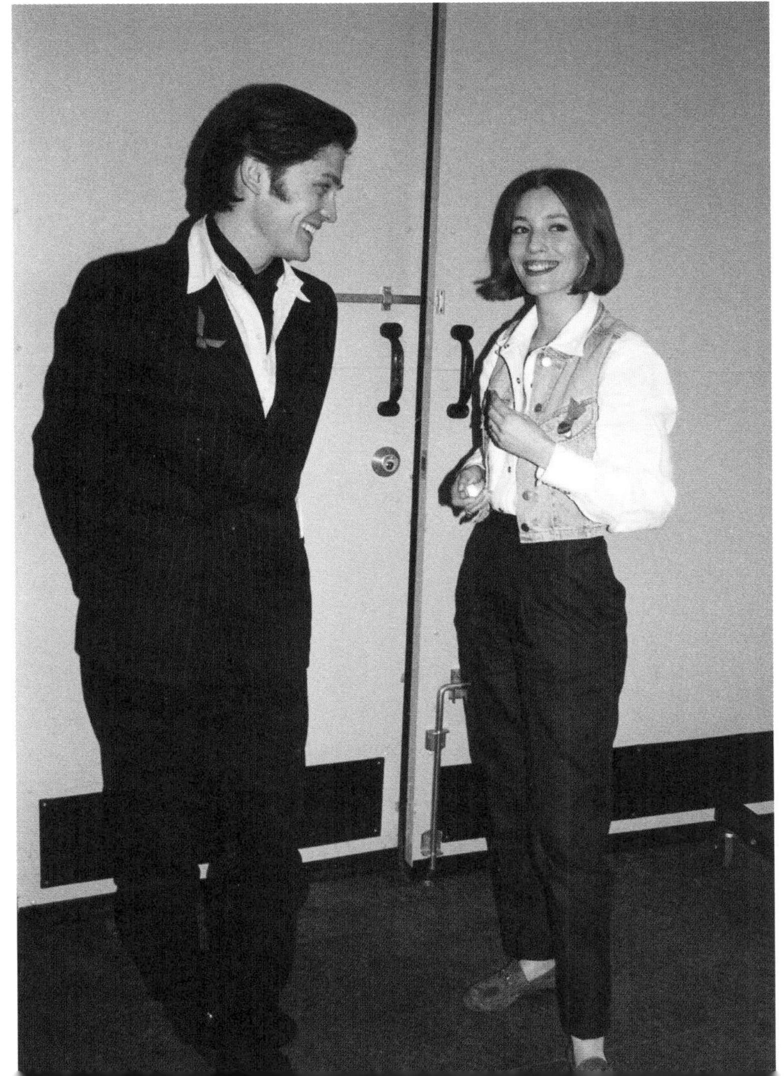

Hamish Bowles, Lucie de la Falaise and Daniel de la Falaise backstage, Fall 1992

André Leon Talley backstage, Fall 1992

Lucie and Daniel de la Falaise backstage, Fall 1992

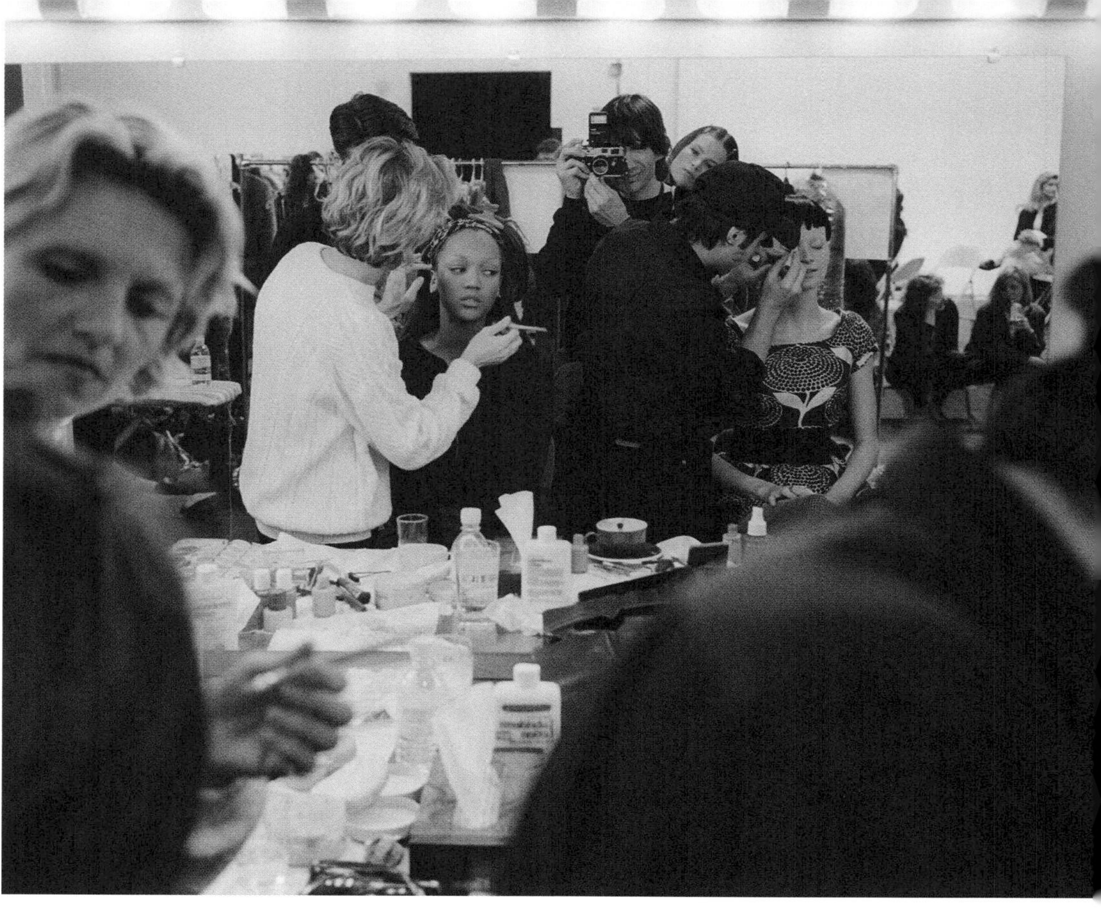

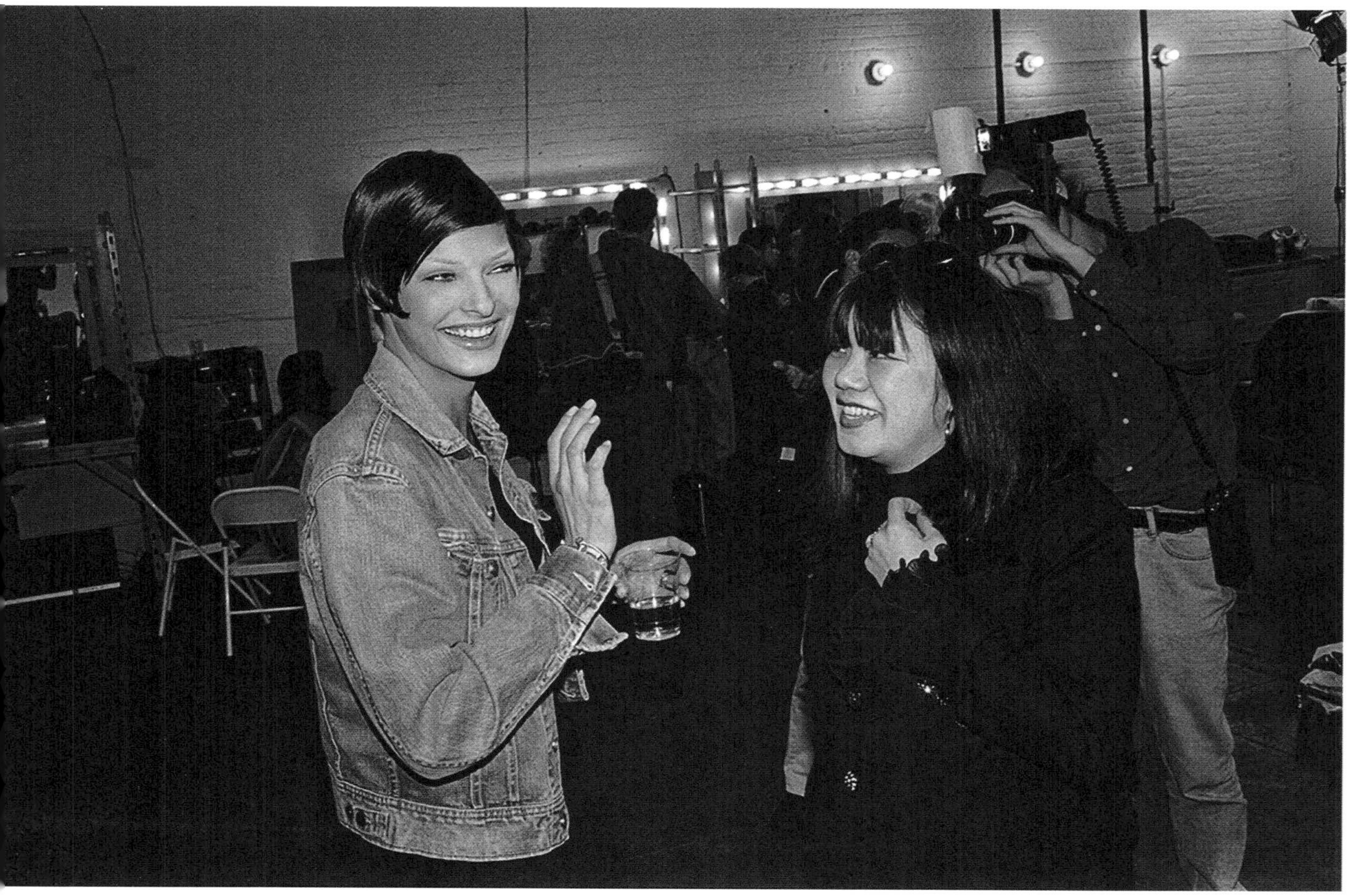

François Nars and his team backstage, Fall 1992
Linda Evangelista and Anna Sui backstage, Fall 1992

Linda Evangelista and Anna backstage, Fall 1992
Tom Priano and Garren backstage, Fall 1992
Naomi Campbell and guests backstage, Fall 1992

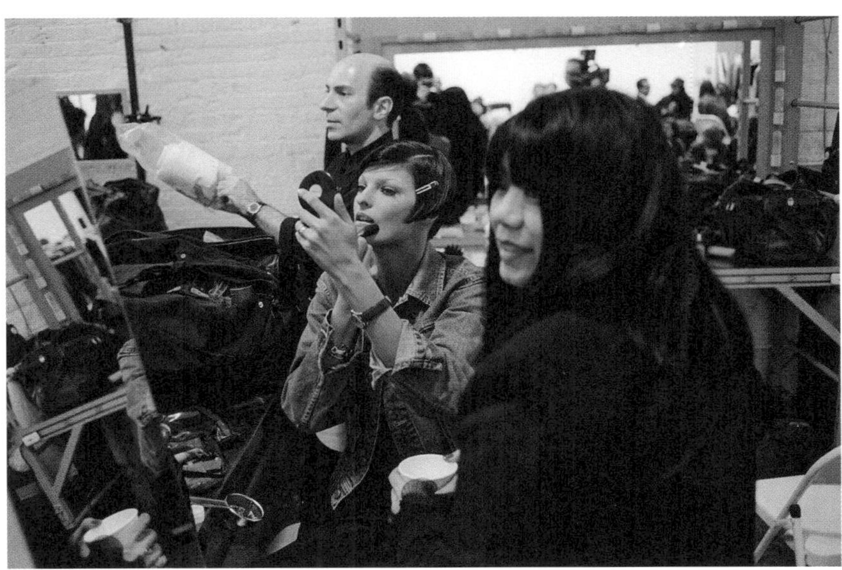

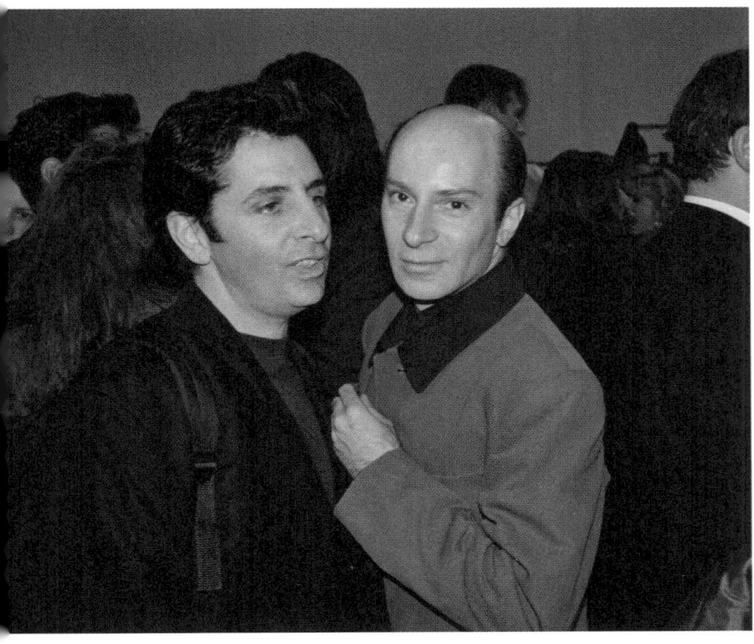

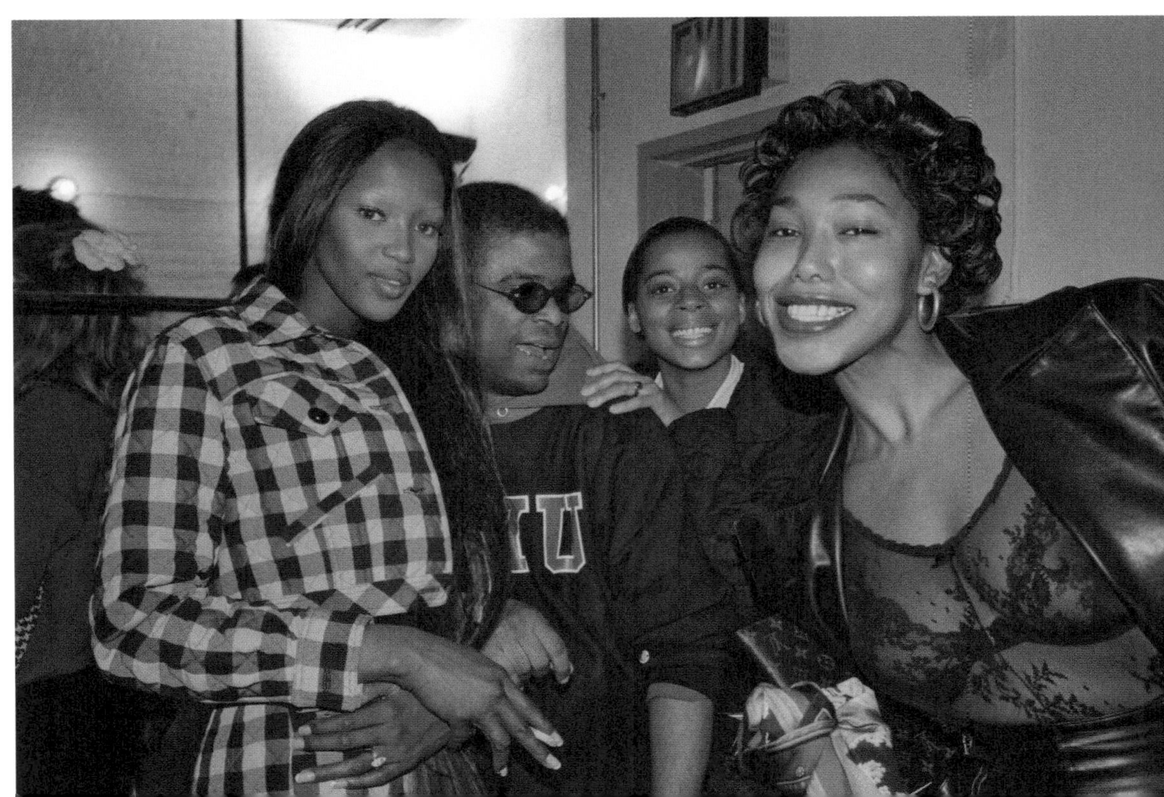

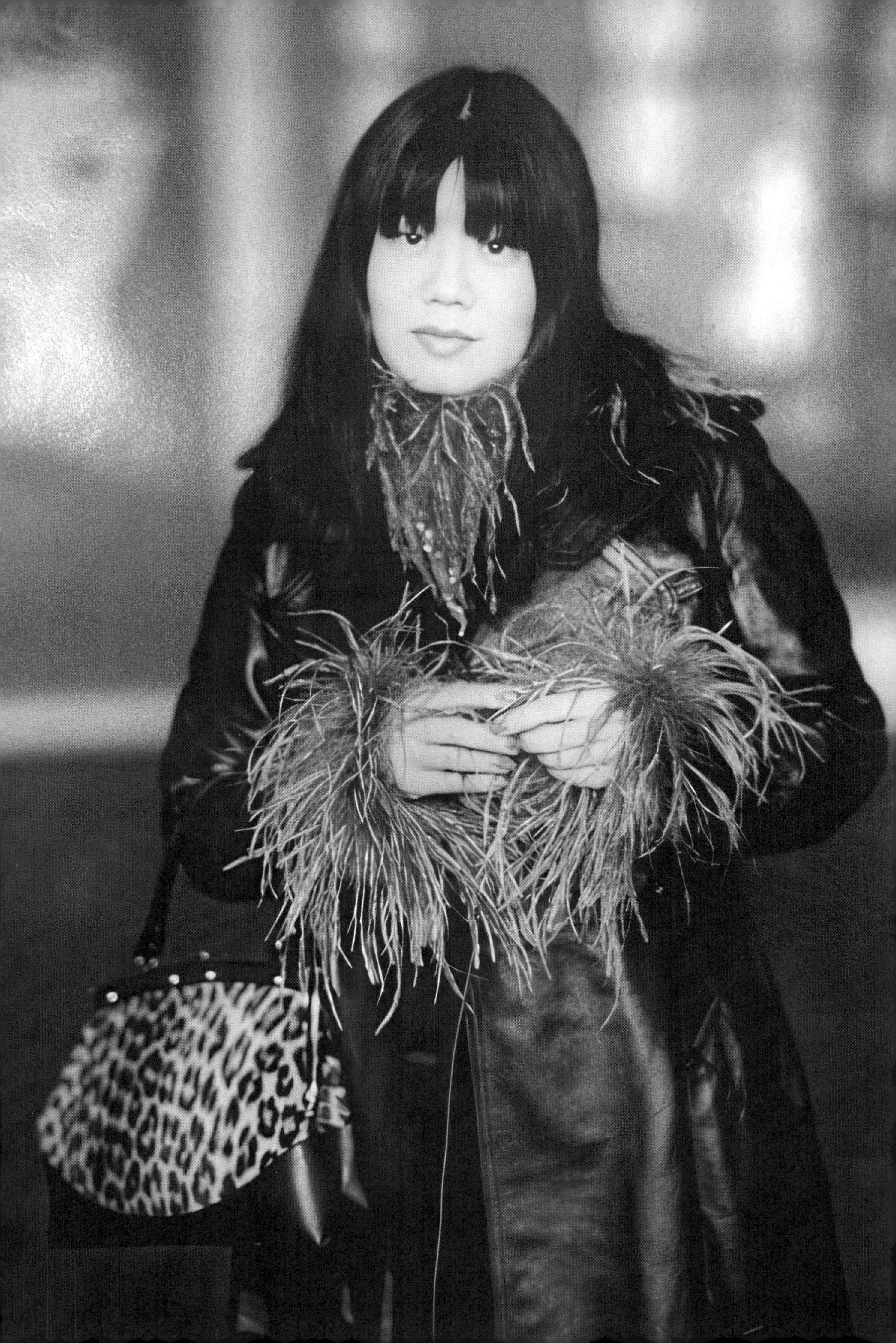

CONTENTS

Anna Sui, 1994

THE 90s

"In the 1990s and early 2000s, Sui's shows were among the hottest tickets during Fashion Week. Models such as Naomi Campbell and Linda Evangelista regularly walked the runway, fashion photographer Steven Meisel was a front-row regular and countless musicians turned up to watch the antics or to participate by providing a live soundtrack. It was a period when fashion and popular culture were still in their honeymoon phase and the combination of models, visual artists, actors, and musicians seemed organic and volatile—not something stage-managed for social media."

The Washington Post, September 13, 2019

Anna Sui and Naomi Campbell at Café Tabac, *New York* magazine, 1993

Matchbooks from Barocco and Café Tabac restaurants in New York City

ANNA SUI

In the '90s there was a small circle of people, and we all went to the same restaurants, clubs, bars, and parties. There was Cafe Tabac, which was the place. And anytime you went there, you would run into at least ten people that you knew. And then there was another a little restaurant on West 10th Street called Piadina and that was a popular place for dinner, too. And then you would hear so-and-so is having a party or a band we loved was in town—you found things out word of mouth in the pre-internet days. And there was so much happening. The MTV Awards was always a really big night. The Paramount and Royalton hotels were huge. There were lots of big parties at Lucky Strike and Barocco—in fact, those famous pictures of Madonna with Tupac were taken at Barocco. And then of course there was the Odeon, Indochine, and Balthazar. It was a movable feast; people would gravitate towards different restaurants, and they'd be the place to go for a while and then you'd move on to someplace else.

When I started doing fashion shows, we had Donovan Leitch in our show. And he was really close friends with Sofia Coppola and Zoe Cassavetes. They came out to New York when Donovan was modeling for us. Then somehow they convinced me to go out to LA to open a store, which I did. When we had our grand opening, they brought all their friends. There were lots of dinner parties in LA. Donovan's sister Ione Skye was married to Adam Horowitz from the Beastie Boys, so we became good friends with the Beastie Boys. Sonic Youth was out there, too. It was very organic and we all just hung out together.

CHRISTY TURLINGTON BURNS

I met Anna in the pretty early days. I got to New York in '84. I started to work with Steven Meisel quite a lot around '86. Steven and Anna were super close from their Parsons School of Design days. There was a clique, a small group of people that included Paul Cavaco [stylist and later founder of KCD]; Richard Sohl, who was in Patti Smith's band; and Louis Chaban [who worked for Anna and then Ford modeling agency]. We did a lot of just hanging out, at Anna's apartment or at the SoHo apartment of the makeup artist François Nars.

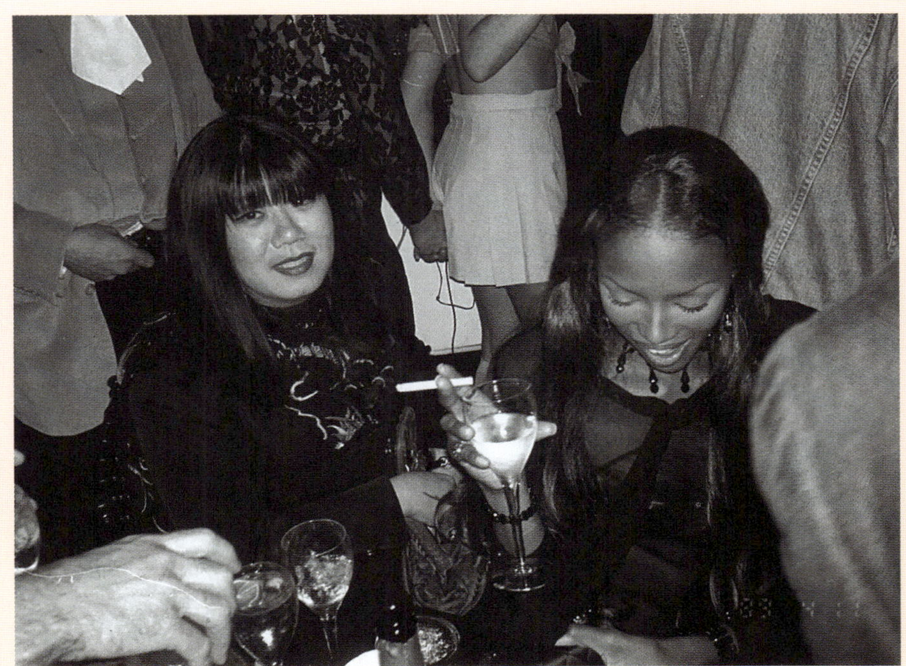

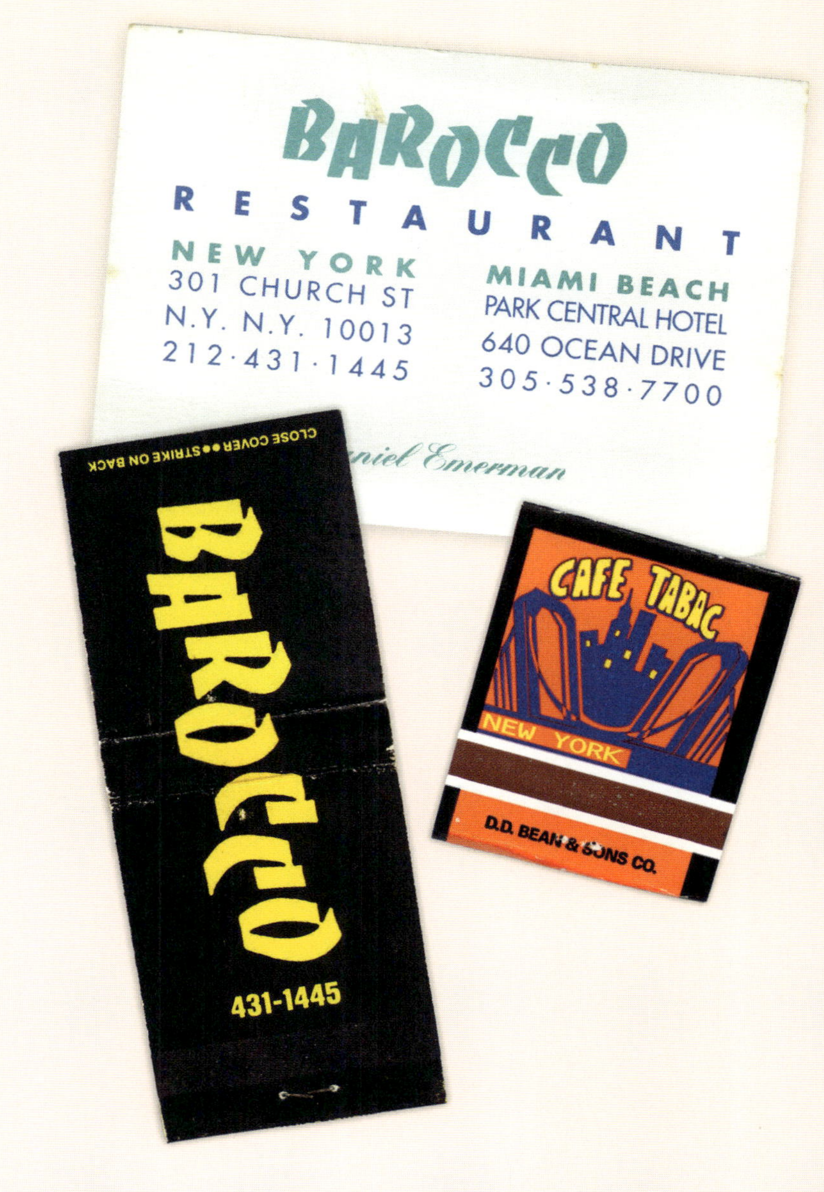

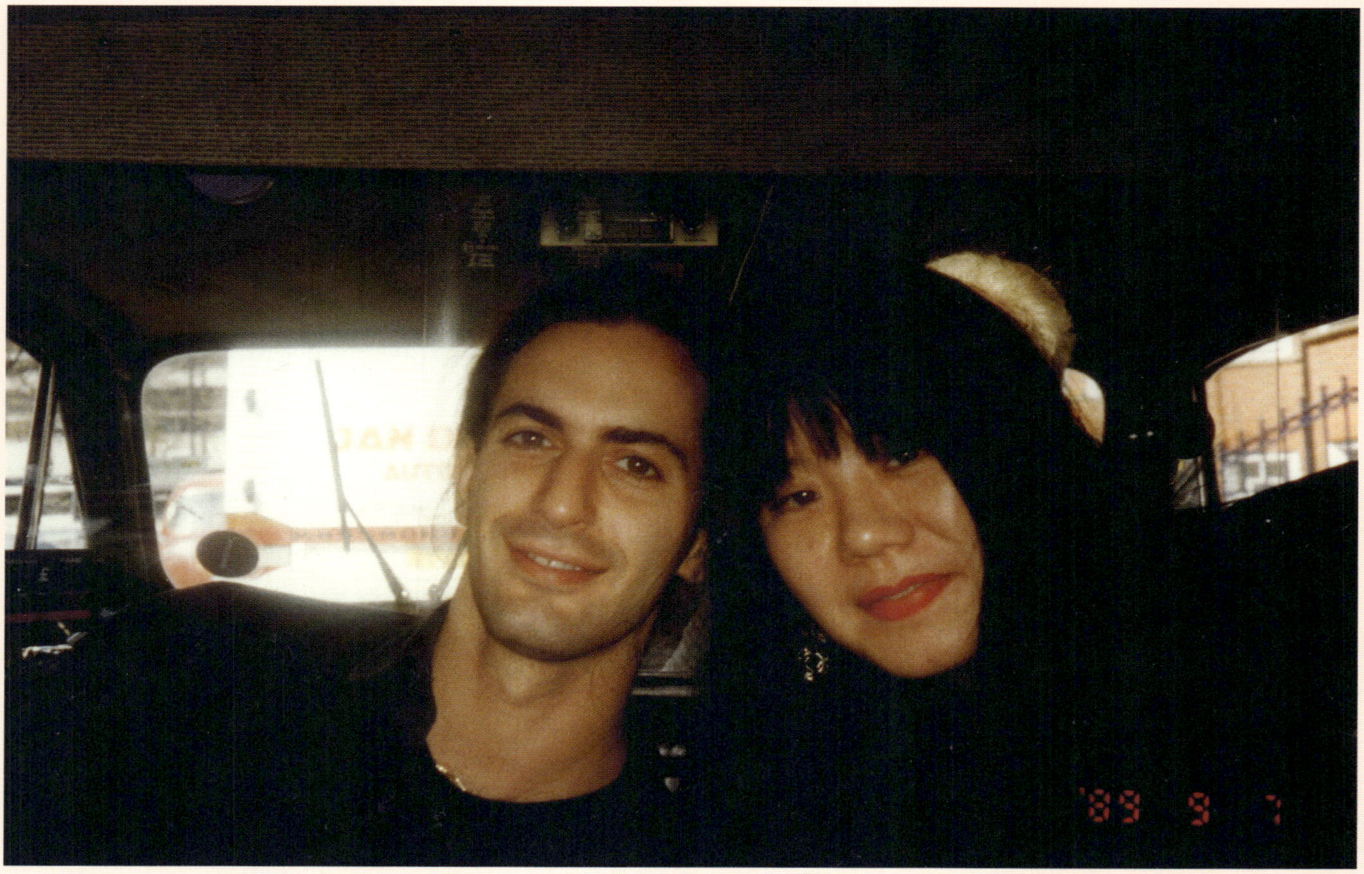

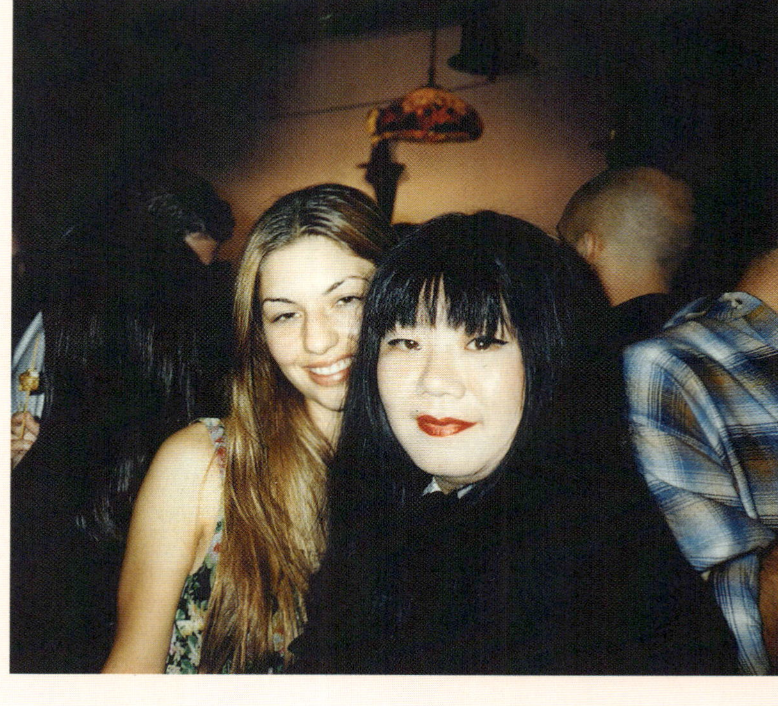

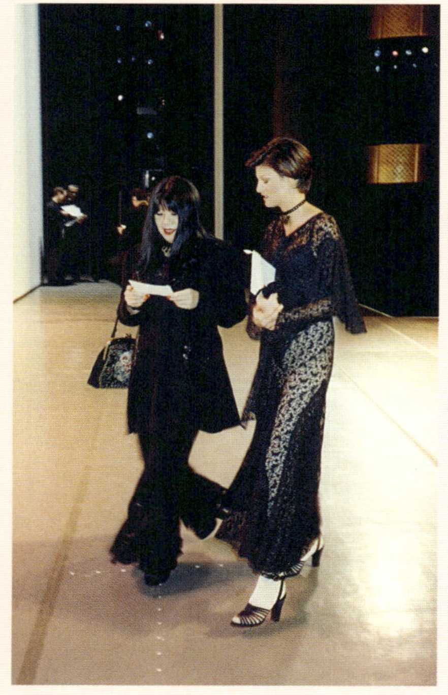

Marc Jacobs and Anna Sui, ca. 1993

Sofia Coppola and Anna Sui at the opening of the Anna Sui store, La Brea Avenue, Hollywood, California, 1993

Anna Sui and Linda Evangelista at the CFDA awards where Anna received the Perry Ellis Award for New Talent, 1992

Lots of dinners. Restaurant culture was emerging then. The McNallys dominated New York eateries in those years. And, if there was a new place, we would go as a group and check it out. There wasn't a lot of clubbing, so there wasn't as much interest to be in those spaces. Although we would often drive around and park across the street from the clubs and just watch people go in to see how people were dressed. They called it "spooking." We would do a lot of spooking around downtown.

Fashion is cyclical, right? If you looked at the '80s, they looked back at the '60s. Generally there would be a generation between the current moment and the moment that inspired it. I think the '90s had a lot of '70s influence, which is why I think Anna was so in the moment and in the right place to make those connections.

The Andy Warhol mythos was still very present at that time. So many people that I've talked to over the years were driven to New York because of how he presented it in his work. There was this sense that if you didn't belong in your hometown, you could come to New York and you could find your people. It's like the land of the misfits. Fashionwise, there was such a weird mix then. There was a convergence of grunge, which was kind of new, but kind of old, too. That was a throwback to the '70s, the flannels and the T-shirts. But then there was also the club kid scene. In the same night, you may go to a Nirvana concert, but then you may also go to a club that had all those club kids. Again, we weren't really going to the clubs that much then, but you couldn't help but notice the scene. The Limelight had a big night for the club kids, and it was kind of infamous. Even before that, there was the drag queen/trans scene and voguing—it was incredible. Steven would do a lot of shoots that brought these worlds together. I remember in one particular shoot where he had Louise Bourgeois, Lady Bunny, and Eagle Eye Cherry. It was this weird eclectic mix. It was such an education for me. I came to New York when I was in my teen years, but by the '90s, I felt like a New Yorker. One of the most beautiful aspects of that time is that you didn't have the kind of ageism that exists today. There was much more flow, and you could be a teenager and sit down with Andy Warhol, or anyone of a much older generation. It was such a cool thing to have that kind of color and flavor and experience. Just to know that you were at a table with people who also knew the Beats and had seen every band and had maybe gone to Woodstock. There was this amazing sense of a continuum at that time, or at least a desire to embrace that continuum. The '90s were unique in that it brought together so many different worlds in a relatively short period of time. I think what people are most nostalgic for from that time is the privacy, possessing a sense of some mystery, not being reachable at all times, making plans and sticking to them. You didn't have the opportunity to constantly change the plan—or maybe you did change your plans but you had to be there in real time and be present regardless.

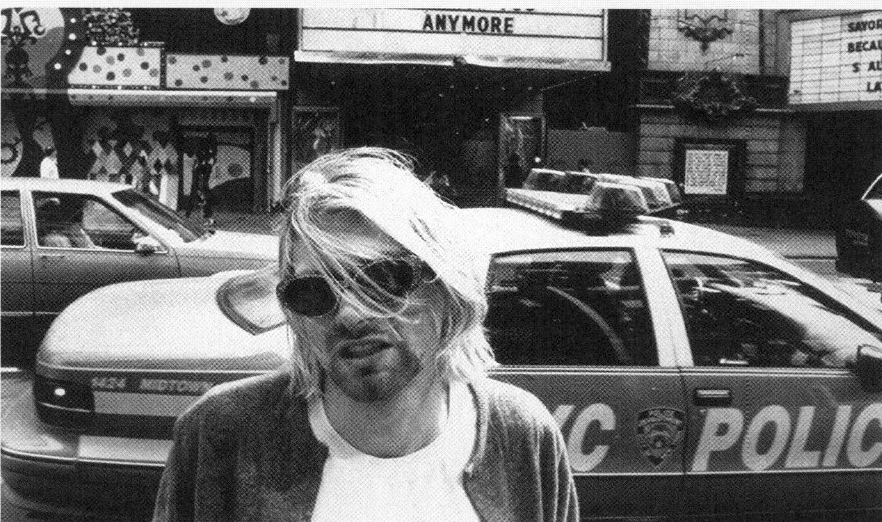

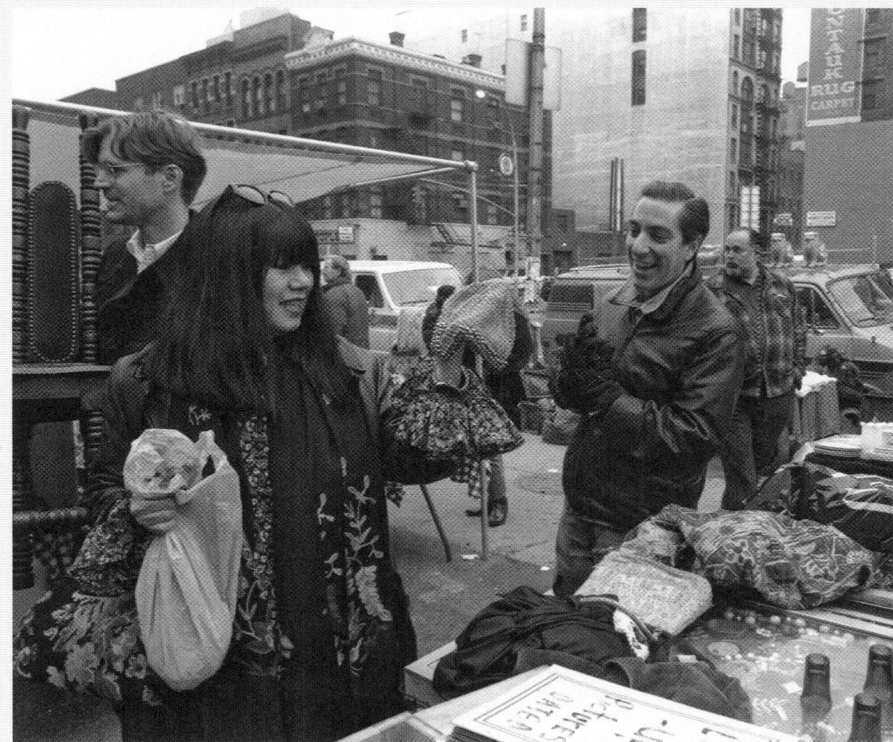

Kurt Cobain, 42nd Street, New York City, July 24, 1993

Anna Sui, Paul Cavaco, and Tim Sheaffer at the 25th Street flea market, New York City, 1992

SOFIA COPPOLA

In the early '90s I lived in LA and spent time in New York. I remember a moment where Fashion Week and the MTV Awards and Halloween were all at the same time. New York was really fun to visit. I met Anna around that time through my friends Zoe Cassavetes and Donovan Leitch. I just hit it off with Anna because we share a lot of interests. She was really into music, design, and culture. We became friends. When she came to Los Angeles to open her store, she asked me where the store should be, and we took her around. I also had a little magazine video show, and we videotaped Anna for it. I loved what she was doing, and it was fun to go to her shows. She was one of the first people to have guys and girls together on the runway, and that was unique to her. When Marc Jacobs and Anna started doing shows, all of a sudden it was like the kids were in charge and they made clothes that spoke to us—it wasn't our mom's generation.

MARC JACOBS

Looking back at the '90s there was this huge change in fashion, and I think a lot of that had to do with the music of grunge and the popularity of alternative and indie music. There was also a whole new group of photographers who saw things differently than the way they were in the '80s: the big hair, the big production shoots, the lights, the type of woman that was being celebrated. What happened in the '90s was that all of a sudden there was a new group of models led by Kate Moss and photographers like Corinne Day, Jurgen Teller, David Sims, and Craig McLean. It was the excitement of this dramatic change in fashion and the idea of what was all of a sudden fashionable. It was a direct contrast to what came before it. The idea of clothes changed greatly, the shoulder pads were gone, and they were replaced by something more edgy and rough, with a slightly bohemian or music-related vibe to it. It's just a completely different vibe and that was what was exciting about it. I think if that didn't stick, or if there wasn't any substance in that change, then you wouldn't see it being popular again today. We felt differently than the people that came before us, the interest in doing something else felt right and genuine.

I had met Anna before that moment, but we really became friends in '92 or '93. I think the first time I saw her it was probably on the rooftop at Danceteria and I didn't know her. And then later, I saw her at Charivari, where I worked. She was dressed in this new romantic style. But it was after we both did grunge collections at the same time that we became closer friends and started hanging out. We had mutual friends, one of which was our dear friend whom we both love very much, Anita Pallenberg. I know she's been a huge inspiration to Anna.

I remember going to her shows and it was like going to a rock concert. The music was great, the boys, the girls, they all looked super cool. There was always this spot-on kind of reflection of youth culture and music culture.

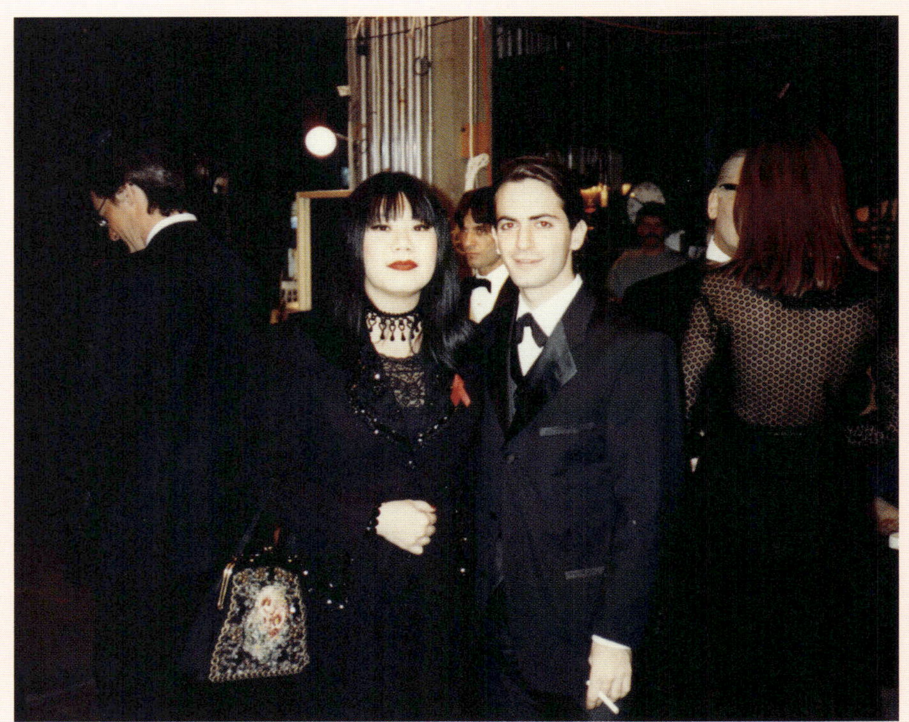

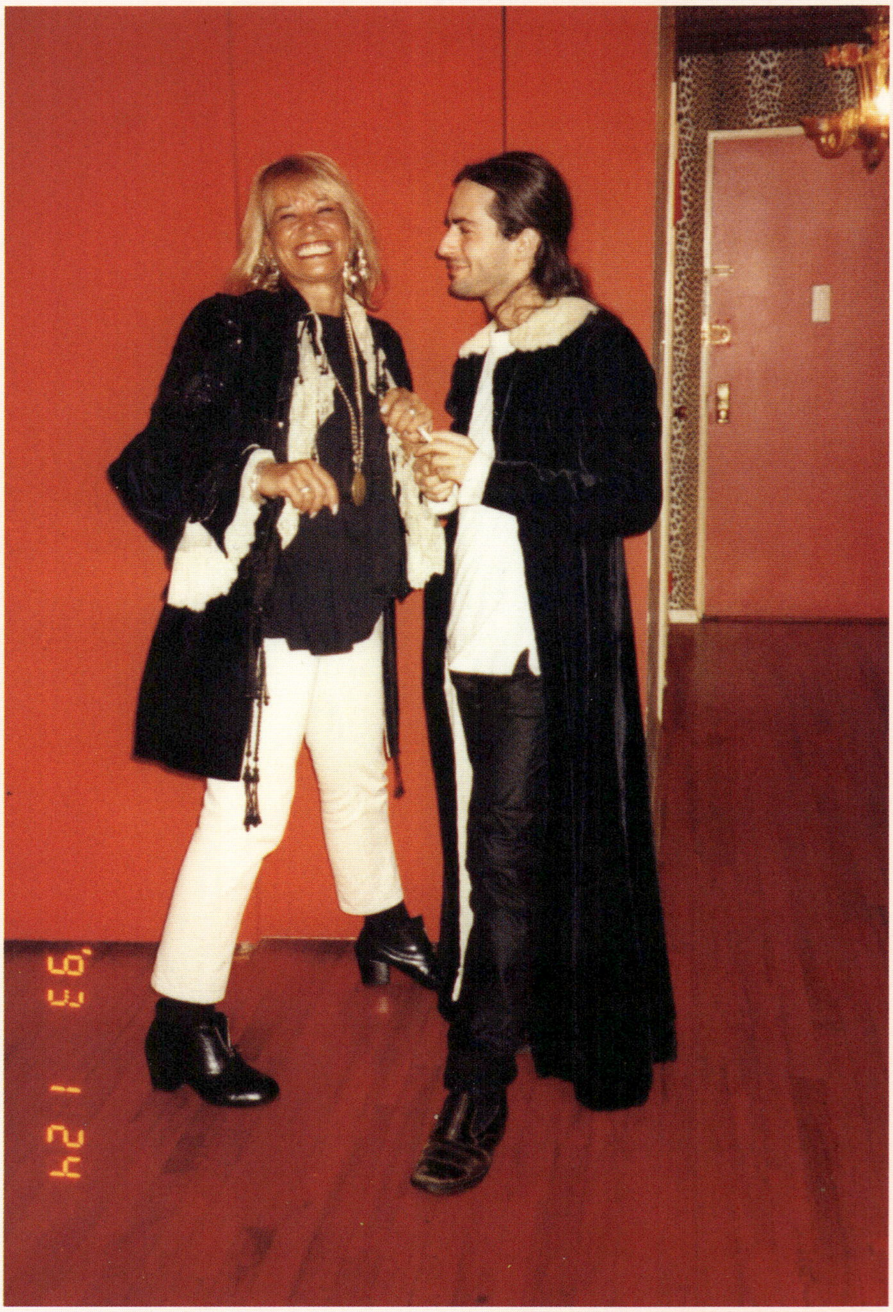

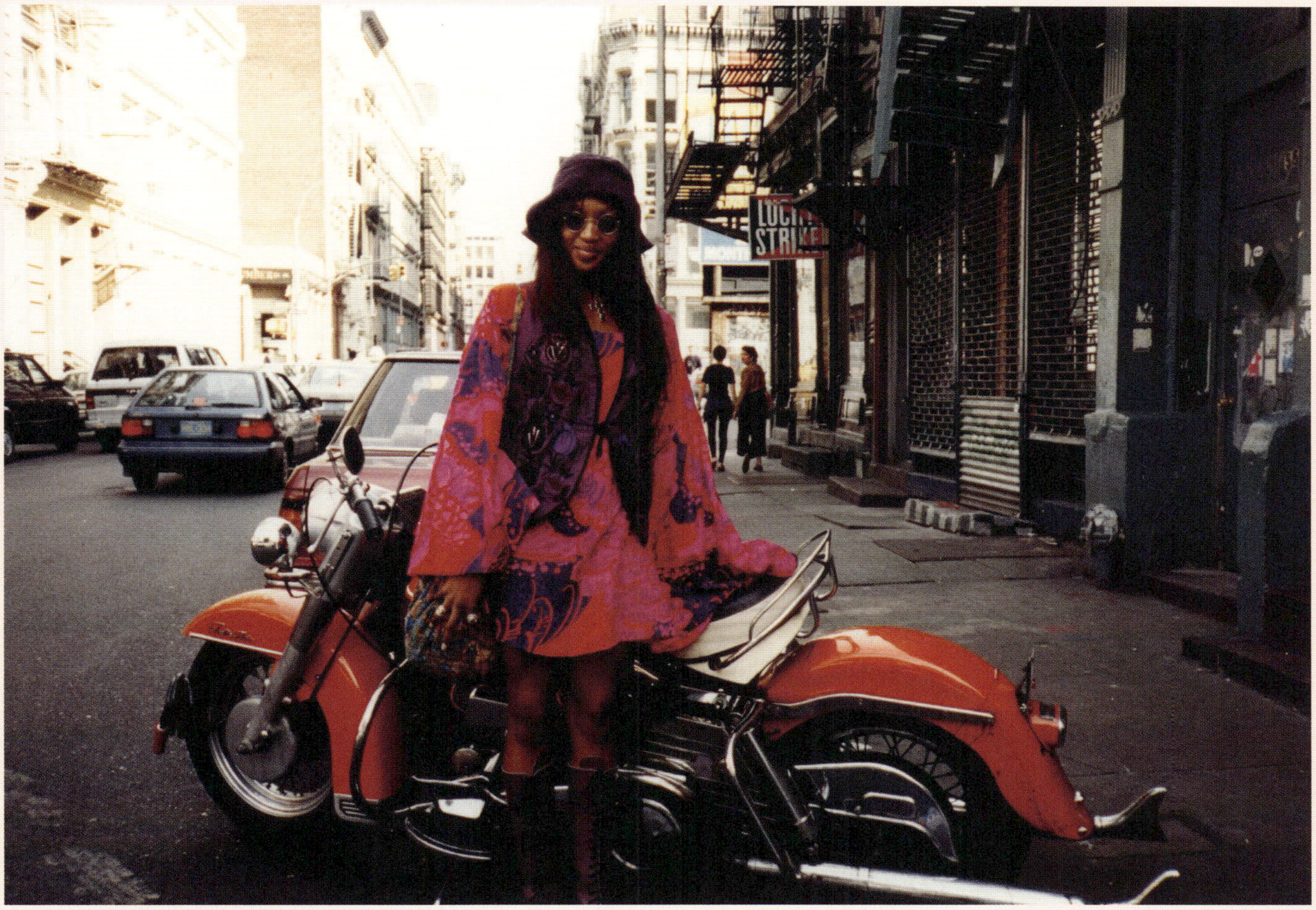

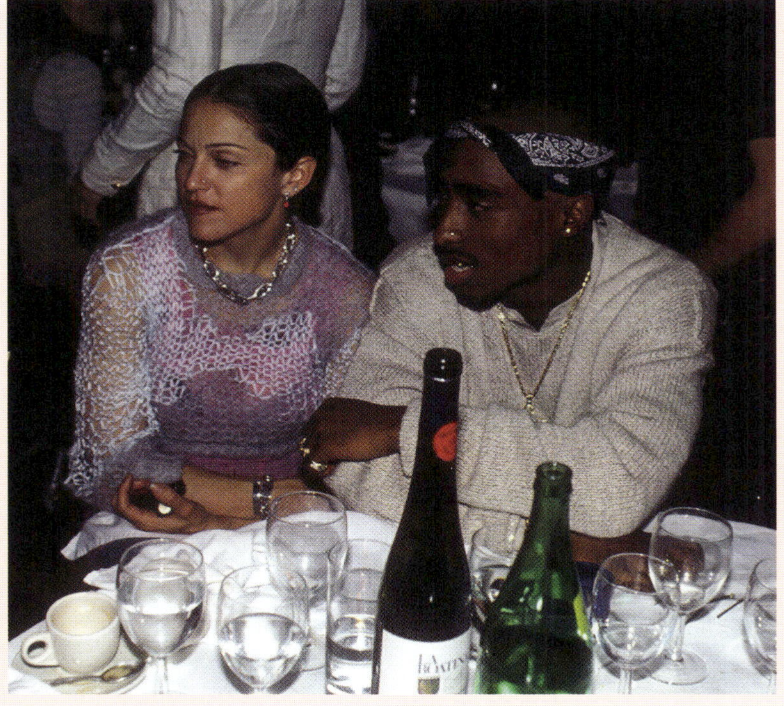

It was a big event to go to an Anna show. You had this beautiful coming together of the most perfect hairdresser, the most perfect makeup artist, and these great girls, and showing these kinds of really youthful, cool clothes, set to great music, and that wasn't what New York Fashion Week looked like—it was very, very specific to Anna.

Anna's clothes had the wonderful quality of youth that you can't buy or fake. I mean, you can buy it as a customer, but you can't as a manufacturer or as somebody else. I feel Anna was very unique at that point and it was so popular because it just didn't exist. And it struck a chord in all the young girls, be they customers or the models who are wearing the clothes.

There is always this kind of cycle in fashion where things come back, of course: people were doing the '30s and '40s in the '70s, that was a big thing. Fashion is cyclical but even more than just being cyclical, I do think that what happened in that moment in the early '90s was a way of dressing and a way of thinking about clothes that hadn't existed before. That was new. And it spoke to people, particularly younger women who were into fashion. Something about that aesthetic in that moment and something about the style has some validity beyond that time and, in many ways, it just never really went away.

Anna Sui and Marc Jacobs at CFDA awards honoring Anna, 1992

Anita Pallenberg and Marc Jacobs at Anna's apartment, 1993

Naomi Campbell in front of the Anna Sui store, 113 Greene Street, SoHo, New York City, ca. 1992

Madonna and Tupac Shakur at *Interview* magazine party, New York City, March 1, 1994

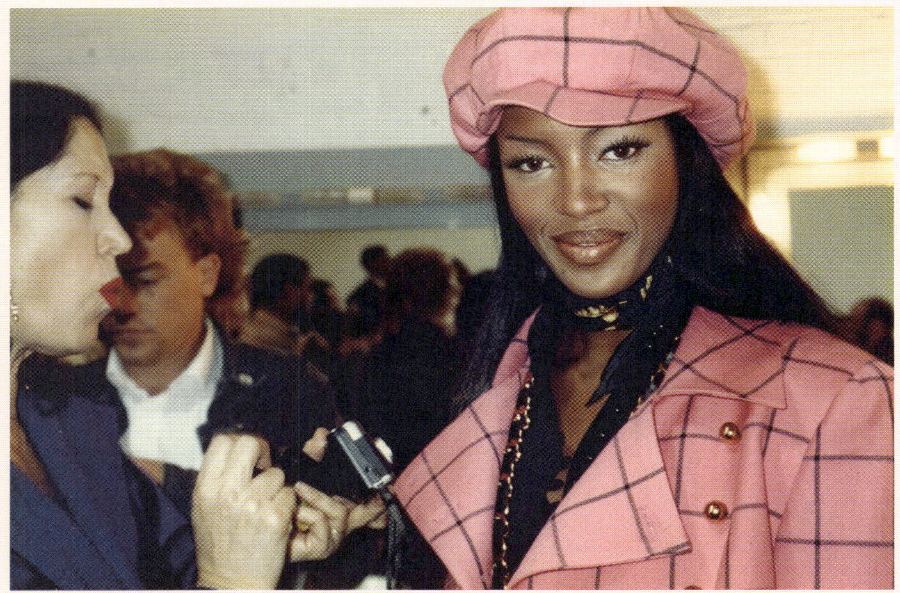

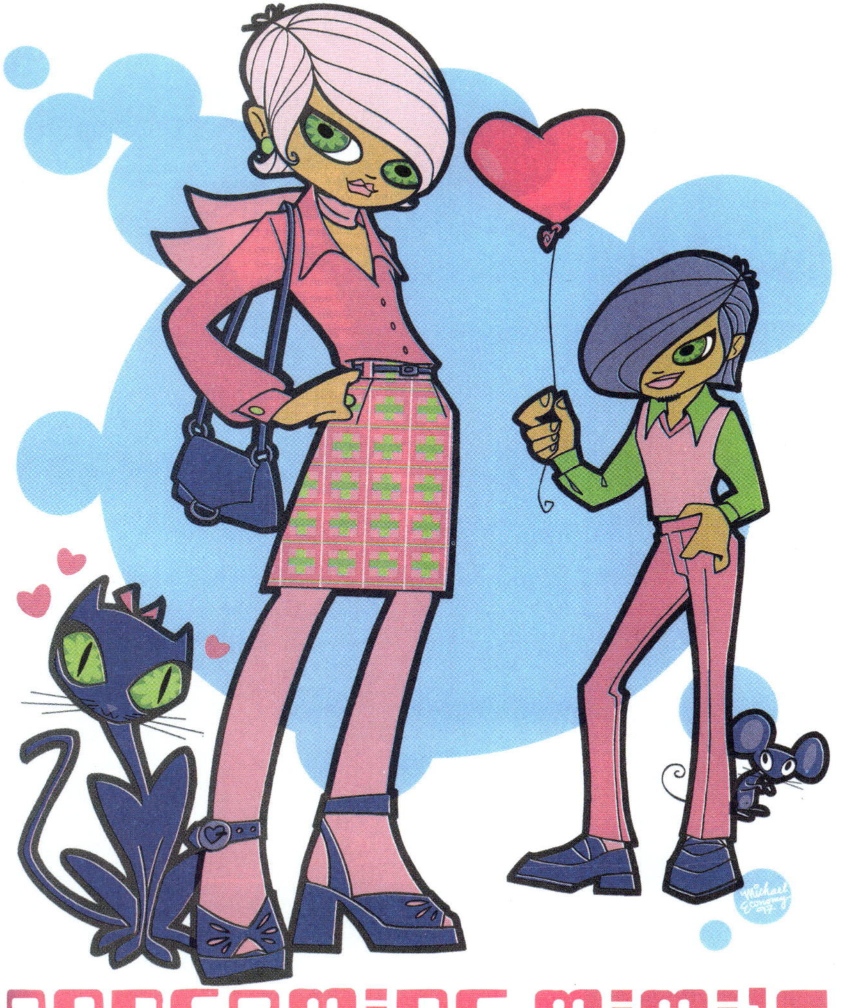

Naomi Campbell wearing Fall 1991 collection backstage, Fall 1992

Screaming Mimi's vintage clothing store advertisement, Michael Economy, *Paper* magazine, March 1997

You can't really compare life today to life then in any way. This digital world is really hard to compare to an analog world, right? There isn't that much visual information about that period, because it was well before the smartphone with cameras, so there are some images and references that get shared, but they can't represent entirely like it was. It couldn't fully be captured. Maybe there was a photographer in the place, but that wasn't typically allowed, so unless it was somebody who was cool enough to be part of that scene, other than their documentation, it doesn't exist.

STEFF YOTKA

It feels like, to someone who wasn't there and didn't live through it, a moment where people, models, and celebrities were dressing really authentically. Not many people had stylists. Celebrities were more likely to pick out their own looks or work directly with the brand themselves to find something to wear. Everything feels a little more unstudied than the fashion of the internet era, where you can call up any image on your phone and recreate that outfit by buying things that look like it. Most famous people are way more calculated about how they dress and the meaning behind what they wear now. The contemporary fascination with the '90s is if you don't know the players or you aren't filled in on the backstory, you just think everyone was really beautiful and well-dressed all the time. Because it seems like that's just how they woke up—they had great taste and were choosing great clothes and were going to great parties where people were actually having fun and not looking at Instagram. I am firmly a millennial. And I lived through a period before cell phones and the internet, but even to me, and even to Gen Z kids who don't know a world without the internet, there's something really romantic about being able to go out and live your life and not feel like you're being observed and that something you were doing could become content. Everyone seemed very free and open. It was also such a great moment for fashion, from Martin Margiela to John Galliano to Anna. The fashion industry seemed to really prize a diversity of ideas during the '90s and going to shows meant you would see different trends or subcultures being represented.

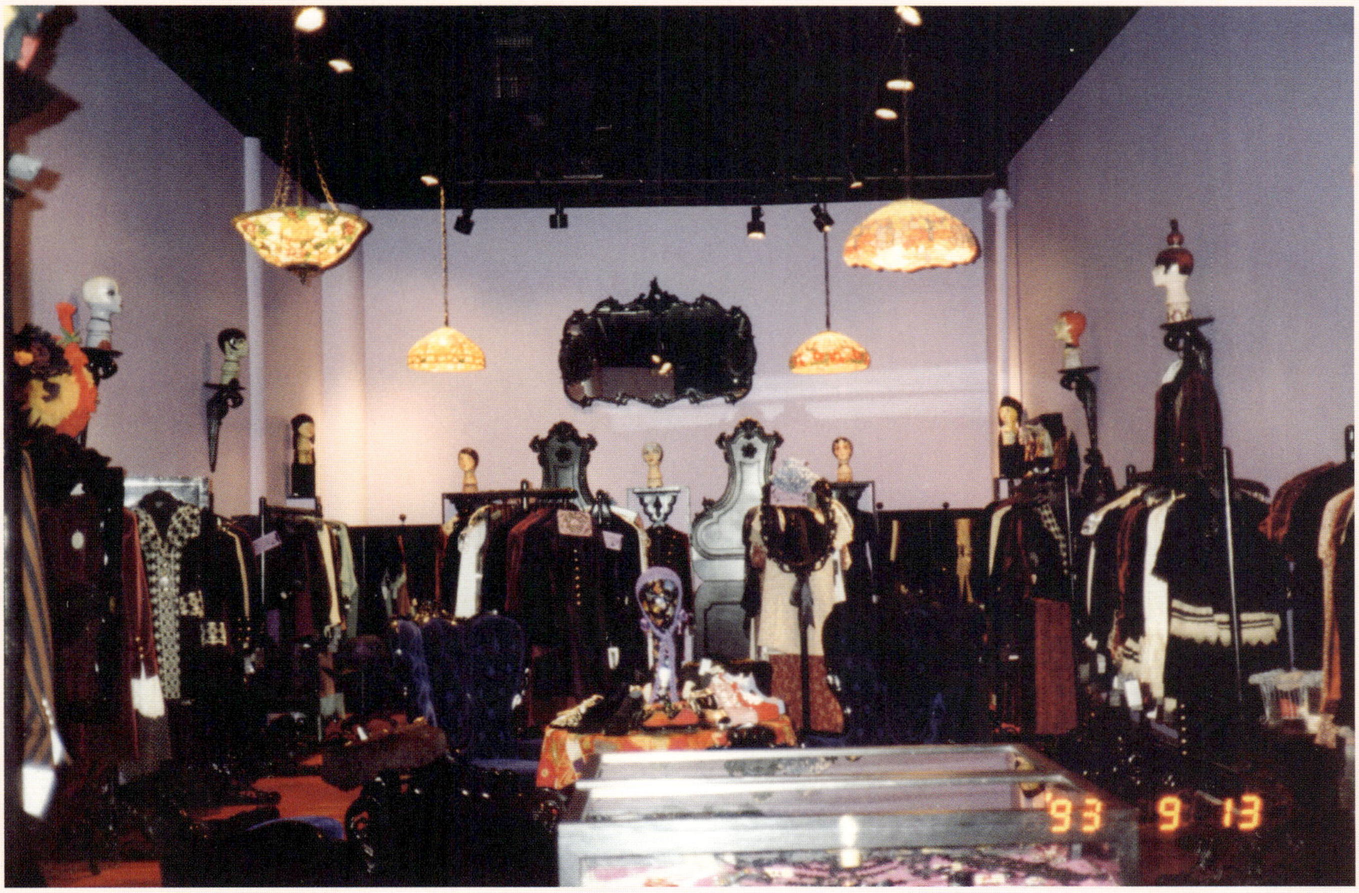

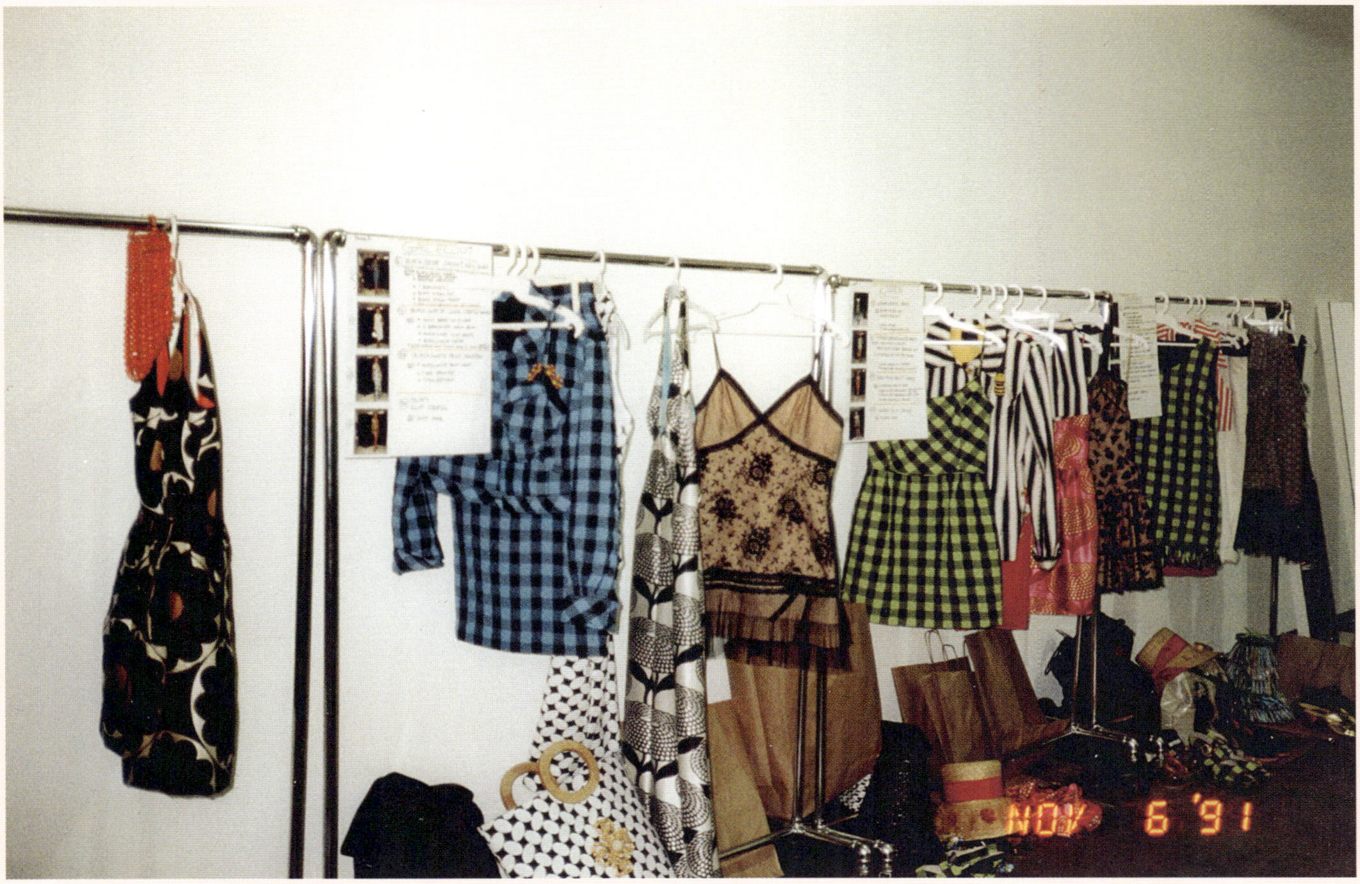

Anna Sui store, 113 Greene Street, SoHo, New York City, 1992

Backstage racks with dresser cards, Spring 1992

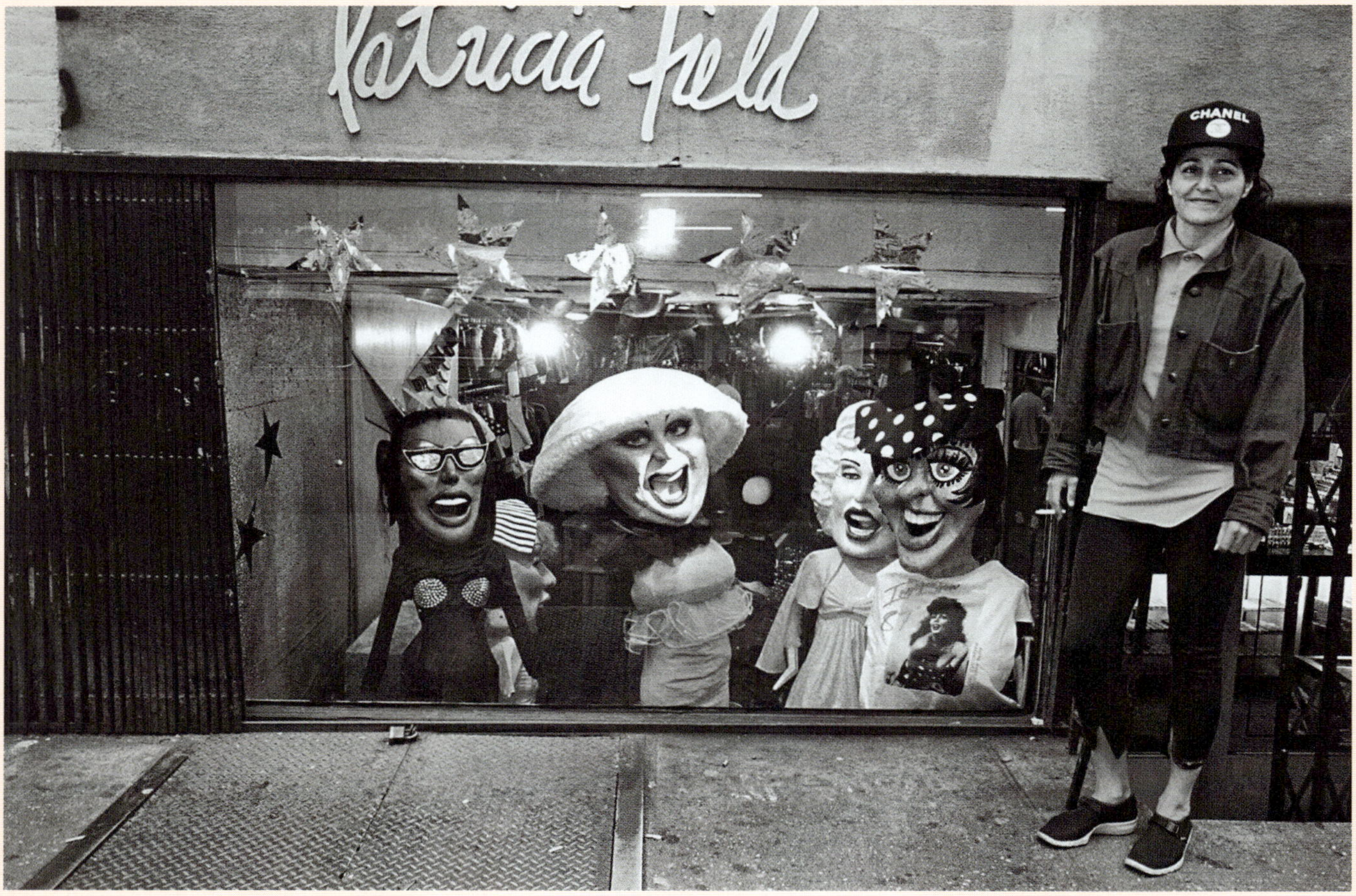

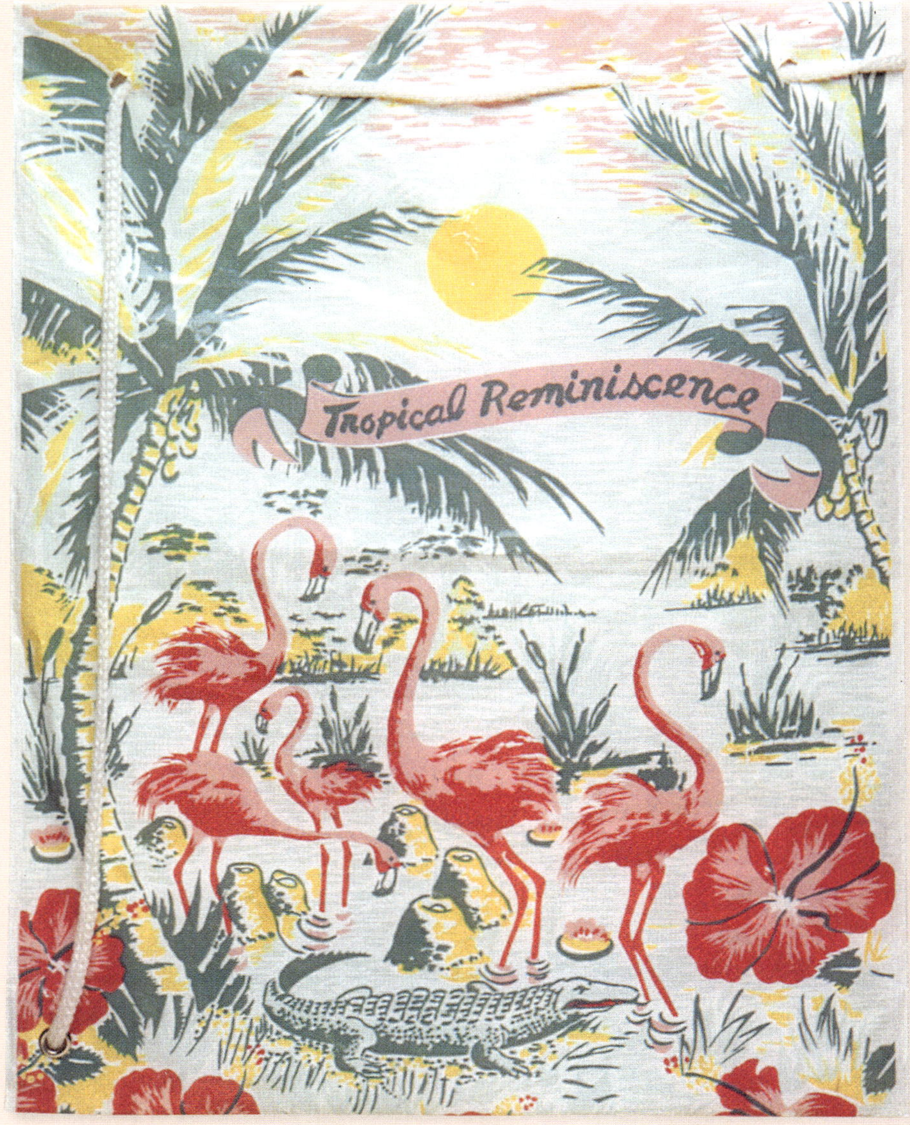

Patricia Field in front of her eponymous store, 8th Street, New York City, 1987

Shopping bag designed by Joan Bedor from Reminiscence vintage clothing store, originally located on MacDougal Street, Greenwich Village

A DAY IN MY LIFE

by anna sui

fashion designer plays photographer; here's her album

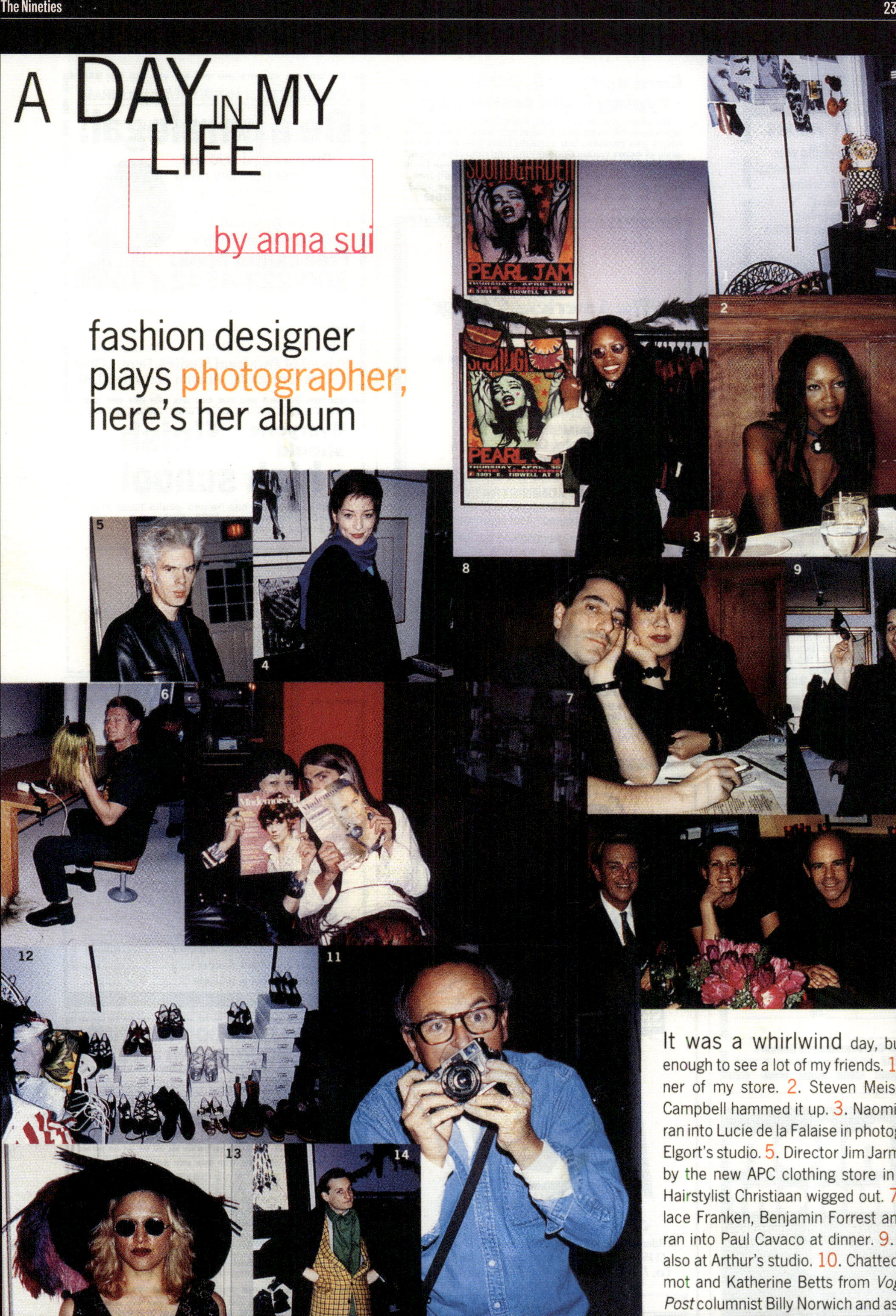

It was a whirlwind day, bu
enough to see a lot of my friends. 1
ner of my store. 2. Steven Meise
Campbell hammed it up. 3. Naomi
ran into Lucie de la Falaise in photog
Elgort's studio. 5. Director Jim Jarm
by the new APC clothing store in
Hairstylist Christiaan wigged out. 7
lace Franken, Benjamin Forrest an
ran into Paul Cavaco at dinner. 9.
also at Arthur's studio. 10. Chatted
mot and Katherine Betts from *Vog*
Post columnist Billy Norwich and as

Downtown L.A.

eye L.A. went "downtown" the other night. Anna Sui's party for the opening of her new La Brea Avenue store was one of the hippest of the summer, drawing **Sofia Coppola**, **Marc Jacobs**, **Donovan Leitch** and **k.d. lang**, as well as a mix of clubgoers, models, actors, artists and writers. It was like Hollywood gone SoHo.

And they were an enthusiastic lot. "I'd give up sex for her latest collection," said Na Na's **Nancy Kaufman**.

Others preferred to part with a little cash. "Can we shop now?" asked a frantic **Rosanna Arquette**, who went straight for the racks with her new boyfriend, **John Sidel**, owner of the Olive.

Cher dropped by for 10 minutes — long enough for paparazzi to note she's looking a bit more robust than in her health club-endorsing days. "I've been ordering directly from her for the past four or five seasons," Cher said. "That's how I know I'm a fan."

"I don't know who most of those people are," said Sui, crushed into a corner of the store, by the cash register. "I am thrilled that Cher is here, but I'm intimidated by k.d. lang. I can't go up and talk to her."

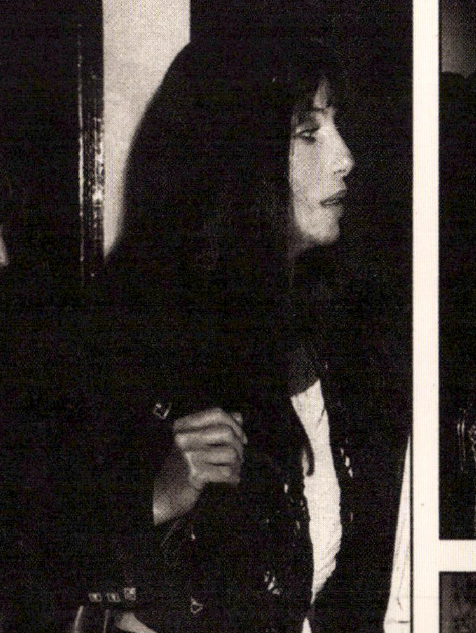

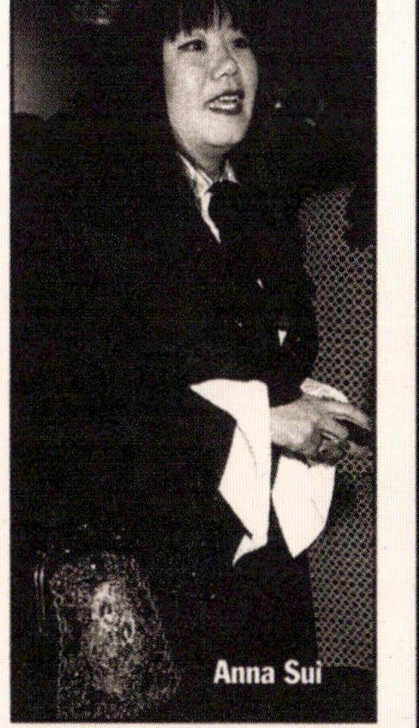

Anna Sui

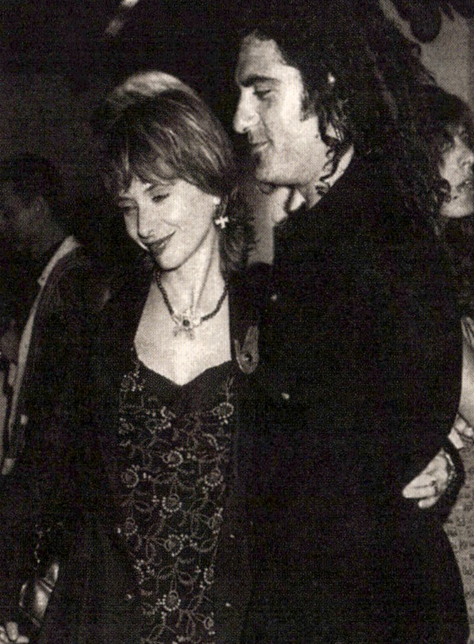

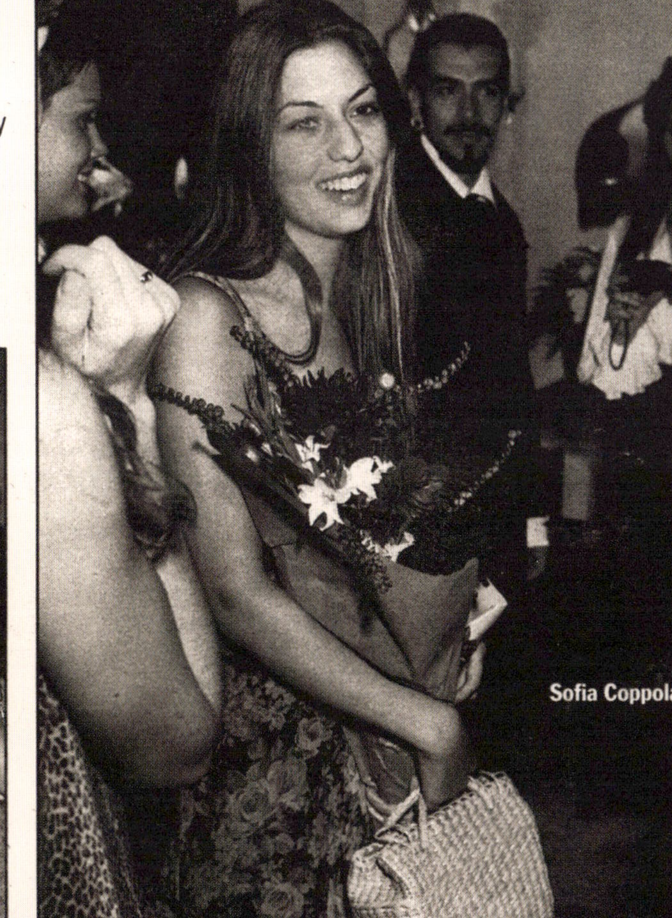

Sofia Coppola

Zoe Cassavetes and

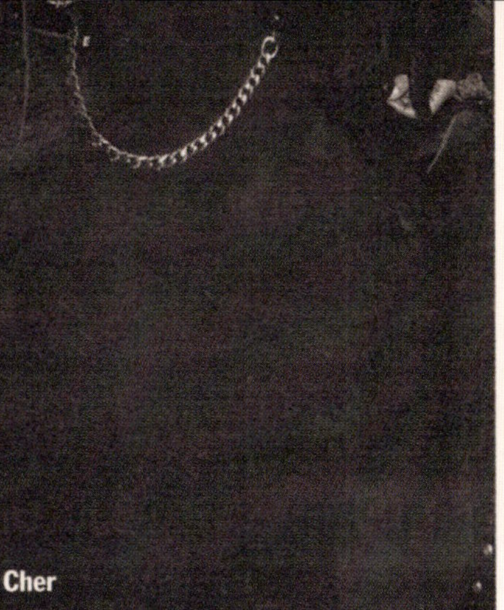
Cher

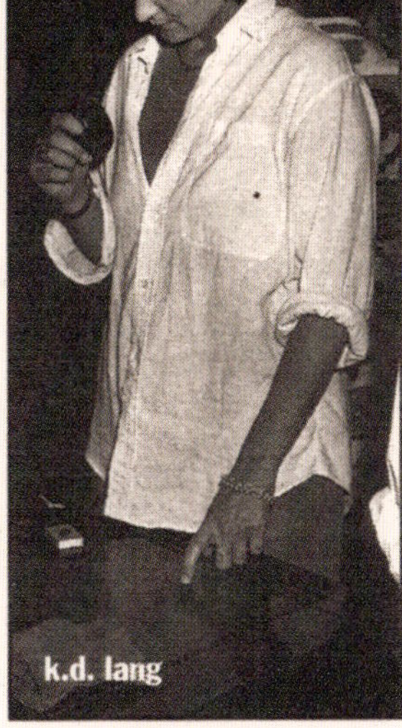
k.d. lang

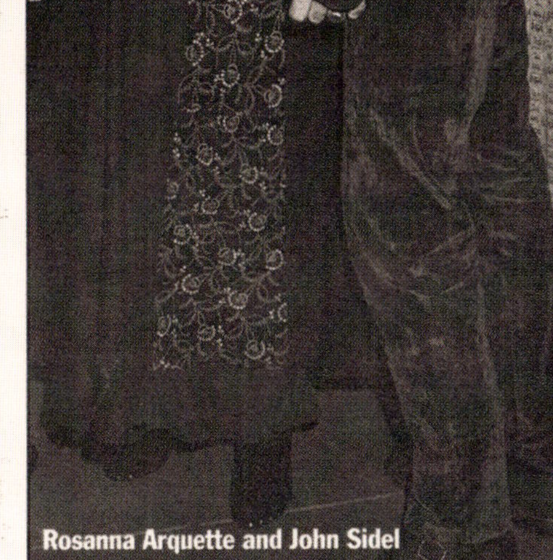
Rosanna Arquette and John Sidel

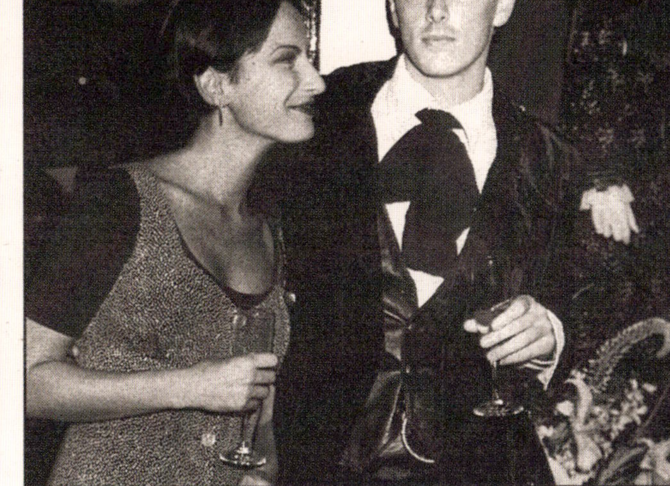

PHOTOS BY TED DAYTON

EYE SCOOP

■ If you think America's model crazy, you should see Australia. The country was in a frenzy last week when **Linda Evangelista** and **Claudia Schiffer** flew down under to launch the spring/summer collections from Myer Grace Bros., one of the country's largest retailers. The media treated them like royals, recording their every move and sending legions of journalists to their press conferences to ask them searching questions about their lives. The press even waited around for more than an hour at one conference for Schiffer, who was said to be finishing up her gym workout.

Schiffer and Evangelista — who traveled with her boyfriend, **Kyle MacLachlan** — were paid a reported $200,000 each to make numerous appearances in Melbourne, Sydney, Gold Coast and Brisbane. Even the prime minister's wife, **Anita Keating**, turned up for one of the three parades the models participated in. And an estimated 2 million people, according to one newspaper, watched the multi-million dollar fashion show, televised live nationwide on **Kerry Packer**'s network.

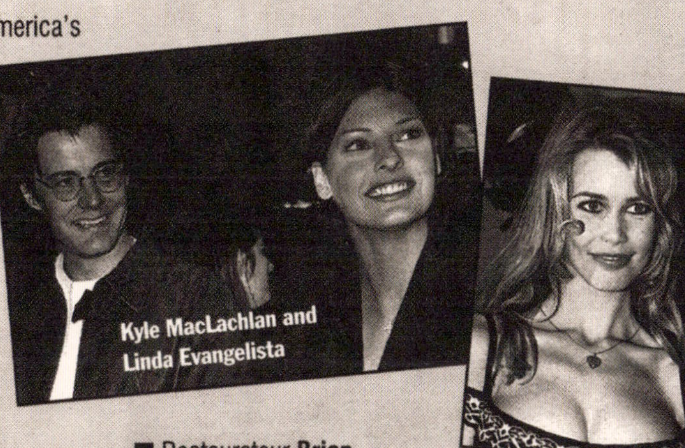
Kyle MacLachlan and Linda Evangelista

Claudia Schiffer

■ Restaurateur **Brian McNally** called Scoop to express his dismay over recent WWD reports that **Richard Gere** had invested and lost $150,000 in his ill-fated 150 Wooster restaurant, causing the two to get into a shouting match at a **Karl Lagerfeld** dinner party in Paris. "Richard Gere never invested $150,000 — directly or indirectly — in any restaurant I've ever owned," said McNally. "I've never been involved in any business transaction with him."

As for the fight, McNally says, "I have no idea what it was about. He was ranting. His performance at Karl Lagerfeld's was his best since his movie, 'King David.'" McNally did suggest, however, that Gere's ire may have been rooted in someone else's investment in the restaurant. "I suppose [Gere] was alluding to his ex-girlfriend, **Sylvia Martins**, who invested $40,000 in 150 Wooster. But she got her money back. He [Gere] wasn't lucid. I can't remember his actual words. You know, I don't understand it; it was I who lost a fortune on that restaurant. She got her money back. And I've seen him since 150 Wooster, and he didn't say anything."

Gere couldn't be reached for comment, but Martins, when reached in London, said she didn't know what the fight was about either. "Richard was not an investor, but I just want all of this to be over," she said, adding that it was possible that Gere's anger might have been out of concern for her.

"Sure, I got my money back," Martins said. "But then there were all these other problems with the restaurant, and after paying all the lawyers' fees, I'm not sure I got anything. I lost money. And after the emotional stress of it all, I'm a wreck. It was only a month ago that this finally got cleared up. Now, I just don't want to think of it any more."

BABY DOLL

"Inspired by the subcultures of New York City's punk and club scenes, the fashion designer has long mixed femme with grunge—from her signature baby-doll dresses to her riotous layers of fabric and trippy saturated colors—and created an inimitable aesthetic all her own. 'You never know if it's a good girl or a bad girl,' Sui says, speaking of the looks she presented; it could also be her mantra. Nowhere is this juxtaposition of innocence and corruption more manifest than that signature baby doll."

T, The New York Times Style Magazine, October 20, 2021

ANNA SUI

I love the baby doll look from the 1960s. A lot of the London designers were doing that look, and even the junior departments in the U.S., there was a lot of baby doll going on. *Seventeen* magazine and *Mademoiselle* would feature it. And it was always my favorite look when I was sewing my own clothes. A lot of times it was that silhouette, the little puffy sleeve and the Empire waist. I remember putting pictures on my wall of Cher wearing a yellow baby doll dress. And there was a really famous Bell Telephone ad that was in every magazine. It featured Naomi Sims, one of the first Black models; Kedakai Turner, one of the first Asian models; and Heidi Wiedeck. They all had ringlet curls and wore baby doll dresses by Bill Blass. It was such a famous ad and it's always stuck in my mind. I wanted to do my version of that.

When I first started my collection, in the 1980s, a lot of the dresses that I made were baby doll, like the one that Madonna wore. That was one of my early dresses. And I did it in so many different fabrics, not only in the chiffon that she wore, but in prints and polka dot, and in lace. It just kept selling over and over and over again, because it had a fit and flair silhouette that's so easy to wear. I think a lot of women found it very flattering. It had a very youthful feel. All those elements appealed to people, and it became my signature. Especially when I sold at Barney's: no matter what I did in those baby doll looks, they kept buying them. That dress was my bread and butter. I started my collections in 1981 and slowly built my business. Around '86 to '88, there was the Barney's Co-op, and they were buying a lot from me, most of which were the baby doll dresses. The one that we had originally done in white cotton lace was our best-selling dress ever. And we kept readapting it. For myself, I wanted one in black chiffon, so we made it in in that fabric one season. Madonna wore that to the first fashion show I went to in Paris with Steven Meisel.

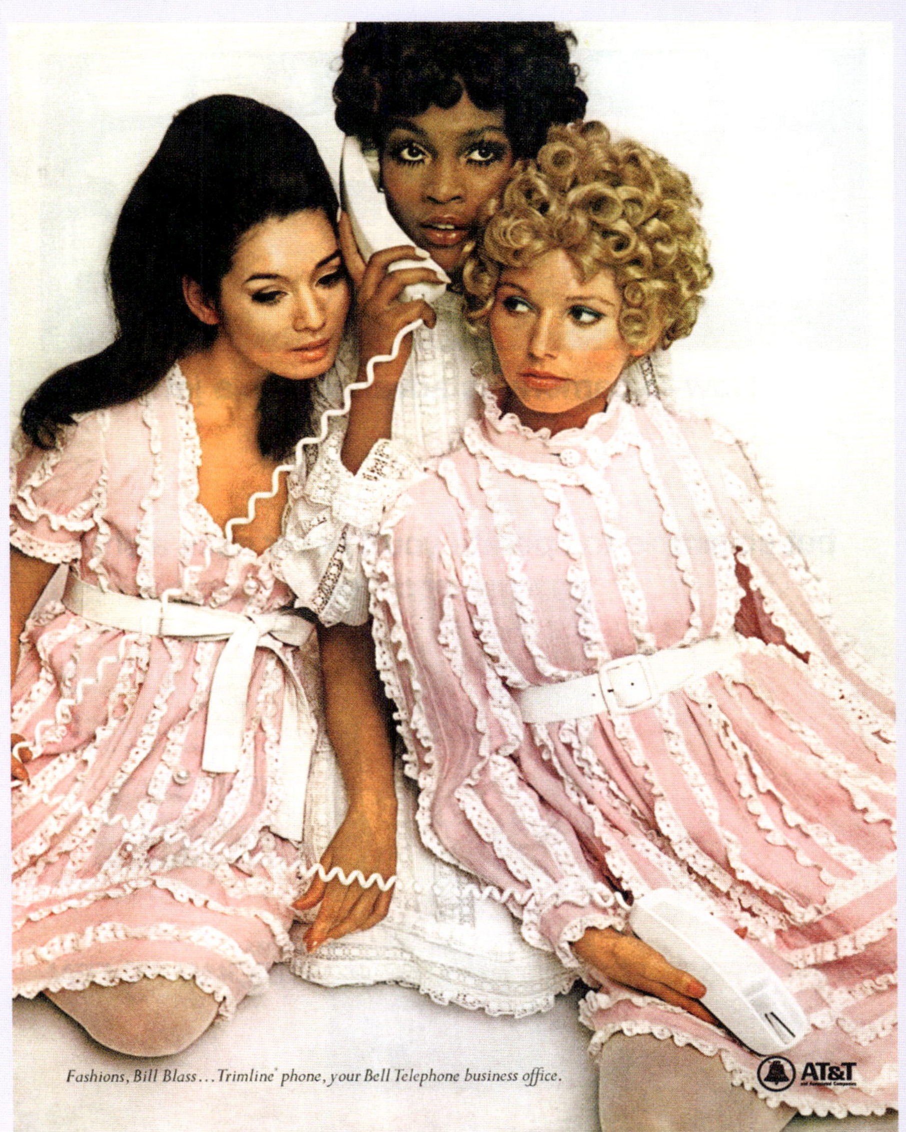

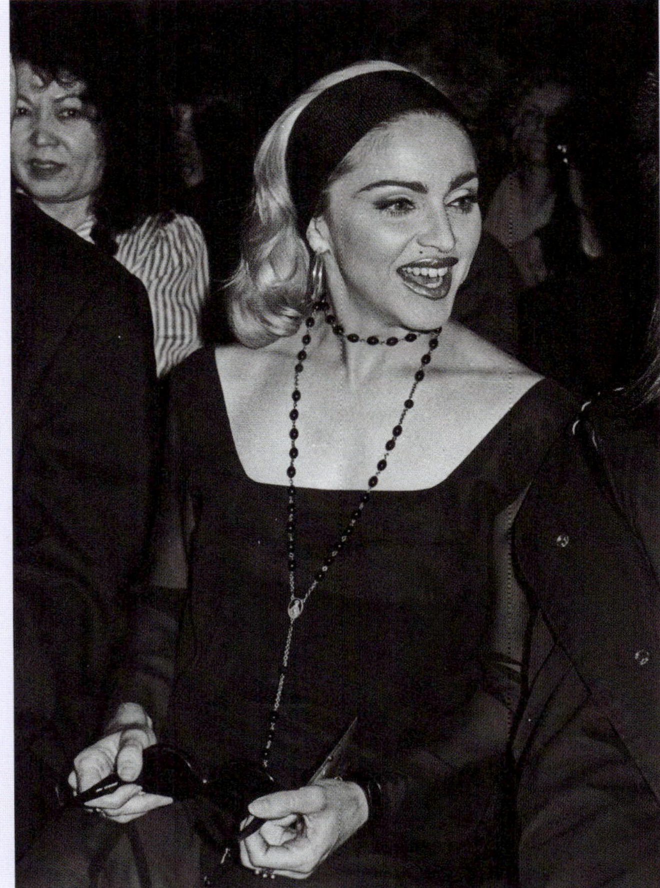

Bell Telephone advertisement for Trimline phone, 1968

Madonna at the Jean Paul Gaultier show, October 1990

There is a picture of Linda Evangelista from 1991—we had gone to Italy with Steven for Valentino's thirtieth anniversary—and she was wearing a polka dot version of the baby doll when we went to the Vatican.

LINDA EVANGELISTA

They would not let me into the Vatican because of that dress. So, I went to buy leggings. They still wouldn't let me in because of my exposed neck. I had a little meltdown since I am Catholic and called my mother. I was very upset. But I got in for a few minutes before they kicked me out. It was that poor sweet little dress that got me thrown out.

ANNA SUI

To me, that dress represented innocence, until I saw how the punk girls were doing it. They were taking old communion dresses or wedding gowns and chopping them off and wearing them with ripped stockings and Doc Marten boots. They flipped it so that the innocence was very subversive. And I think that's what appealed to me, that's what I tried to capture in that 1993 collection, getting that tongue-in-cheek version of innocence.

The baby doll endures to this day because of that ambiguity, that good girl / bad girl aspect, which is what a lot of what people say about my clothes. There's always ambiguity and that is very intentional. I don't want it to be clear which side of the divide the clothes fall—it was dependent on how you style it and how you wear it to suit your personality.

During the '90s, there were a lot of girl bands, especially from California. They were all dressing in little communion dresses or wedding gowns and on stage they wore them with their sneakers and fur hats. Everybody was dressing this way and then of course that famous *Spin* magazine cover with Courtney Love, and her white lace dress with the orchid-colored bow and the tiara. That look was very of the moment.

Naomi Campbell, Christy Turlington, and Linda Evangelista had been doing my shows regularly at that point. They just all happened to be in the 1993 show and that whole moment was very spontaneous. Linda just stopped right in the middle of the runway as the other two were walking by and signaled to them to come back and stop. And they just did it very spontaneously.

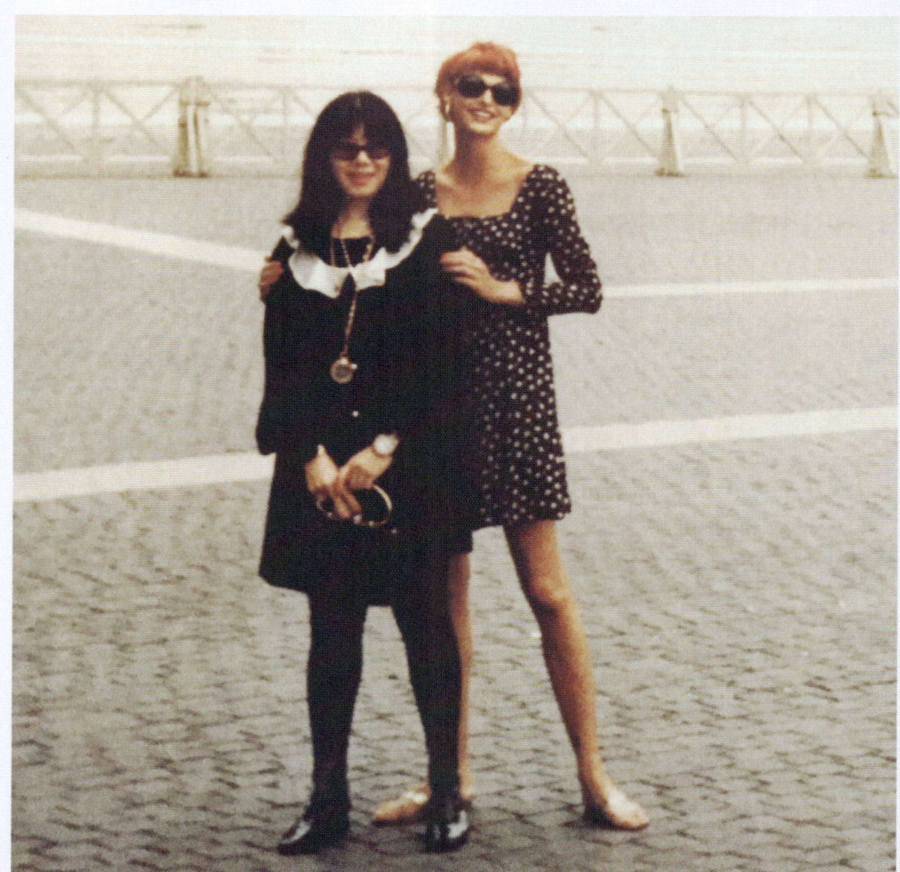

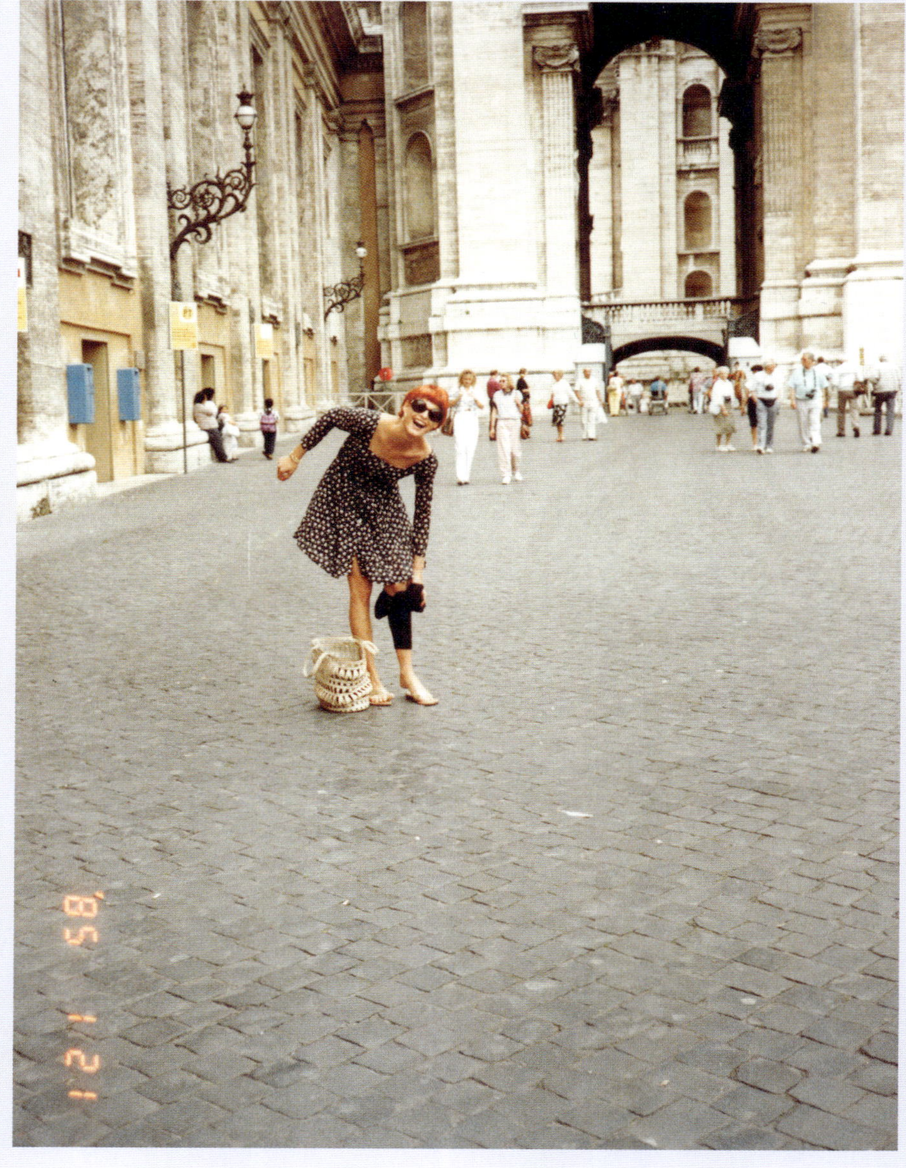

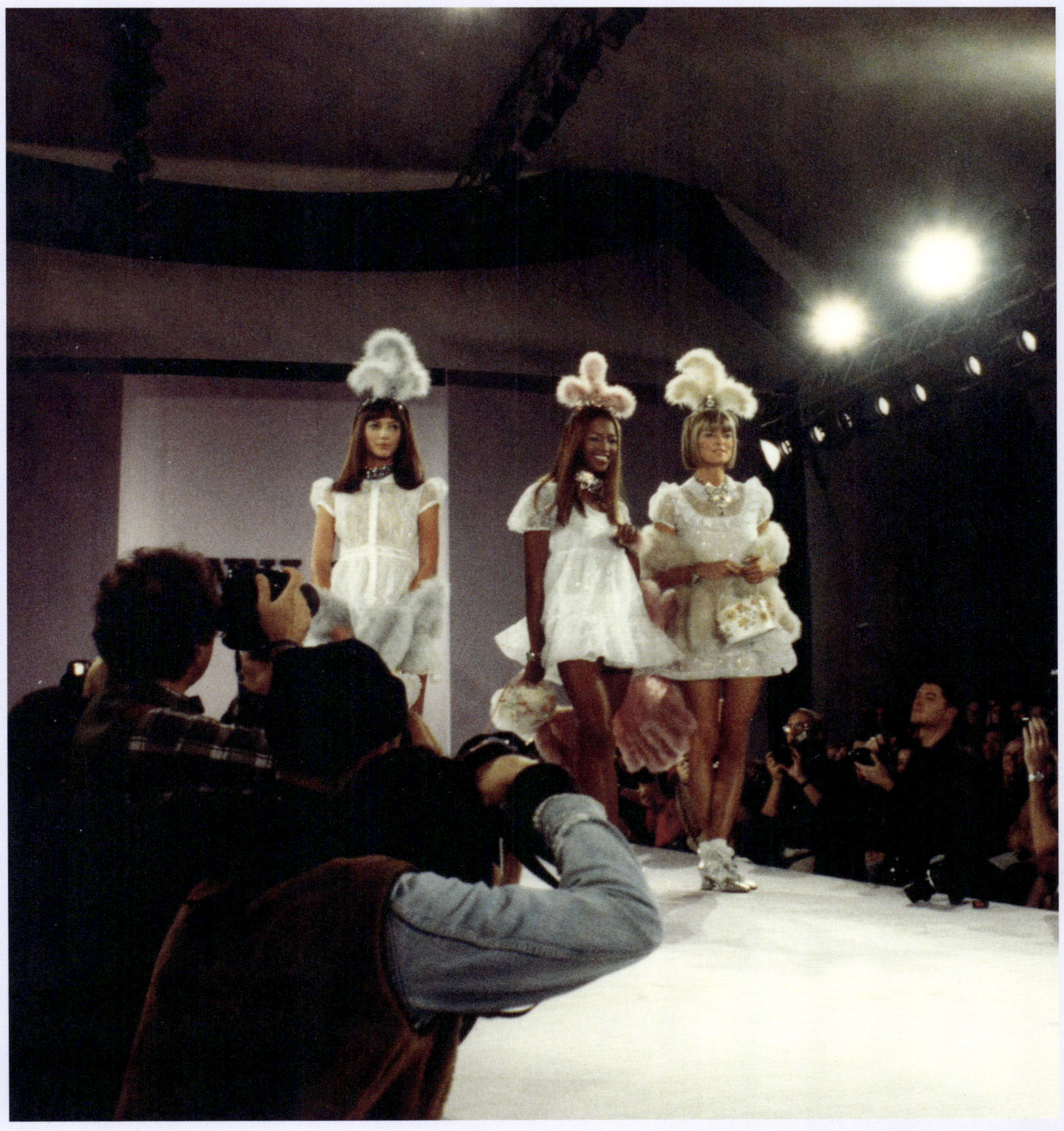

Anna Sui and Linda Evangelista outside the Vatican, Rome, 1991

Linda Evangelista outside the Vatican, Rome, 1991

Christy Turlington, Naomi Campbell, and Linda Evangelista, Spring 1994

CHRISTY TURLINGTON BURNS

Naomi, Linda, and I got to know Anna and hung out with her. She was creating her business and had a showroom in the fashion district. She did these really cute dresses, and we all wore her summer dresses. In 1993 she hadn't built out the Anna Sui brand as it became known just a couple years later. The Spring/ Summer 1994 show was a big moment for the three of us. We'd obviously known each other for a long time and hung out with each other. We had been grouped in many different ways with others of our peer group. But in that moment, it catapulted this trifecta. It was definitely one of the bigger highlights in my career from the runway days.

I guess we just passed the thirtieth anniversary of that time. It's funny, there's a thing about fashion that does not want women to grow up. And so, had it been anybody but Anna, because Anna has that sense of humor and irony, it could have felt very different. Her intention when she presents these kinds of ideas of girls and women is unique. There's something very playful about Anna's brand. I know women of all ages who wear her clothes, but they do have a youthfulness to them.

STEFF YOTKA

The baby doll dresses are iconic. Christy, Linda, and Naomi wore them. She took three of the most famous and sexy women in the world at that time and created what today we would call a viral moment by embracing their girlhood and their girlishness without them looking like they're wearing a costume. At that time, they were young women who, in their other jobs, were being dressed like adults. That's the other important thing about Anna's clothes: she allows women to be girly, in a moment when you're being told you have to grow up. Anna really allows you to indulge yourself in the beauty and the freedom of being young, or girly, or whimsical. It's a time when you're told you have to be serious, you have to speak more professionally. And you have to dress that way, too: you need to wear a blazer in a meeting, for example. Anna has always really embraced this idea of being yourself and not overly corporate or serious. I think that may be the purest thing that she did in the '90s. And that continues today. She gave people an alternative to being so formal and polished and proper. The idea of dreaming is so fundamental to what she does. This is something that has never really been cool in popular culture. It's cool to be tough. It's cool to be authoritative. It's cool to be icy, especially for women. Many of the ways to express female power require a kind of cold exterior. Anna gave us something different: her clothes are warm and she is warm. You can feel like yourself, feel like you're living the dream—you can feel the sense of wonder that we associate with being young. That girlishness in her aesthetic was never demeaning though, which is so key. You don't lose your power by embracing that girlishness.

Jenny Shimizu, Spring 1994

Honor Fraser, Spring 1994

Fabric swatches, Spring 1994

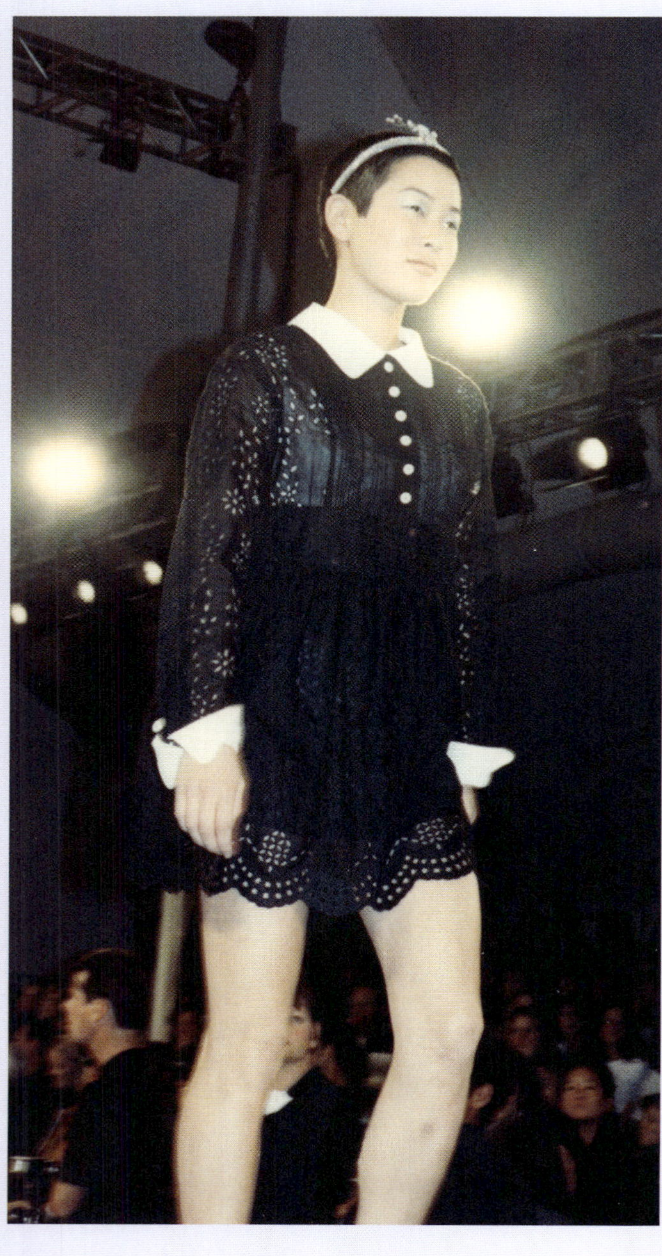

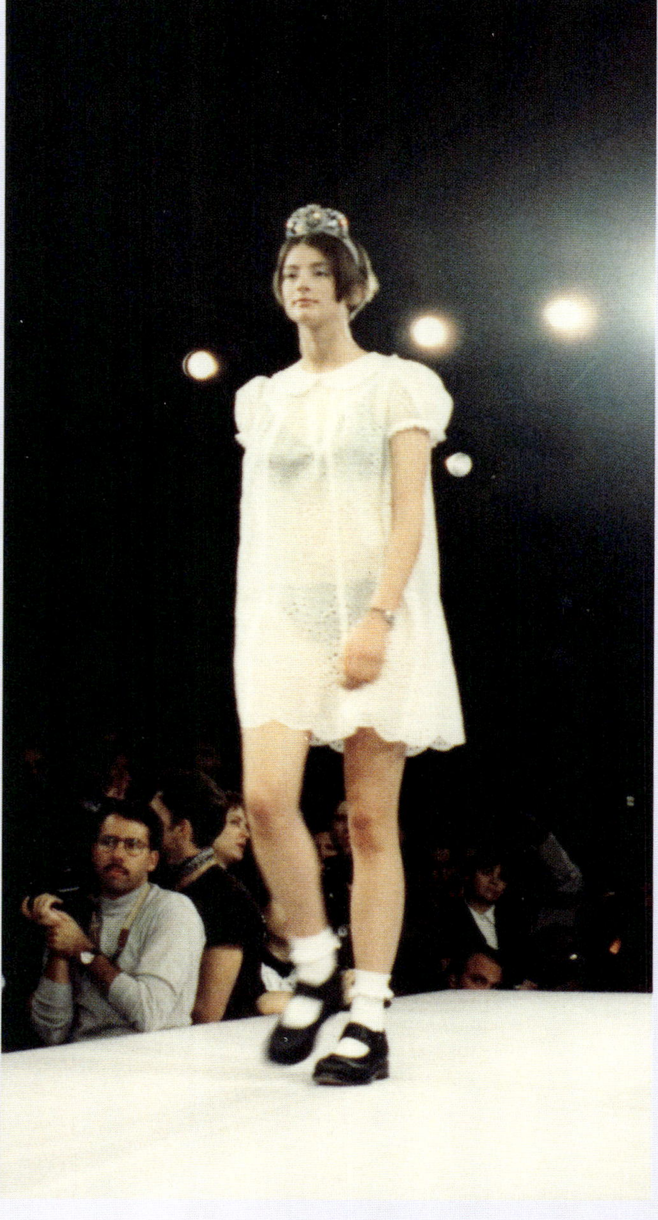

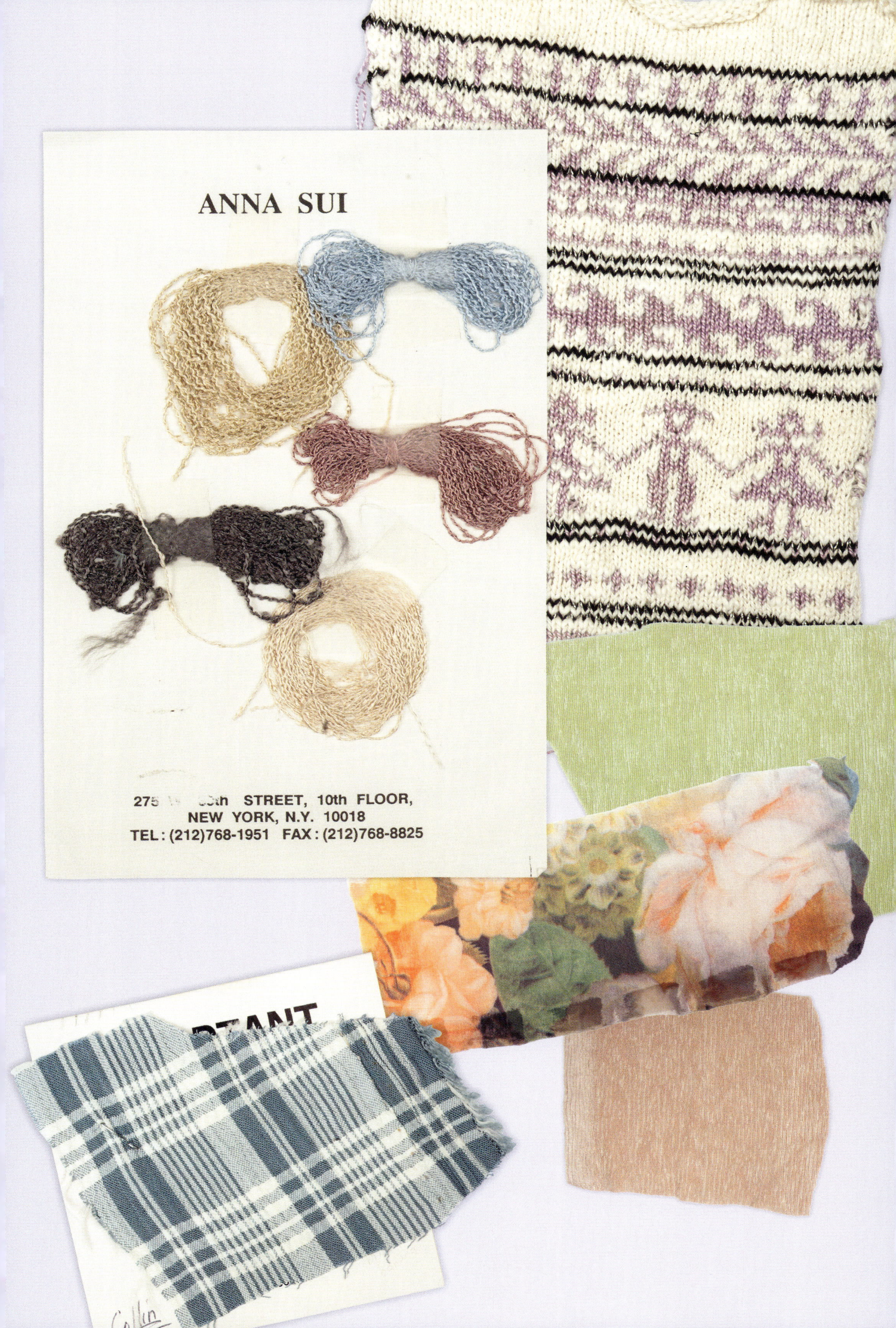
ANNA SUI
275 STREET, 10th FLOOR,
NEW YORK, N.Y. 10018
TEL: (212)768-1951 FAX: (212)768-8825
RTANT

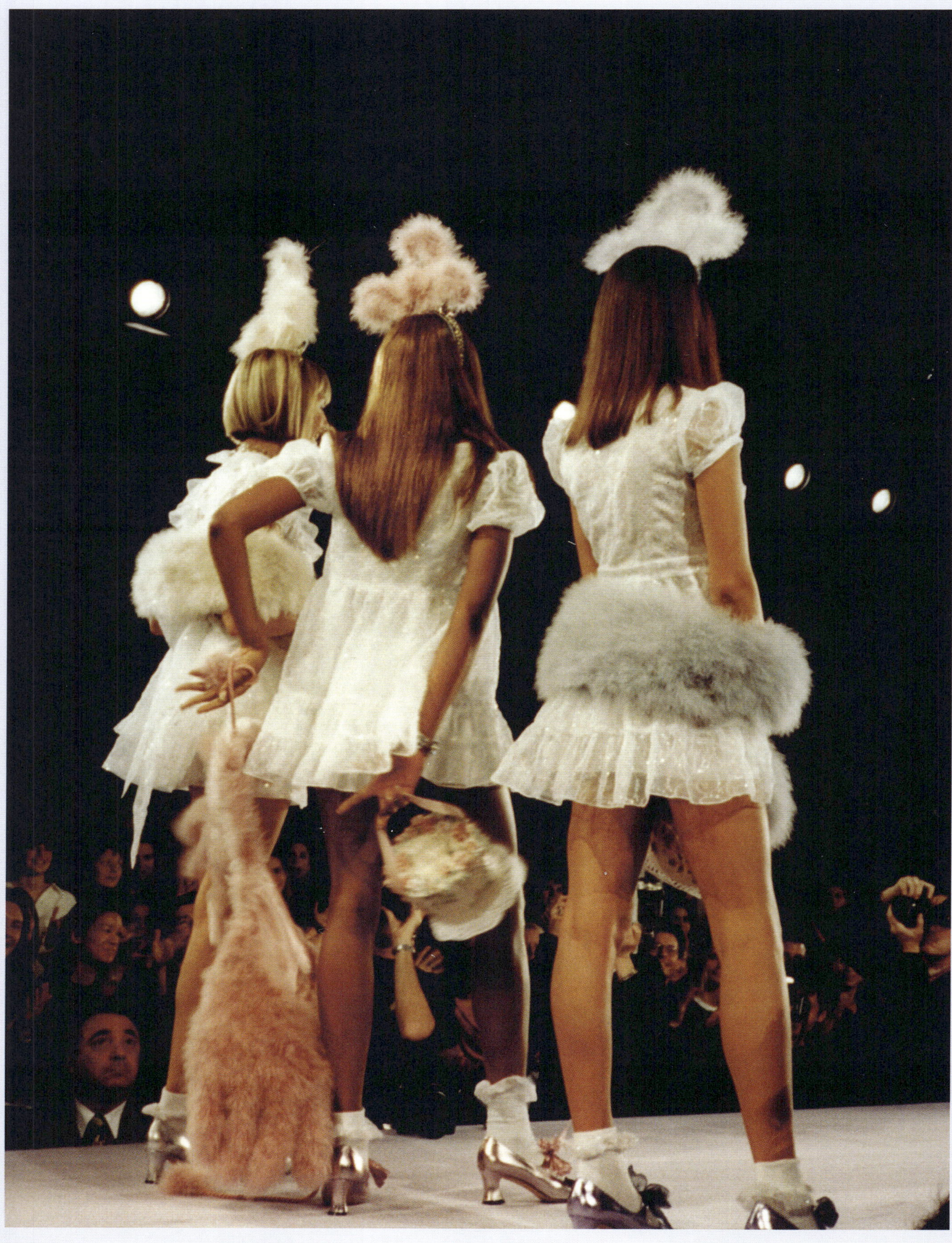

Linda Evangelista, Naomi Campbell, and Christy Turlington, Spring 1994

Potential model list, Spring 1993

Please list with agencies-

Gill:
Models for Anna —

If you need to call Steven Studio about anyone its okay.

Naomi Campbell
Linda Evangelista
Christy Turlington
Lucie de la Falaise
Amber Valletta
Janine Giddings
Michele Hicks
Benedicte Loyen.
Shalom.
Patricia Hartman
Courtney
Barry Smithers
Brandy
Jaimie
Jenny
Stella.
Bridget
Nadja
Jade.

Anna Sui Music

★ New CD's

Denim ① Bjork (#4) There's more to life than This
NOTES: Great!

★ Peruvian ② Jane's Addiction (#5) Been Caught Stealing
NOTES: edit out 1st 10 seconds (noise

SeerSucker ③ Breeders (#3) Cannonball

Chiffon ④ Smashing Pumpkins (#3) TODAY

Metallic ⑤ Suede (#?) Metal Mickey

★ Eyelet ⑥ Lush (#7) Thoughtforms

★ Sports ⑦ Cypress Hill (#2) I ain't going out like tha
Notes: shorten intro - start with bass

★ ~~[illegible]~~ Punk Evening ⑧ Pearl Jam (#1) GO

notes: shorten intro, take out 1st 12 seconds; edit out guitar solo ~~[illegible]~~ (begins at 1:45 seconds) ~~[illegible]~~

Finale ⑨ Iggy (#15) Louie Louie

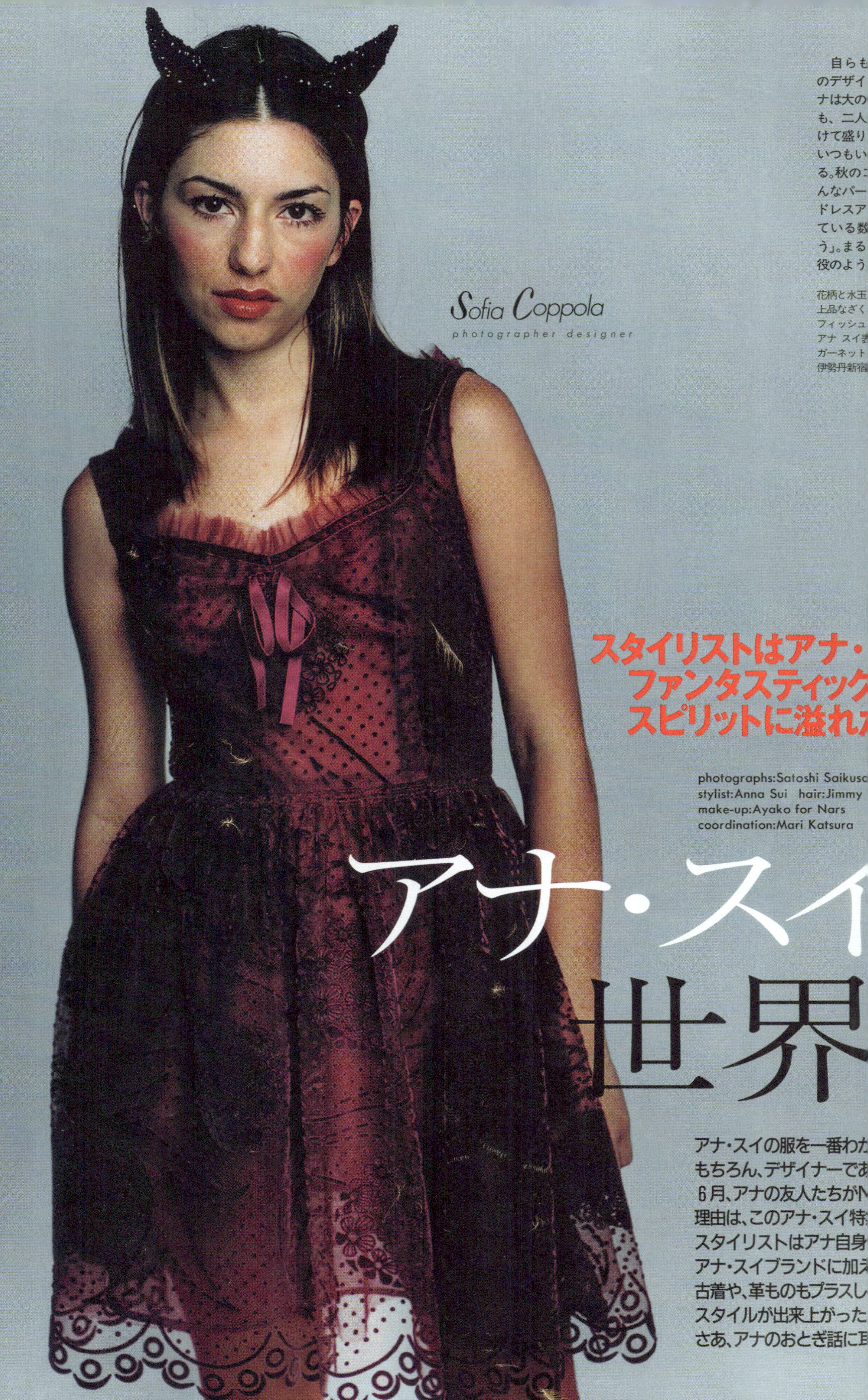

Sofia Coppola
photographer designer

アナ・スイ
世界

スタイリストはアナ・
ファンタスティック
スピリットに溢れた

photographs:Satoshi Saikusa
stylist:Anna Sui hair:Jimmy
make-up:Ayako for Nars
coordination:Mari Katsura

アナ・スイの服を一番わか
もちろん、デザイナーであ
6月、アナの友人たちがN
理由は、このアナ・スイ特
スタイリストはアナ自身
アナ・スイブランドに加え
古着や、革ものもプラスし
スタイルが出来上がった
さあ、アナのおとぎ話に耳

自らも
のデザイ
ナは大の
も、二人
けて盛り
いつもい
る。秋のコ
んなパー
ドレスア
ている数
う」。まる
役のよう

花柄と水玉
上品なざく
フィッシュ
アナ スイ表
ガーネット
伊勢丹新宿

(29) Linda
Black short sleeve ribbon dress
black shorts

accessories
black lace tights
black satin shoe

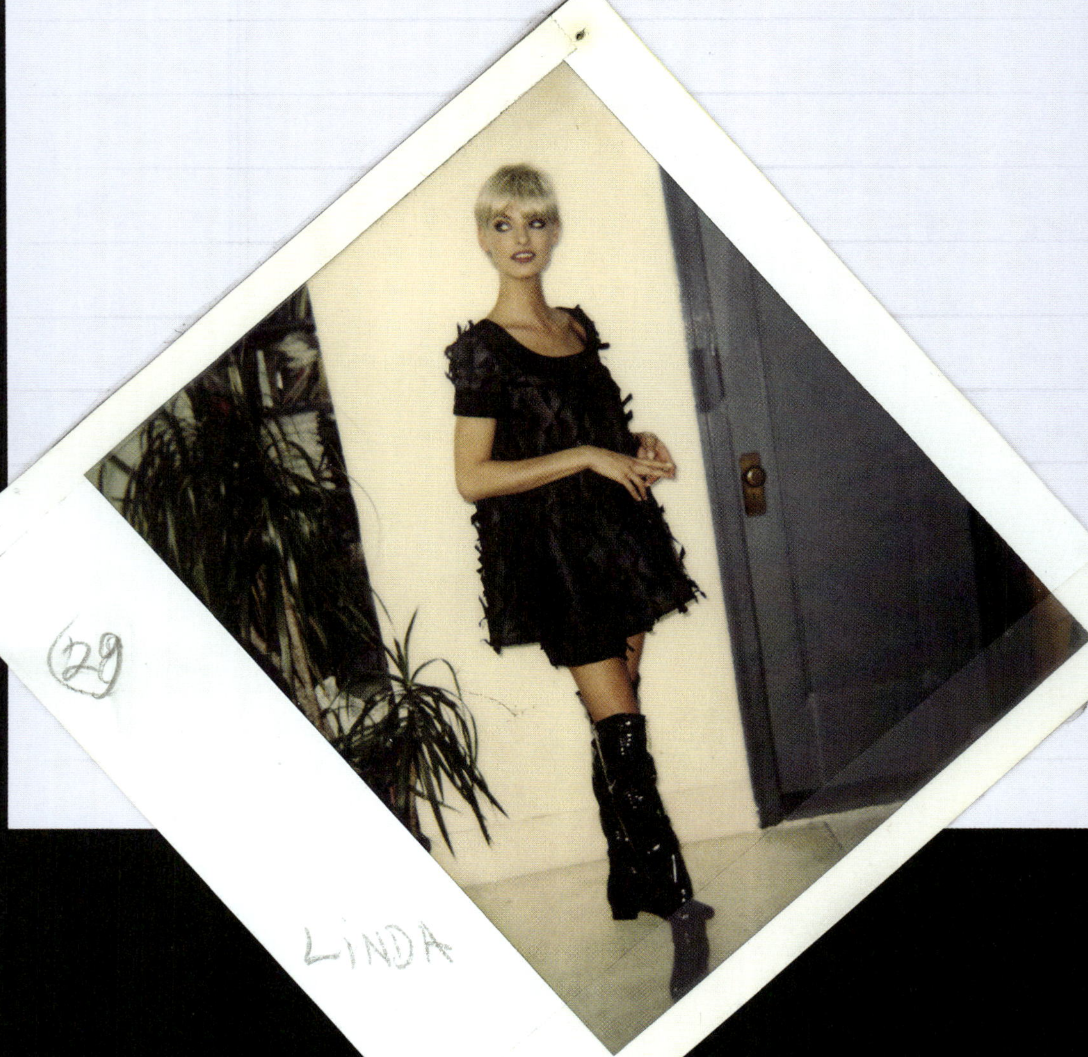

Dresser card, Linda Evangelista, Fall 1991
Dresser card, Nadège Du Bospertus, Fall 1991

(27) Nadege
long sleeve black ribbon dress

accessories
black lace tights
black satin shoes
choker

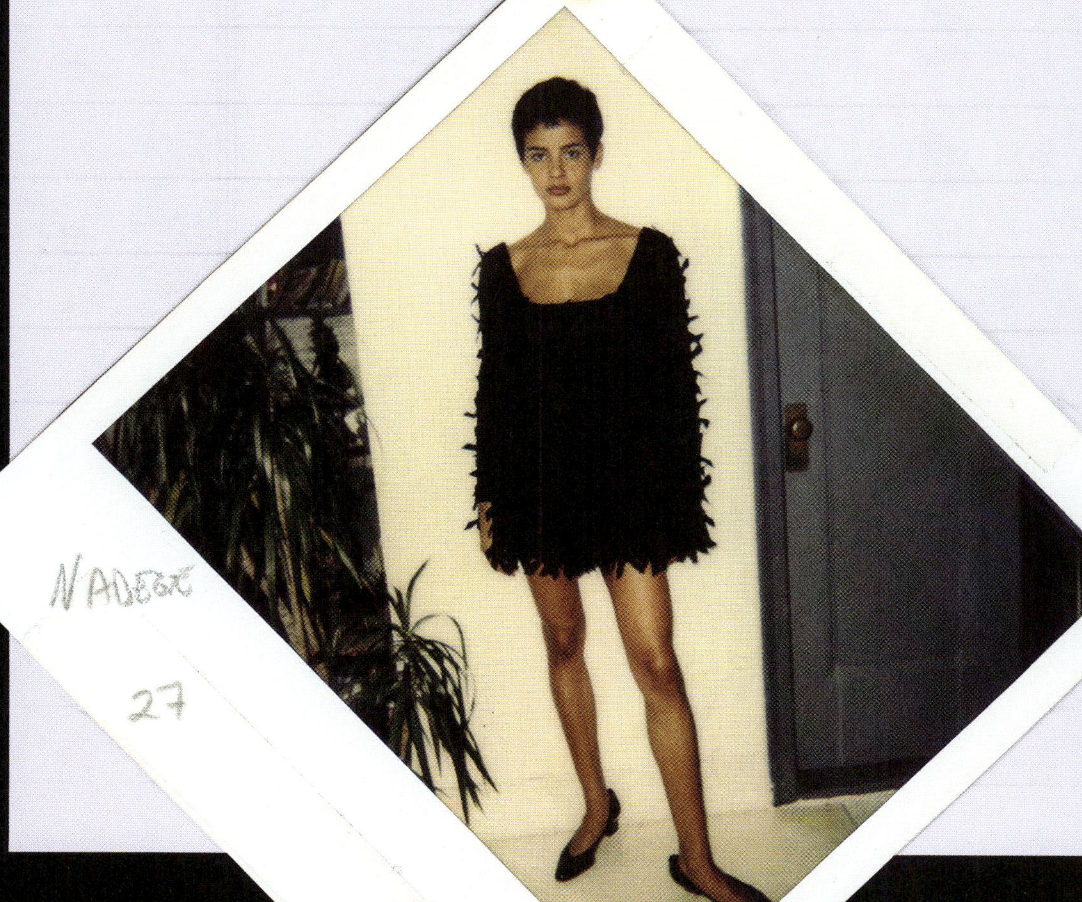

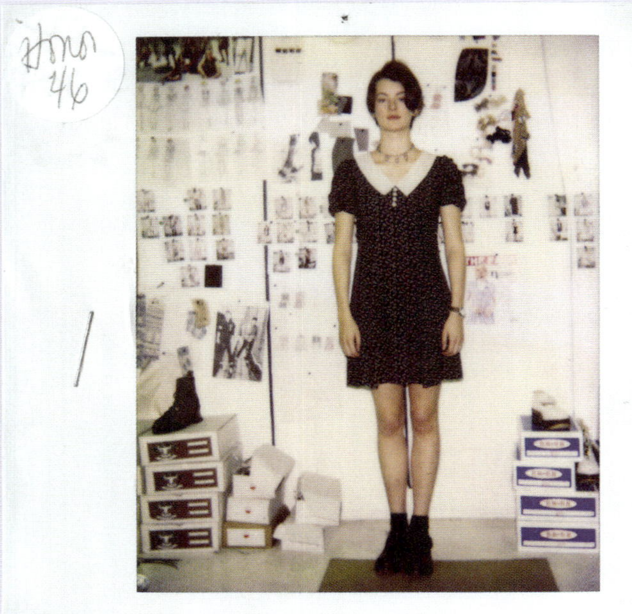

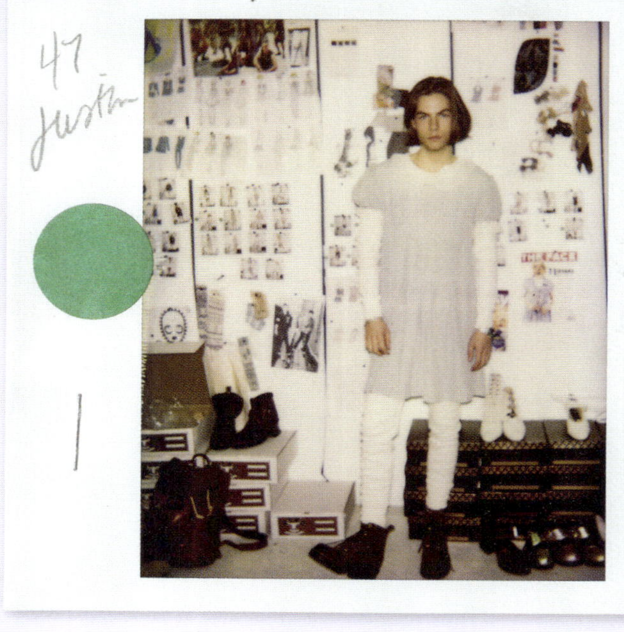

46. Honor
Black print dress
(Black bra) (Honor's own bra; keep on for look #63)

46. ACCESSORIES
- **_Red heart necklace_**
- **_Black anklet w/lace ruffle_**
- **_Black Maryjane shoe_** (shoe 7)

47. Justin
Blue print baby doll dress
(closed; buttons in back)
(Cream union suit) (top 2 buttons open)

47. ACCESSORIES
- **_Black lace up boot_** (size 10)
- Black socks (from #6)

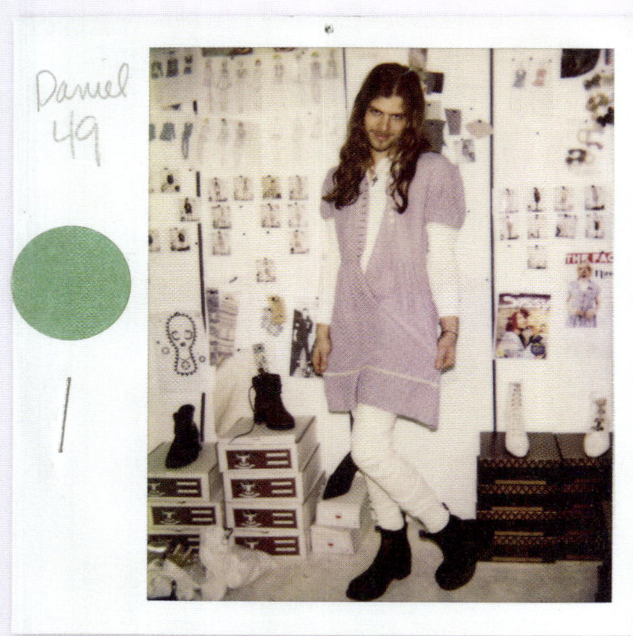

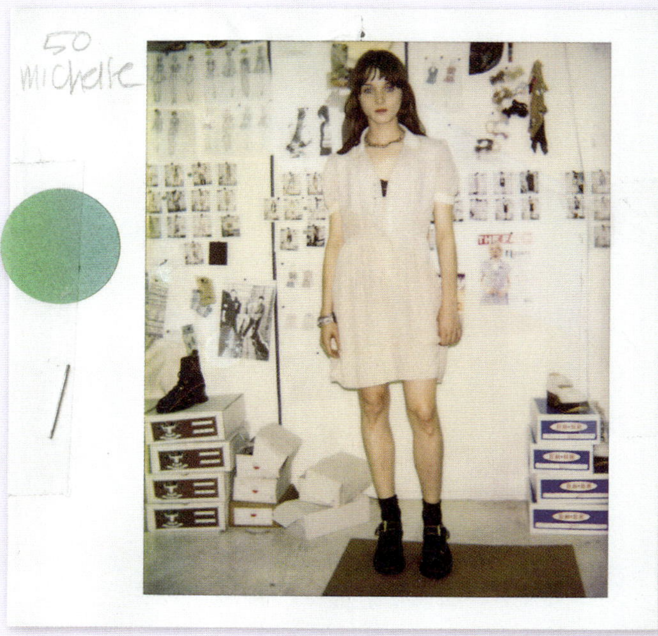

49. Daniel
Purple print dress (unbuttoned)
(Cream union suit) (buttoned; pull down leg)

49. ACCESSORIES
- **_Daniel's cross necklace_**
- **_Black pull on boot_** (size 11)
- Black socks

50. Michelle
Pink print dress (bottom 9 buttons closed; bra shows)
(Black lace trim bra and panties) (keep on for look #64)

50. ACCESSORIES
- **_Pink rhinestone bagette necklace_**
- **_Pink and black rhinestone bracelet_** (on right wrist)
- **_Pink and clear rhinestone bracelet_** (on left)
- **_Black anklet w/lace ruffle_**
- **_Black leather Maryjane with top stitching_** (size 8)

Dresser card, Honor Fraser, Spring 1994
Dresser card, Justin Scott, Spring 1994
Dresser card, Daniel Baylock, Spring 1994
Dresser card, Michele Hicks, Spring 1994

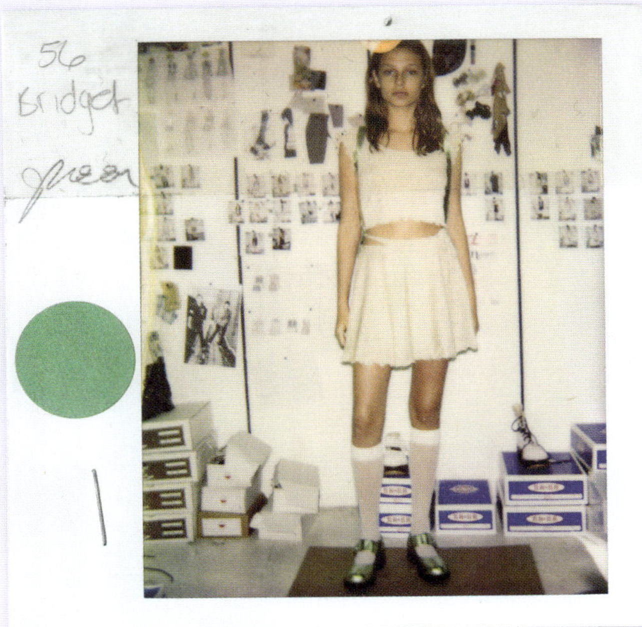

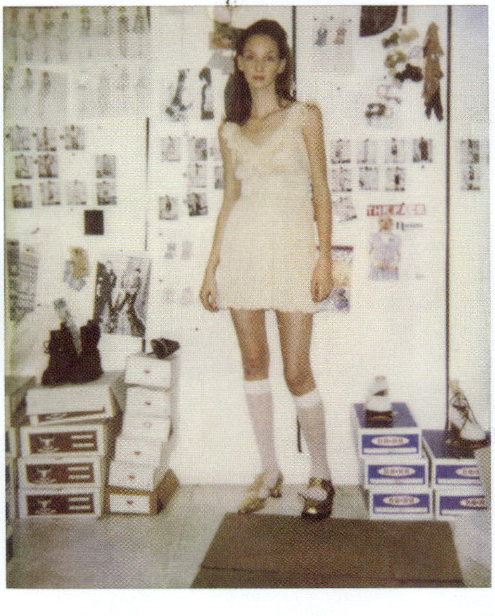

56. Bridget
Green lettuce edge cap sleeve top
Green lettuce edge wrap skirt

56. <u>ACCESSORIES</u>
- ***Green mini knapsack*** (on back)
- ***White fine net knee-hi***
- ***Green Maryjane shoe*** (size 8)

57. Debbie
Butterscotch v-neck lettuce edge pinafore dress

57. <u>ACCESSORIES</u>
- ***Gold backpack*** (on back)
- ***White fine net knee hi***
- *gold pointed toe pump w/bow tie* (39)

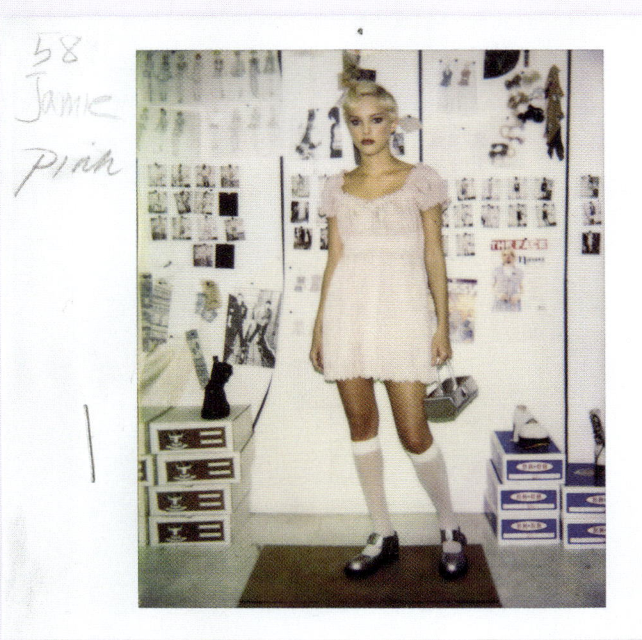

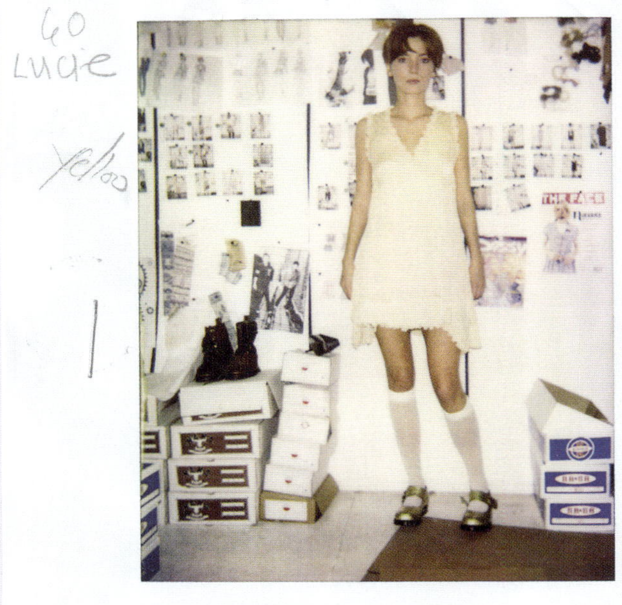

58. Jamie
Pink lettuce edge puffed sleeve dress

58. <u>ACCESSORIES</u>
- ***Pink knapsack*** (stuffed; on back)
- ***White fine mesh knee-hi***
- ***Pink Maryjane shoe*** (size 6)

60. Lucie
Butterscotch lettuce edge wrap dress

60. <u>ACCESSORIES</u>
- ***Gold backpack*** (on back)
- ***White fine net knee hi***
- ***Gold Maryjane shoe*** (size 7; needs shoe pad)

Dresser card, Bridget Hall, Spring 1994
Dresser card, Debbie Deitering, Spring 1994
Dresser card, Jaime Rishar, Spring 1994
Dresser card, Lucie de la Falaise, Spring 1994

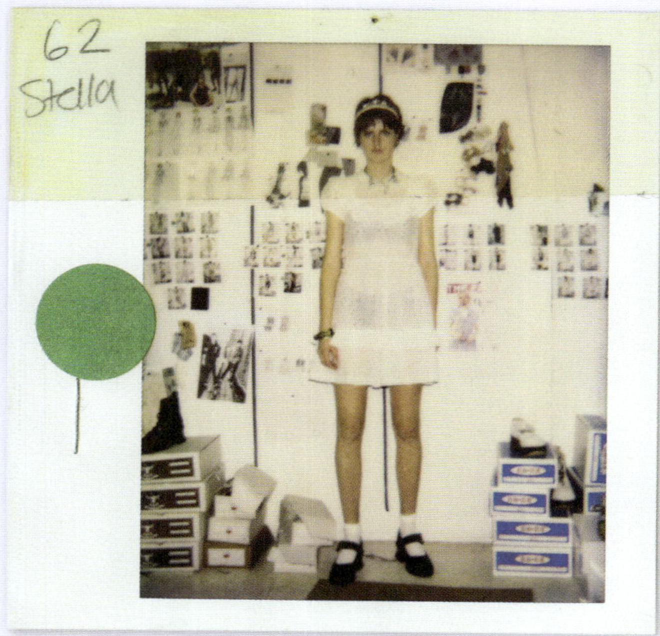

62. Stella
White lace party dress
(Black bra and panties) (from look #41)

62. ACCESSORIES
- **Green rhinestone tiara**
- **Green rhinestone 3-tier necklace**
- **Green rhinestone bracelet** (on right)
- **White anklet with lace ruffle**
- **Black leather Maryjane with topstitching** (from look #41)

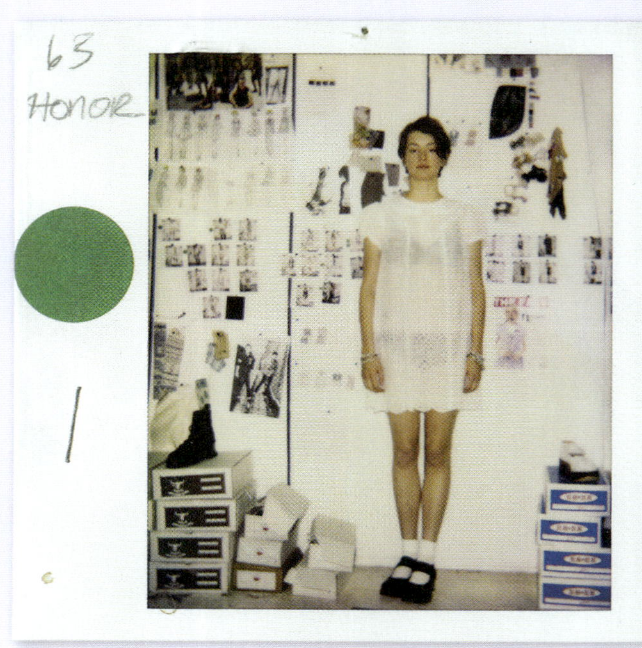

63. Honor
White lace baby doll dress
(Black lace panties and bra) (Honor's own bra; from look #46)

63. ACCESSORIES
- **Rhinestone tiara**
- **Multi color rhinestone bracelet** (on right)
- **2 Multi color rhinestone bracelets** (on left)
- **White anklet with lace ruffle**
- **Black Maryjane shoe** (from look #47)

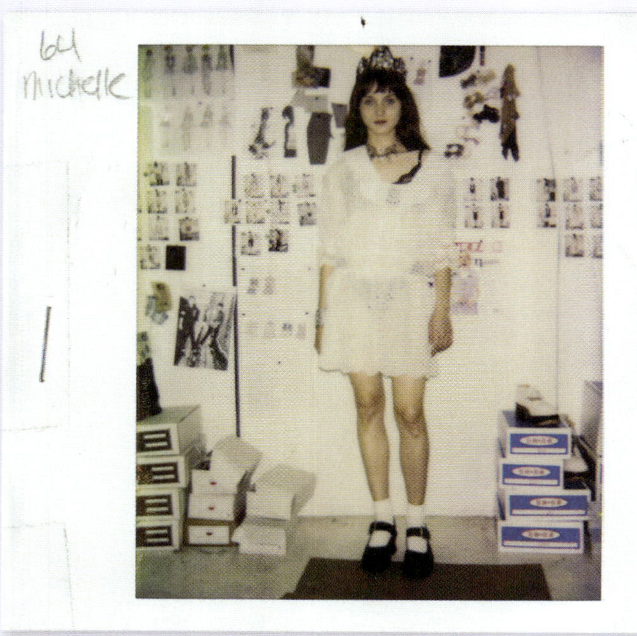

64. Michelle
White lace drop waist dress (pull down dress so bra shows)
(Black lace bra and panties) (from look #50)

64. ACCESSORIES
- **Tall b/w tiara**
- **Rhinestone 4-drop necklace**
- **Rhinestone multi-strand bracelet** (fix bracelet)
- **White anklets with lace ruffle**
- **Black leather Maryjane with topstitching** (from look #50)

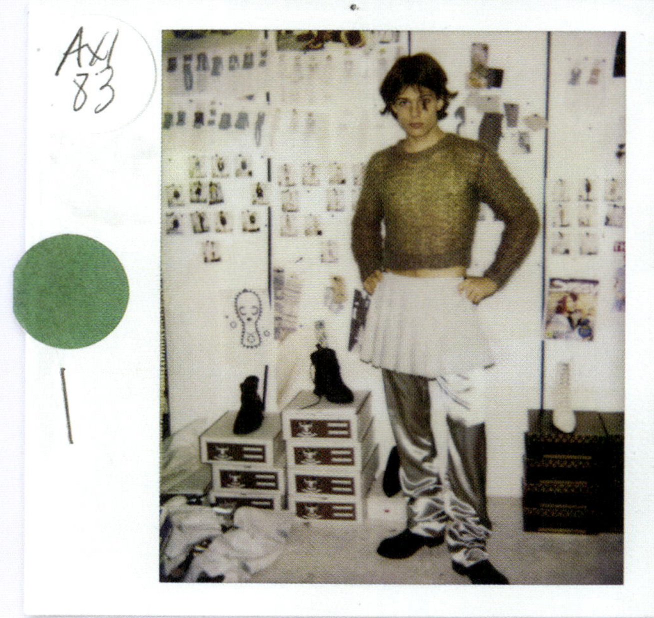

83. Axl
Silver mohair sweater (pull down sleeves)
Silver trouser with pleated satin panels (pin front and back together w/lg. saftety pins at sides)

83. ACCESSORIES
- **Silver pull on boot** (size 9)

Dresser card, Stella Tennant, Spring 1994
Dresser card, Honor Fraser, Spring 1994
Dresser card, Michele Hicks, Spring 1994
Dresser card, Axel Maas, Spring 1994

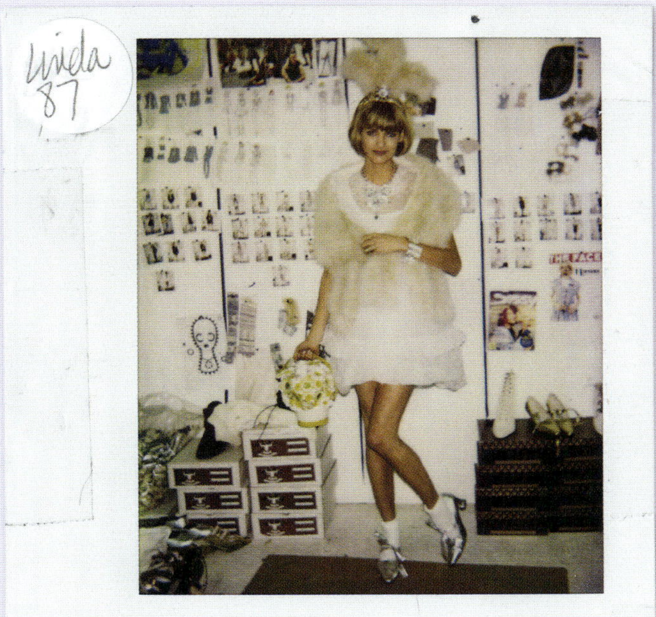

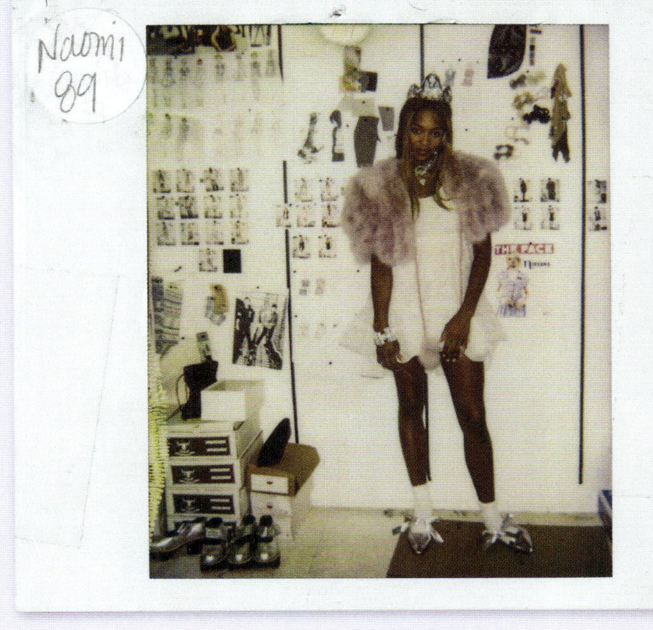

87. Linda
White party dress with irridescent sequin embroidery and bow in back
(Peach maribou stole)
(White panty)

87. ***ACCESSORIES***
- ***Peach maribou rhinestone tiara***
- ***Clear rhinestone necklace***
- ***Clear rhinestone bracelet*** (on left writs)
- *Birthday cake bag* (on right hand)
- ***White anklet with ruffle to match dress***
- ***Silver high-heeled EH pump with bowtie*** (size 39)

89. Naomi
Party dress with sequin irridescent embroidery
(Pink maribou stole) (open)
(White panty)

89. ***ACCESSORIES***
- ***Birthday cake handbag***
- ***Pink maribou tiara***
- ***Pink rhinestone necklace w/heart drop***
- ***White rhinestone chunky bracelet*** (AS might change)
- ***White anklet w/chiffon ruffle*** to match dress
- ***Pink pump with bow tie*** (size 40; from look #53)

Dresser card, Linda Evangelista, Spring 1994
Dresser card, Naomi Campbell, Spring 1994

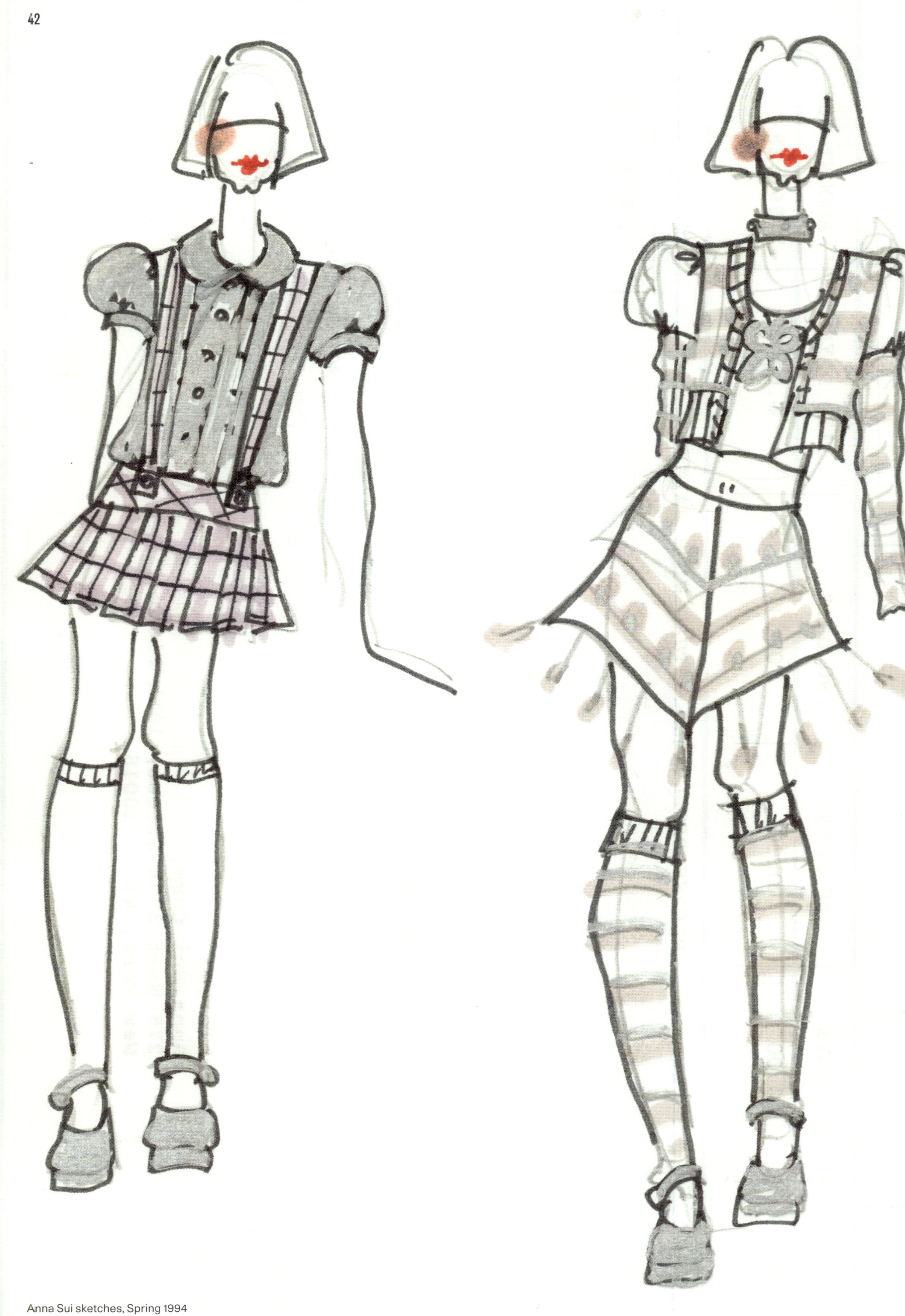

Anna Sui sketches, Spring 1994

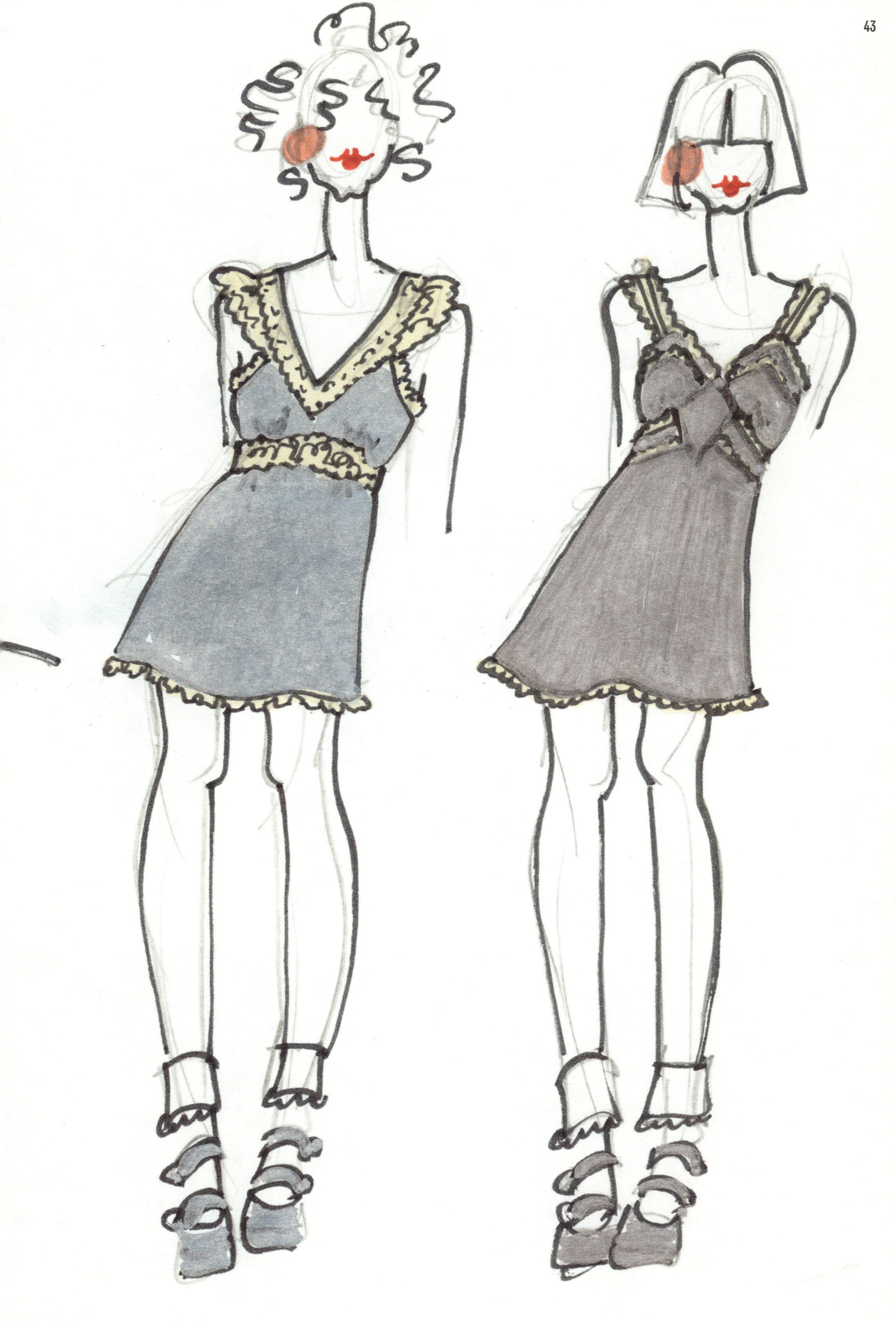

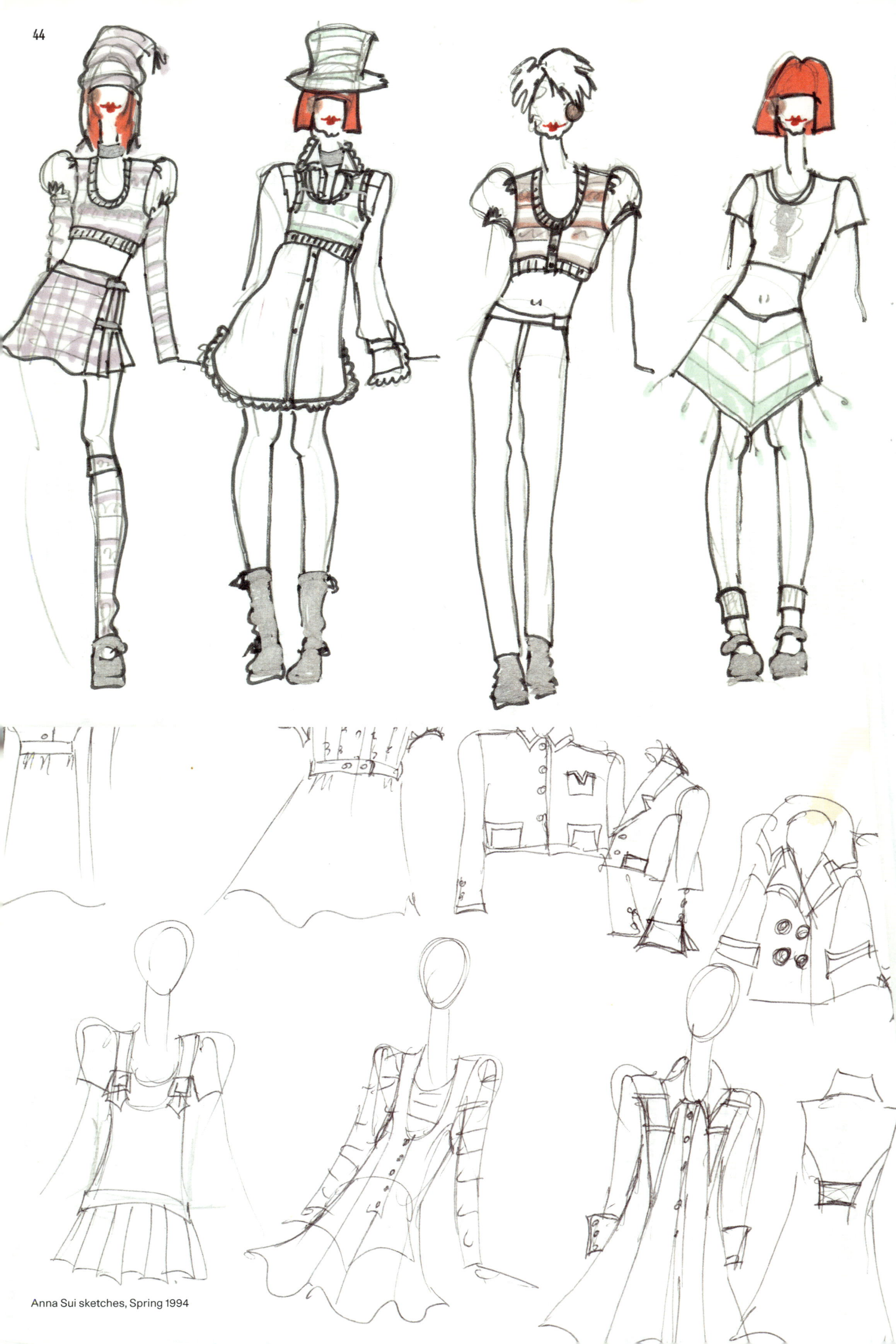

Anna Sui sketches, Spring 1994

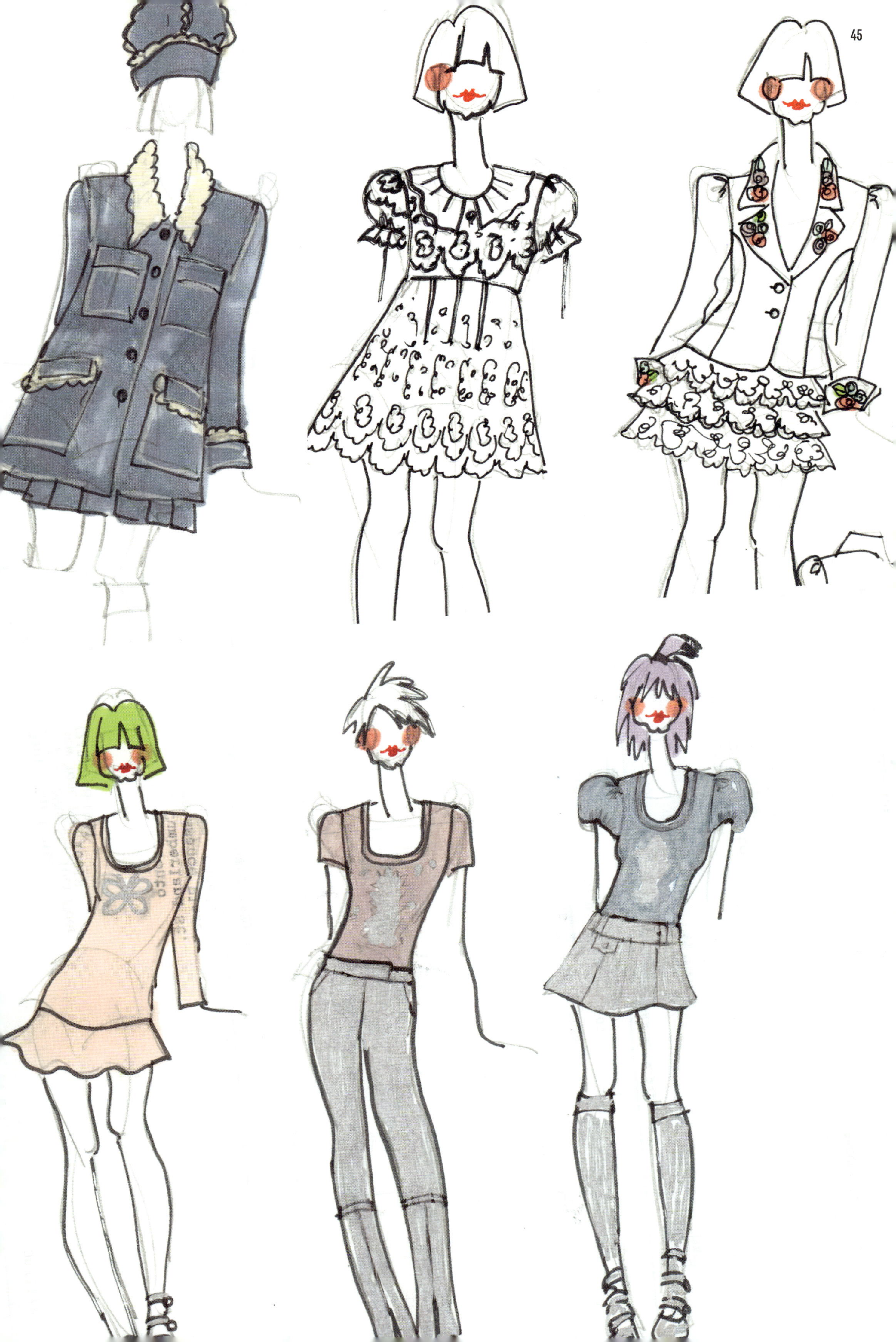

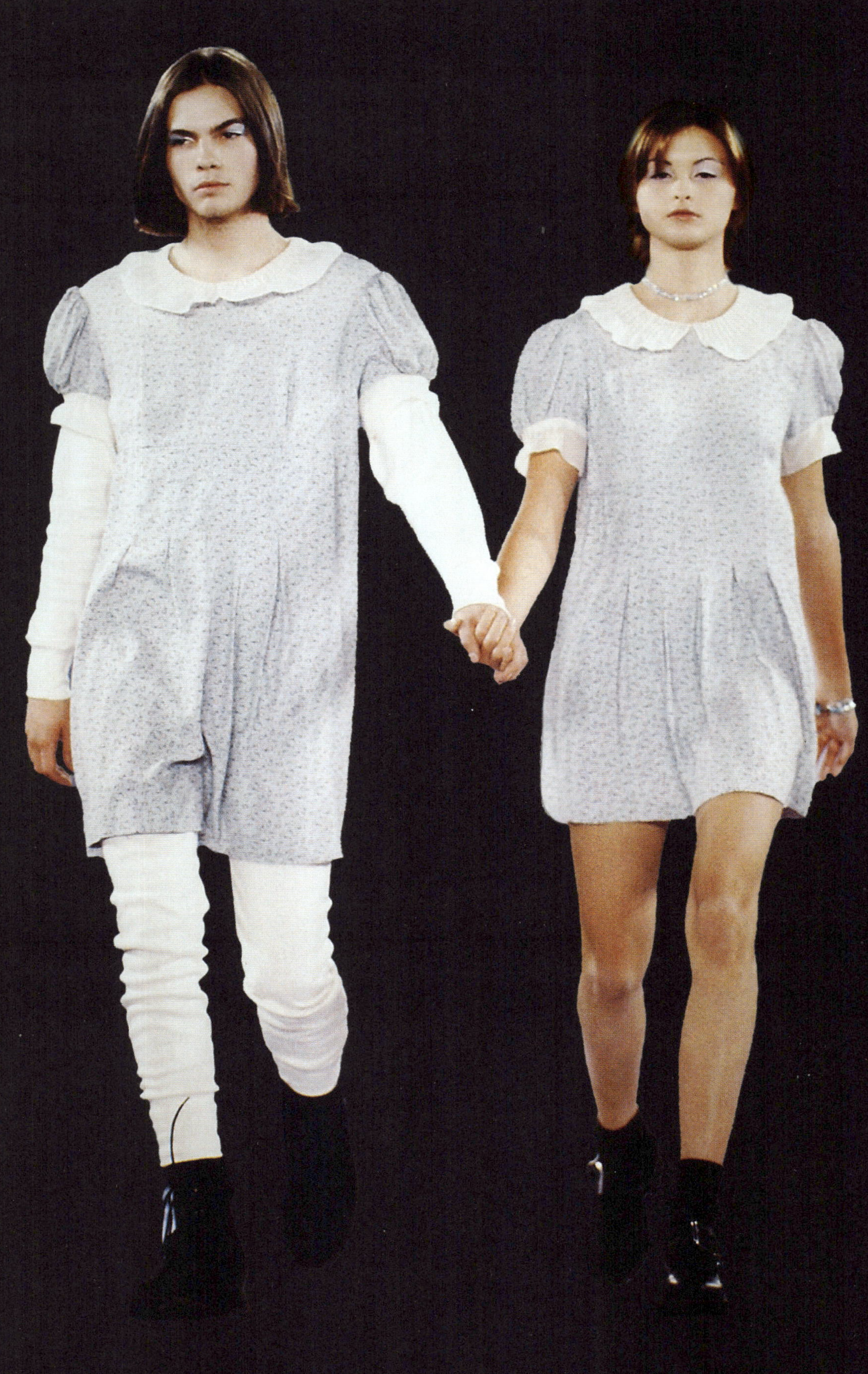

Justin Scott and Trish Goff, Spring 1994
Anna Sui sketches, Spring 1994

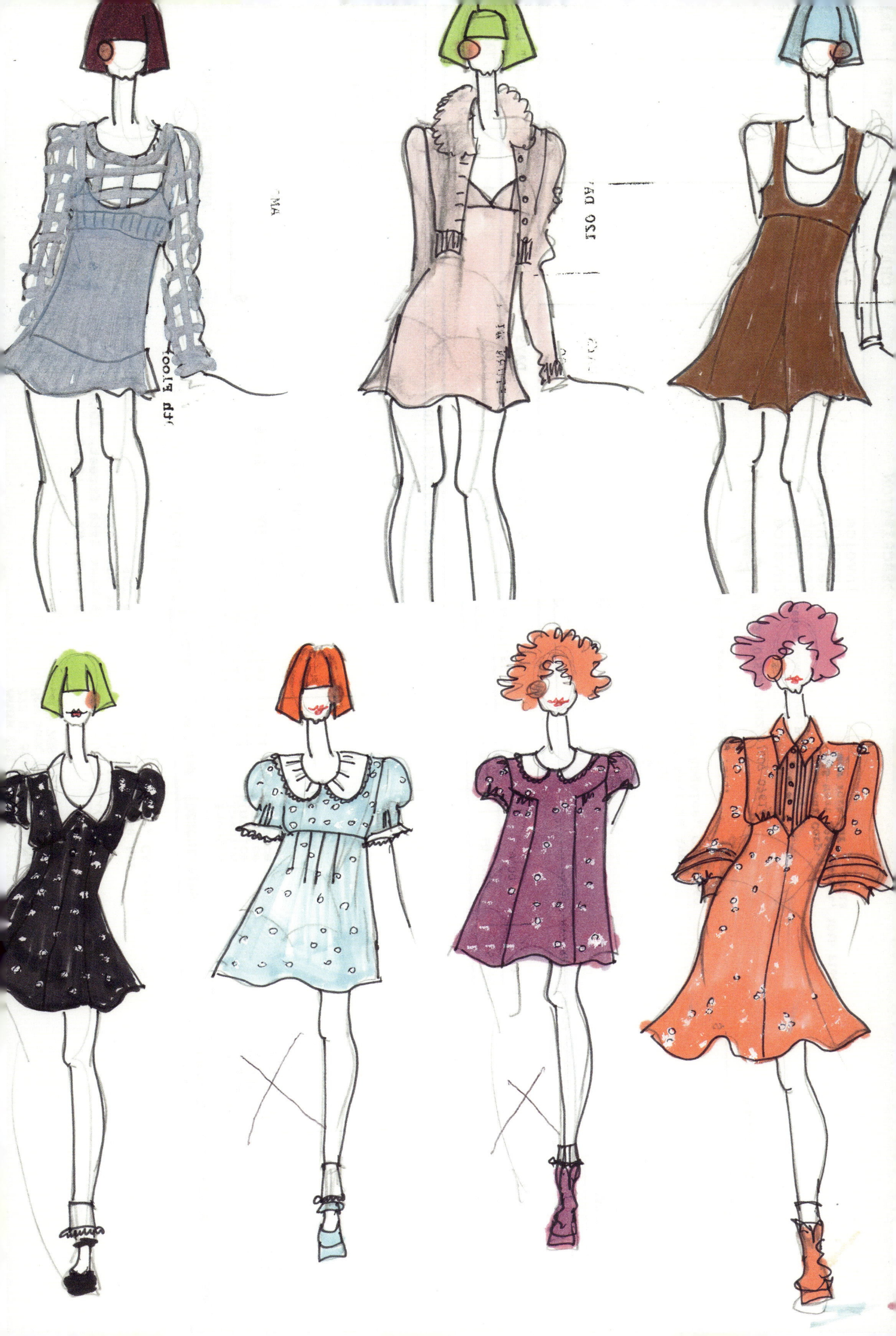

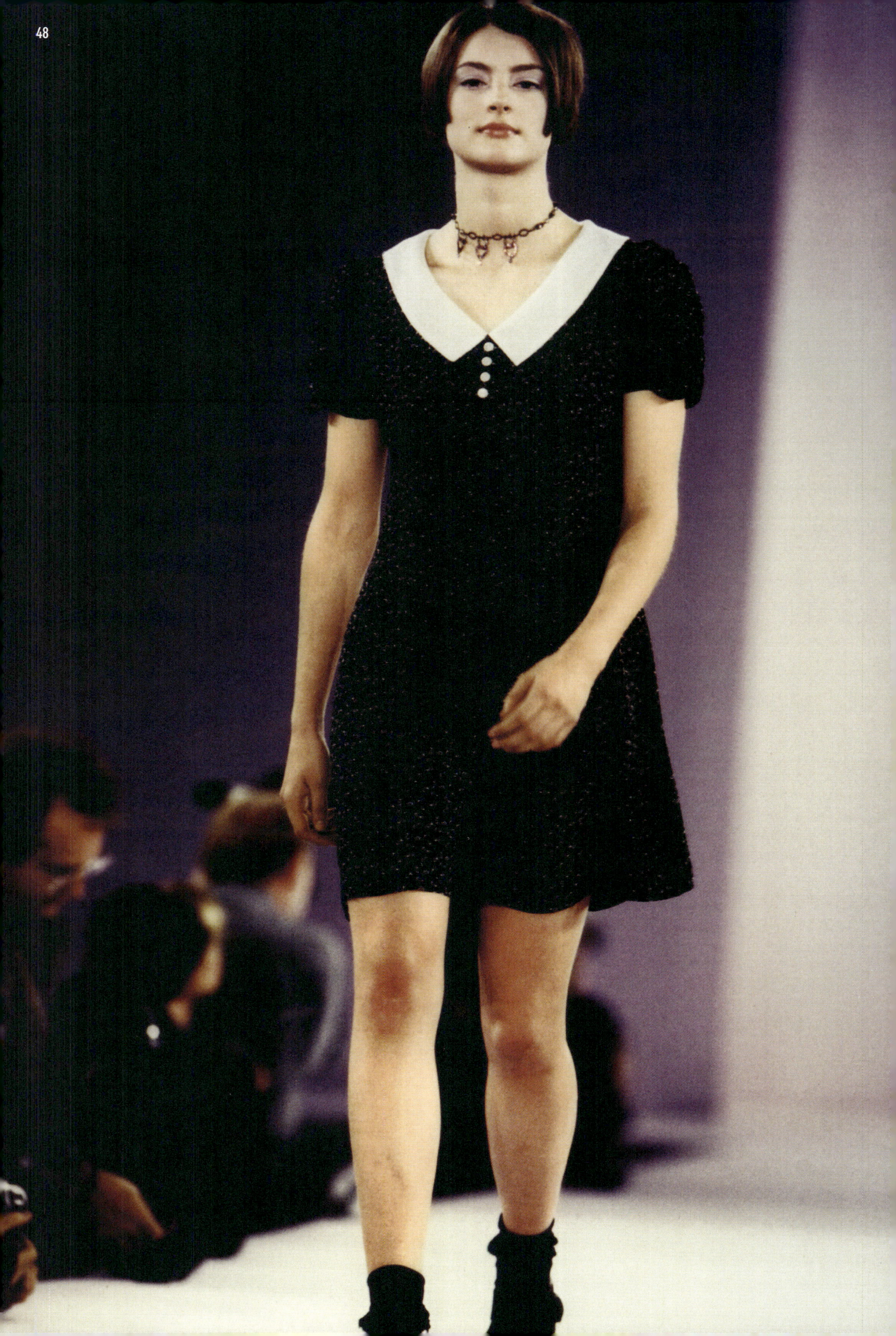

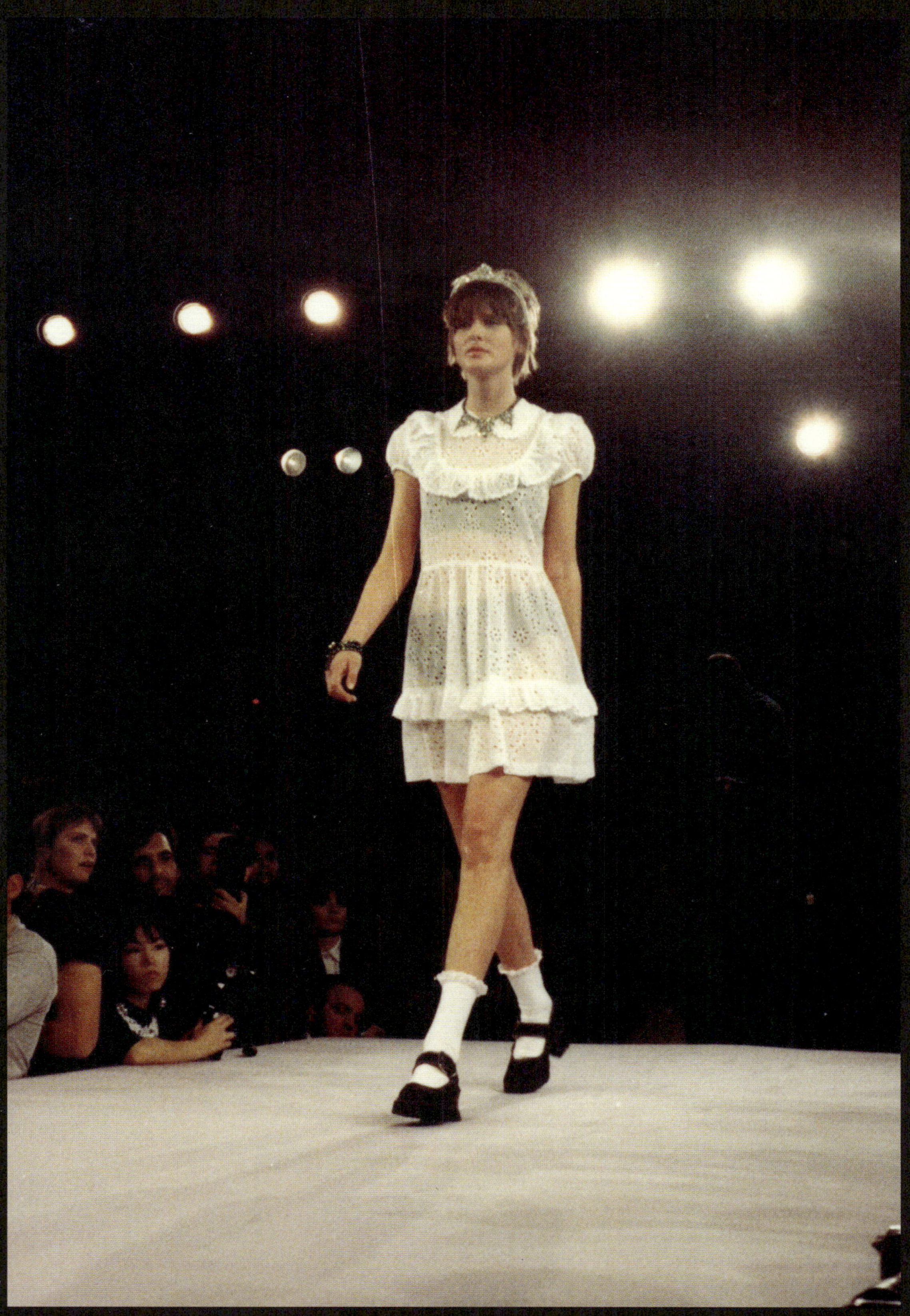

Honor Fraser, Spring 1994
Stella Tennant, Spring 1994

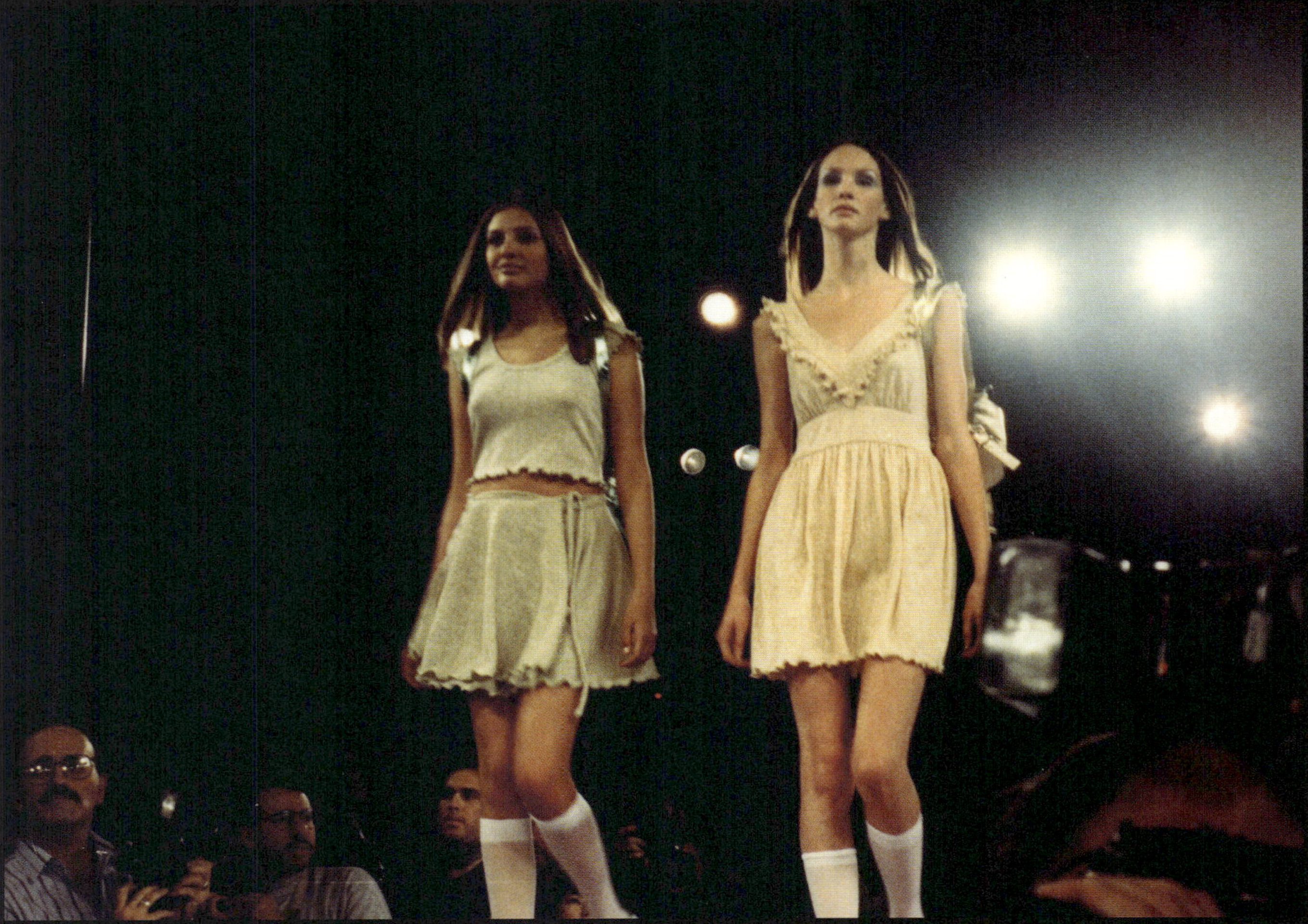

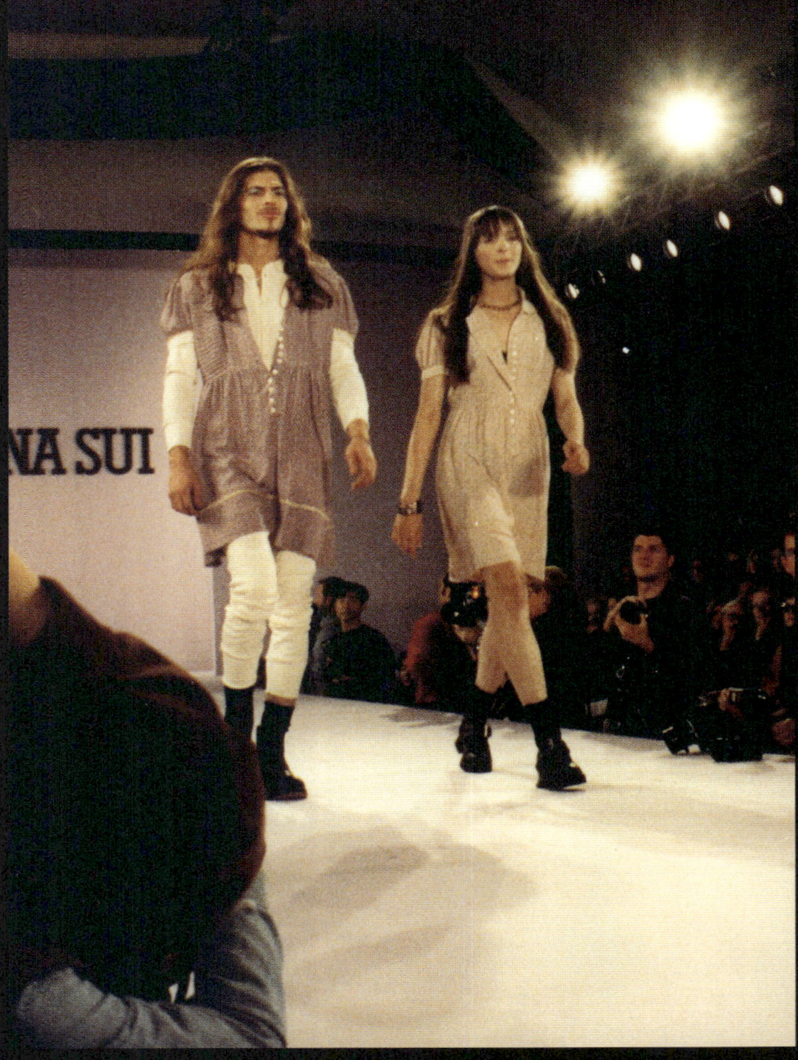

Bridget Hall and Debbie Deitering, Spring 1994
Daniel Baylock and Michele Hicks, Spring 1994
Kate Moss, Spring 1994

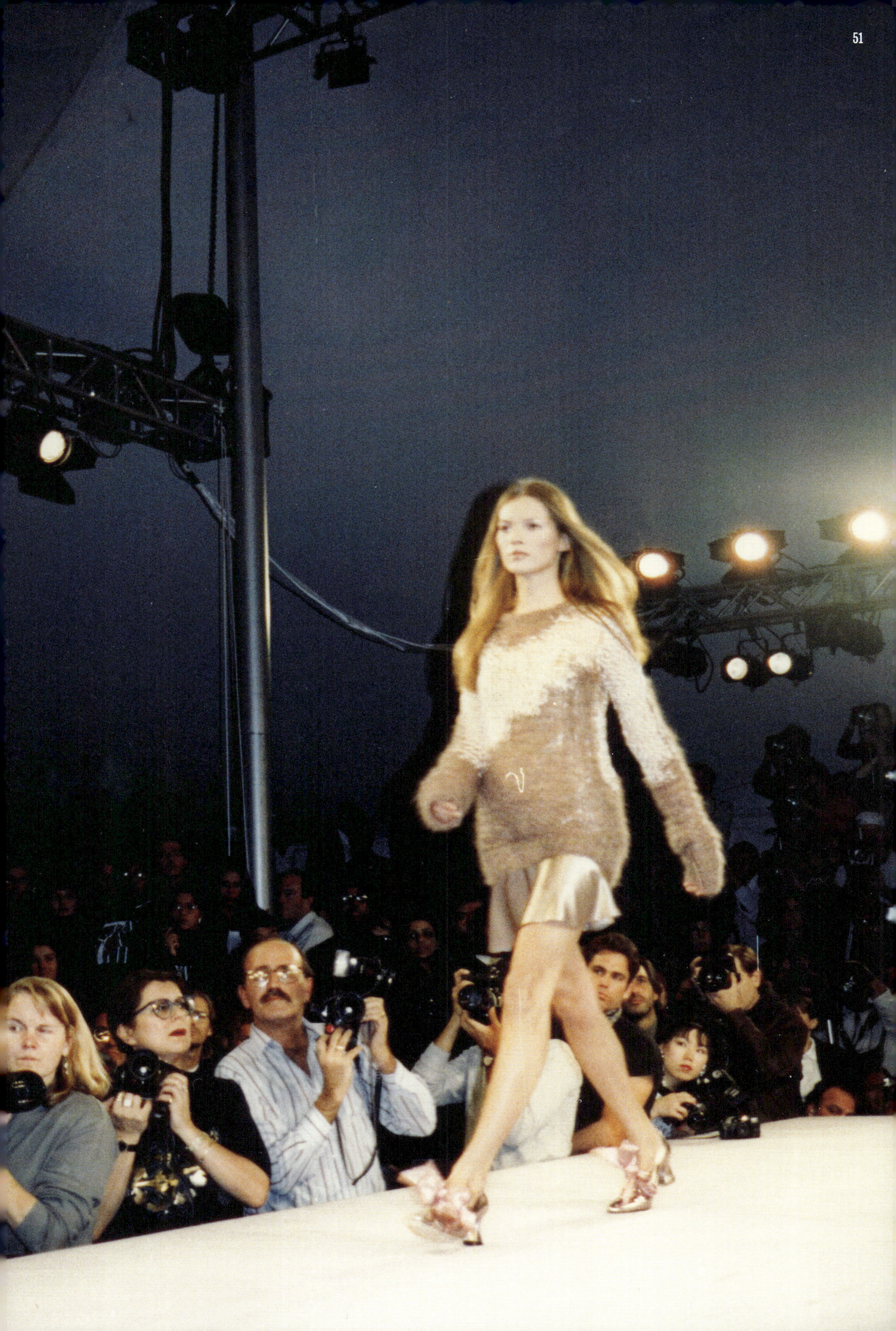

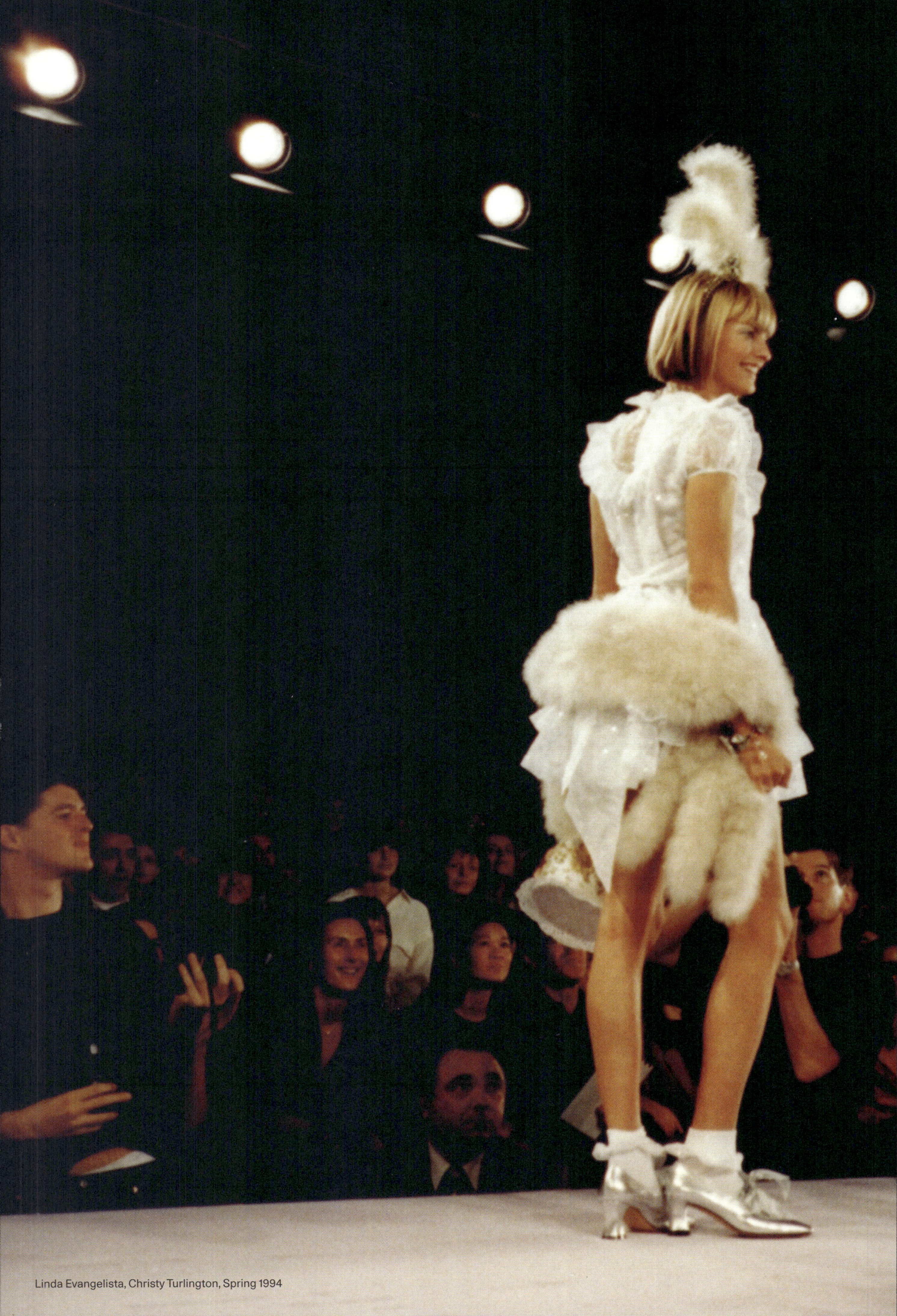

Linda Evangelista, Christy Turlington, Spring 1994

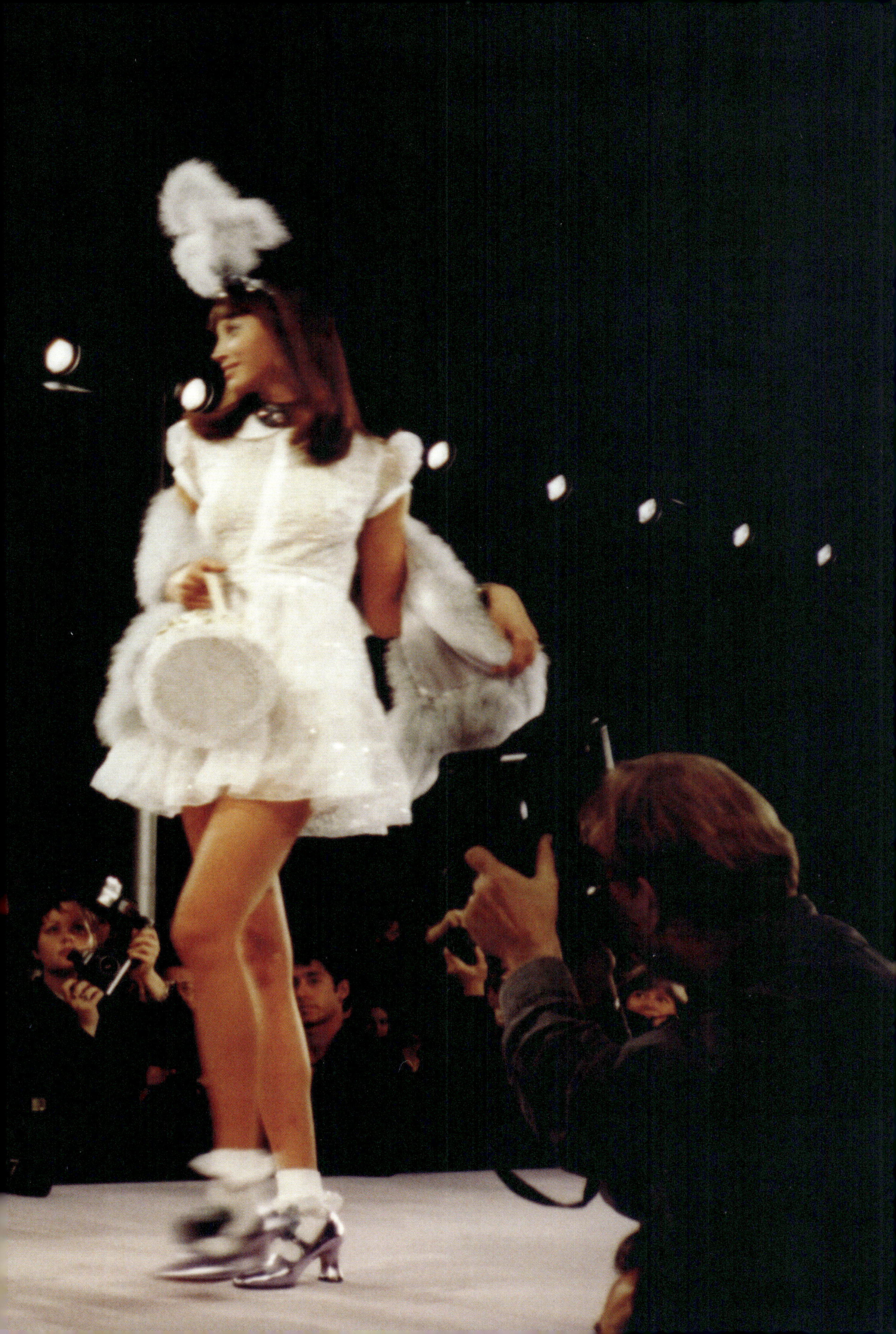

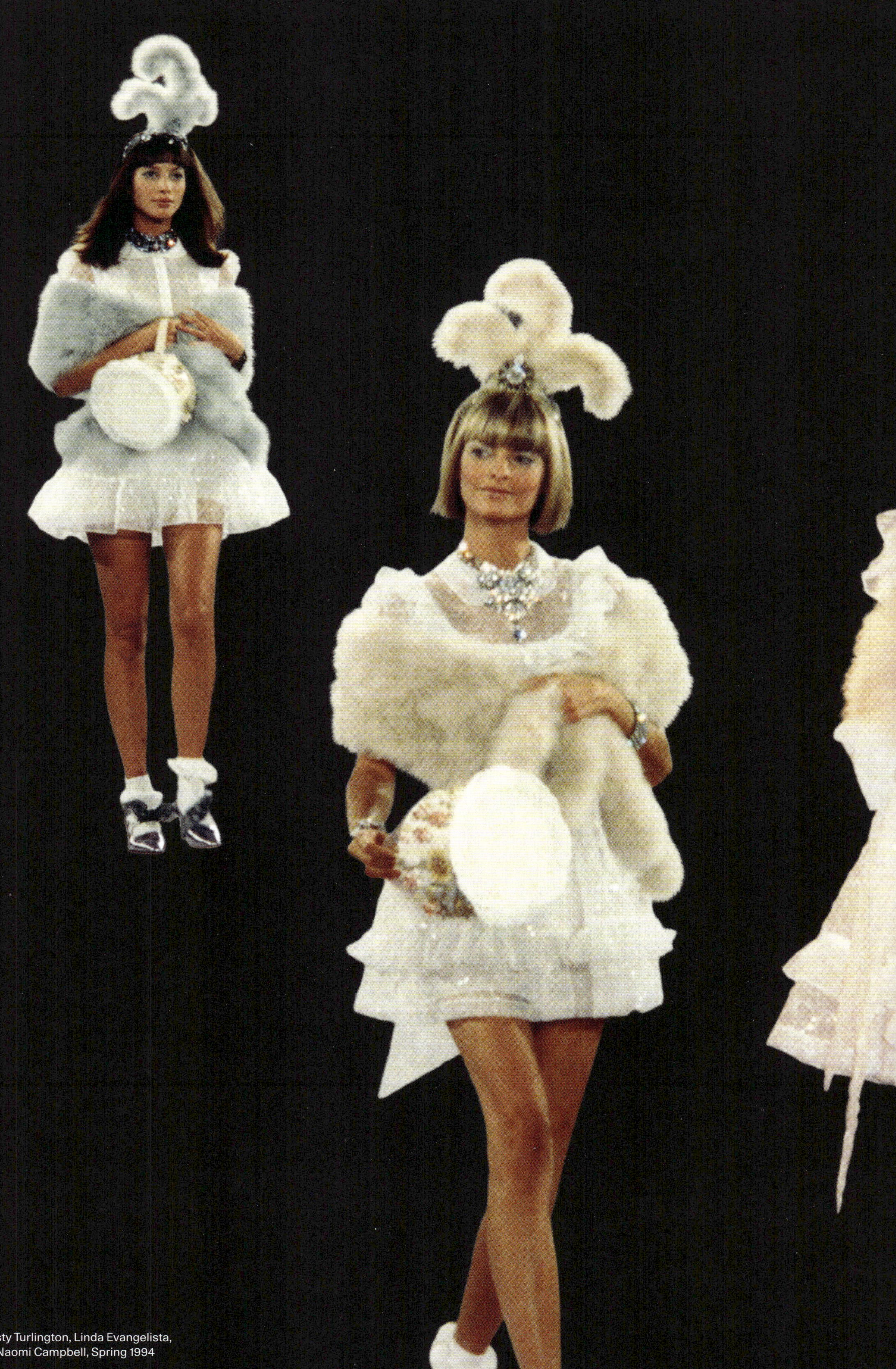

Christy Turlington, Linda Evangelista,
and Naomi Campbell, Spring 1994

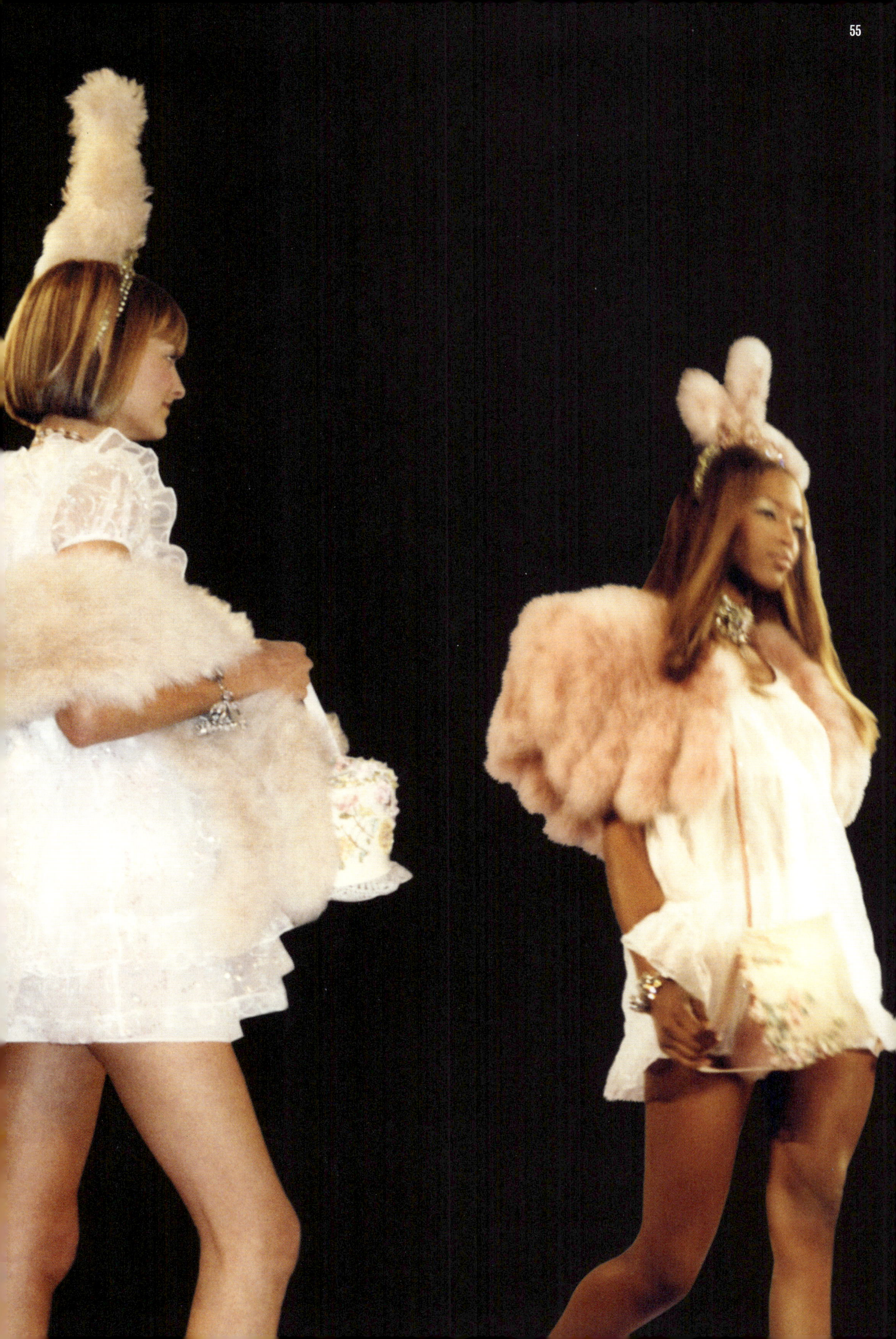

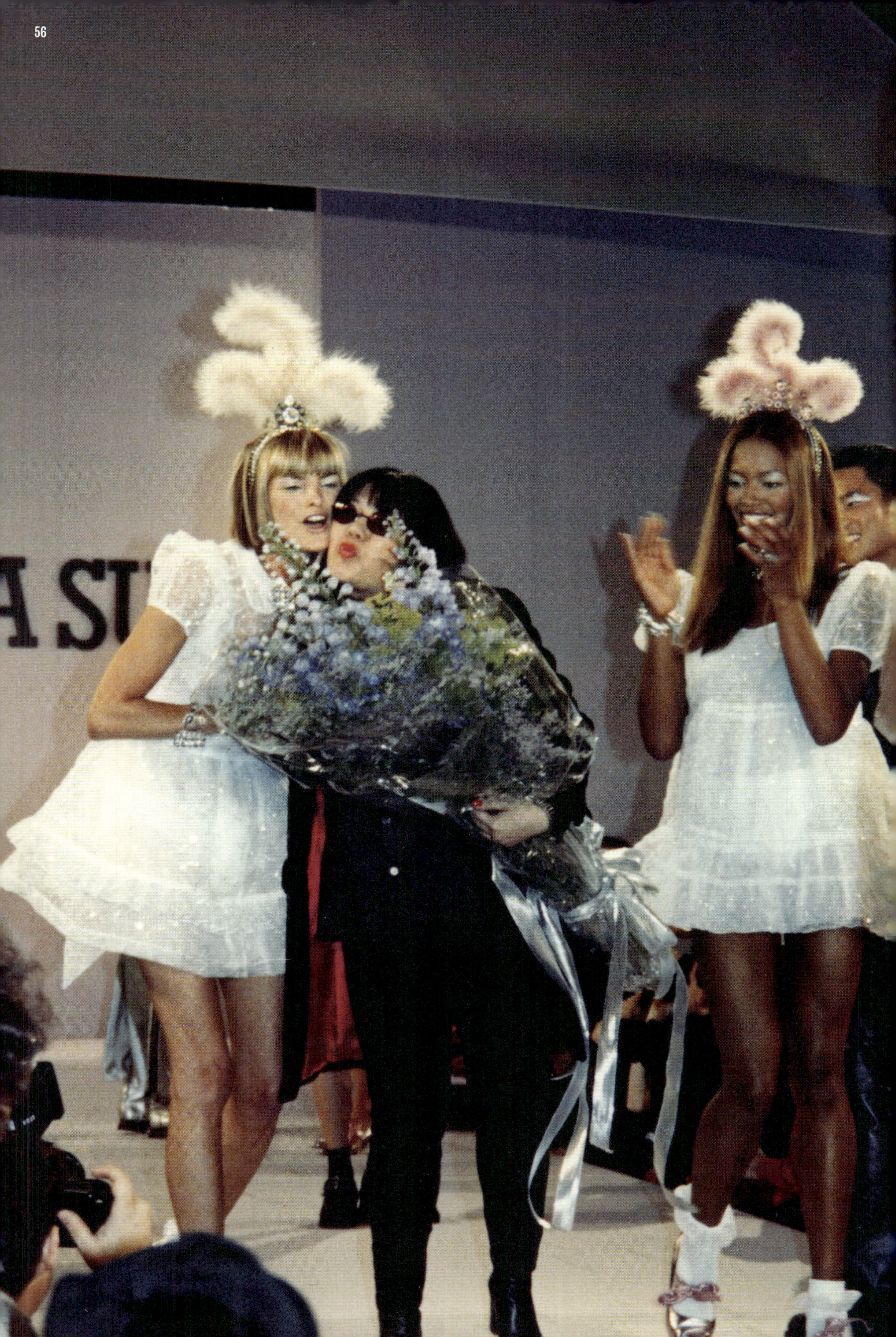

Anna Sui Pounds Out the Beat

By ANNE-MARIE SCHIRO

Today's question is "Who will wear all ıose baby-doll dresses designers are show- g for spring?" They're decidedly not meant r the nursery-school set nor for a fashion- ıle sophisticate. Who then?

Anna Sui came up with one answer in her ıllicking show on Tuesday night in Bryant ark. Her twentysomething customers who ıve enough style and wit to wear them the ay the designer shows them: with black ıderwear peeking through white eyelet, ith a marabou stole and headdress, with ıkle socks and high heels, with silver back- ıcks and lug-soled Mary Janes. Or, if you're man, over longjohns (the men's wear she ıowed last season had no dresses).

The dresses themselves in eyelet, tulle or ıral chiffon had an old-fashioned charm, ıt Ms. Sui did her best to give them a funky vist for her club-hopping fans.

Ms. Sui is not a one-note designer, though. ith rock stars like Adam Clayton and An- ıony Kiedis and movie stars like Matt Dillon ıd Christian Slater in the audience, along ith Jaye Davidson and Sofia Coppola, there ere bound to be touches of punk and rave in ır show. Silver, of course, in satin, organza ıd leather, and also metallic blue, pink, 'een and copper leathers.

lver and Lurex

She used Peruvian sweaters in ways the ıdians never dreamed, chopping them off ıches above the waist and pairing them with aid minikilts and terry-cloth vests or with lver hot pants and Lurex knee socks. And ere was Linda Evangelista wearing a tas- ıled Peruvian knitted cap with a studded lver biker's jacket and a studded silver iniskirt.

A sports-inspired group featured metallic ıtin pants or shorts with racing stripes and ıspenders hanging loose. The designer's ıst ideas for evening combined mohair veaters with satin miniskirts or pants. The en's pants had kiltlike overskirts.

Anyone can buy Anna Sui's clothes, but not 'eryone has the style to carry them off.

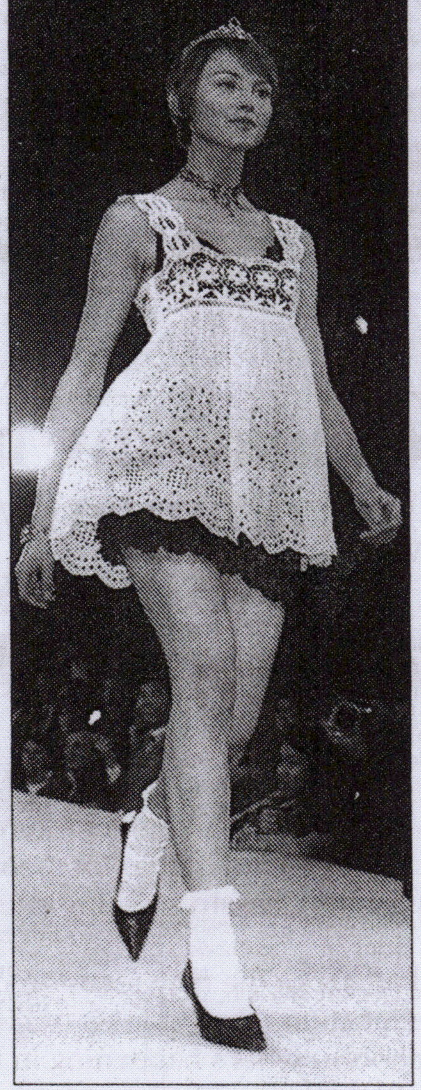

ABOVE White eyelet baby-doll dress by Anna Sui is worn over black bloomers.

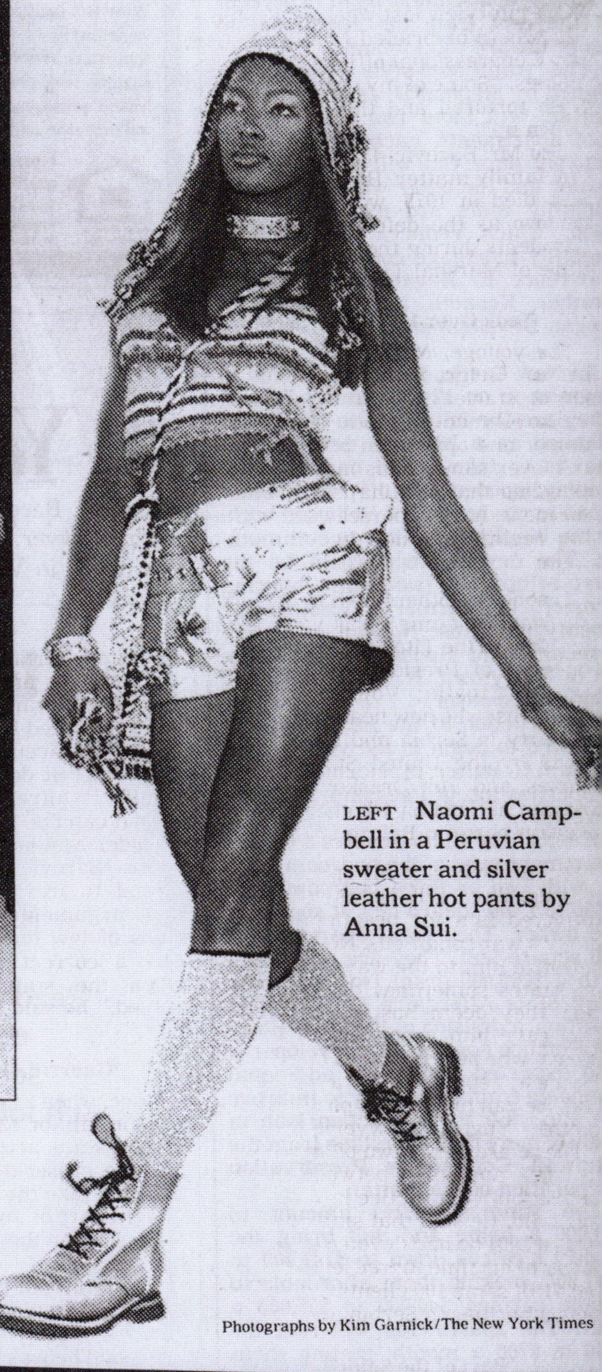

LEFT Naomi Campbell in a Peruvian sweater and silver leather hot pants by Anna Sui.

Photographs by Kim Garnick/The New York Times

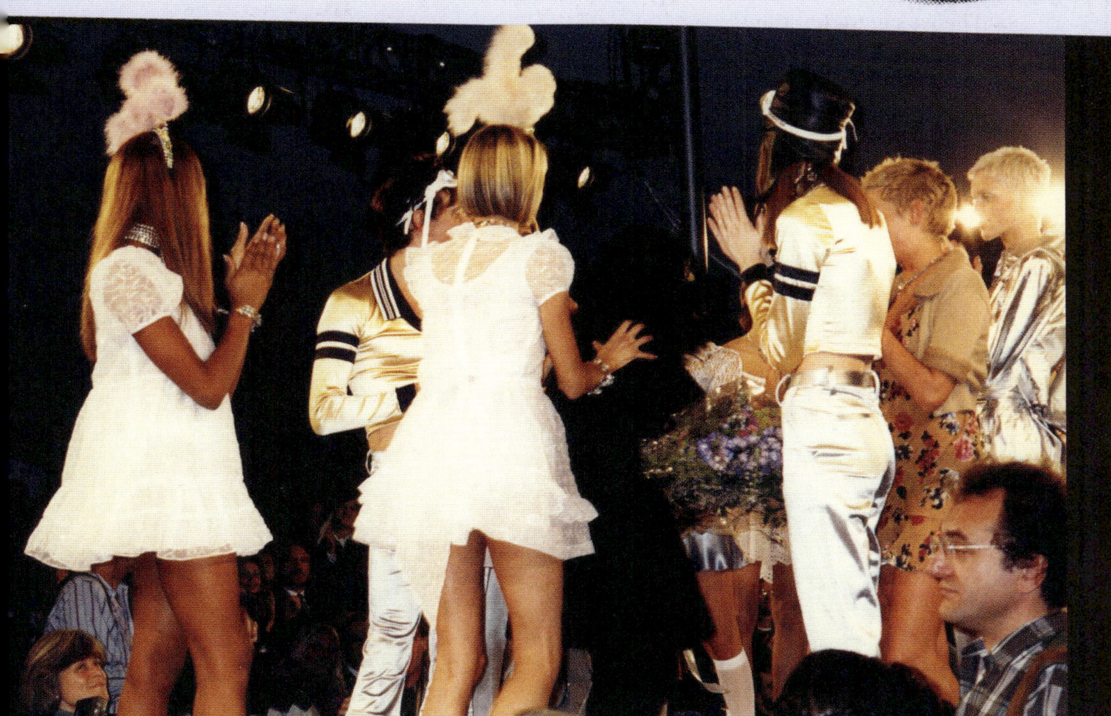

Linda Evangelista, Anna Sui, and Naomi Campbell, Spring 1994

The New York Times, November 5, 1993

Show finale, Spring 1994

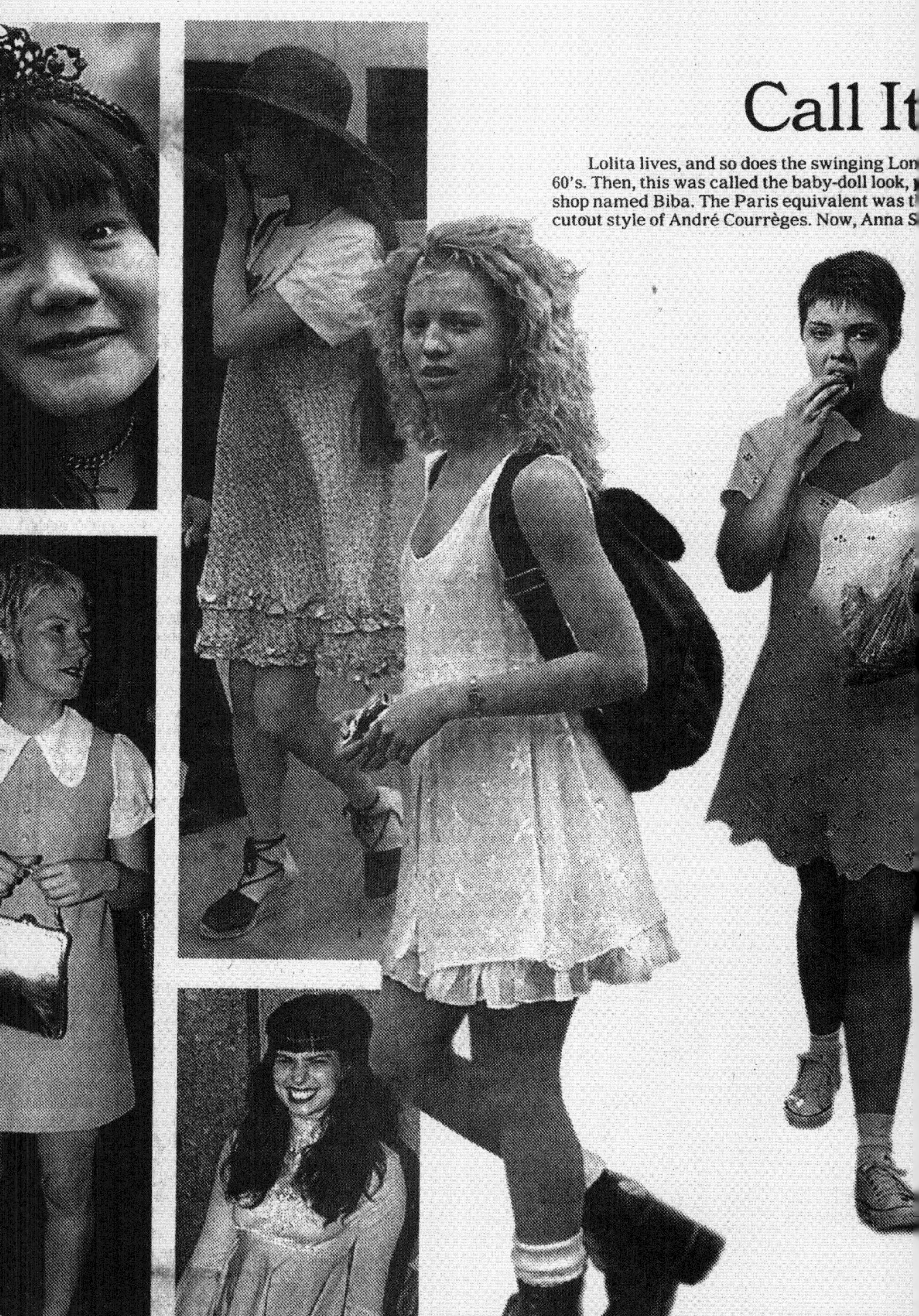

Call It

Lolita lives, and so does the swinging Lon
60's. Then, this was called the baby-doll look,
shop named Biba. The Paris equivalent was t
cutout style of André Courrèges. Now, Anna S

The New York Times, July 24, 1994

ON THE STREET

Neo-Baby Doll?

of the
eyed by a
per-doll
p left, is

leading the charge, and the new designs are distinguished by the fluidity of the fabric and cut. While these dresses used to be worn with patent-leather Mary Janes, today's styles are being seen with lace-up boots.

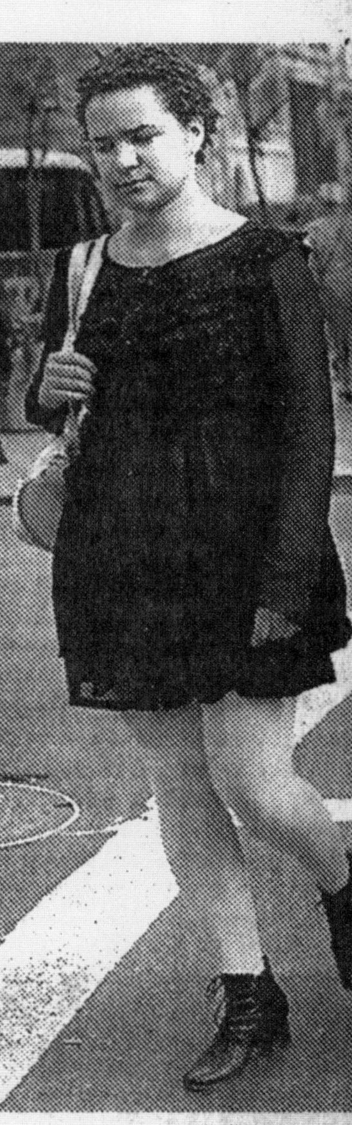

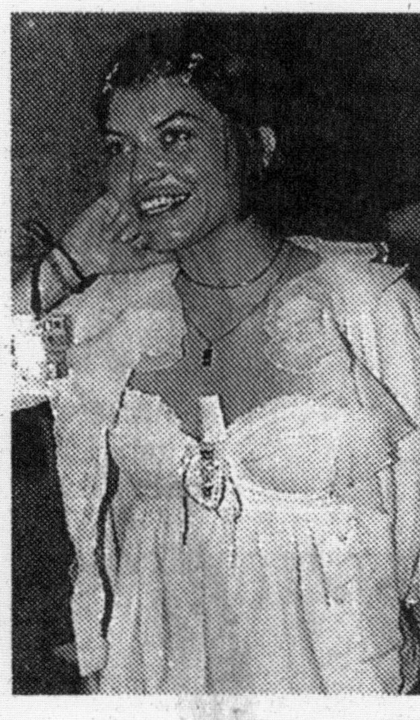

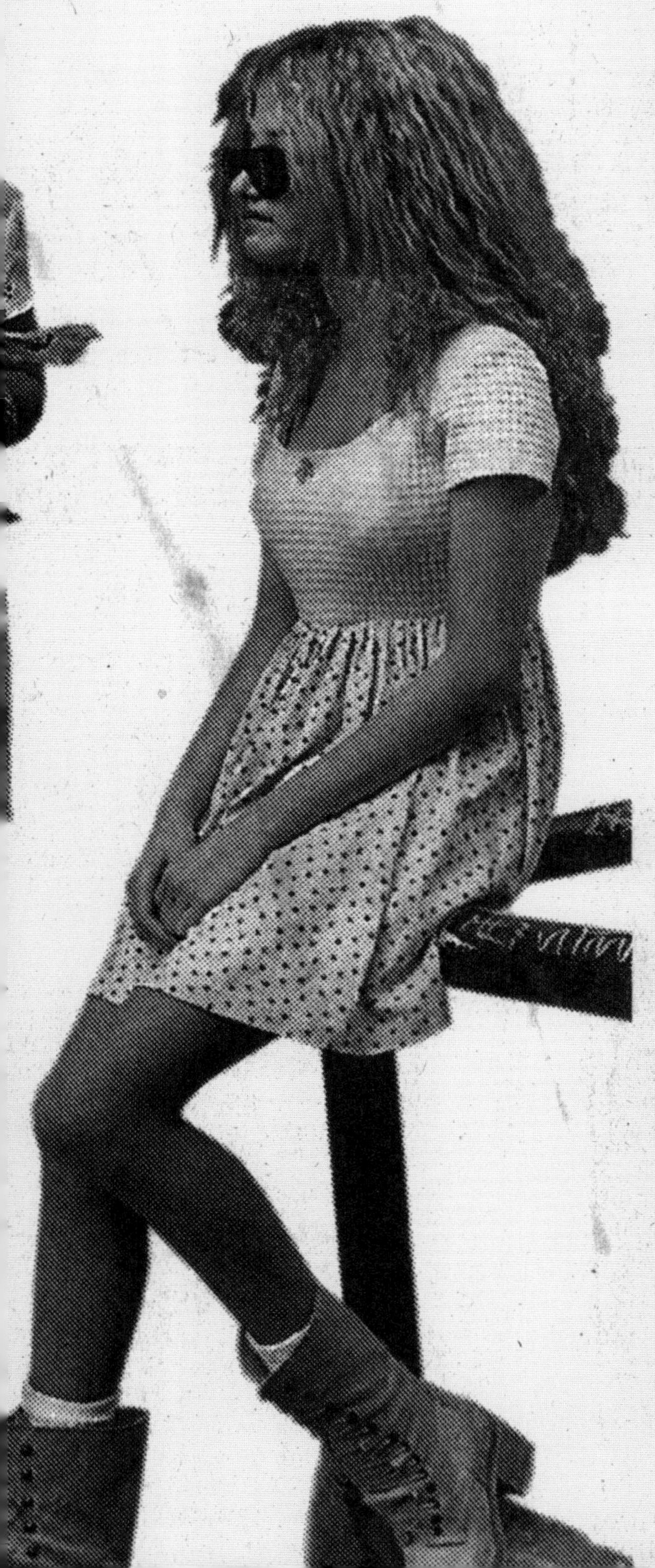

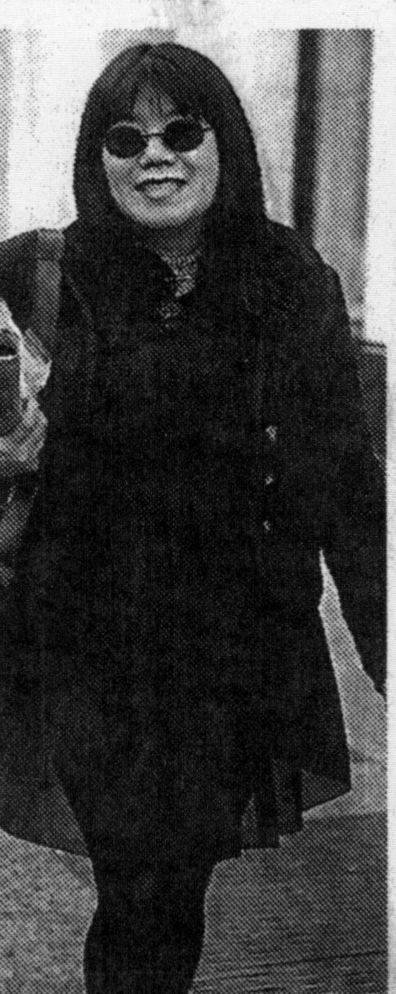

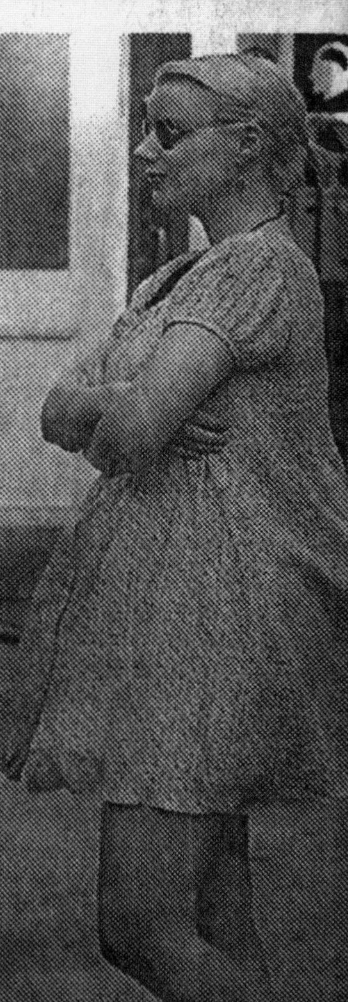

GRUNGE

"Sui's famous 'Grunge Collection' (1993), which honed in on the emerging influence of Kurt Cobain on MTV and Claire Danes on regular TV by taking slinky striped sweaters and floor skimming dresses (worn with combat boots, of course), and cranking up their color saturation and ultra-femme details like butterfly embroidery and glitter accents." *Associated Press*, April 13, 2023

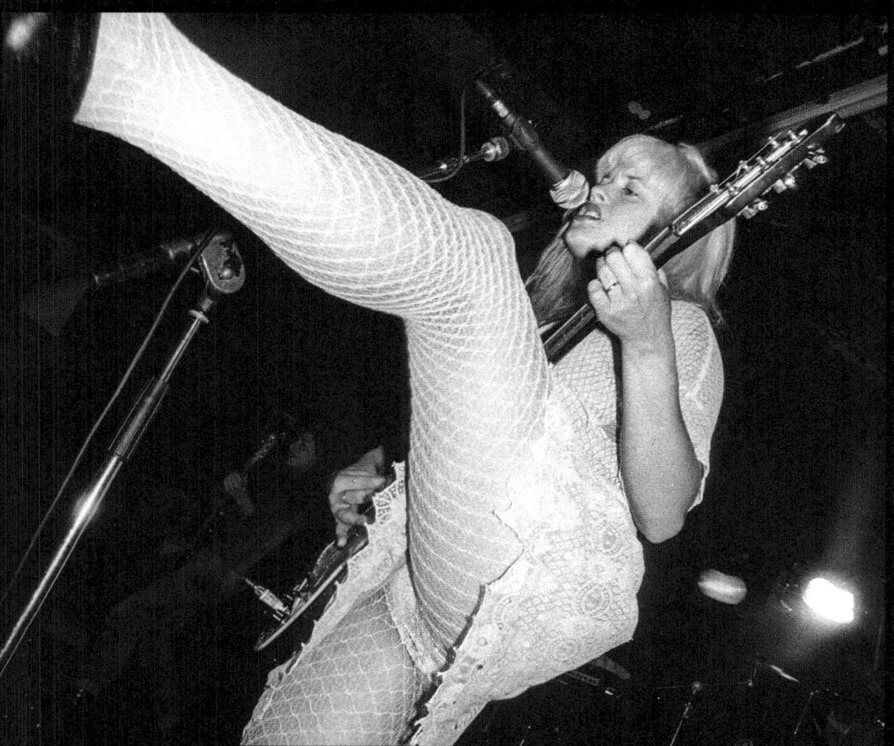

ANNA SUI

The arts on every level were changing. Suddenly there was a new music movement where bands were coming out of smaller towns like Seattle. They were more lo-fi emerging out of the '80s big hair bands that were very LA and very metal. All of a sudden, there was a much quieter thing going on. It was very exciting to see this authentic sort of music that wasn't reminiscent of anything before it. It was something that felt very fresh, very much in tune with the times. It was not just a music movement but an entire art movement. There were alternative filmmakers and a lot of new artists. There was a seismic change going on with this generation.

Kat Bjelland of Babes in Toyland, on stage at Esquires, England, 1990

Courtney Love playing at Reading Festival, Reading, UK, August 26, 1994

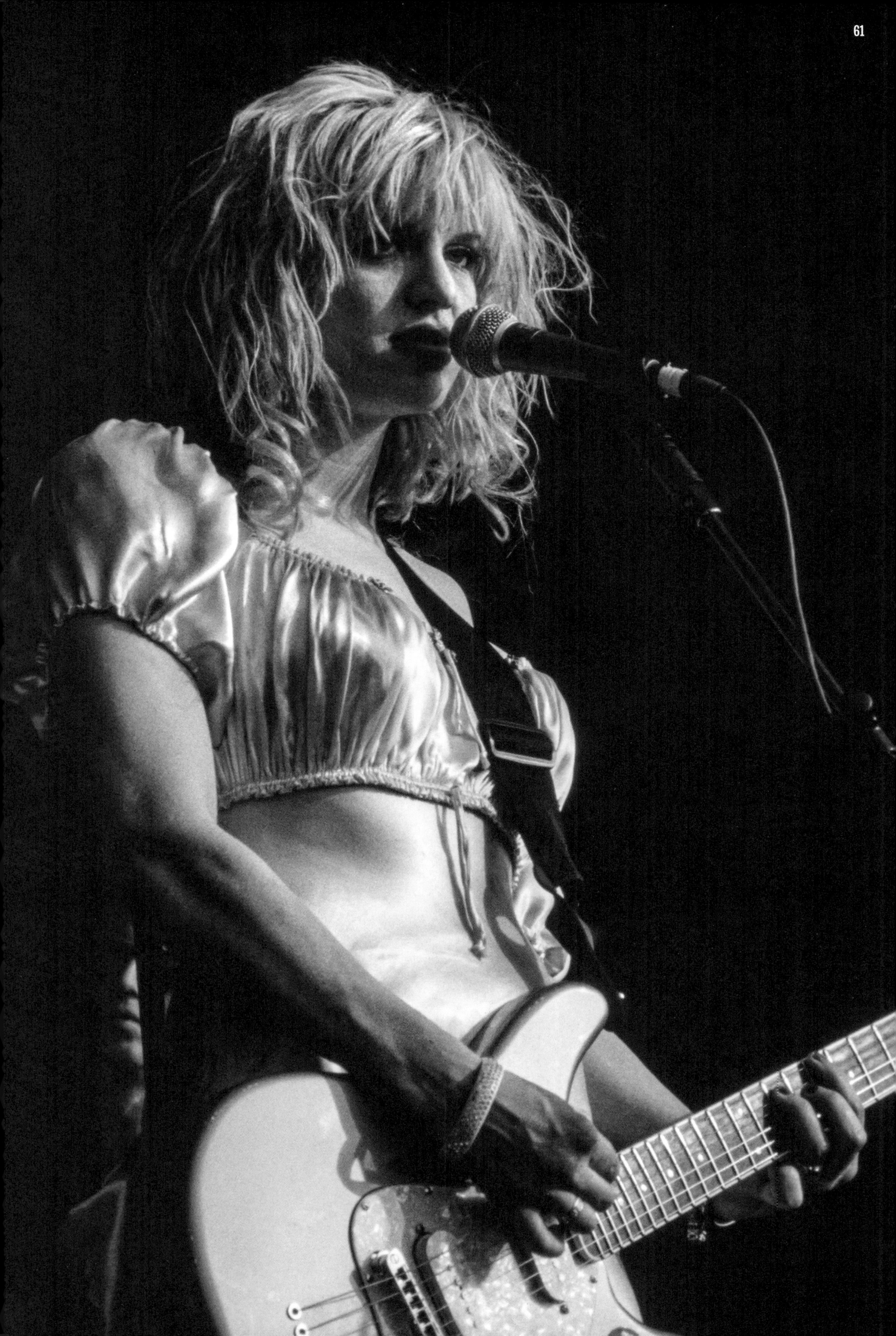

There were so many interesting people around at that point and so many were influencing me a lot. I wanted to capture that, but in a fashion way, because it was something that came out of suburbia. The Seattle scene was very suburban, and I wanted to do my take on it and give it a fashion spin. I thought I was in a unique position because I understood what that movement was about, but I could also take it to a different level with style.

It was so exciting to go see bands that weren't playing in a stadium—they played small venues and it felt so original. In the fashion world, a lot of the models were dating members of these bands, and they would be hanging out and coming to our shows. It was a really nice moment when the worlds mixed.

The first bands that I had seen were Nirvana and Smashing Pumpkins, and then all those Seattle bands started playing all the time in New York. I went to some festivals, and I saw pretty much all of them. And they were good friends, too. I remember Chris Cornell from Soundgarden, and Pearl Jam. Sonic Youth was huge, and we would go see them play. The Beastie Boys—we were really good friends and they put on that big festival, and we all went out to San Francisco. It was a two- or three-day event and every band that was happening at that moment played.

I saw Nirvana at theNew York Coliseum when it was still open. And the bigger venue was Madison Square Garden or the Felt Forum. Sometimes there would be festivals in the park, and Sonic Youth or Nick Cave would be playing, and then everybody would go to hang out just to see each other. It was a real scene.

And then there was Blind Melon that had that one hit about the little bee that was dancing "Bee Girl." It was a huge hit on MTV. MTV was very connected to the fashion world because Alisa Belletini started *House of Style* [hosted by Cindy Crawford], and brought together music and fashion. All of that went hand in hand with what was going on in the fashion scene in New York. And when those bands were in town, they would come to see the fashion shows. It was all very interconnected.

Grunge was seismic because think about the '80s and how it was flamboyant, big shouldered and all about power dressing—it was very Ivana Trump. Then suddenly everything got deflated, the hair got deflated, and the clothes looked worn—the more worn the better—and then that was mixed with vintage. It could not have been more different than the bright gold buttons on jackets and shoulder pads from the '80s.

At the time, I was very nostalgic about the '60s or the '70s or the Victorian era. It was one of the few collections I did at the moment. And it was how people were dressing. It was '93, just two years into me doing fashion shows. There was just a big change in how models were dressing. Everybody was dressing down rather than dressing up. There was a lot of vintage thrown in. And I remember at the big festival in San Francisco saying to some of my friends that I can see the next collection. I noticed in the audience everybody was wearing something Army fatigue mixed with an "ethnic" look, mixed with sportswear, mixed with punk, and it just all started blending. Tribal tattoos were really popular at the time. People were traveling a lot and that exposure to different cultures showed up in the clothes. It was not a designer look. It was not a head-to-toe look. It was very much dressing down. And it just became very clear that was the right look at that time.

Naomi Campbell embraced the grunge look more than anyone. She had to have those outfits right away. She's in that first Steven Meisel photoshoot in *Vogue* where she's wearing one of my Chinese cheongsam dresses, which actually came from the collection before grunge, and it was styled with a man's overcoat, a knit cap, and some kind of army boots. She would wear that kind of look when she went out. She liked going to vintage stores and wearing old '40s dresses mixed with army boots and men's cardigans or coats.

Everyone was wearing long underwear layers, thermal layers. My version of the thermal layer was a brightly colored stripe. The Iraq War was raging at the time and that piece was my protest against war because I wanted peace and love. There were the army fatigue pieces that layered over it, and belts that I got from the army surplus which we put flowers on. Everything seemed to be blanketed with love and rainbows and peace, even though we incorporated an army surplus feeling to it.

John Fluevog was making boots inspired by army boots, but we made them with a multicolor platform. There was a guy in the East Village that made custom platform layers for your boots. We color coordinated those layers. It was taking things that I saw people wearing but making them more "Anna Sui" and crafting a designer collection from it.

Naomi Campbell, *Vogue* magazine, December 1992

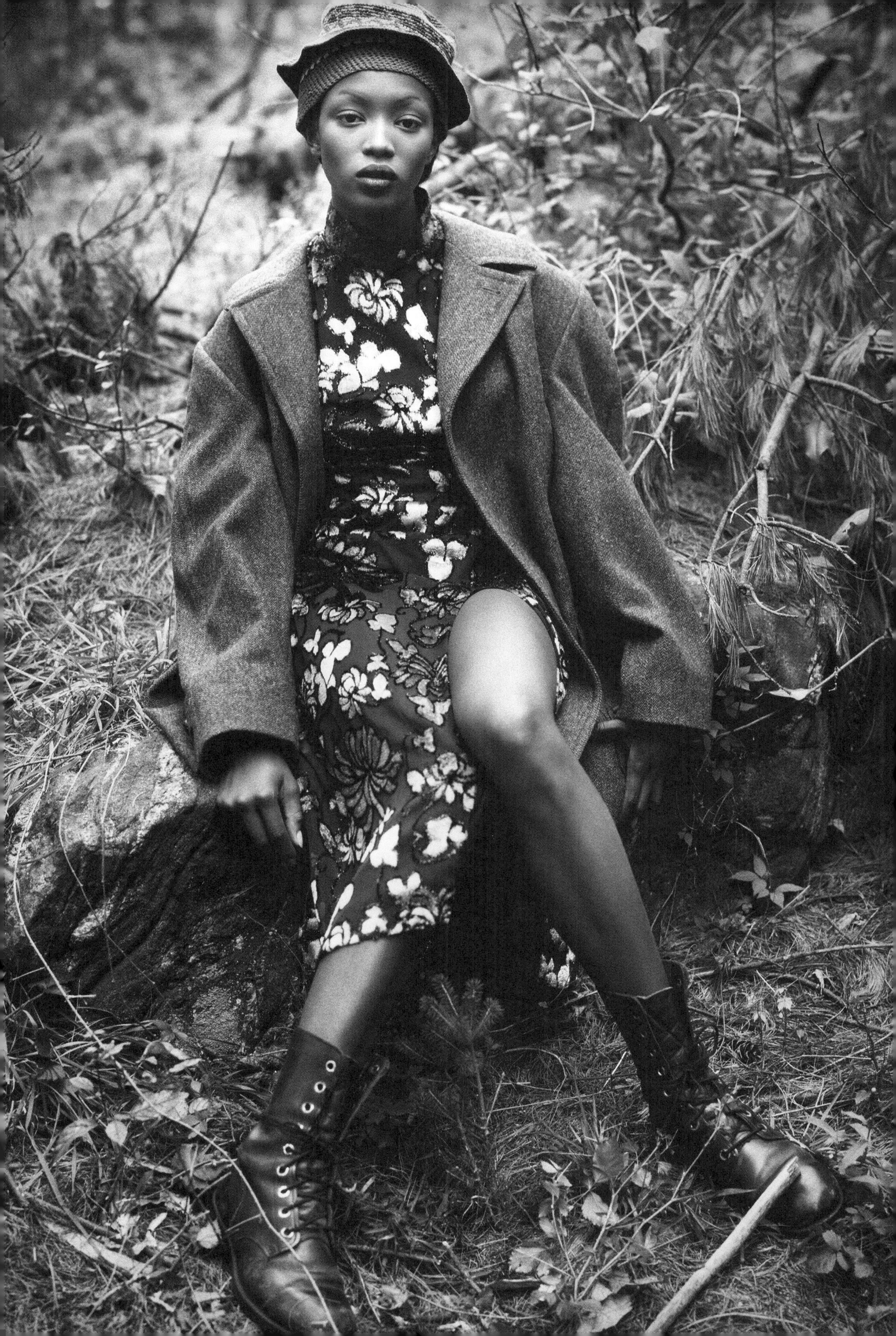

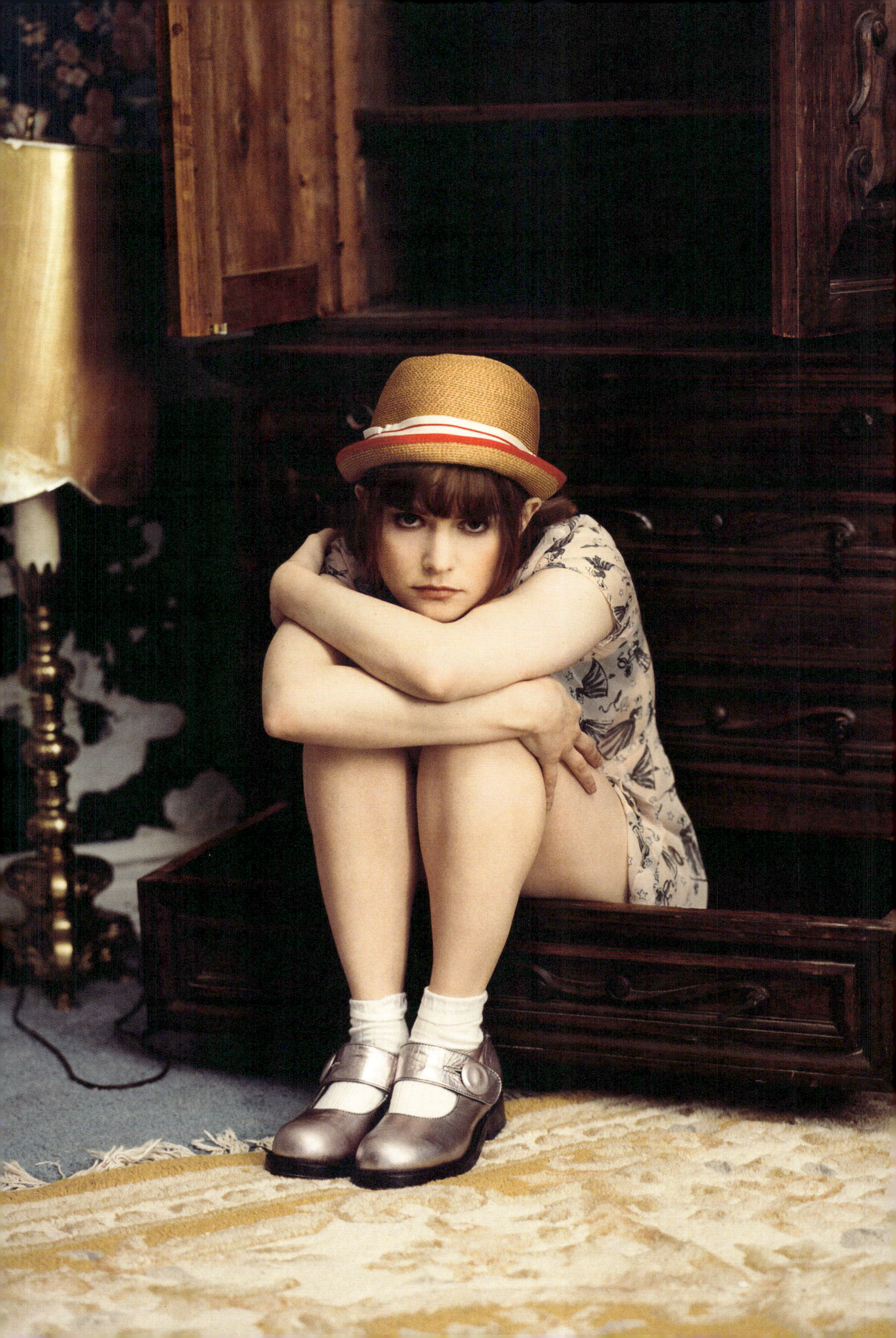

Jennifer Jason Leigh, *Vogue* magazine, February 1994

Young people especially find that period very romantic—you can craft your version of it easily. On the runway I was showing how to create the look, but you can easily adapt. Hippie fashion was kind of like that, too.

Grunge never really went away—there's an element of it that continues. The Brooklyn hipster, that's really grunge. The combination of army fatigues and the plaid shirt and oversized T-shirt and the sneakers or the combination of skater mixed with surfer mixed with the beanie caps and the beards. All that comes from grunge. The moment when grunge emerged, though, was such a different moment, the music and fashion worlds were so in sync. And I think that's why it was such an impactful thing.

MARC JACOBS

I started to see friends and other girls running around the city in a bit of a slip dress with an old '50s cardigan over it and with sneakers—it just looked so good to me. It's kind of poor, dowdy, and it's very eclectic, like mixing out-of-context sensibility and style. I just thought it looks so right. The girls who wore it looked so stylish, and it's probably very similar to what happened in the '70s, when those girls discovered the '40s. There was Courtney Love, and Kim Gordon from Sonic Youth, who were huge influences. And there were all these girls in music who had great style—they played a big part in it, too. When Courtney wore those white baby doll dresses that were torn. And she'd wear these tiny little dresses, but she wasn't diminutive at all—she's six feet tall— and they were busting at the seams. They weren't really baby doll dresses, but they had that kind of naive innocence about them, but stained and almost tattered. Courtney called it—it's not my word—"kinderwhore." It was this sort of twisted, demented style.

There was a huge shift in music at that time, and then having the visuals just added to the importance of the movement. I'm not a music critic, and I can't speak with any real knowledge of music history, but I think grunge was very different than the type of rock 'n' roll music that came before it. It was dismissive of metal and dismissive of other things that were super popular.

There was also something about grunge that I remember really well—a word that I always loved: it was that the heroes of grunge were shoegazers. There was something uncomfortable about them. It didn't feel like they were the cool kids, and they didn't want to be like the cool kids. They were cool in spite of themselves. There was an awkwardness. The music was totally strong and confident and had all of this edge and energy. But the message in the music and the performers themselves was that they were shoegazers, people who look down and didn't want attention and I think that's a such a good description of the way those thrift shop clothes were worn.

STEFF YOTKA

It seems like a moment when super casual clothing was permitted to be on the runways. Flannels were never allowed to be fashion. It was very much clothing from the mall. But Naomi Campbell in striped pants and a jean vest walking the runway was revelatory at that time. It's how kids dressed or wanted to dress. And I think grunge, as an idea, resonates with young people today because it doesn't feel studied or precious—it's easy and authentic. When I was growing up, the worst thing you could be called was a sellout or a phony. It would give you anxiety for days. If I went to school wearing a T-shirt with a skateboarding brand logo and I didn't skateboard, I would be roasted and end up in the bathroom crying. Today everyone is totally happy to be a sellout. That's why grunge remains like a real cultural fixation because it was about authenticity and subversion. It was also one of the last musical genres to really see success before the internet created a new way of consuming and remixing music. Now so much of the music comes to the audience as singles rather than an entire album. There's a real fascination and freedom around grunge. And Anna makes grunge so glamorous. Even if you would never be caught dead hanging out with skateboarders, you would still want to wear a fabulous sheer T-dress that Anna made in a grunge collection. This is the beauty of Anna's work: she can take anything and make it seem more beautiful and more glamorous and more exciting than maybe even the original idea is. Don't you wish someone could just do that to your closet every day?

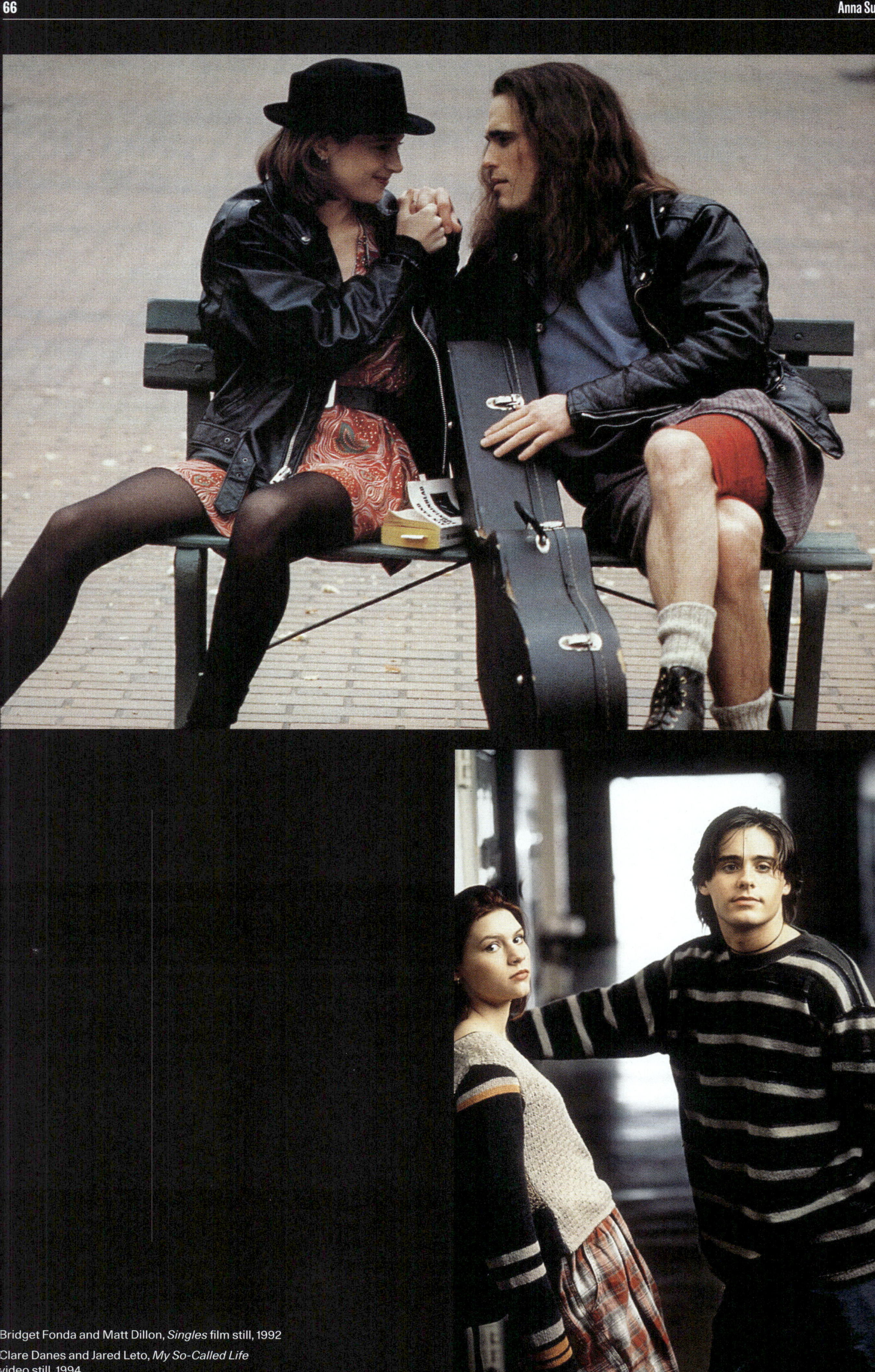

Bridget Fonda and Matt Dillon, *Singles* film still, 1992

Clare Danes and Jared Leto, *My So-Called Life* video still, 1994

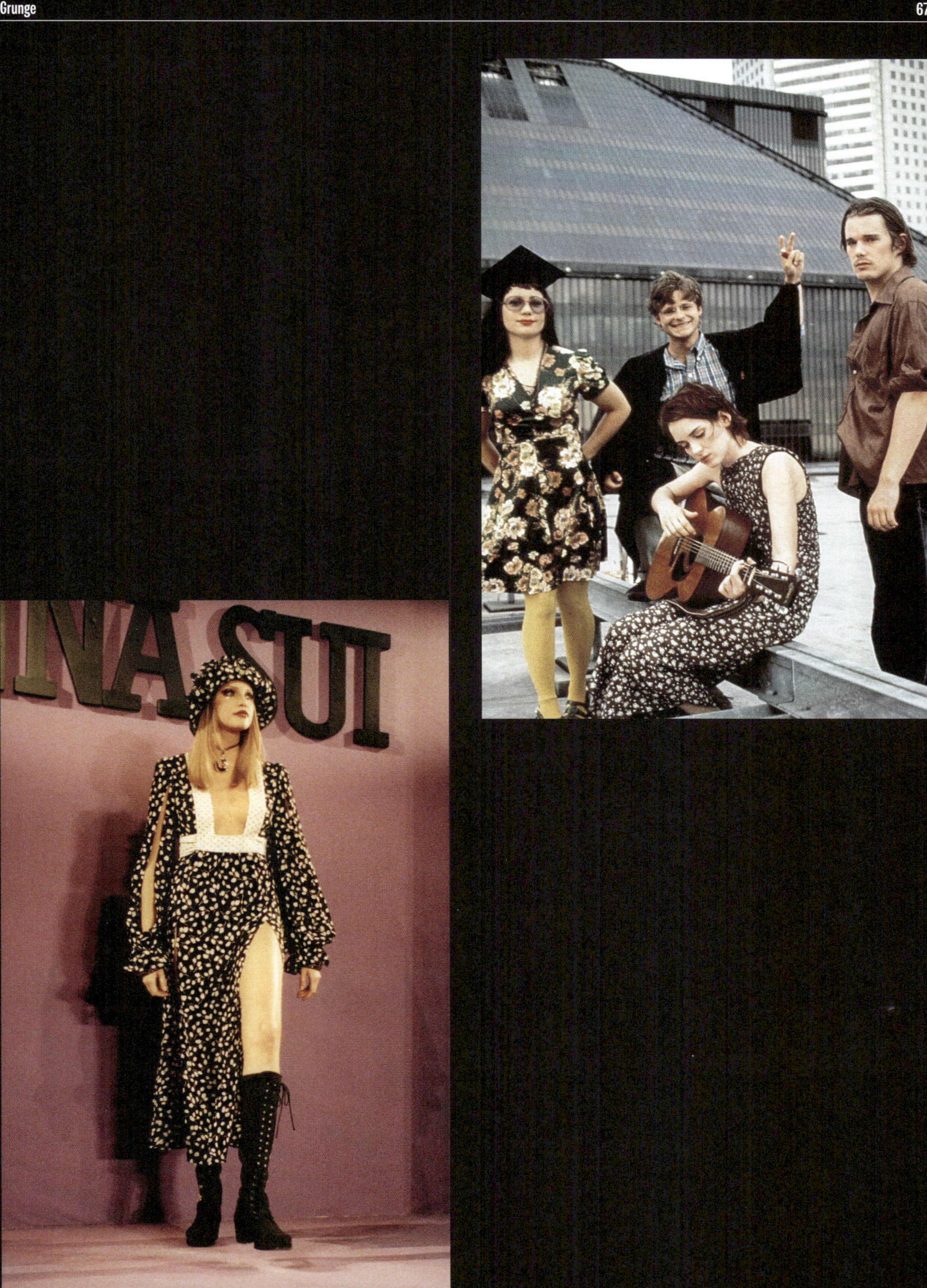
NA SUI

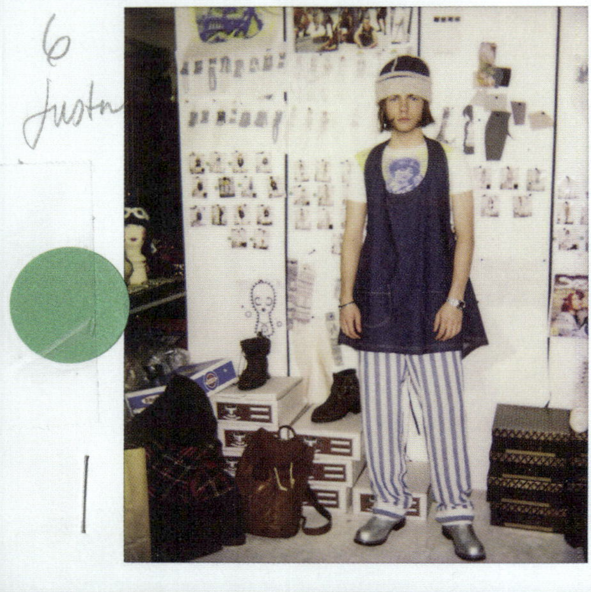

6. **Justin**
Indigo patch pocket apron
Blue cleopatra mini tee
Blue/white stripe pajama pant w/matching panels

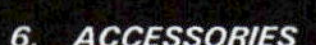

6. ***ACCESSORIES***
- ***denim fleece lined hat***
- ***silver lace up boot*** (size 9½)
- black socks (leave on for #47)

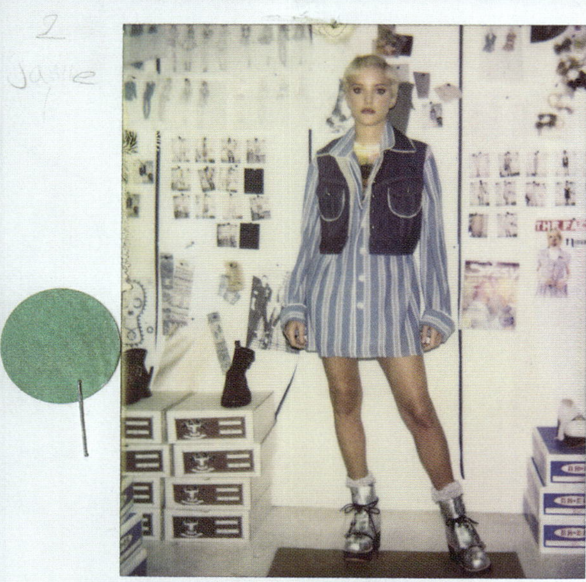

2. **Jamie**
Indigo jean fleece lined crop vest (open)
Blue and white stripe pajama top (buttoned)
Orange cleopatra mini tee

2. ***ACCESSORIES***
- ***silver glitter knee-hi*** (pushed down around ankle)
- ***silver lace up buckle boot with wood platform*** (size 6)

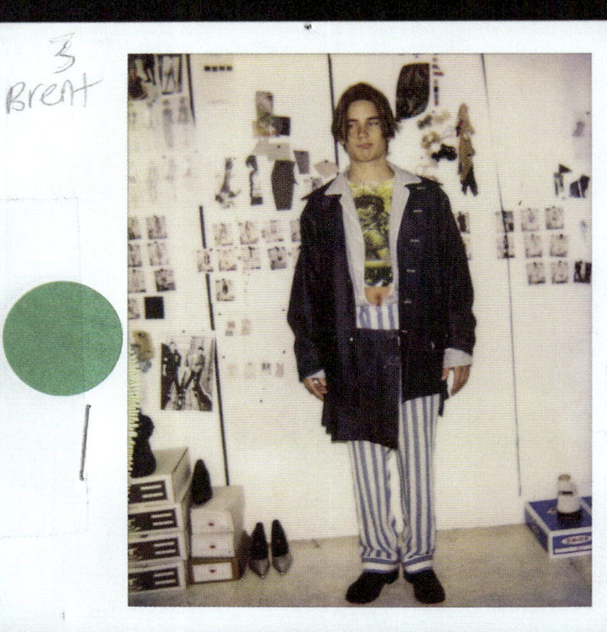

3. **Brent**
Indigo barn jacket (open; cuffs open and turned up; take jacket off on runway)
Blue pajama top (open and tucked in)
Blue cleopatra mini tee
Indigo kilt (open; fastentop buckle with safety pin on left hip)
Blue/white stripe pajama bottom

3. ***ACCESSORIES***
- ***silver pull on boot*** (size 10)
- tube sock (leave on for look #38)

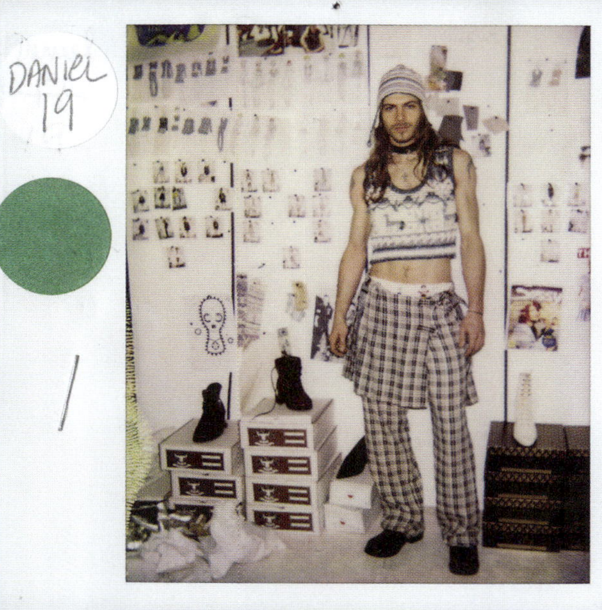

19. Daniel
Blue Peruvian vest
Black/cream plaid pant
(open; pin top buckle w/lg. safety pin; boxers should show)
Silver glitter boxer shorts

19. ACCESSORIES
. Blue and cream Peruvian hat (untied)
. Daniel's cross necklace
. Silver pull-on boot (size 10)
. silver suspenders (hanging down on pant)

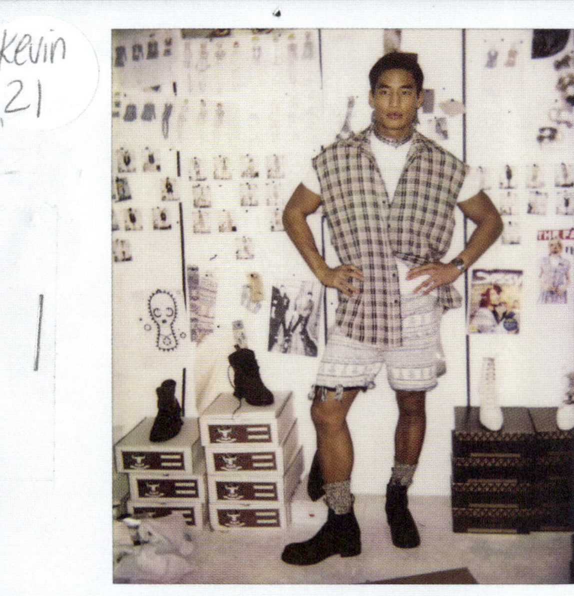

21. Kevin
Black/cream plaid sleeveless shirt
(out; button 4 & 5)
White Dolly Head mini tee
Blue jacard knit short

21. ACCESSORIES
. Dog collar
. Silver suspenders (on shorts; hanging down)
. Tube sock
. Silver pull on boot (size 9)

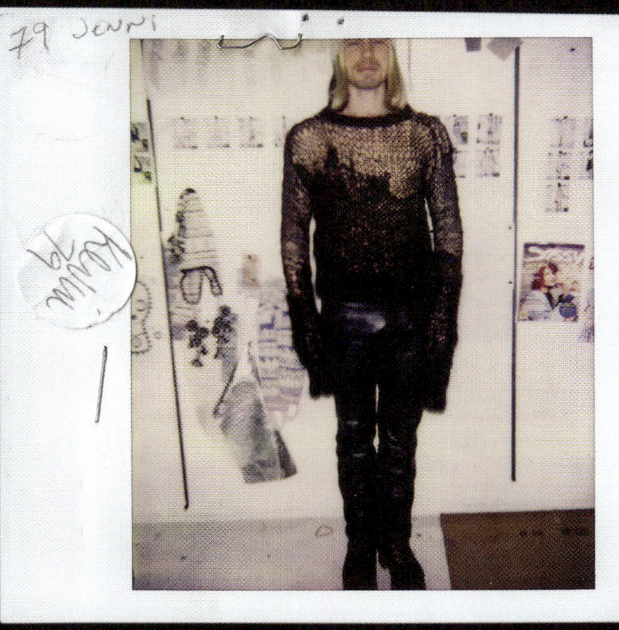

79. Kevin
Black leather lg. trench coat
(open; take coat off runway)
Black mohair sweater (out; pull down sleeve from under coat)
Black leather pant (leg over boot)

79. ACCESSORIES
. Black pull on boot (size 9)

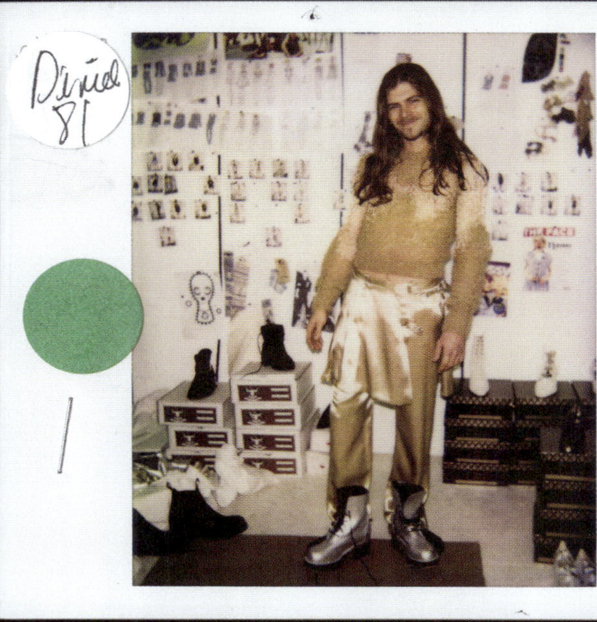

81. Daniel
Gold mohair sweater (pull down sleeve)
Gold satin kilt (open; pin top buckle w/lg. silver safety pin)
Gold satin trouser

81. ACCESSORIES
. Daniel's cross necklace
. Silver pull on boot (from look #19)

Dresser card, Daniel Baylock, Spring 1994
Dresser card, Kevin Louie, Spring 1994
Dresser card, Kevin Louie, Spring 1994
Dresser card, Daniel Baylock, Spring 1994

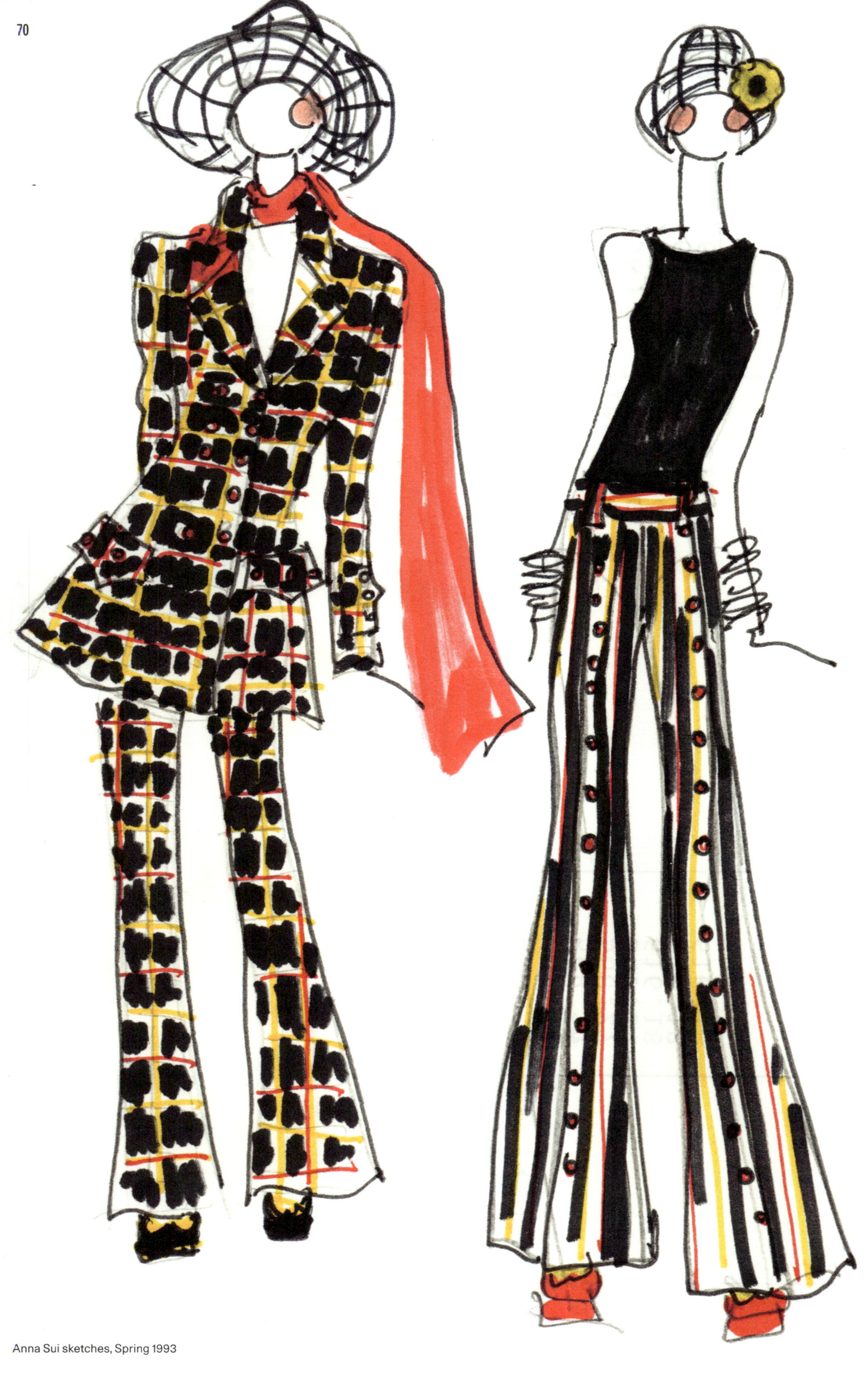

Anna Sui sketches, Spring 1993

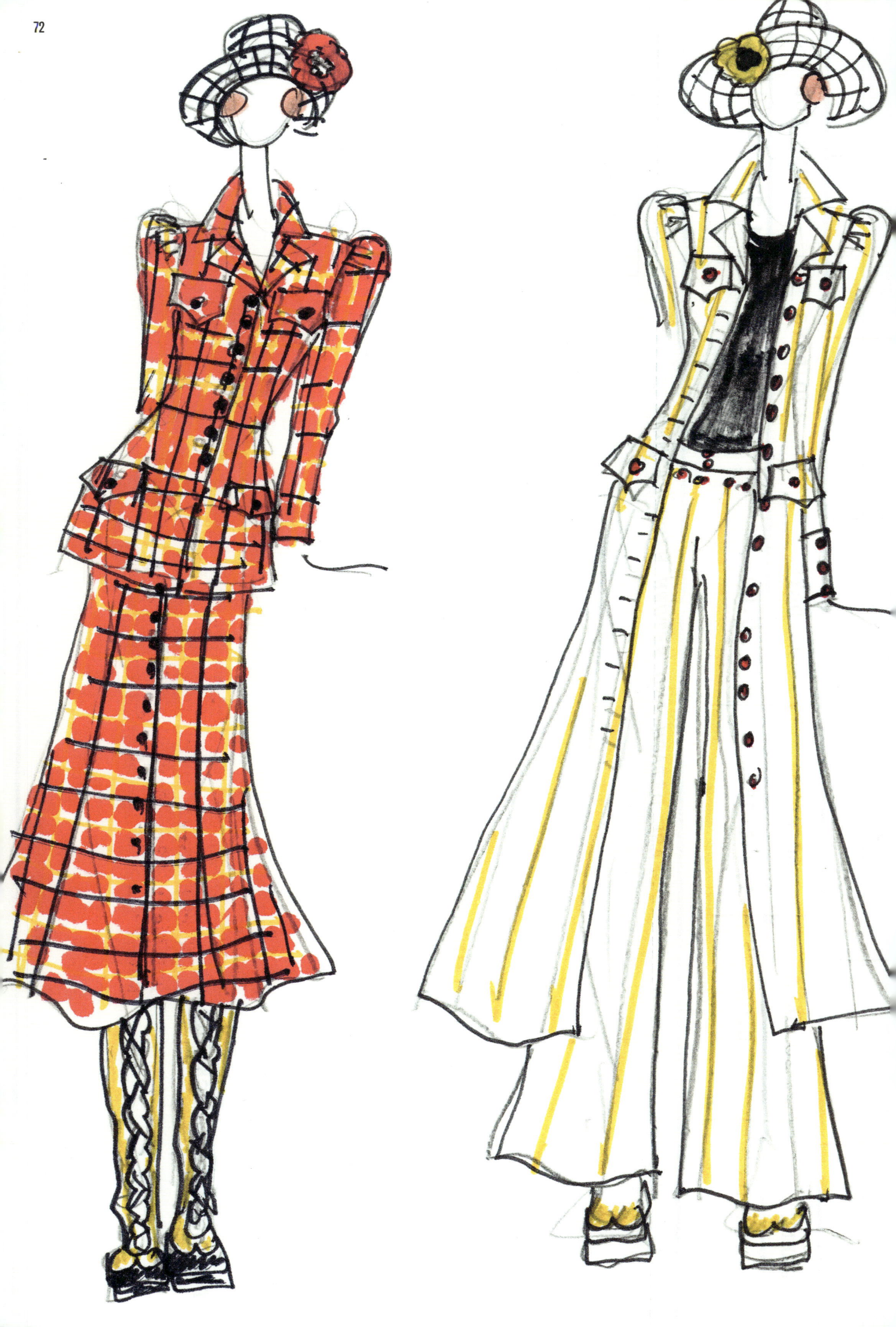

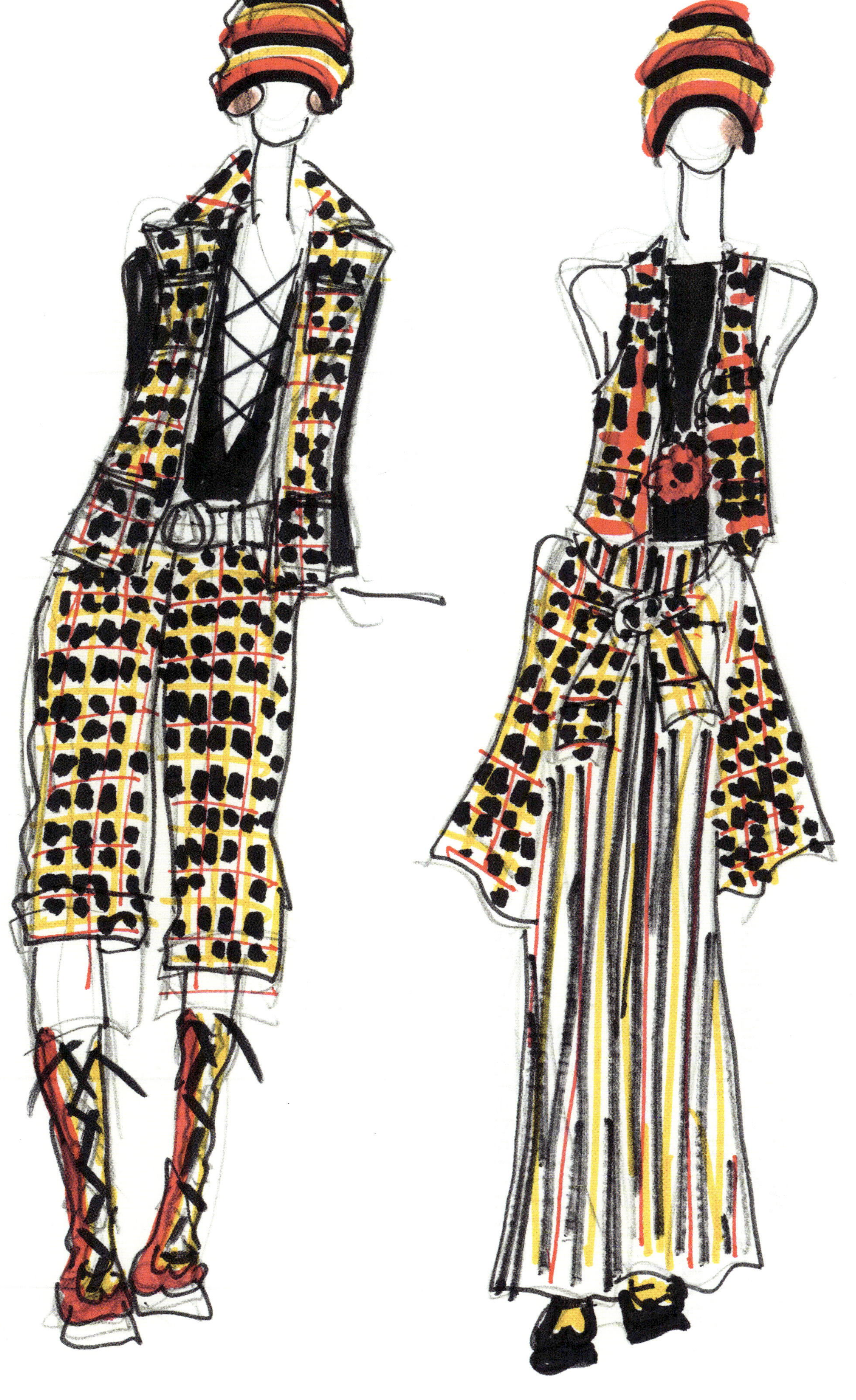

Anna Sui sketches, Spring 1993

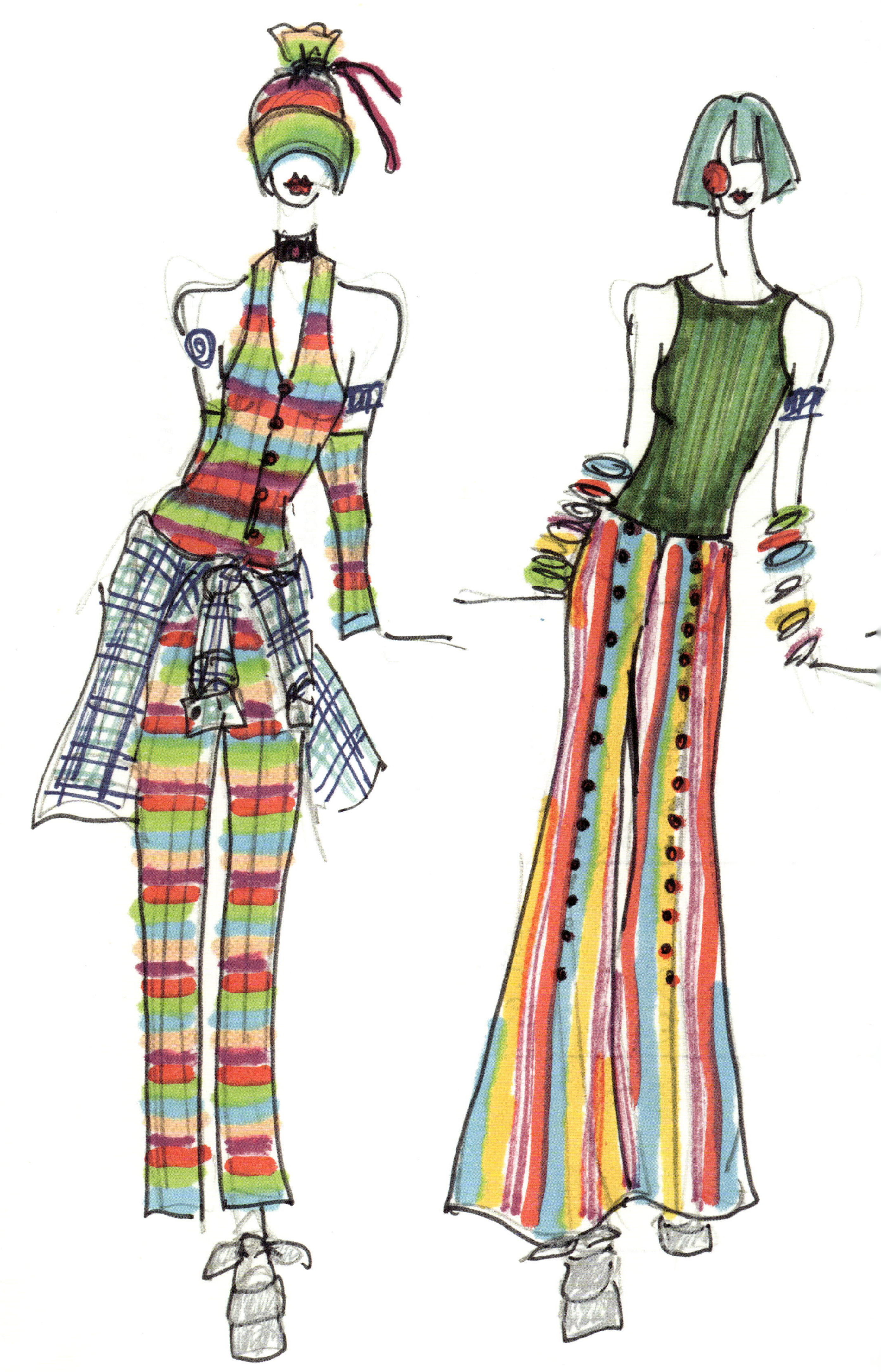

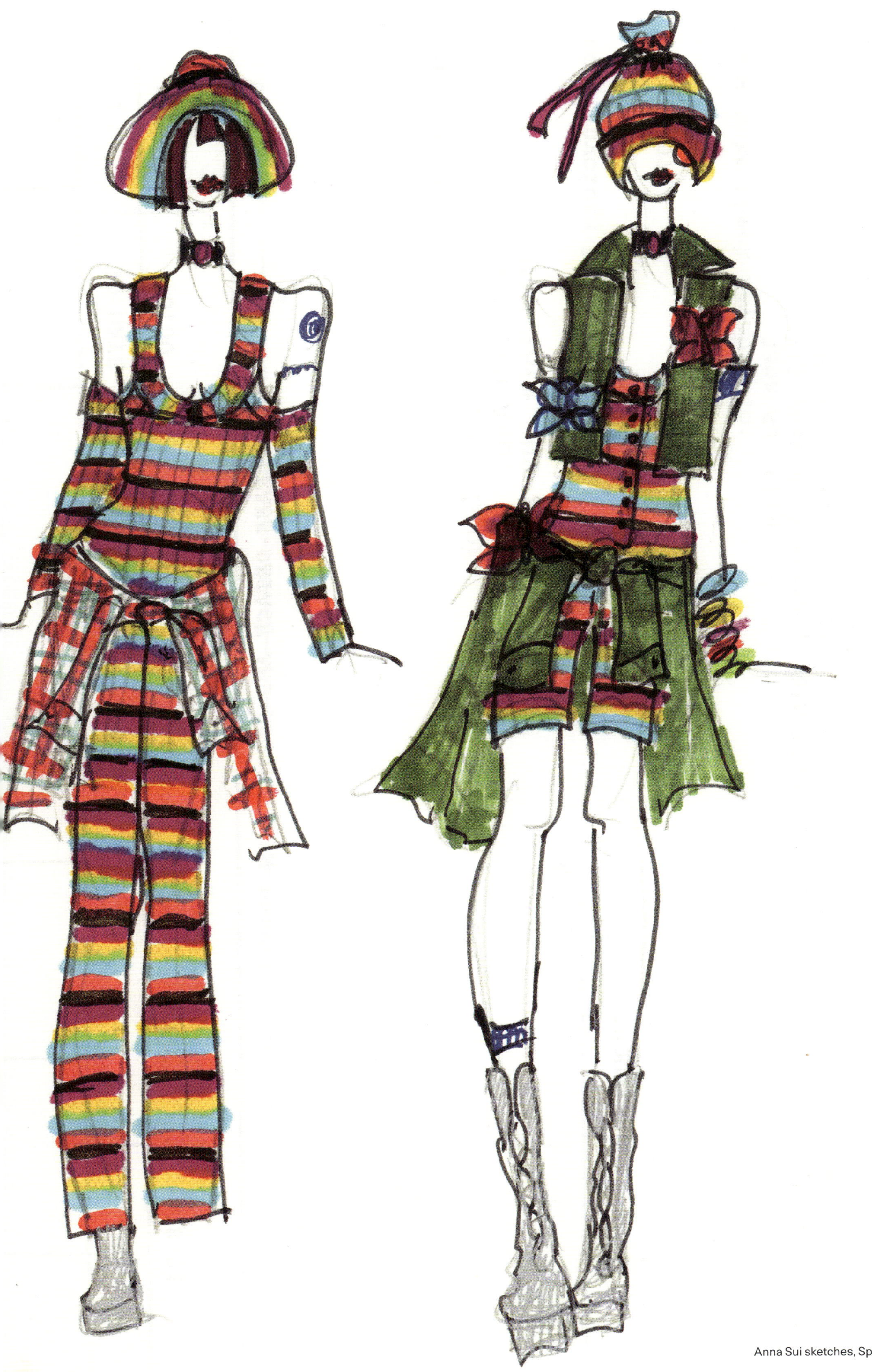

Anna Sui sketches, Spring 1993

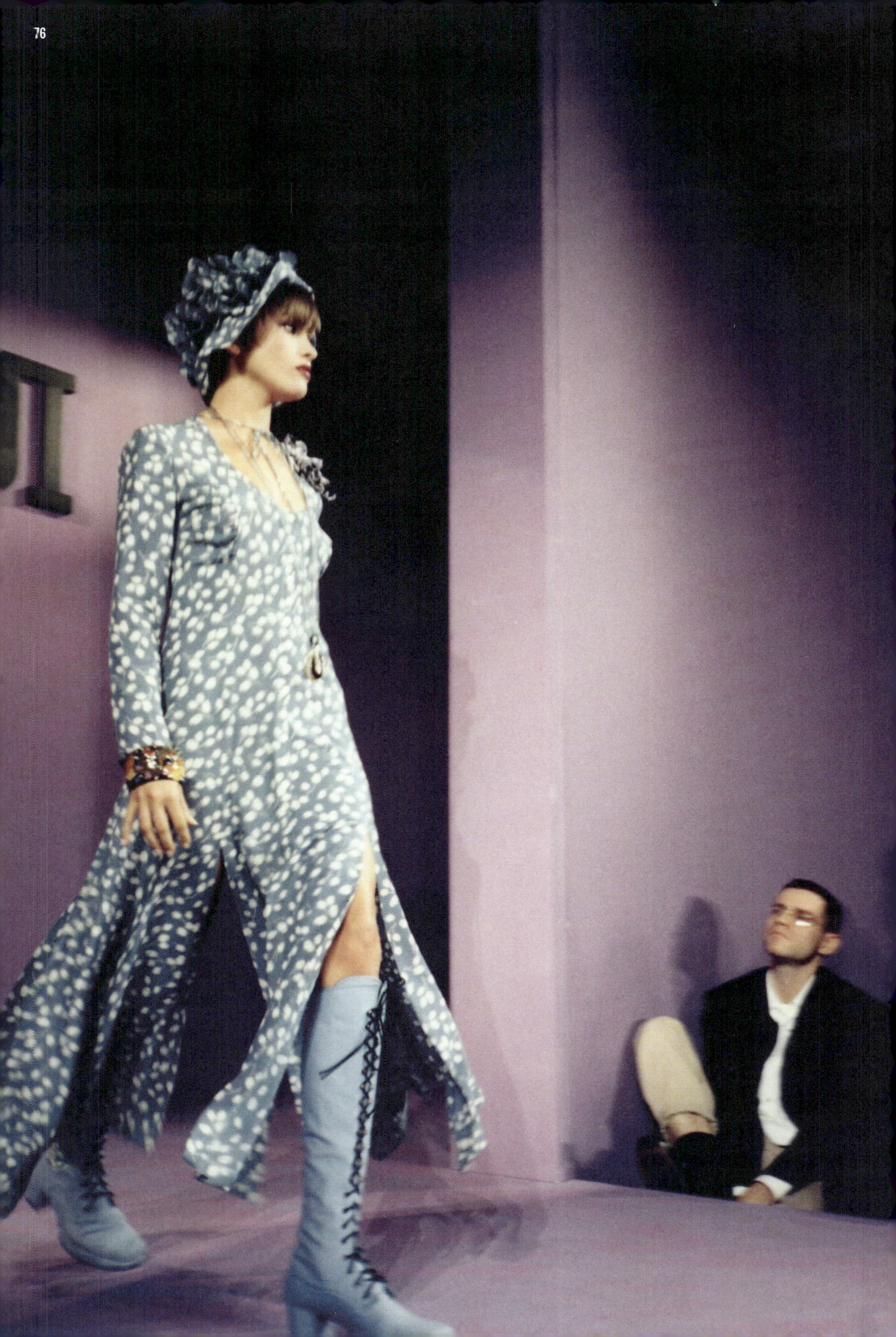

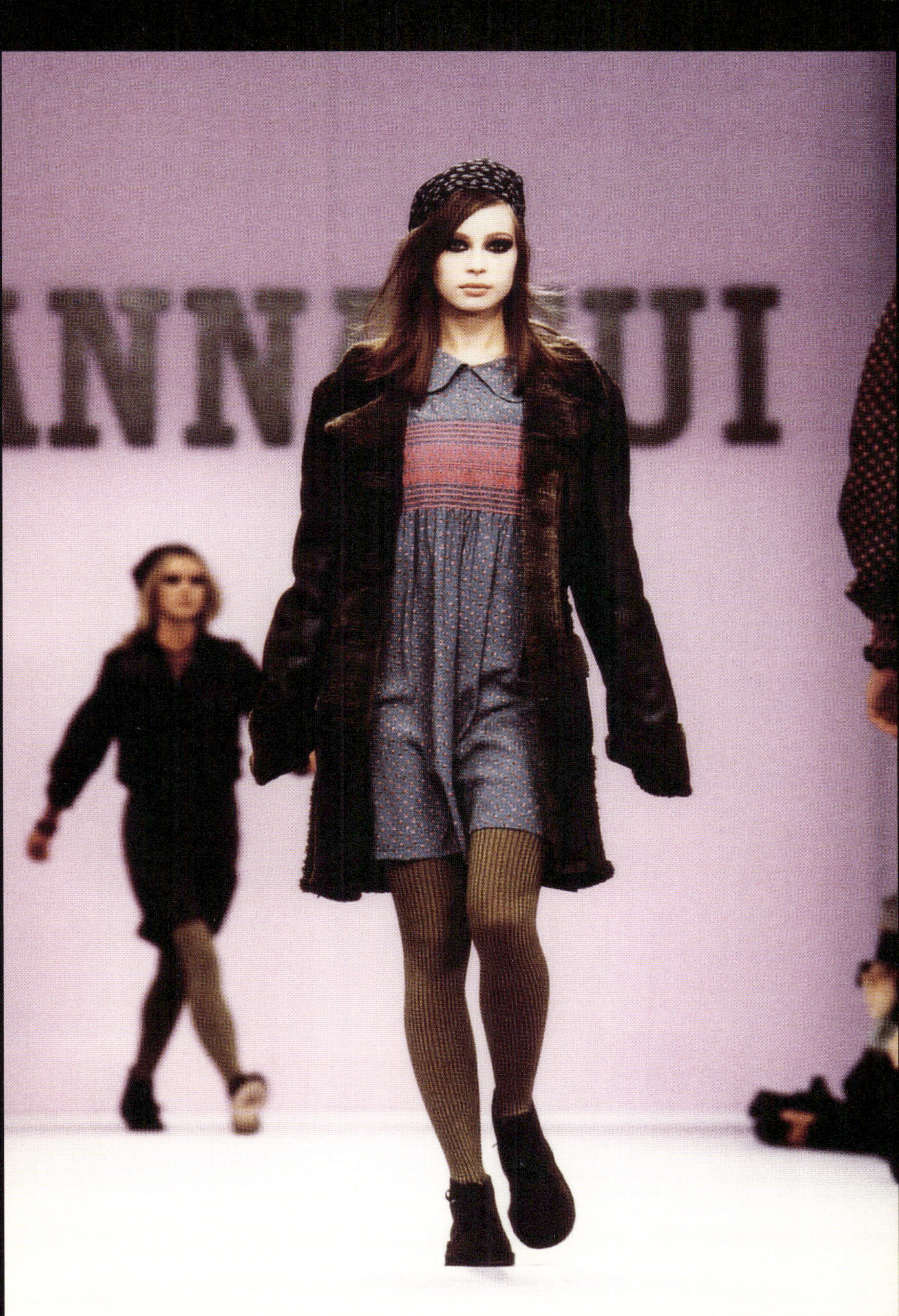

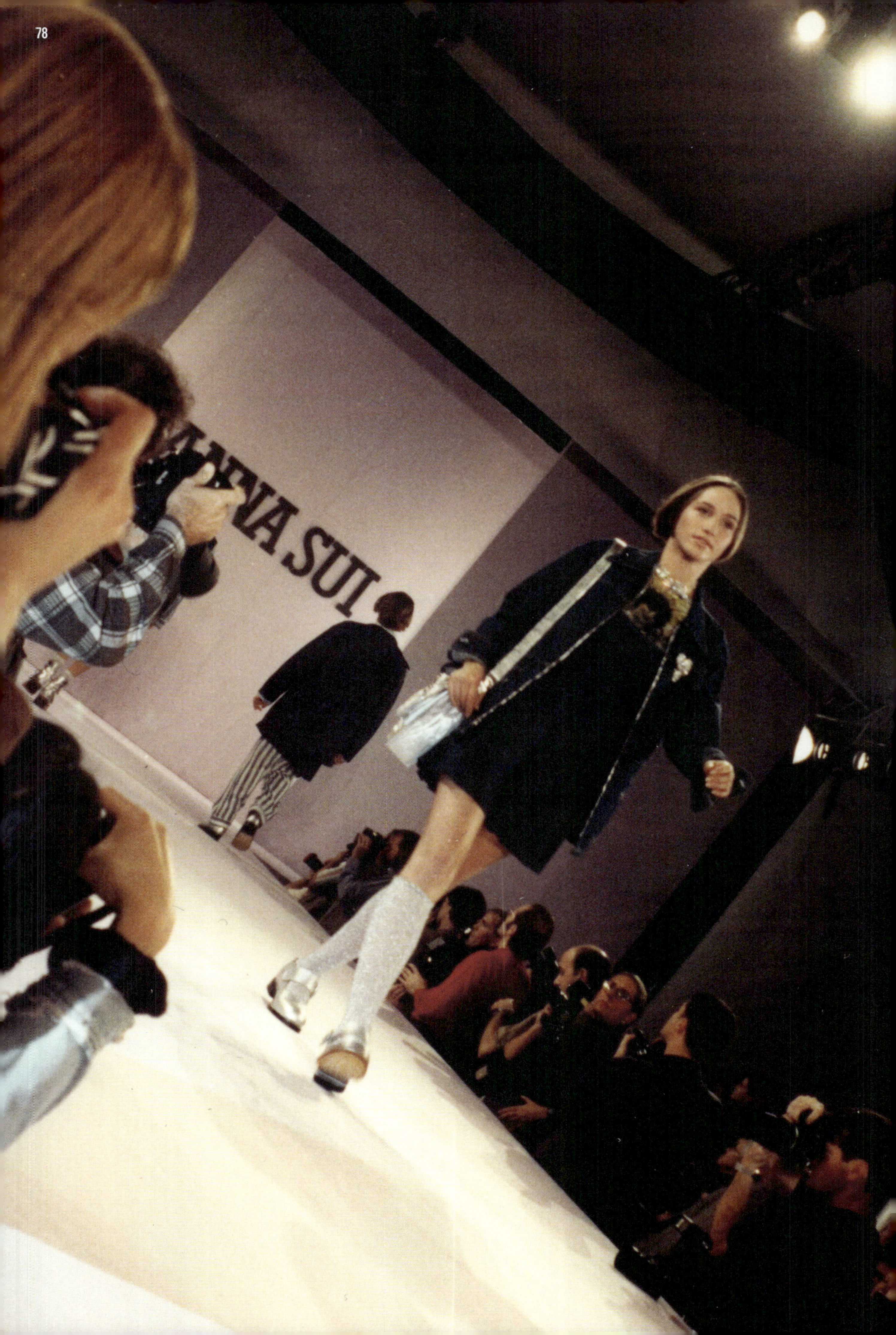
NA SUI

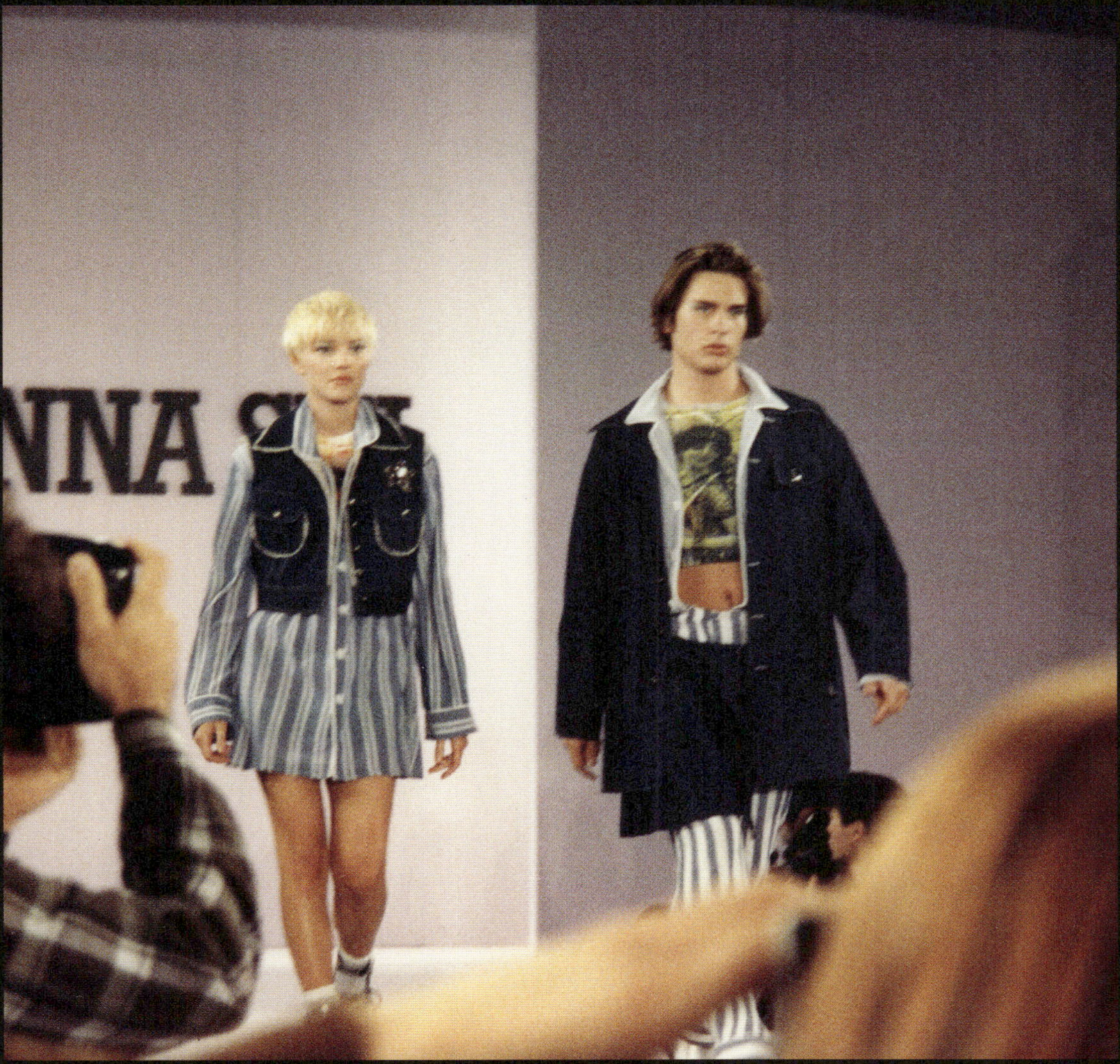

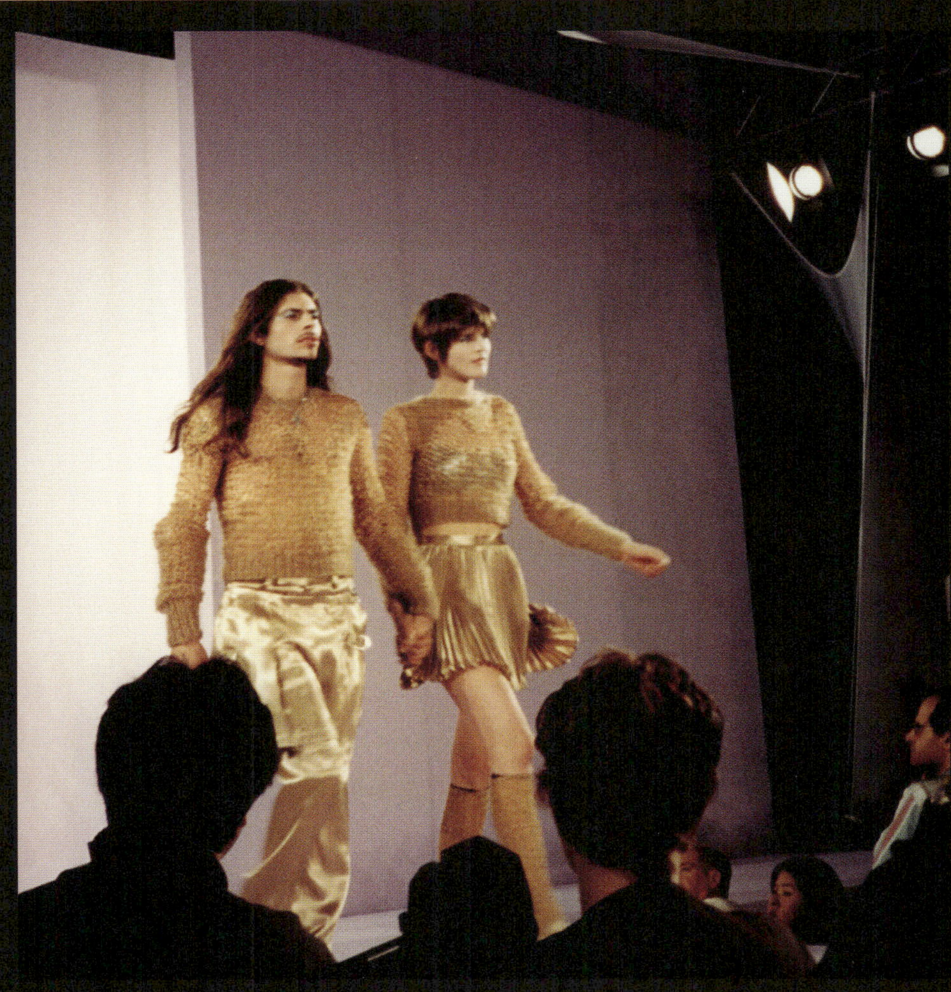

Rosemary Ferguson, Spring 1994
Daniel Baylock, Stella Tennant, Spring 1994
Jaime Rishar, Brent King, Spring 1994

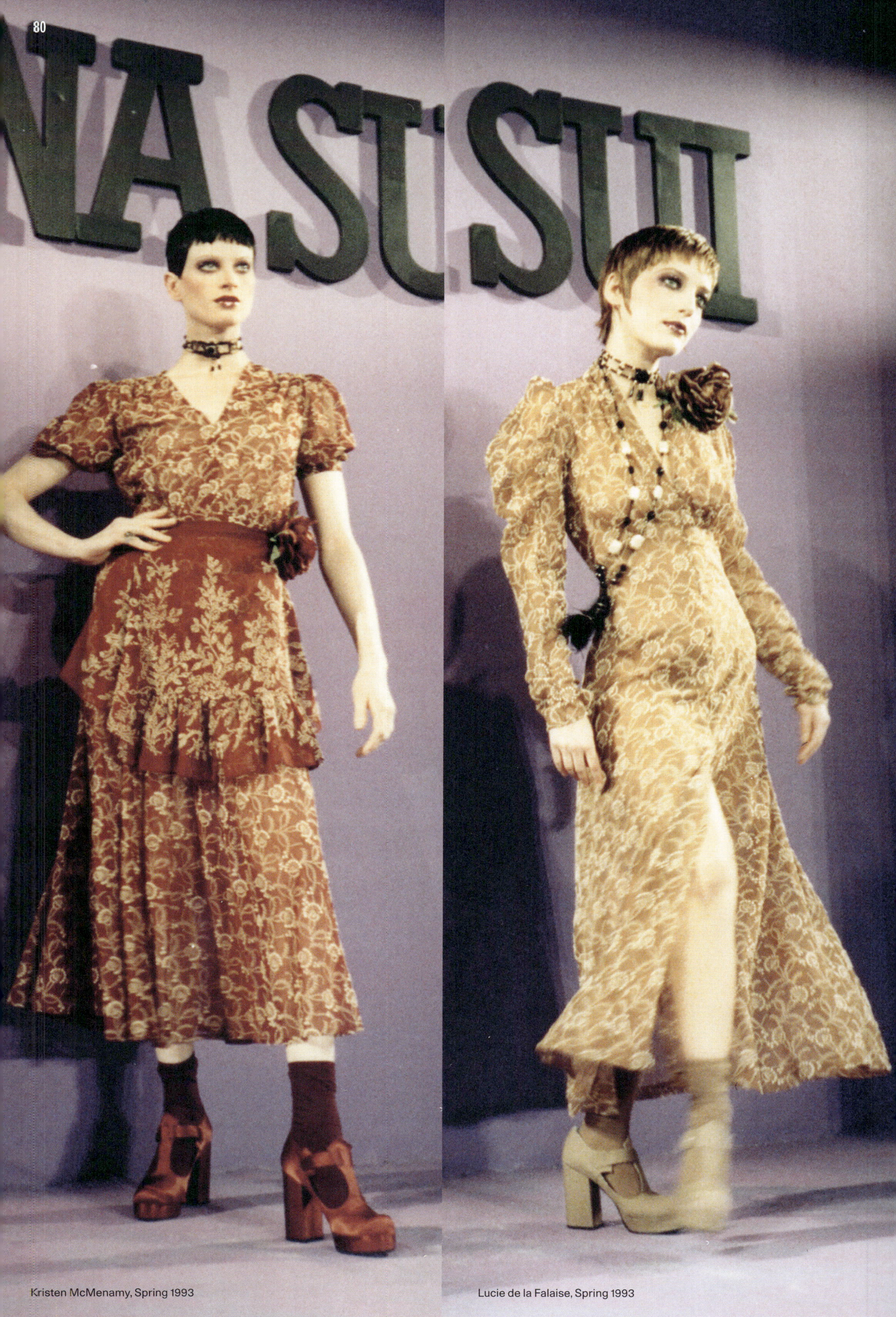

Kristen McMenamy, Spring 1993

Lucie de la Falaise, Spring 1993

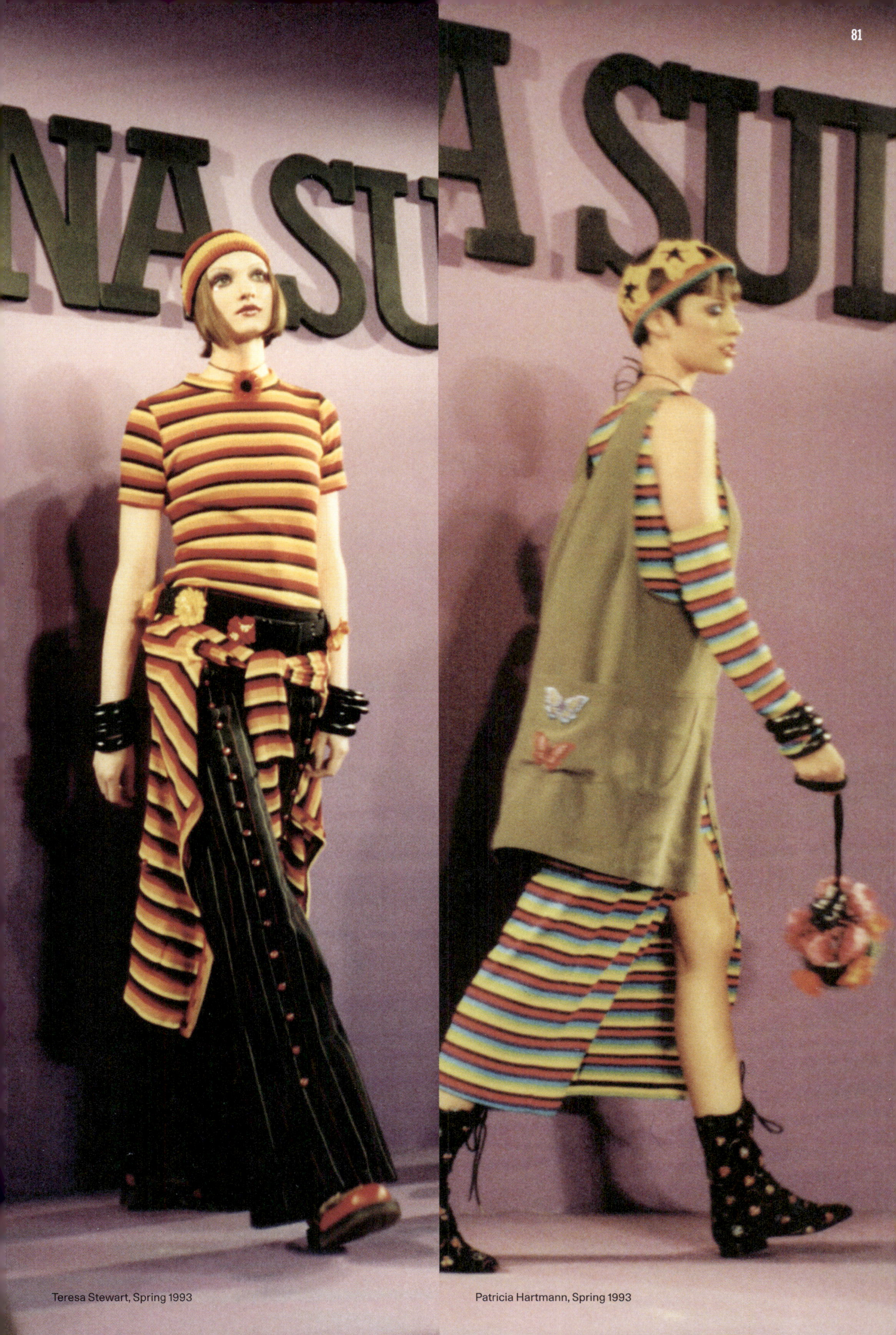

Teresa Stewart, Spring 1993

Patricia Hartmann, Spring 1993

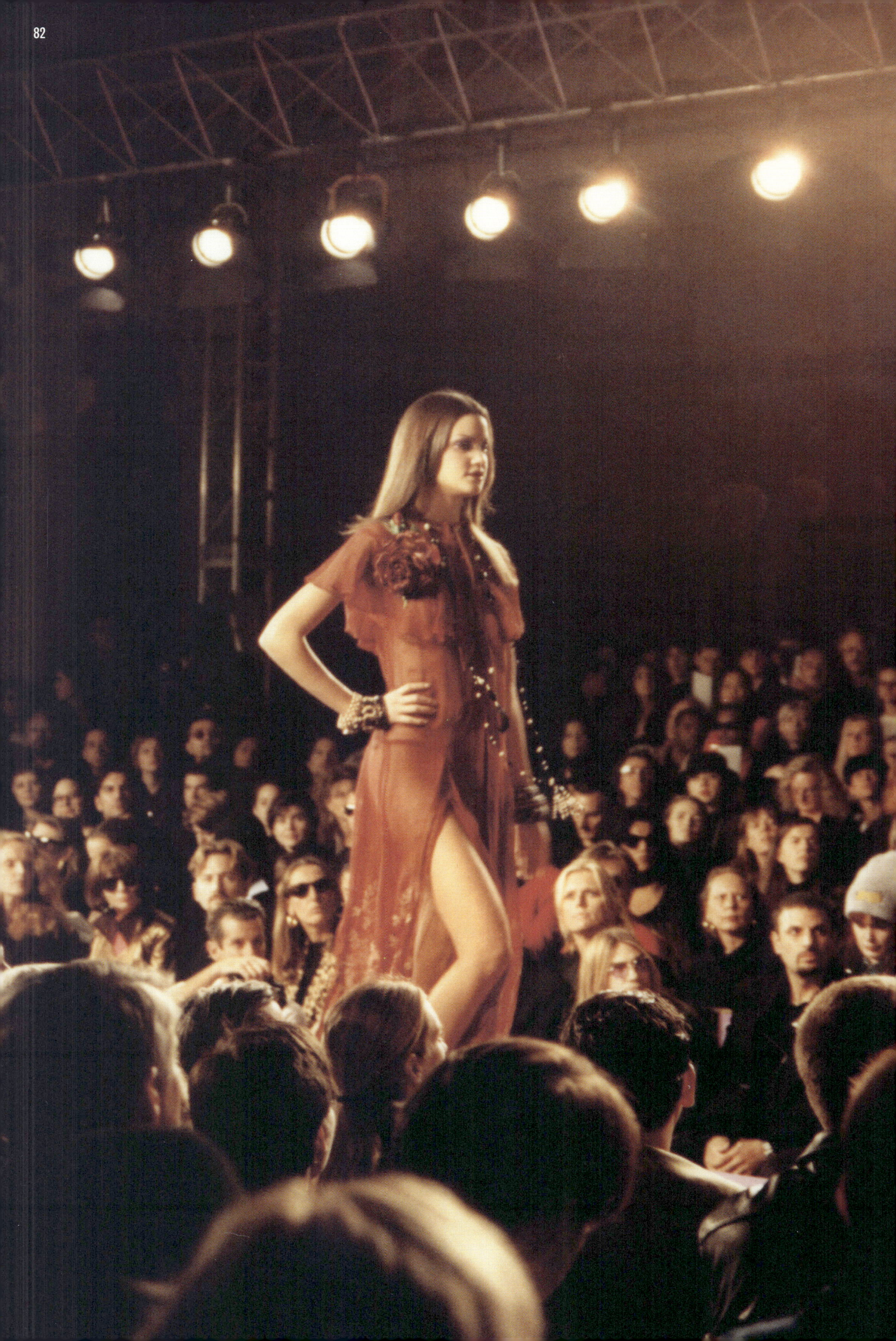

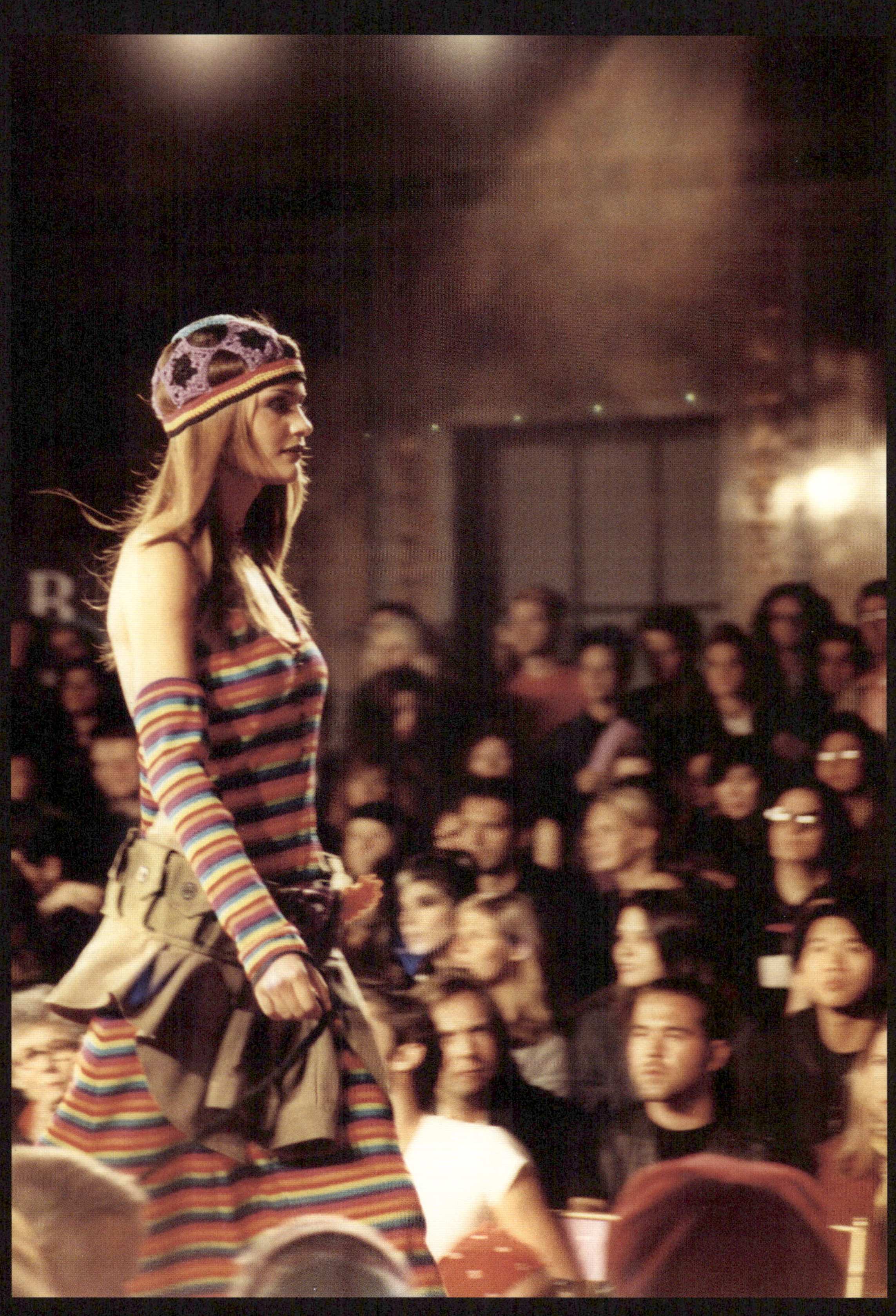

1993

pring 1993

SLIP-DRESS

"When slips were revived in the post-modern 1990s, they were representative of several different trends, among them innerwear as outerwear (think: Madonna), vintage and thrift (Courtney Love), the revival of Old Hollywood glamour (Ginger, of course, and other screen goddesses like Greta Garbo and Jean Harlow); and minimalism. Over time the slip dress has become almost synonymous with the 1990s, a focus of continued fashion."

Vogue.com, November 29, 2020

Linda Evangelista, Spring 1992

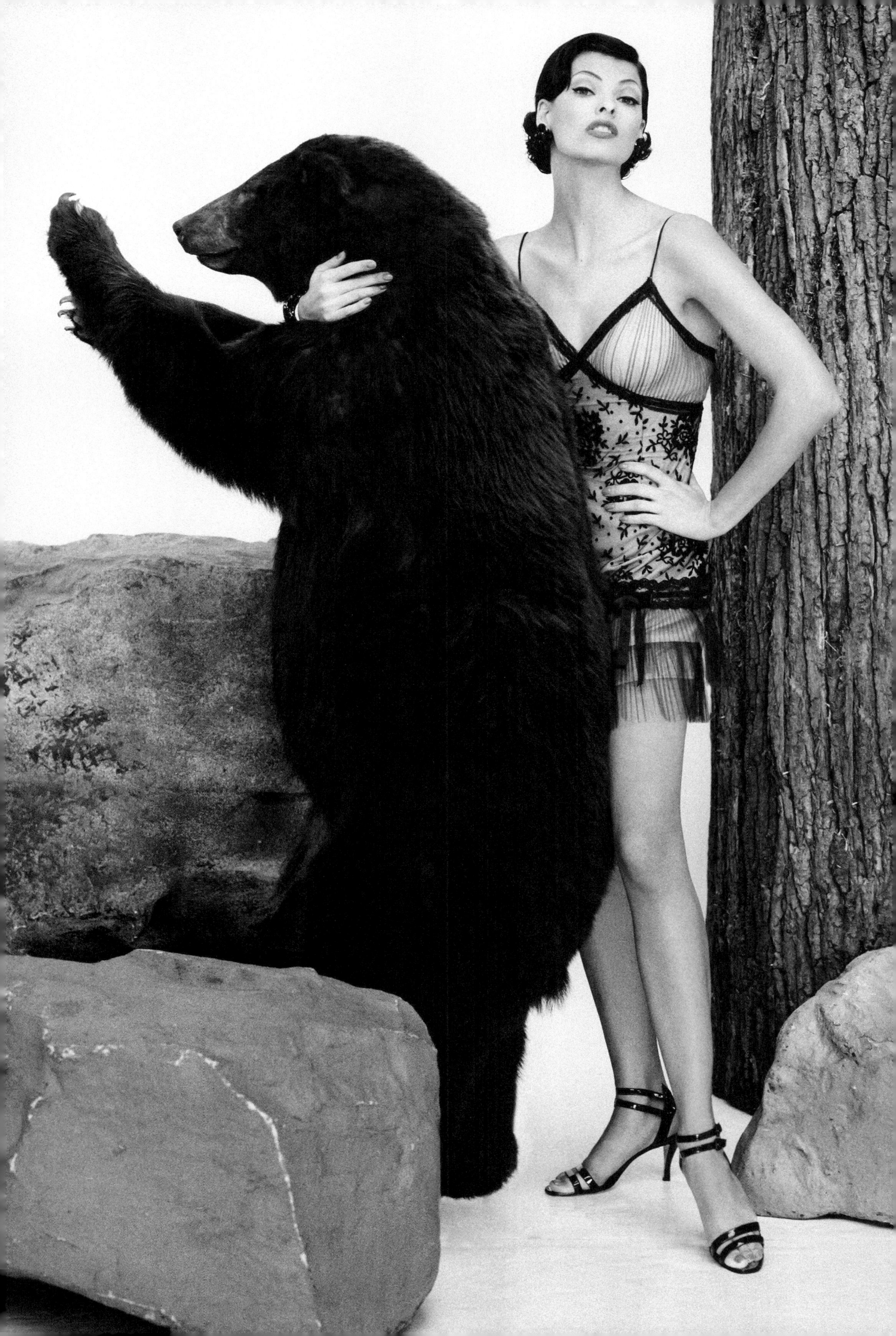

ANNA SUI

Even in my first show, there were slip dresses, because I loved that look. I loved Elizabeth Taylor in *Butterfield 8*, when she walked out with the sable coat with just a slip underneath it. When I was a kid, I dressed up as her for Halloween wearing my mom's slip. I had a fake fur leopard coat, because Elizabeth Taylor and Jackie Kennedy were both wearing leopard coats. And I wore plastic heels. I went trick or treating at a nearby house, which was known in our neighborhood as the "bachelors" house. I didn't know what that meant. They opened the door and said, "And what are you, young lady?" I told them I was Elizabeth Taylor from *Butterfield 8*. They started screaming—I didn't understand what that reaction was about. But looking back now I realize they loved the camp of it all.

Slip dresses were huge. And we were buying them from the flea markets and vintage stores, like the old '30s nightgowns, and just wearing those as dresses. And they were so beautiful because they were in that peach satin with the lace around them. Or if you were lucky, you'd find a black one. Some people were tie-dyeing or dip-dyeing them. Everyone was wearing and then adapting it from vintage into their wardrobe.

When I was working on the Spring/Summer '98 collection I had gone uptown in a cab and in the window of Bergdorf Goodman's there was a patterned sari. I got out of the cab and ran over to the window—it was the most incredible dress I had ever seen. I was not happy with my fabric selection and wondered where this dress came from. It turned out to be the Duchess of Windsor's dress. Sotheby's was auctioning off her collection and they had some pieces in the window. That night I went to Little India and found these saris and asked if they could supply more and that is how we got the fabric for the collection.

I started making them in our signature prints and there was one group that I made in a kind of a heavy satin, all cut on the bias, and we made some mohair sweaters that layered over them. They were in pastel colors and a lot of people bought them and were wearing them out. It's funny when I go back and look at pictures of how many people actually had those sets—I found a picture of Sofia Coppola wearing it in a smoky gray. Madonna had it in the periwinkle blue with the matching sweater. Before this, people dressed up

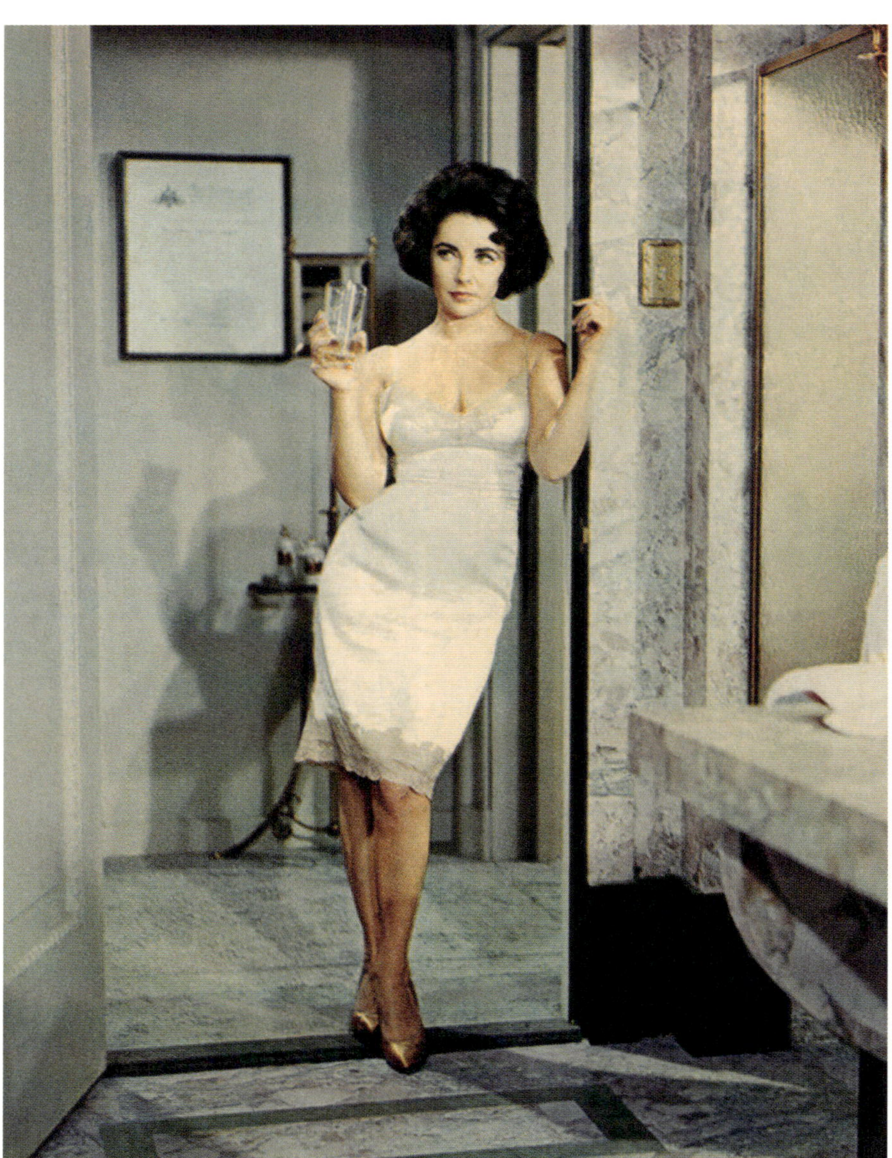

Elizabeth Taylor, *Butterfield 8* film still, 1960

Carolyn Murphy, Spring 1998

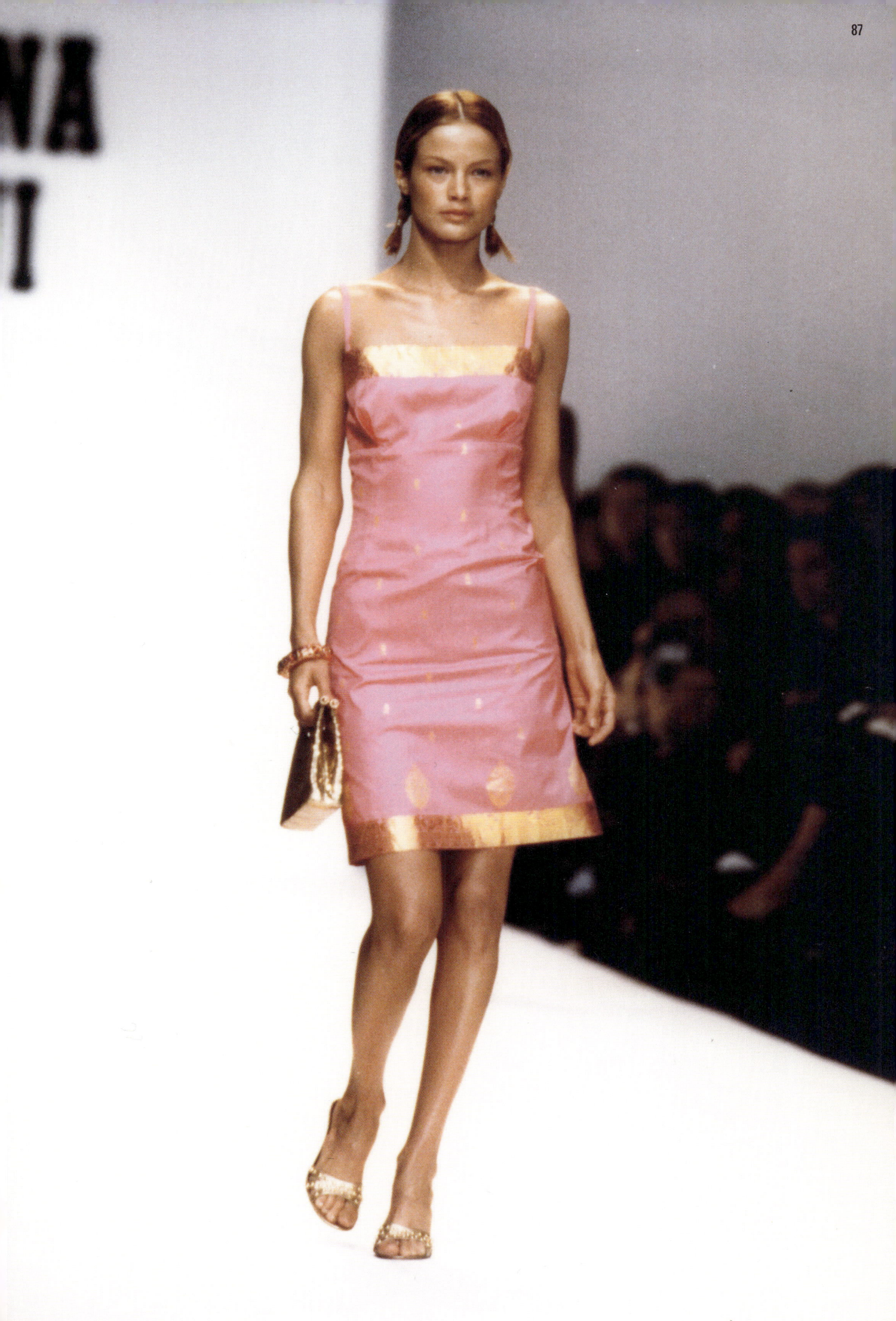

to go out-and-about but suddenly style was downplayed a lot.

Even in the Mudd Club days in the summer, we would wear those slips from the '50s as a dress. I still have all mine from that period—you could find such beautiful ones at that time. I always loved that look. In my first show, there's a whole section of lingerielike clothing. During my punk collection show in '94 there's that satin slip dress with the mohair sweater over it, like the one Madonna's was wearing. In that collection there were a lot of these dresses and mohair sweaters looks.

When we showed them on the runway, it was slightly before Carolyn Bessette started wearing them. Then Calvin Klein did his slip dresses.

The style reminds you of a movie star like Jean Harlow, wearing those satin bias-cut dresses in the '30s, or the beautiful lingerie slips from the '50s that you saw in movies. There was always a scene where the actress would take off her clothes and she'd have on a beautiful slip. In the Mudd Club days, there's lots of pictures of Lydia Lunch wearing those slips. You could find them so easily in the flea markets at that point. In my first show I had to put a slip dress in there and I think there's usually a similar kind of piece throughout my work. I've done that slip dress so many different times.

CHRISTY TURLINGTON BURNS

Some designers started to make them. I feel like even Comme de Garçons made some version of a slip dress during those years. Galliano was doing slip dresses—everybody's doing their take on the slip dress, but I think part of it came from street culture. Courtney Love was wearing old, more ratty versions of them, and then Naomi was wearing them, too. Anna was making them and incorporating them into an overall look. Then other designers were like, wait a minute, let's get on this.

SOFIA COPPOLA

Anna understood how girls wanted to dress—she was in touch with that. It was those slip dresses in that moment and how she mixed different elements to make it her own. This, like everything she's done, was so unique and that is how she has made her mark over all these decades.

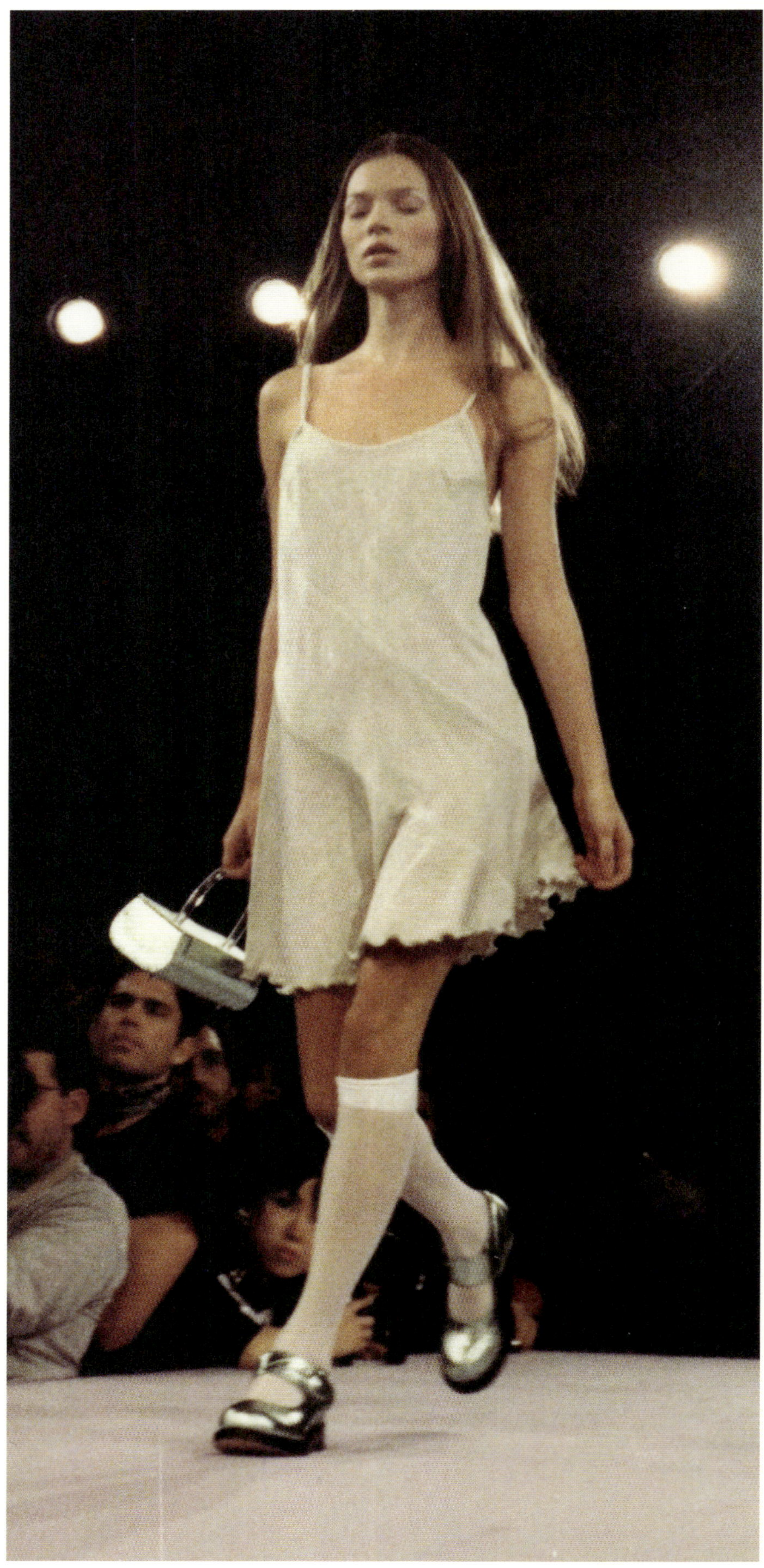

Kate Moss, Spring 1994

Winona Ryder wearing Fall 1993 collection, September 1994

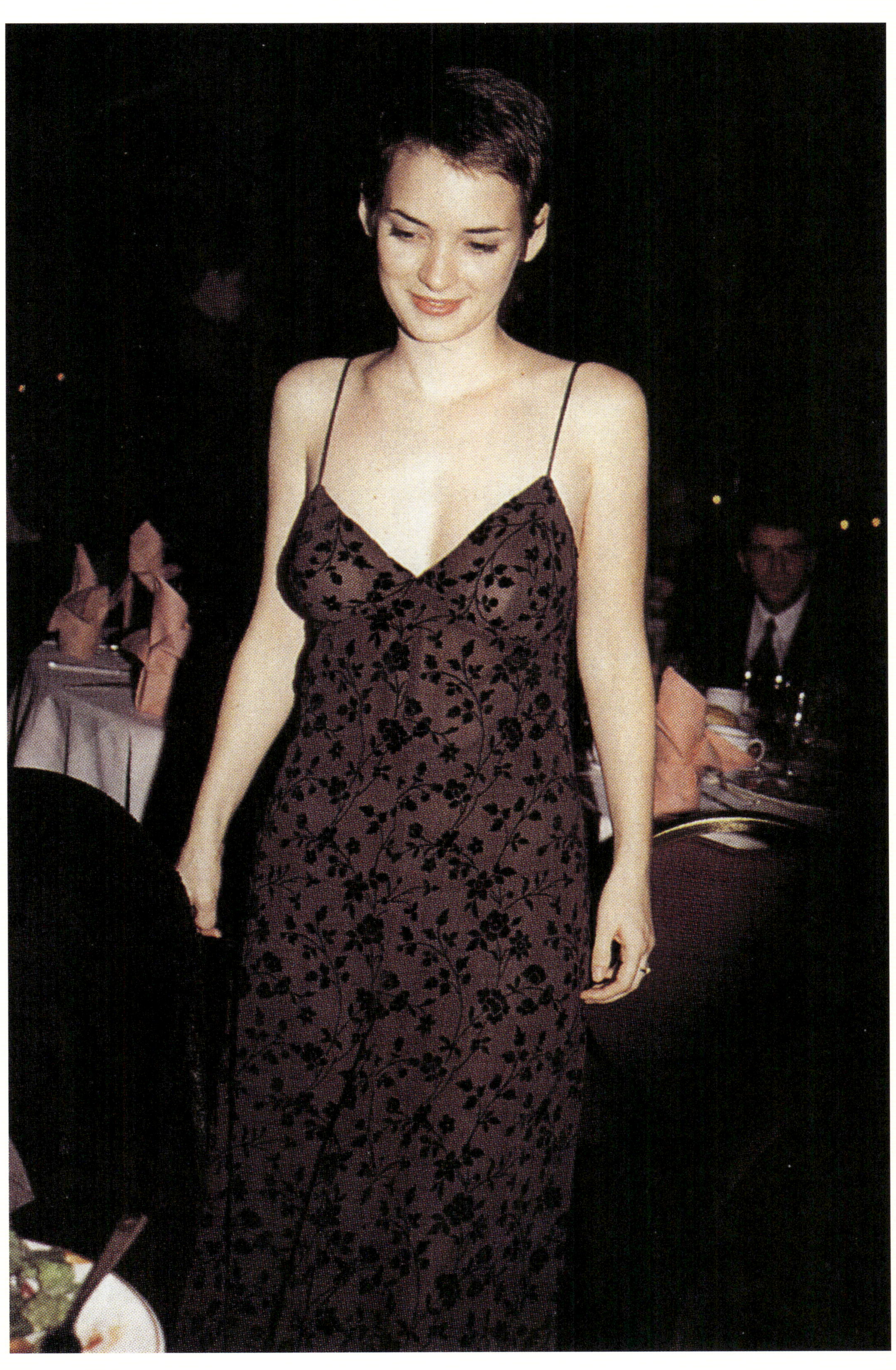

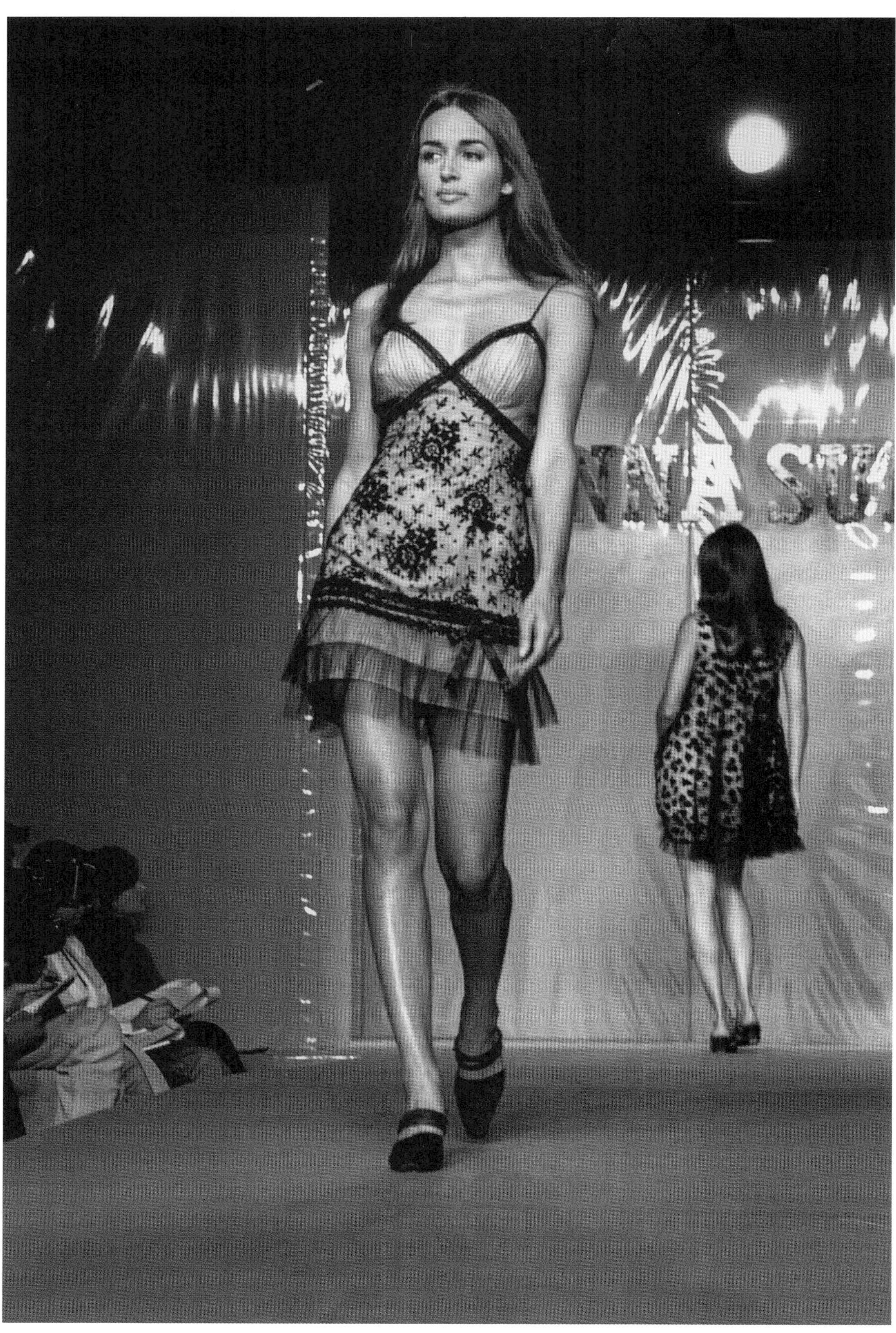

Gail Elliot, Spring 1992

Jenny Shimizu, Spring 1994

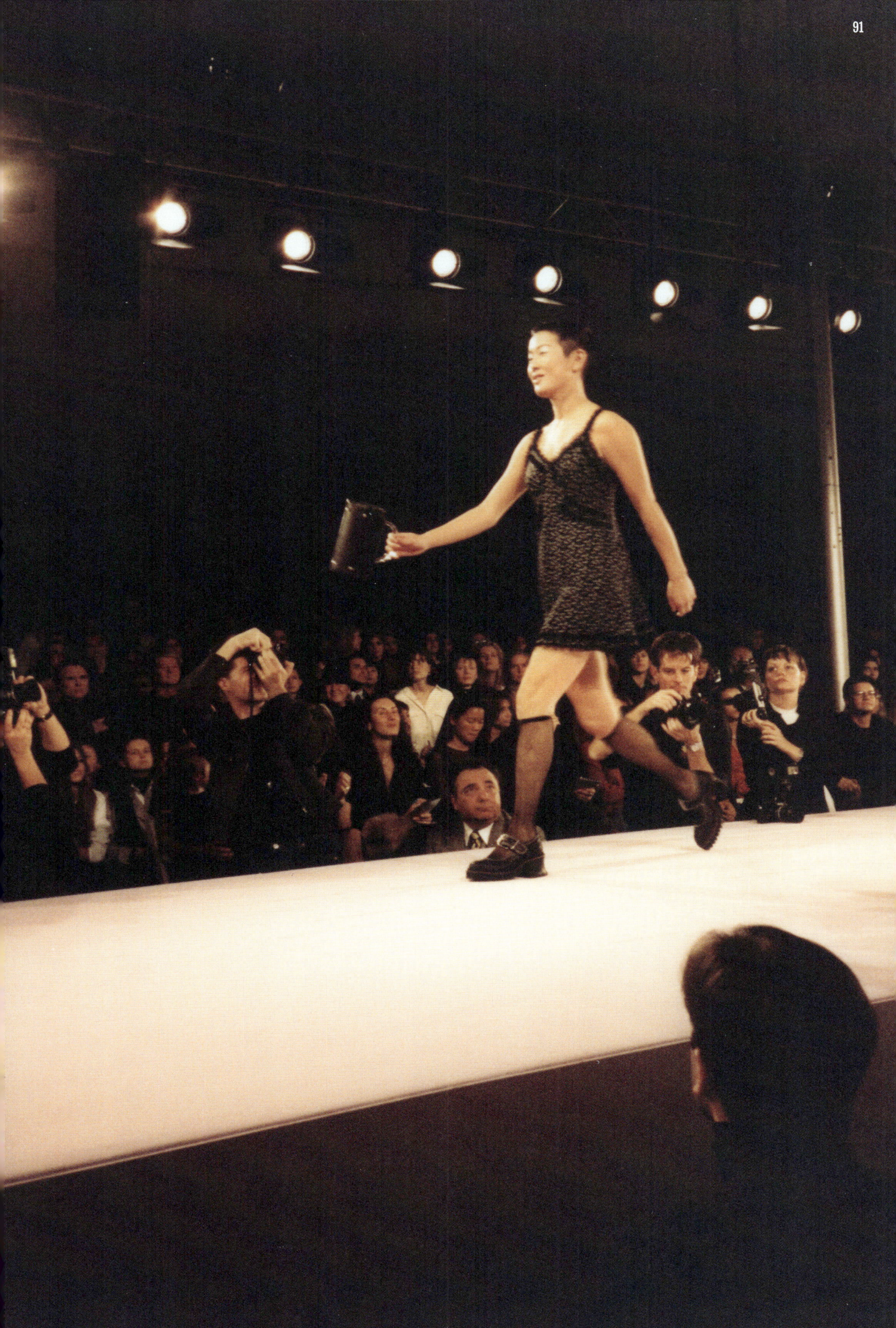

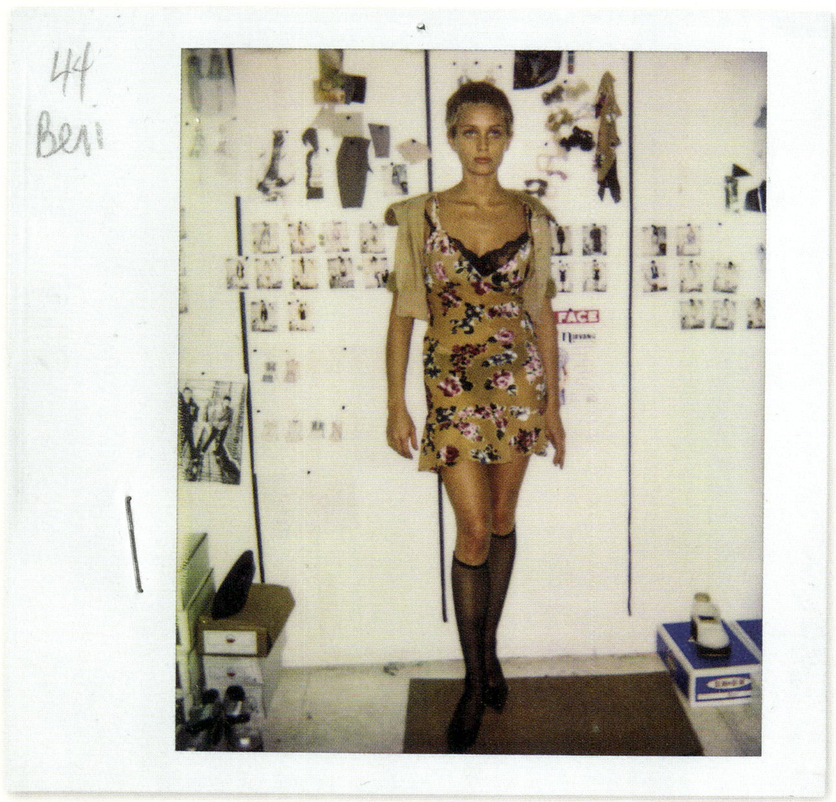

44. Berry

Tan s/s sweater with mohair collar (open)

Tan silk slip dress with velvet flowers

(Black lace trim bra and panty)

44. ACCESSORIES

- *Green rhinestone necklace with center teardrop*
- *Black fishnet knee hi*
- *Black pointed pump* (size 6)

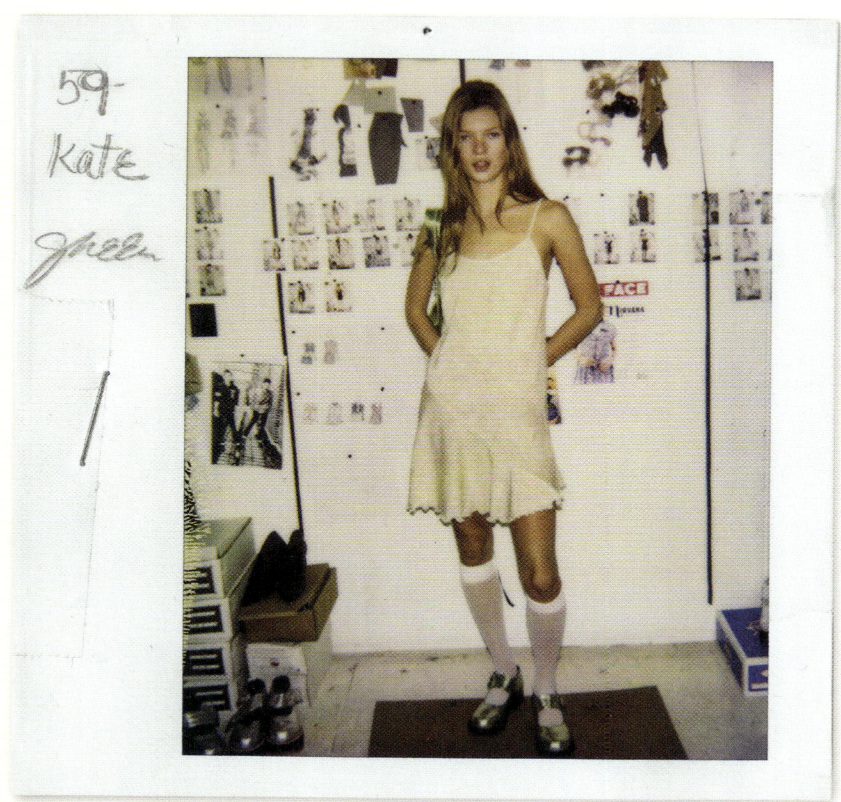

59. Kate

Green lettuce edge slip dress

59. ACCESSORIES

- *Mini green leather knapsack* (on back)
- *White fine net knee hi*
- *Green Maryjane shoe* (size 7)
- Green bag with glass handle

Dresser card, Beri Smithers, Spring 1994

Dresser card, Kate Moss, Spring 1994

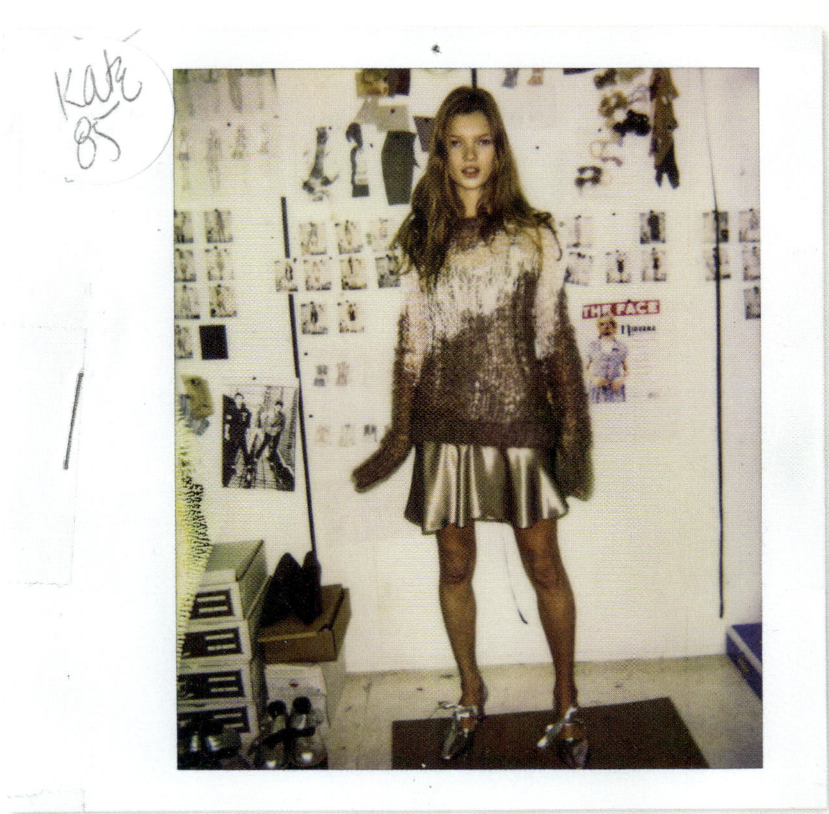

85. Kate

Pink mohair sweater

Pink satin bias dress

85. ACCESSORIES

. *Pink pointed pump w/bow tie* (size 39)

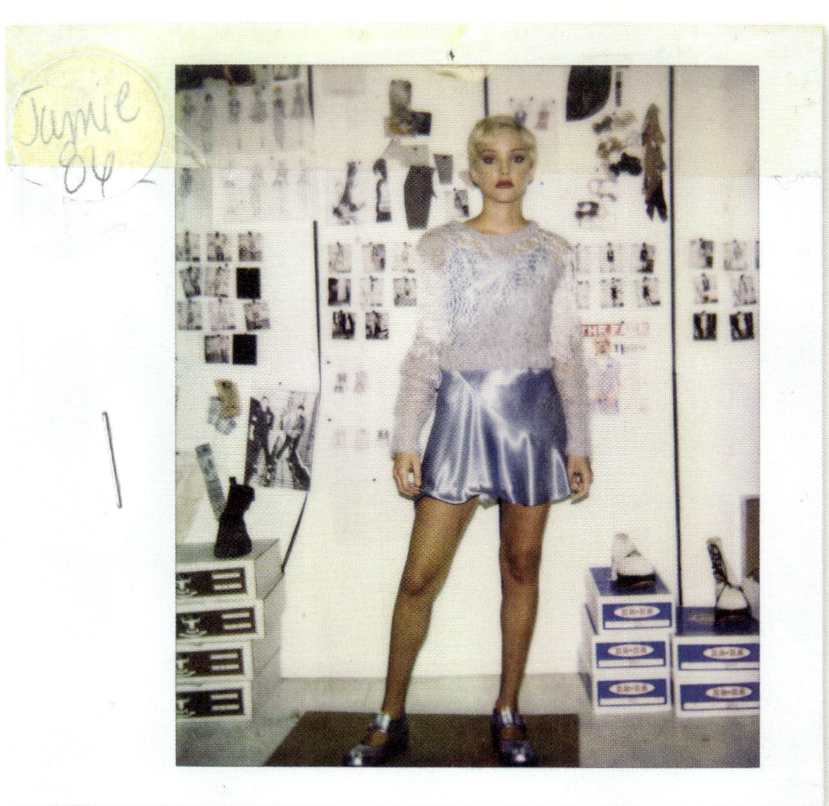

86. Jamie

Blue mohair open weave sweater

Blue satin slip dress

86. ACCESSORIES

. *Blue Maryjane shoes*

Dresser card, Kate Moss, Spring 1994

Dresser card, Jaime Rishar, Spring 1994

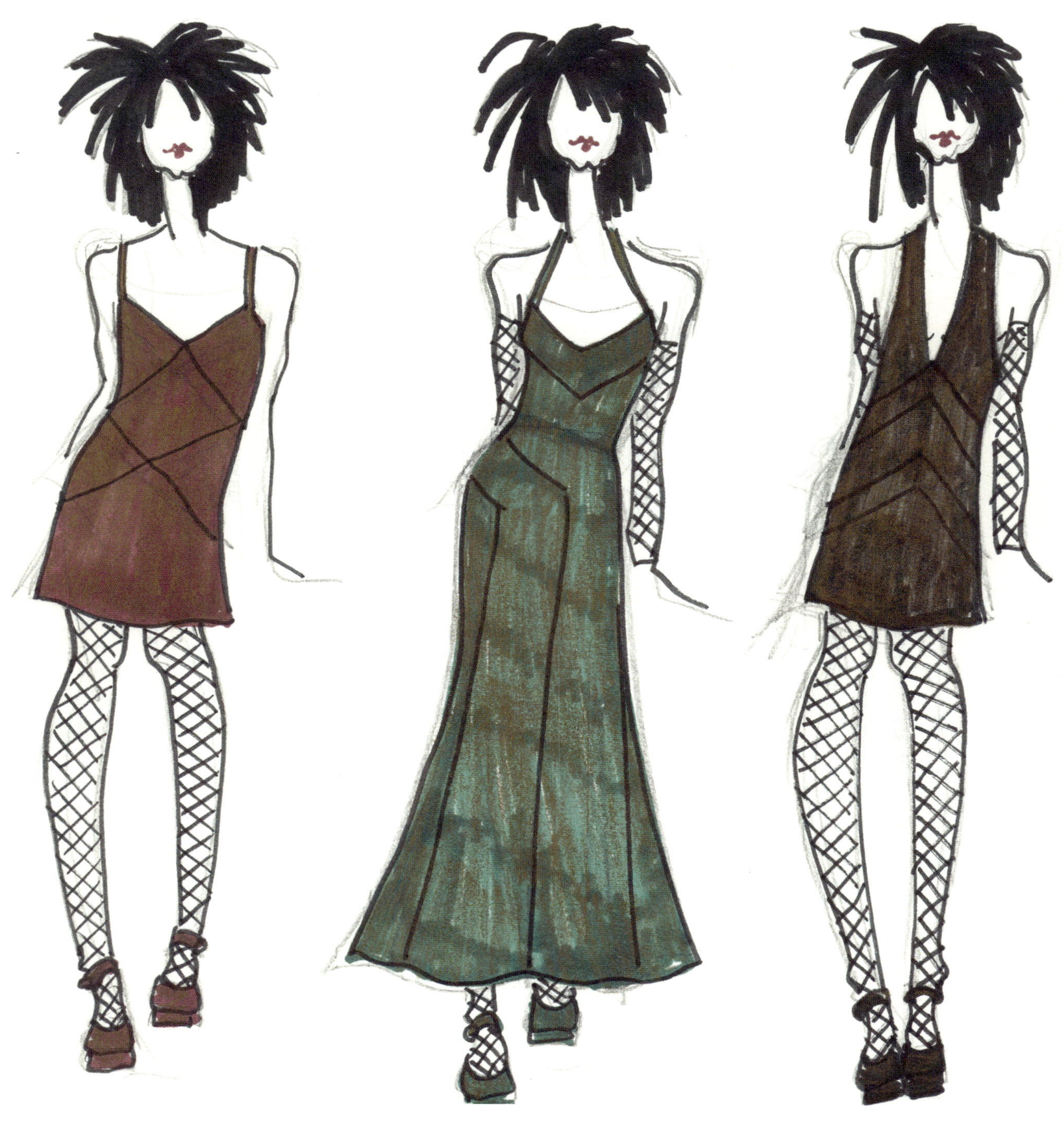

Anna Sui sketches, Fall 1997
Kiara Kabukuru, Spring 1998

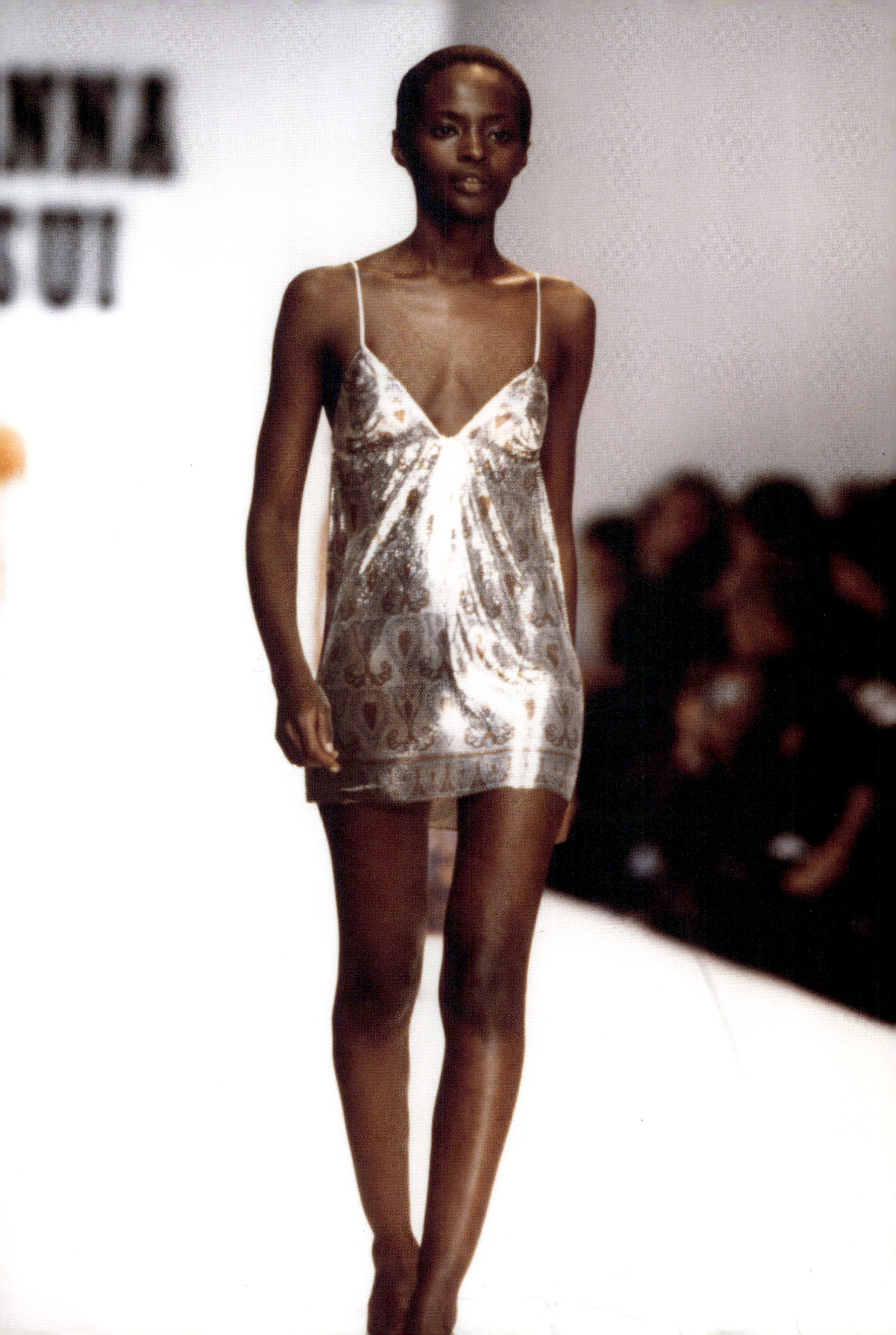

MUSIC

"Having a rocker-slash-celebrity walk the runway felt new—and spoke to Sui's focus on hosting dynamic shows that felt celebratory, fresh, and different. Sui first met Navarro at a festival in San Francisco, chatted him up, and asked, spur of the moment, if he would ever want to be in her show. 'Then he said, 'Well, only if there's lingerie involved,' Sui recalls. 'He flew in for his fitting and walked into our office, took off all his clothes and he said, 'You're the artist. I'm the clay. Mold me.' Everybody in the room just about dropped dead.'"

Vogue, June 8, 2022

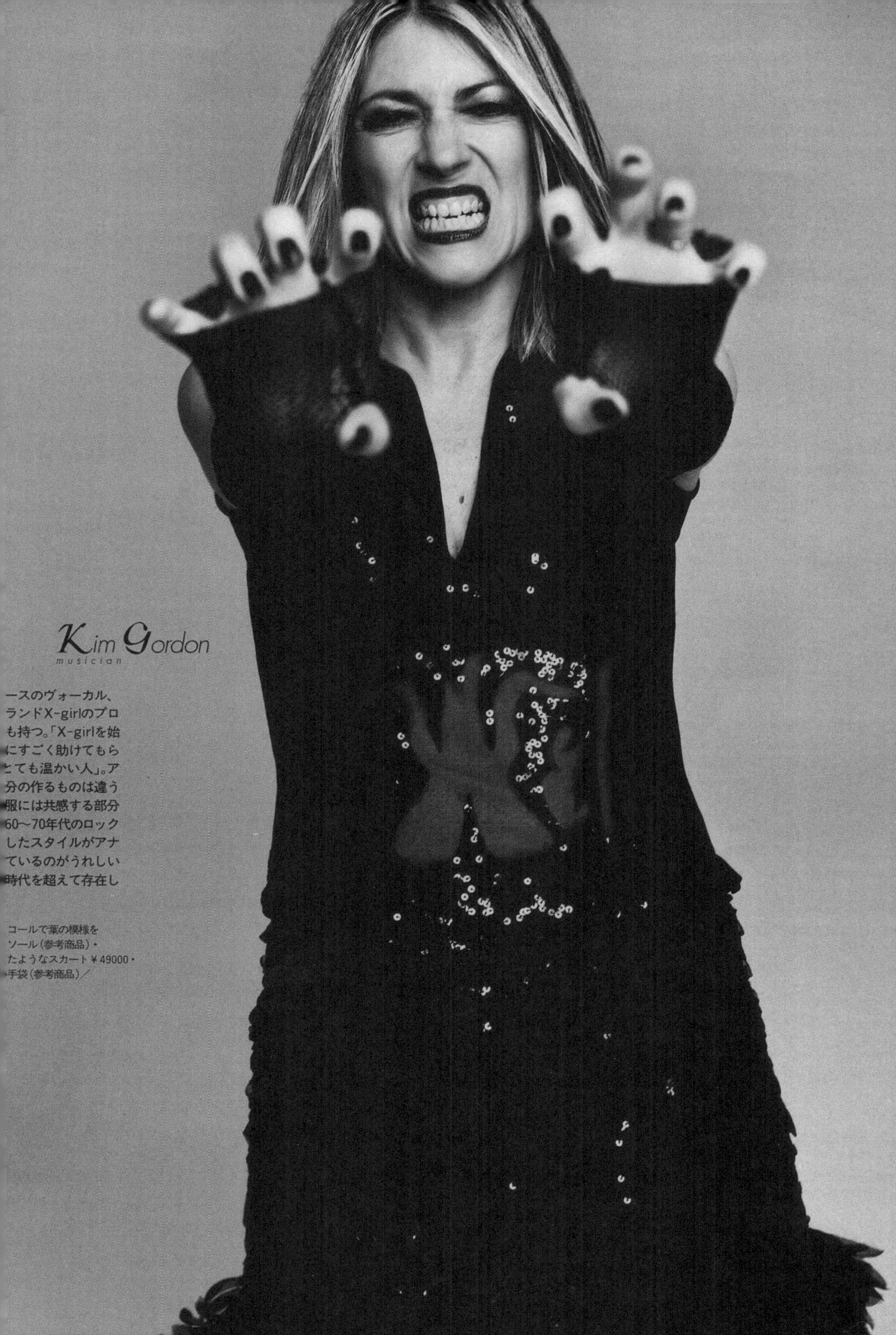

Kim Gordon

musician

ースのヴォーカル、
ランドX-girlのプロ
も持つ。「X-girlを始
にすごく助けてもら
とても温かい人」。ア
分の作るものは違う
服には共感する部分
60～70年代のロック
したスタイルがアナ
ているのがうれしい
時代を超えて存在し

コールで葉の模様を
ソール（参考商品）・
たようなスカート￥49000・
手袋（参考商品）／

ANNA SUI

Music has always been an important inspiration—I am of that generation. Probably the earliest music and visuals I remember are Elvis Presley on TV singing "Hound Dog," or the first transistor radio song. I remember somebody running up to me on the playground with a transistor radio and asking me to listen to "I Want to Hold Your Hand." All those things happened in my lifetime. So, I've lived through rock and roll, the British invasion, metal bands, alternative rock and grunge, and then hip hop. The music thing is pretty much ingrained in my generation.

Rock stars have always influenced me. My number one influence for rock was Anita Pallenberg, and then Keith Richards and the Stones and how they dressed, and the movie *Performance*. I remember tearing out pictures from *Seventeen* magazine. Sometimes the clothing was a little more sophisticated than you would have thought. There would be an article like "Granny Takes a Trip" or a piece on girlfriends of the rock band members wearing something you weren't sure where it came from, but it was probably Ozzy Clark or Biba. I was drawn to how Anita looked or Alice Cooper's girlfriend, Cindy Lang, whom I saw at parties in Detroit where I grew up. When I went to New York, I saw that her clothes were from the upscale department store Henri Bendel and they were European. The discovery of this other world was exciting. Eventually fashion magazines started covering these looks more, and they would have a little story about Biba or Ozzy Clark. In the front of *Vogue*, there was a section called "Vogue's Boutique," and they would feature Marissa Berenson or Penelope Tree wearing those British fashions. I was starved for information on where this incredible clothing was coming from. It's been my life's quest to find those designers and meet a lot of them, get to know them, and see exhibitions of their work. I found a lot of similar kinds of clothes in the flea markets and was able to understand more what it was about. But as a teenager, I didn't have access. I would only get glimpses of it in magazines.

By the time I got to New York, the style was glam. I was friends with the band the New York Dolls and they were wearing glitter, patent leather, platform shoes, and makeup. And that's right when Bowie broke as Ziggy Stardust. We went together to see Bowie at Radio City Music Hall, and eventually he started showing up at the New York Dolls shows.

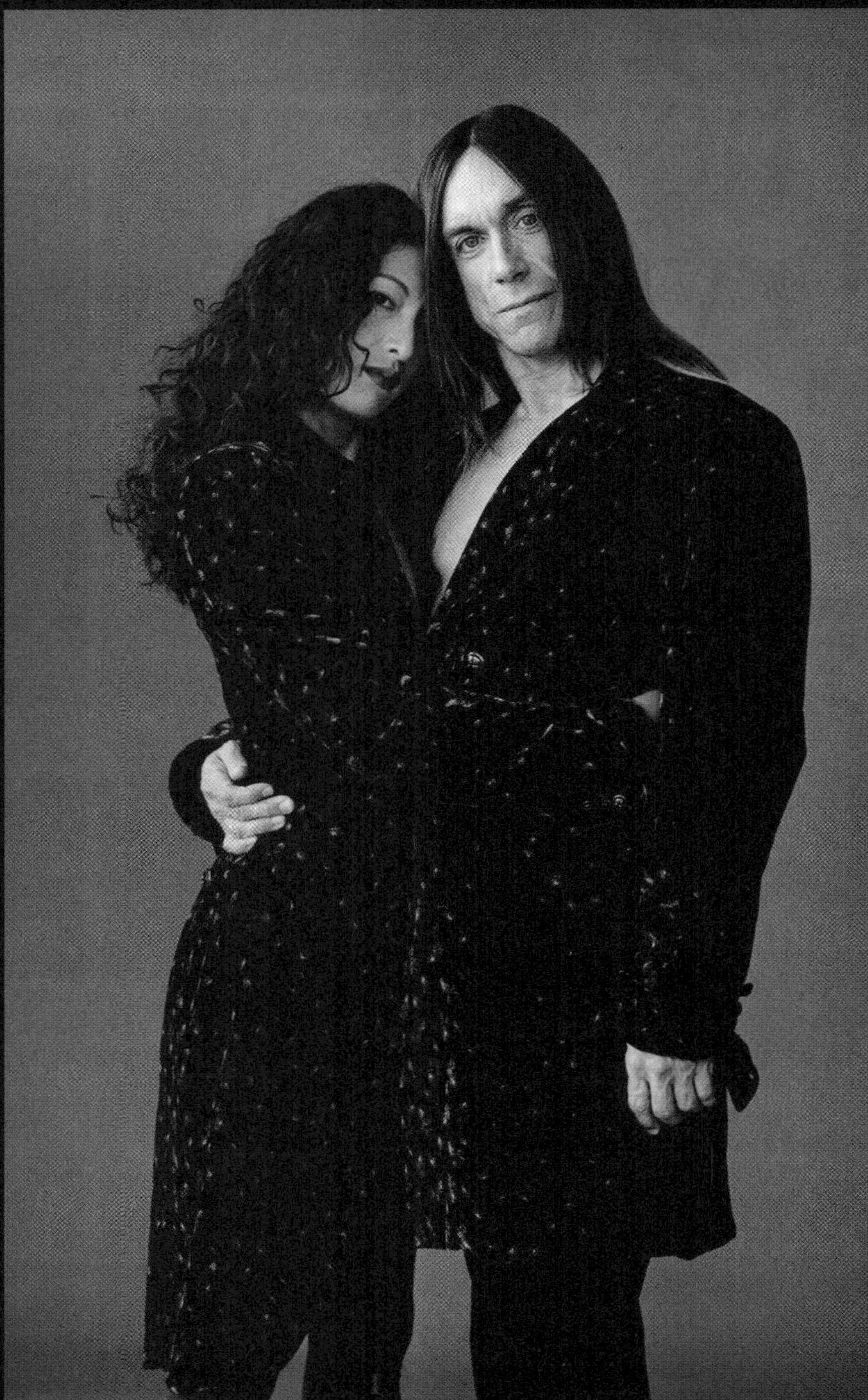

I went to this big concert in San Francisco that the Beastie Boys put on and Dave Navarro was playing with Jane's Addiction. We were all staying at the same hotel and I ran into him in the hotel elevator and we said hello to each other but then we ran off in different directions. I should have said something to him, but that night there was a big party at Trader Vic's in the Fairmont Hotel. I saw Dave across the room, and I asked him if he would ever consider being in my show, and hesaid, "If lingerie is involved, then yes." He flew in for his fitting and walked into our office, took off all his clothes and he said, "You're the artist. I'm the clay. Mold me." Everybody in the room just about dropped dead.

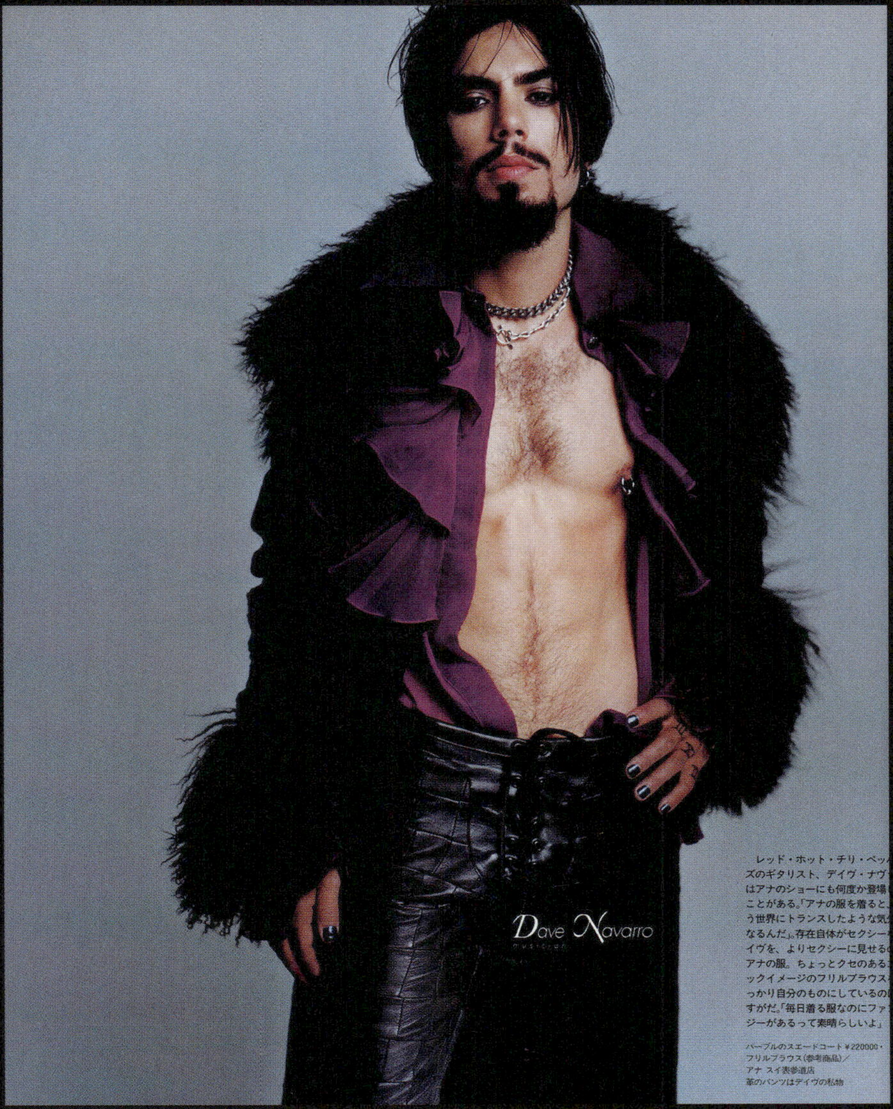

Dave Navarro

レッド・ホット・チリ・ペッ
ズのギタリスト、デイヴ・ナヴ
はアナのショーにも何度か登場
ことがある。「アナの服を着ると
う世界にトランスしたような気
なるんだ」。存在自体がセクシー
イヴを、よりセクシーに見せる
アナの服。ちょっとクセのある
ックイメージのフリルブラウス
っかり自分のものにしているの
すがだ。「毎日着る服なのにファ
ジーがあるって素晴らしいよ」

パープルのスエードコート ¥220000・
フリルブラウス(参考商品)／
アナ スイ表参道店
革のパンツはデイヴの私物

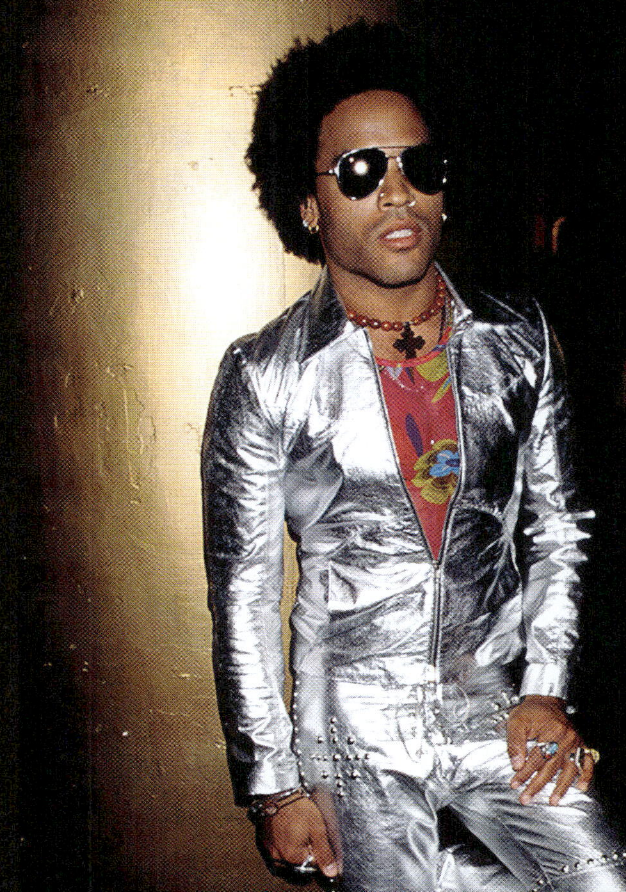

Suchi Asano and Iggy Pop, 1990s

Dave Navarro, *Spur* magazine, October 1997

Lenny Kravitz in Anna Sui Spring 1999 at Tommy Hilfiger Fall 1999 show, February 1999

STEFF YOTKA

I think whether Anna will admit it or not, music may be her most frequent starting point. She told me about sneaking into nightclubs when she was underage in Detroit. I guess being from Detroit, which has had such a great alternative music scene, I'm not surprised that she's been plugged in to music since her earliest days. Music is a really prominent through line in many of her collections because it's the thing that is most likely to connect people. If you don't care about fashion, you're still buying records or listening to CDs or making a Spotify playlist. I think you can track popular music of the past fifty years through Anna's collections because she's been inspired by it so much. And it's not surprising that musicians want to wear her clothes. I know the pop star Olivia Rodrigo is obsessed with her and the bands No Doubt and Paramore and so many other great bands have looked to Anna to dress them because they have the same references—they're all obsessed with PJ Harvey and Courtney Love and Björk and Cool Human.

SOFIA COPPOLA

Anna and I are both big music fans. We both really love music and it's a big part of our work. She knows so much about the history of culture and music in general. I always learn something from being around her. Anna was in New York at such an exciting time in the late '70s and '80s. And I'm always excited to hear about all the bands that she sees. Even just the other day, she was talking about the Jesus and Mary Chain, whom I love. She's loved being around punk, seeing Blondie's early shows, and the Ramones and so many other classic New York bands. In the early '90s I was really into the Smashing Pumpkins with James Iha, and I know she was really inspired by them and the look of rock bands and their groupies and just that whole scene and incorporated it into her work.

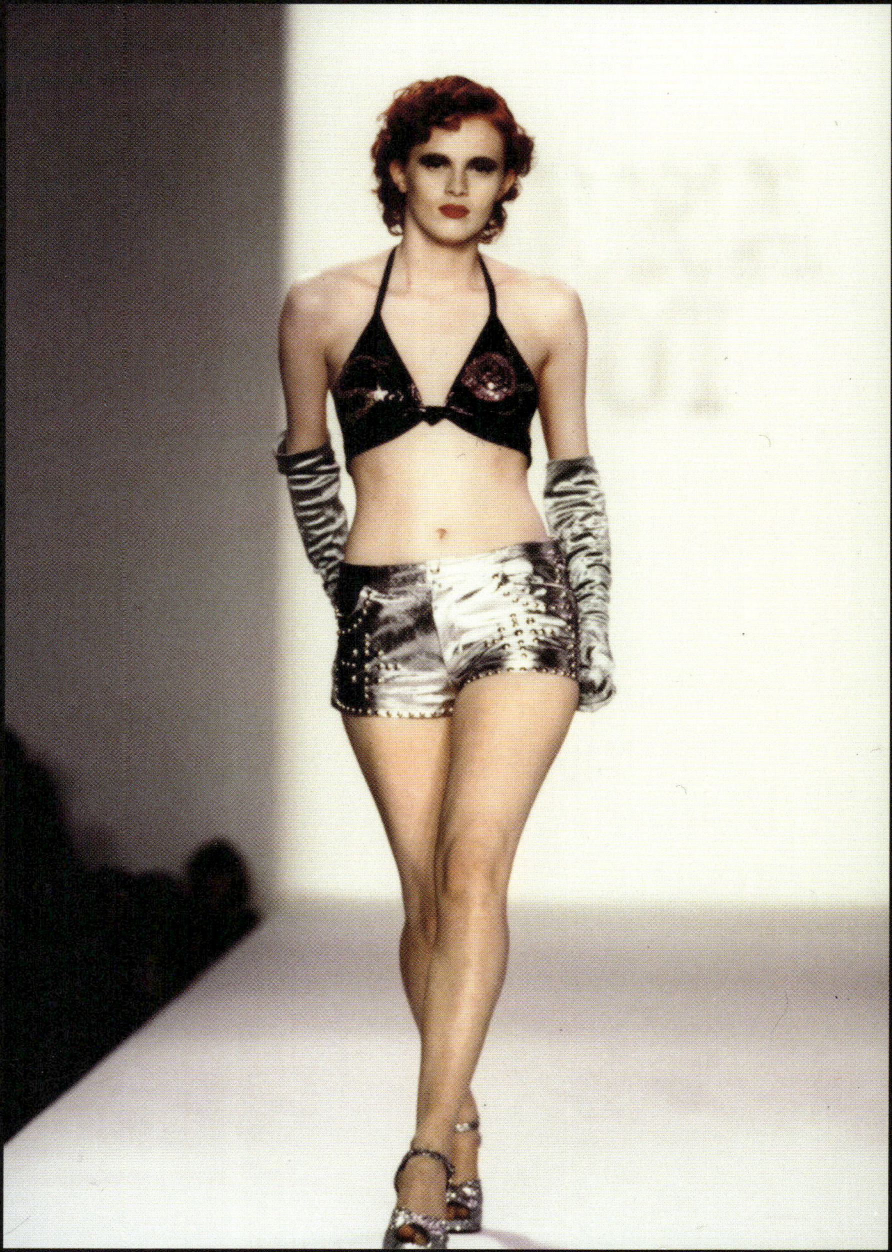

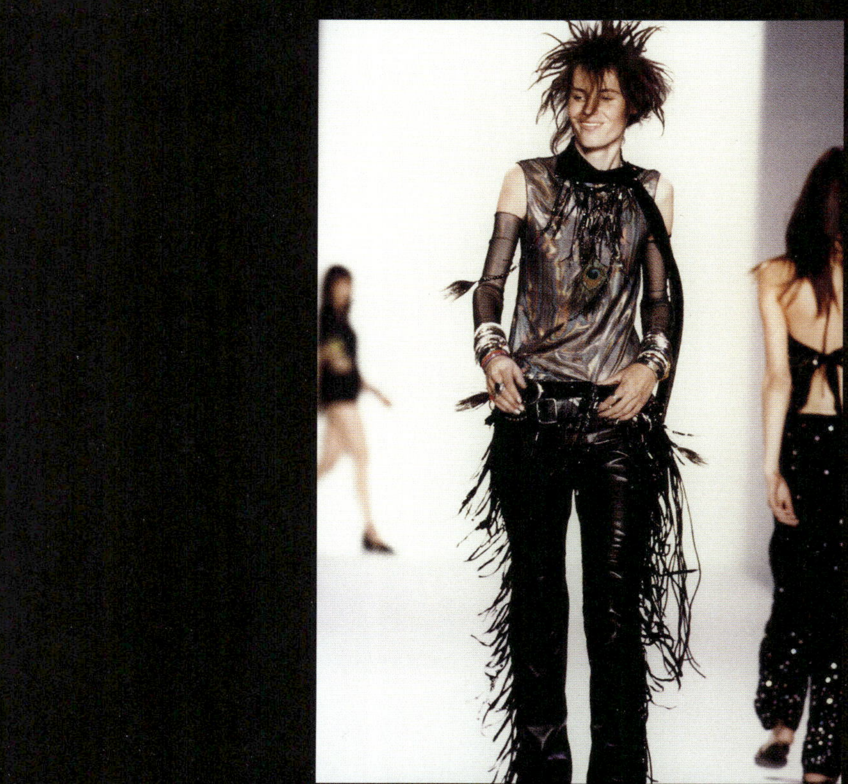

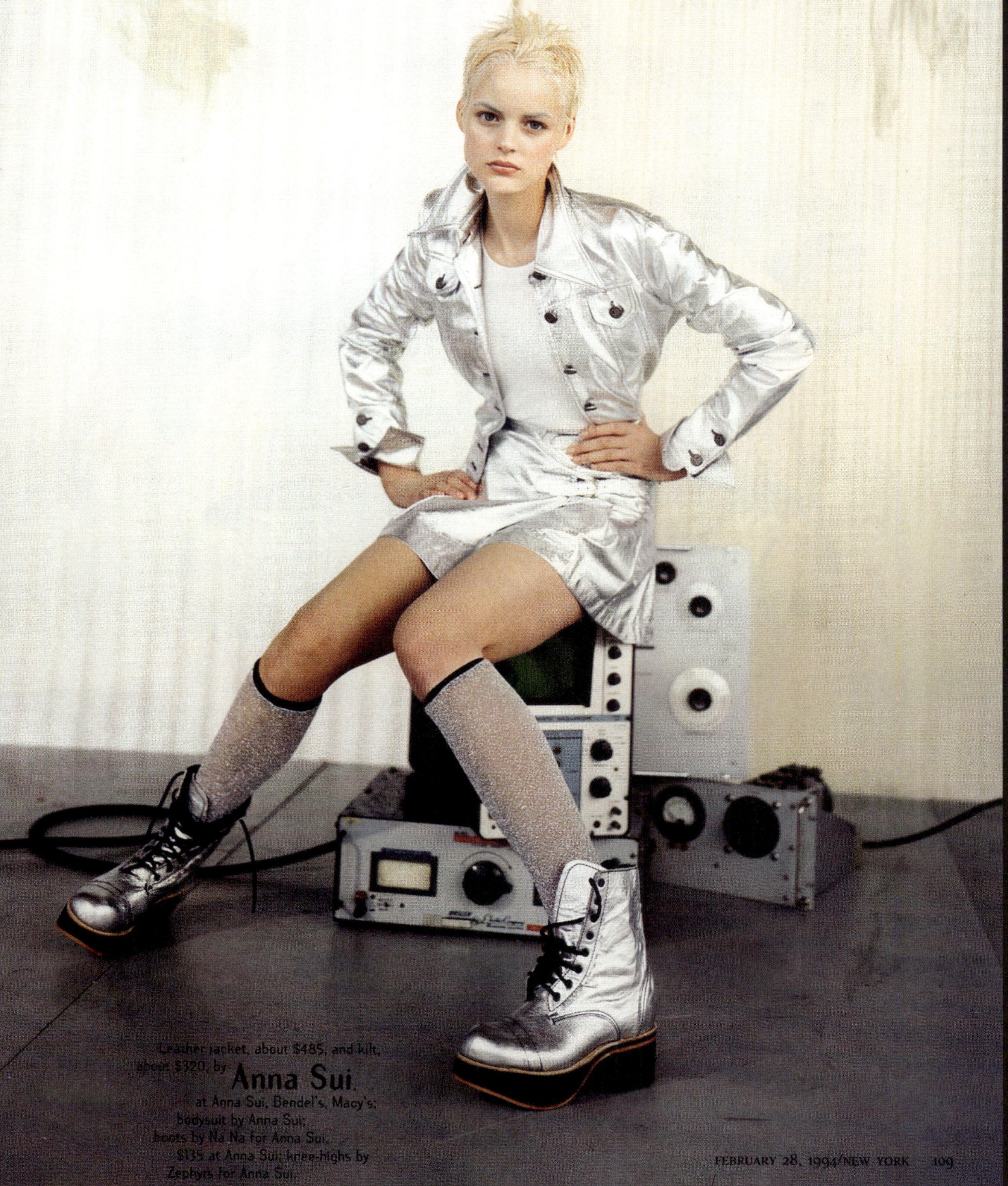
Taking their cues from movies like **Blade Runner** and **Total Recall**, designers are moving the action from the screen onto the **street.**

Leather jacket, about $485, and kilt, about $320, by **Anna Sui**, at Anna Sui, Bendel's, Macy's; bodysuit by Anna Sui; boots by Na Na for Anna Sui, $135 at Anna Sui; knee-highs by Zephyrs for Anna Sui.

FEBRUARY 28, 1994/NEW YORK 109

Karen Elson, Spring 1999

Jesse Camp, Spring 1999

Farrah Summerford, *New York* magazine, February 28, 1994

The New York Times,
October 18, 1998

The New York Times
Sunday Styles
Sunday, October 18, 1998
Section 9

Golden Years 2: Is Glam's Return Real or Fantasy?

In Britain in the 70's, glam rock glittered, and men wore eye shadow and feather boas. As a new movie and magazines proclaim a new glam era, it sounds as artificial as the first time.

By DAVID HANDELMAN

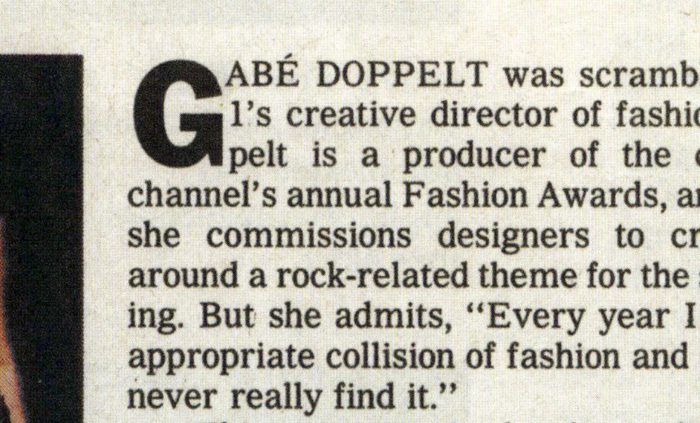

GABÉ DOPPELT was scrambling. As VH-1's creative director of fashion, Ms. Doppelt is a producer of the cable music channel's annual Fashion Awards, and each year she commissions designers to create outfits around a rock-related theme for the show's opening. But she admits, "Every year I look for the appropriate collision of fashion and music, and I never really find it."

This year promised to be no different, until Ms. Doppelt heard that a movie about the glam rock movement had won an award at the Cannes Film Festival, and her antennae began buzzing. Todd Haynes's "Velvet Goldmine" is a fictional-

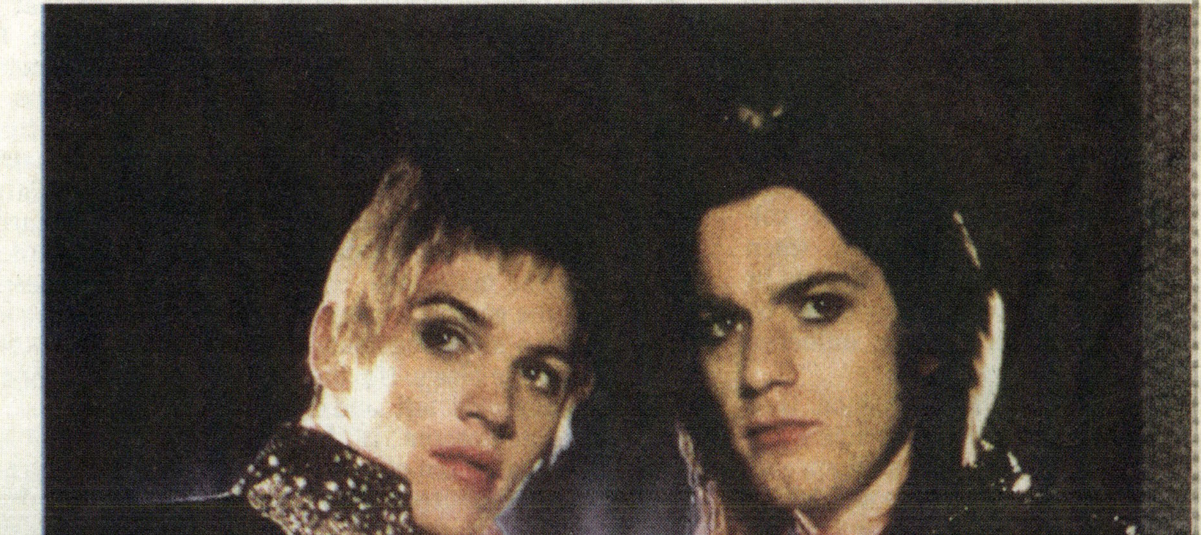

Corina Lecca for The New York Times

Rex's lead singer, Marc Bolan, started wearing glitter and women's clothes, and the former folkie David Bowie decked himself out as the sexually ambiguous spaceman Ziggy Stardust. For a brief, shining moment, men wore eye shadow, feather boas, platform shoes and the tightest outfits the era's fabrics allowed.

Ms. Doppelt, who as a teen-ager in England had once worn a Bolan-inspired leopard-print catsuit, called Miramax, the distributor of "Velvet Goldmine," to screen the movie. Seeing the eye-catching period costumes designed by Sandy Powell, she knew she'd found her motif. She sent "Velvet Goldmine" stills and vintage 70's videos to designers she thought would respond, including Tom Ford, Michael Kors, John Galliano and Anna Sui.

They not only delivered fanciful concoctions to VH-1, which will telecast its awards show Oct. on 27, but some of them also carried the theme into their own work.

Ms. Sui got so excited that when she sat down to design her spring 1999 collection (which will be presented on Nov. 4), she plastered her studio walls with images of the film's co-stars, Ewan MacGregor and Jonathan Rhys Meyers (who play fictionalized versions of Iggy Pop and Mr. Bowie), while blasting songs like T. Rex's "20th Century Boy."

"The movie captured that whole excitement when there's something going on, rules to be broken," Ms. Sui said. "That hasn't happened for the longest time."

Now, as myriad glam influences seem to be percolat-

Continued on Page 6

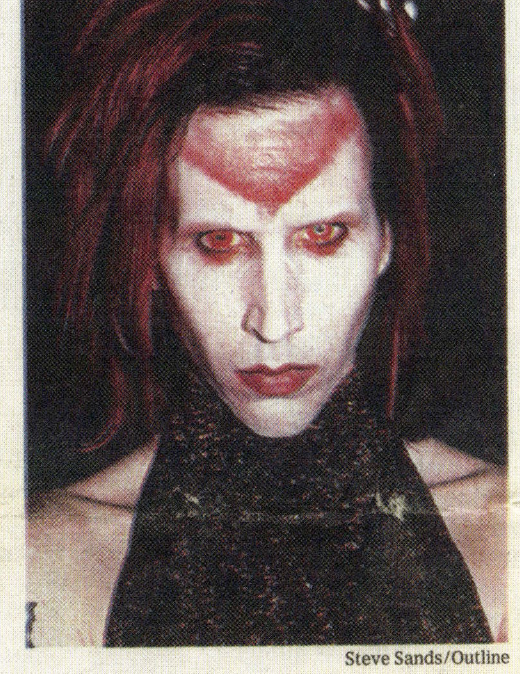

Steve Sands/Outline

Peter Mountain/Miramax Films

In "Velvet Goldmine" Jonathan Rhys Meyers, right, and Ewan MacGregor, far right, play glam rockers. Tom Ford's glittering dress for Gucci, top, and Marilyn Manson's new glam image, above.

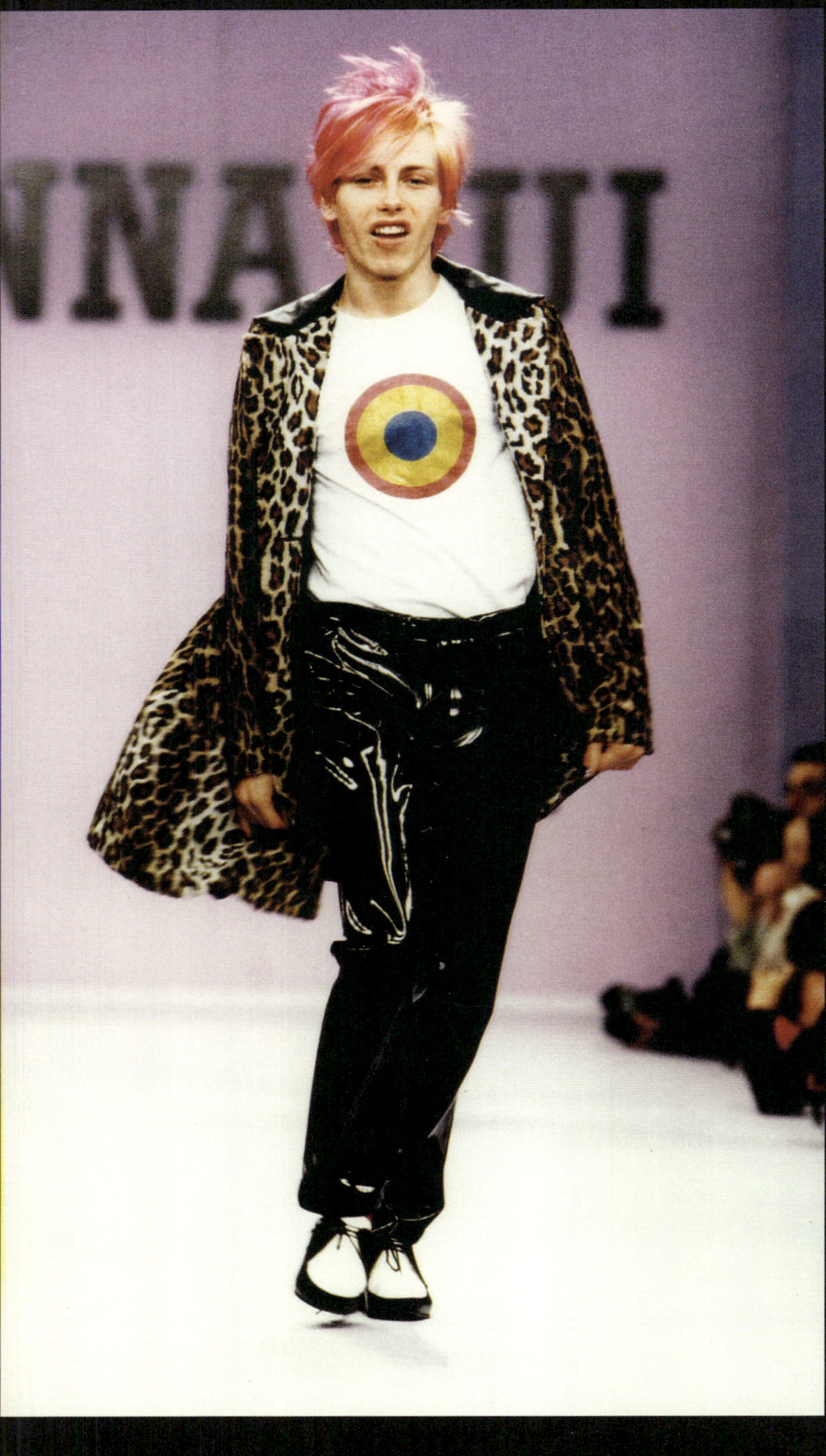

CHRISTY TURLINGTON BURNS

I was obsessed with music and so was Anna—and we both had crushes on some of the guys in bands. There was this guy that I was friends with who I loved, Charlie Sexton. He was super cute—a Texan. Anna was also friendly with the Duran Duran guys, and Ian Astbury from the Cult. Anna knew all of them, and she knew their girlfriends. She was part of a rock 'n' roll subculture. I would see shows as much as I could. I had such a crush on David Bowie, and then got a chance to hang out with him a bit in those early years. We went to the Modern Love Tour at Madison Square Garden. But we also loved the polar opposite of rock 'n' roll—we were obsessed with Liza Minnelli. We went to see her at Radio City Music Hall for a big show—we liked a little bit of the kitsch and some show tunes.

MARC JACOBS

I think when there's a big shift in music or there's something that's really popular that strikes a chord, then people want to look like their pop star heroes: they wanted to look like Bowie, they wanted to look like Elvis, they wanted to look like the Rolling Stones. With music, there's the message, the voice, and the sound, but then there's also the visual, and, for me, the Rolling Stones looked amazing. I didn't think about other groups that were more popular than the Rolling Stones. Mick Jagger as a front man and Keith Richards, they looked incredible. They dressed so stylishly and ticked all the boxes for me.

PUNK—ANNA SUI

When I did the punk collection, I had been in London in the beginning of the punk days and met all those bands, the Sex Pistols, the Clash, saw Siouxsie and went to Vivian's [Westwood] store and bought clothes. And I loved everything about punk except for the nihilistic Idea behind it, and so when I did the punk collection, Spring/Summer 93, I decided to make it optimistic. So instead of black leather, I did the silver leather and did the pastels and gave it like sweetness and optimism rather

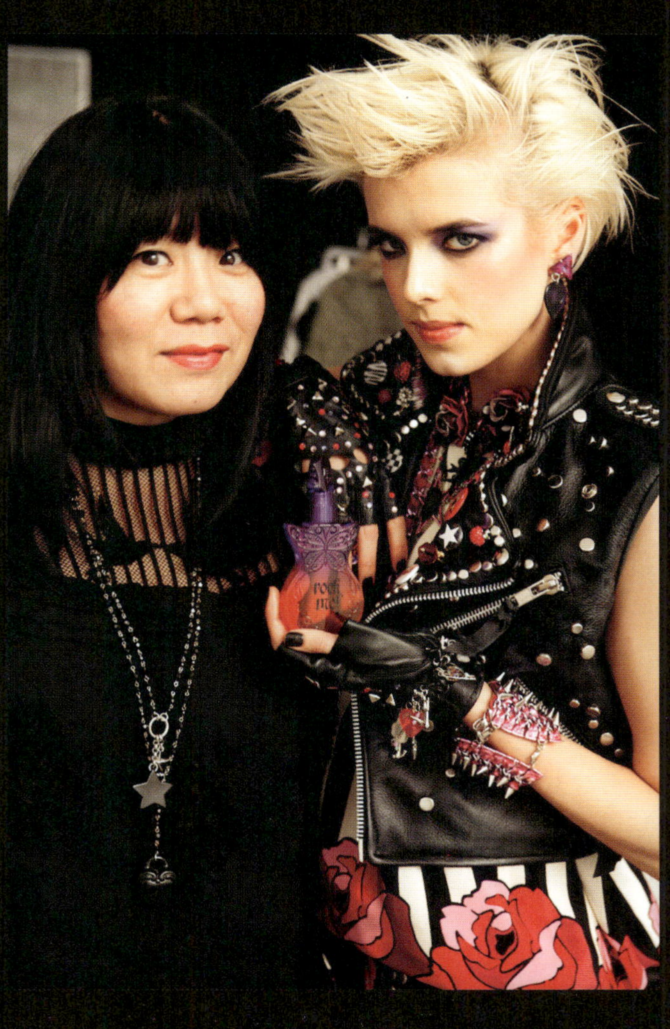

> **"She is one of the only designers who recognize that women have a rock fantasy, also."**
>
> *The New York Times*, November 1, 1996

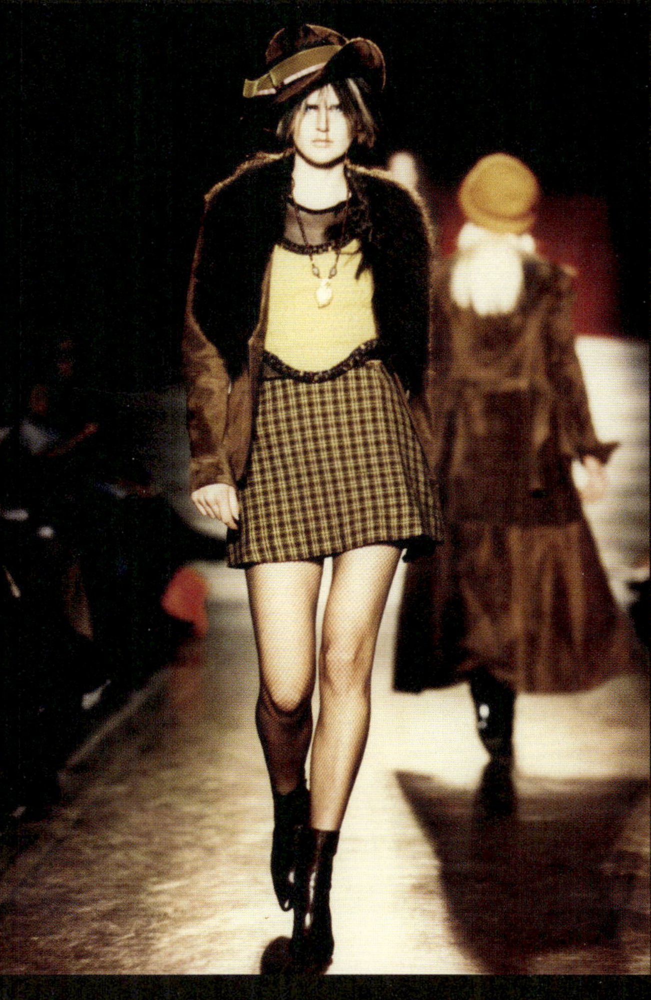

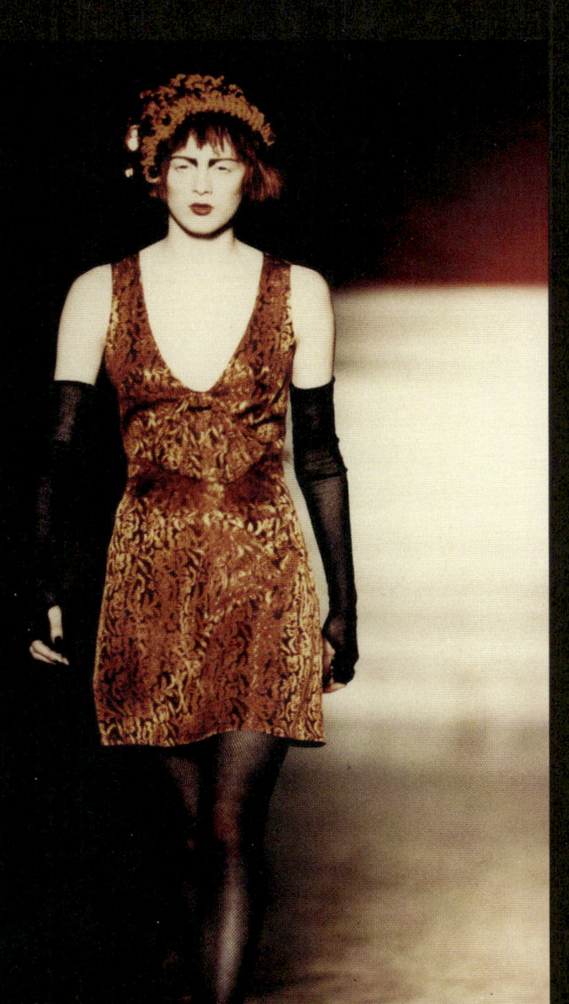

Anna Sui and Agyness Deyn, photo shoot for Rock Me fragrance ad, October 2009

Karen Elson, Fall 1997

Stella Tennant, Fall 1997

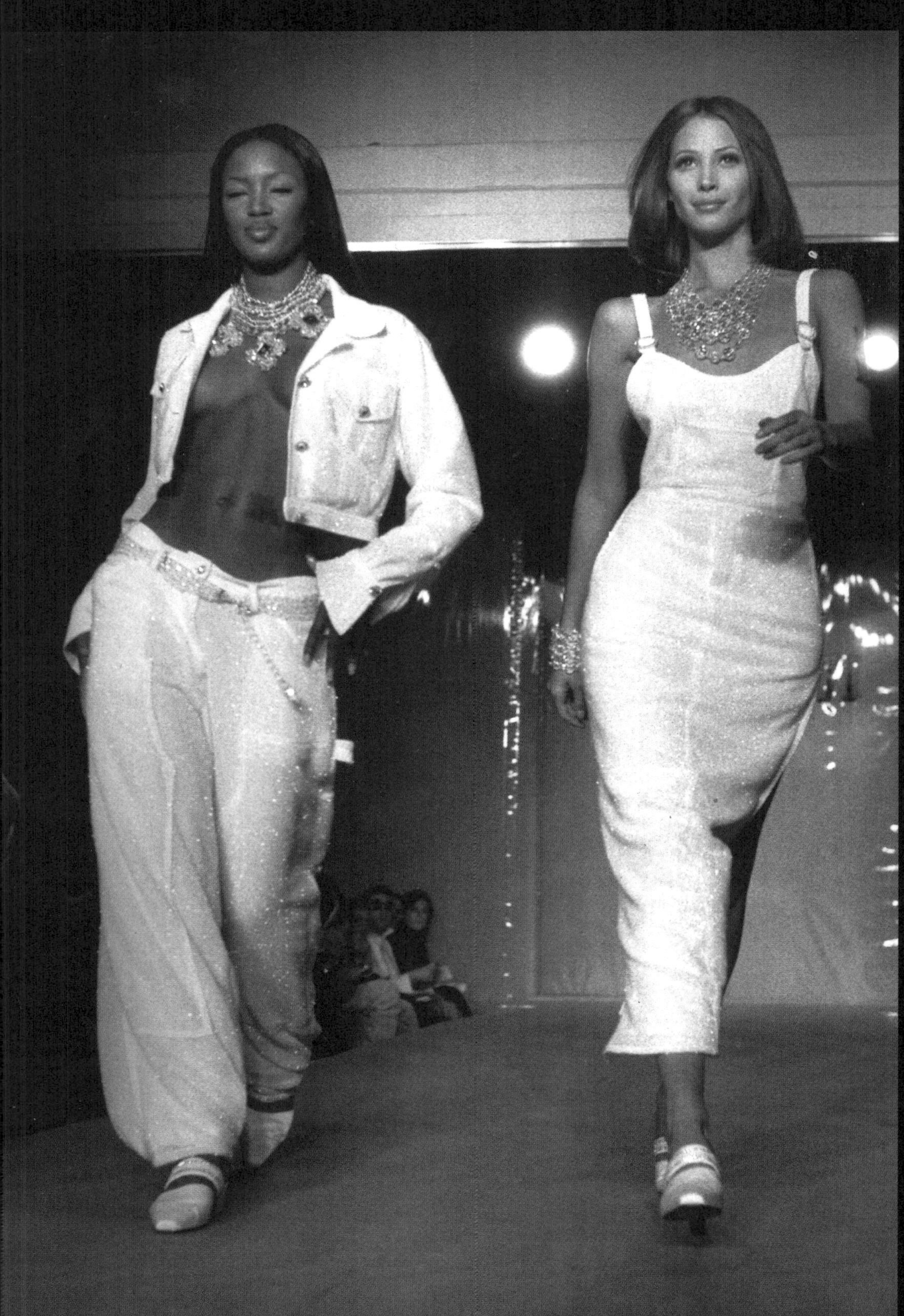

all the motorcycle jackets and quilted things that we did in the leather, they were all in silver, but everything was very optimistic.

HIP HOP— ANNA SUI

Hip hop definitely had an influence, and especially in my first collection, if you look at the jewelry, it was very hip hop inspired. In fact, I worked with Erickson Beamon on the jewelry, we went up to Harlem and bought all those big gold chains. And then we embellished them these big clocks, and we attached them to these big chains and we put grosgrain ribbons on them and just kind of again made them very Anna Sui, but the basis was very hip hop.

We also put baggy "homeboy" pants on Naomi over a bikini and gave her that whale tail look where you see the top of the bikini and the pants are really low, and then we did those durags, but we made them out of our fabrics, our prints. And Naomi opens that show [Spring/Summer 98], where it's kind of a combination of all those looks, with some athletic elements too.

Naomi Campbell wearing "homeboy" pants and Christy Turlington, Spring 1992

Jewelry, Erickson Beamon for Anna Sui Spring 1991

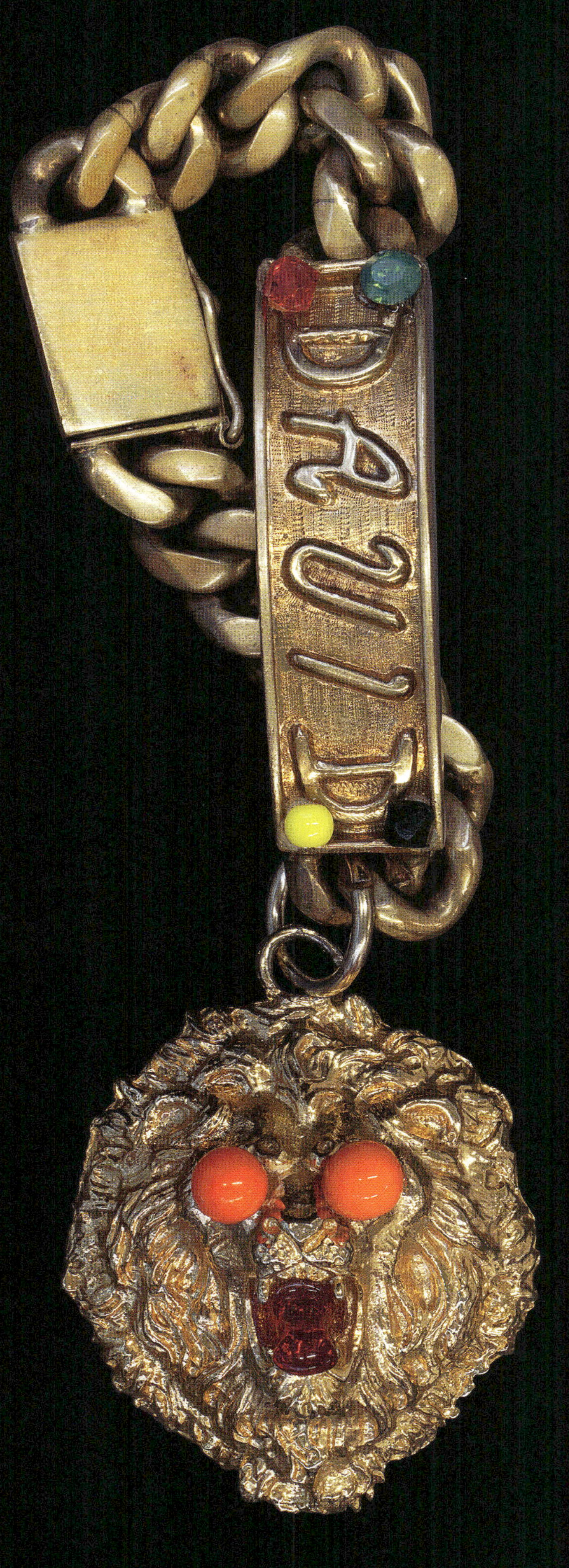

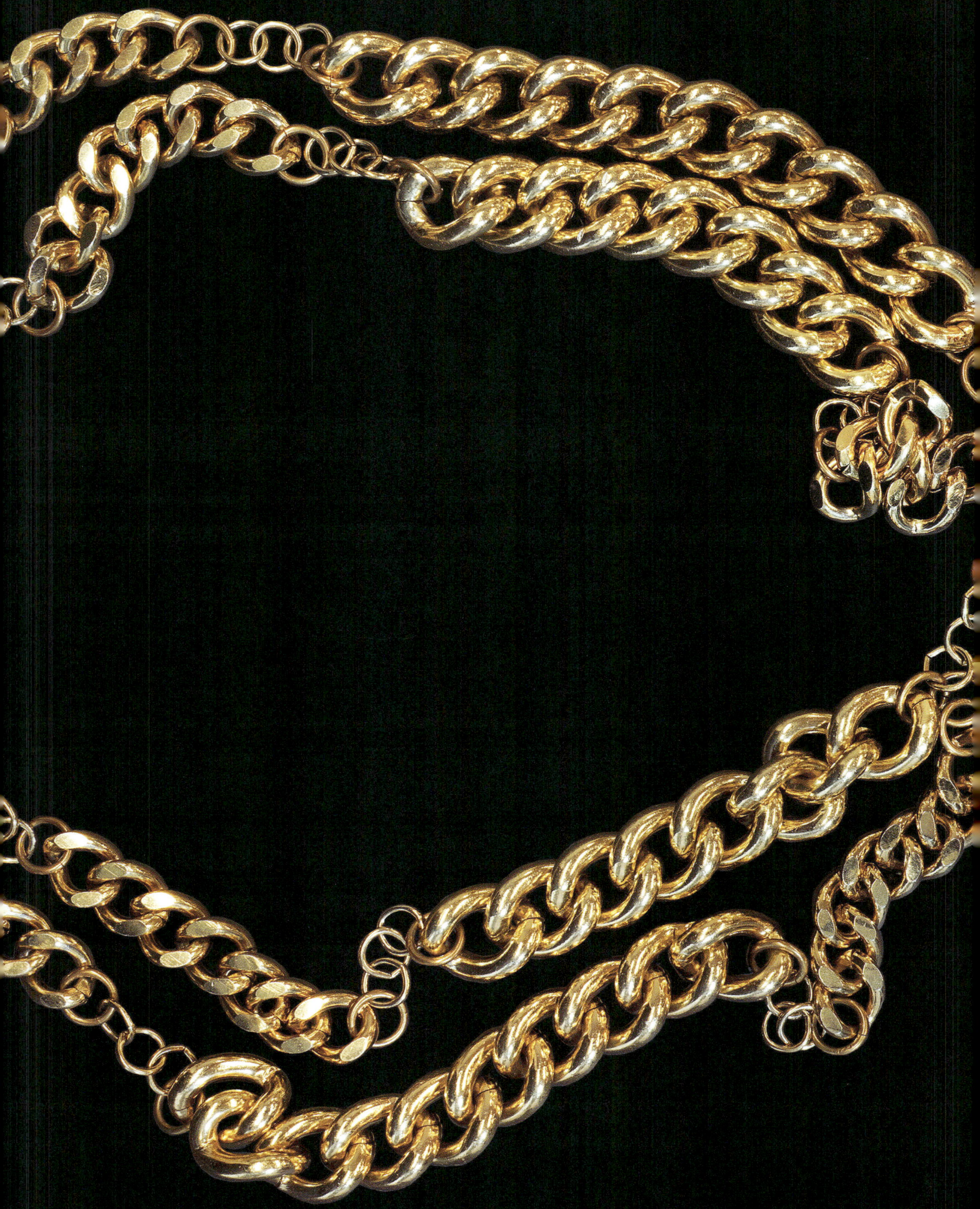

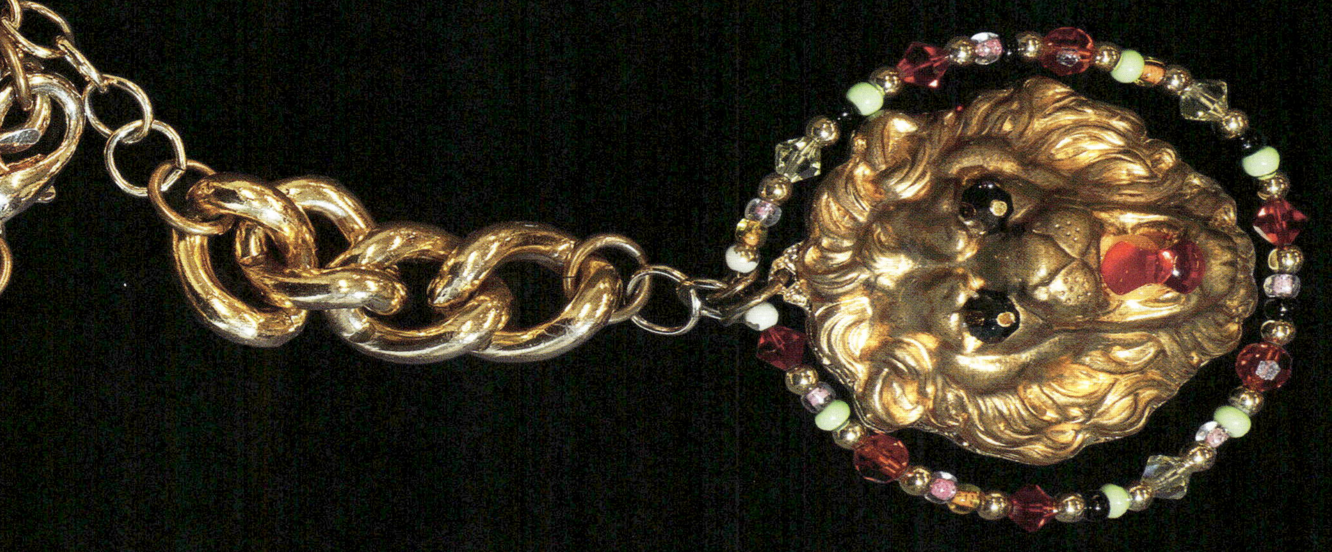

Jewelry, Erickson Beamon for Anna Sui Spring 1991

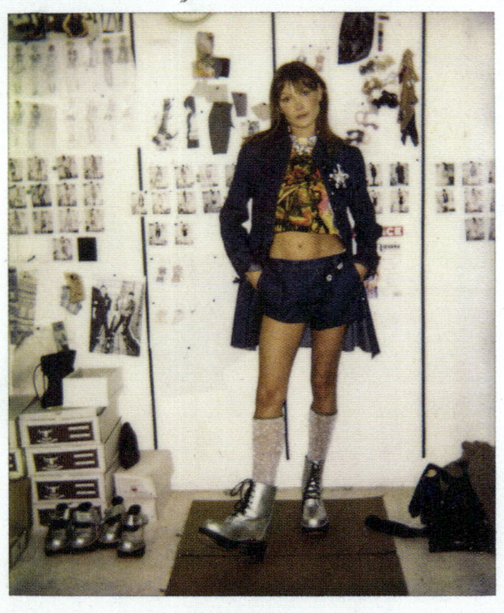

12. Carla
Indigo shirt dress (open)
Orange cleopatra mini tee
Indigo hot pant

12. ACCESSORIES
- *Rhinestone flower cross necklace*
- *Rhinestone star pin* (on left side of coat)
- *Rhinestone flower safety pin* (through belt loop on hot pant
- *Silver glitter knee high*
- *Silver boots* (size 10)

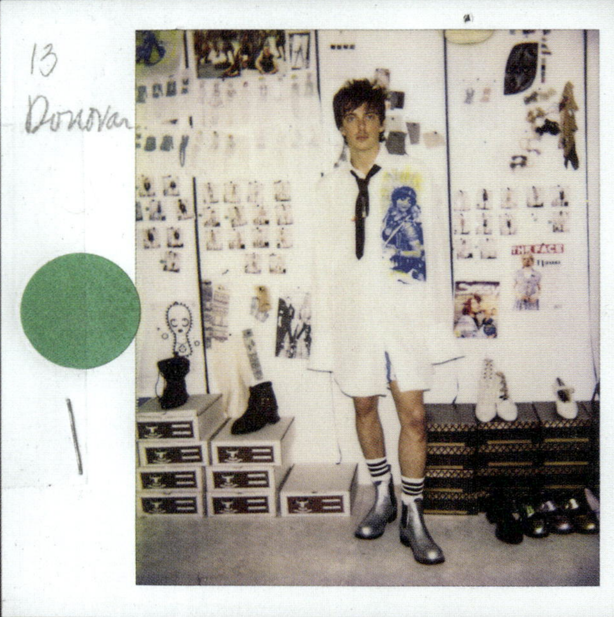

13. Donovan
White silk screened shirt
Blue/white stripe boxer

13. ACCESSORIES
- *black leather tie*
- *white tube sock w/blk stripes*
- *silver lace up boot* (size 10)

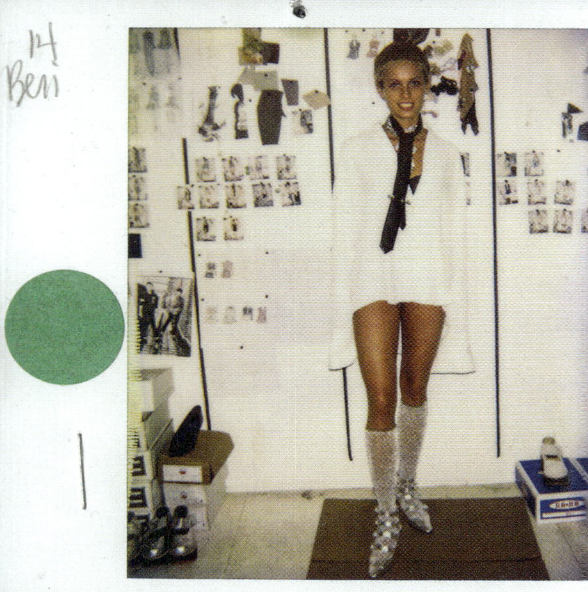

14. Beri
White silk screened shirt (5th button closed; cuffs down & open)
Black bra and panty with lace trim

14. ACCESSORIES
- *Black leather tie w/rhinestone pin*
- *Rhinestone multi-strand choke w/medallion*
- *Silver glitter knee hi*
- *Silver P. Cox lace up boot* (size 39)

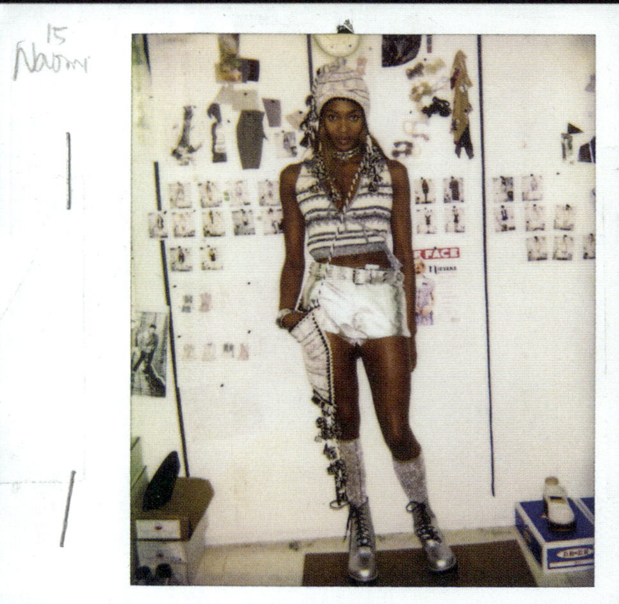

15. Naomi
Blue Peruvian wrap front vest (closed)
Silver leather hot pant

15. ACCESSORIES
- *Pom Pom Hat* (untied)
- *Peruvian handbag* (across chest; on right hip)
- *Dog collar*
- *Silver bracelet*
- *Silver belt with holes* (buckle in center)
- *Silver glitter knee hi*
- *Silver lace up boot w/wood platform* (size 7)

Dresser card, Carla Bruni, Spring 1994
Dresser card, Donovan Leitch, Spring 1994
Dresser card, Beri Smithers, Spring 1994
Dresser card, Naomi Campbell, Spring 1994

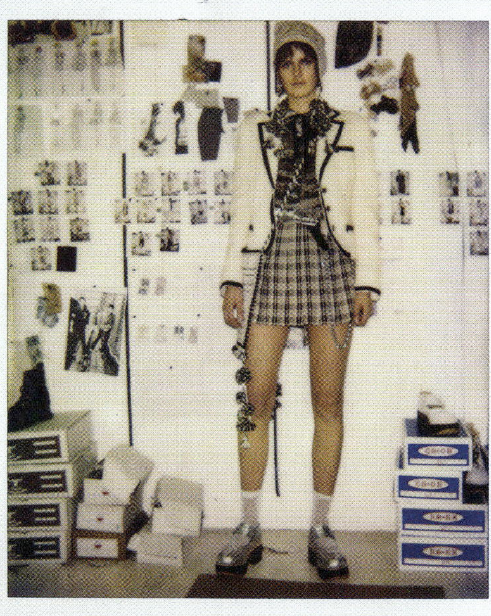

16. Stella
~~Cream~~ Aqua terrycloth jacket w/blk trim (open)
Silver organza pleated blouse (closed)
Black/cream plaid kilt
Black lace trim bra and panties (leave on for #41)

16. ACCESSORIES
- Pom Pom Hat (untied)
- black ribbon tied in a bow (at neck)
- Peruvian bag with tassels (over left shoulder; on right hip)
- Thin silver studded belt (wear buckle on right with silver chain on left)
- Silver glitter anklet
- Silver Maryjane w/wood platform (size 8)

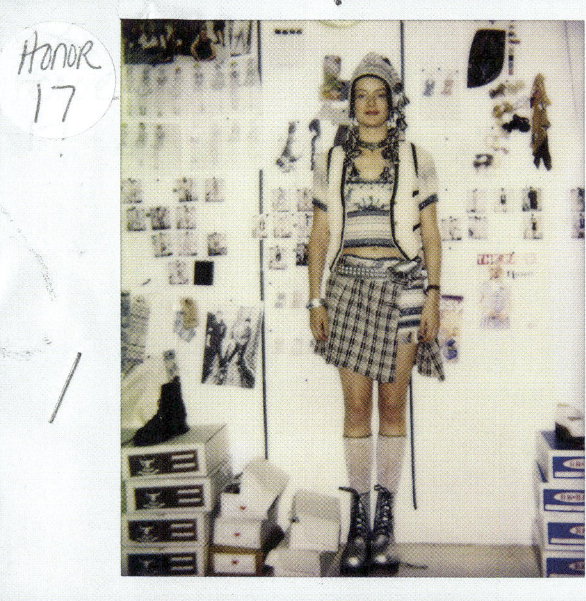

17. Honor
Cream terrycloth vest (open)
Blue Peruvian puff sleeve sweater and fringe short
~~Black/cream plaid kilt (open; (fasten top buckle w/safety pin over left hip)~~

17. ACCESSORIES
- Pom pom hat (untied)
- Silver studded shoulder bag (on right)
- Dog collar (to come)
- Silver studded belt (buckle on left hip)
- Silver glitter knee-hi
- Silver lace up boot with wood platform (size 7)

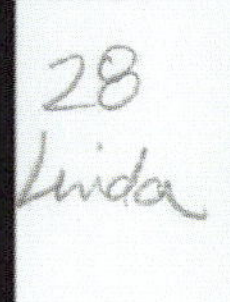

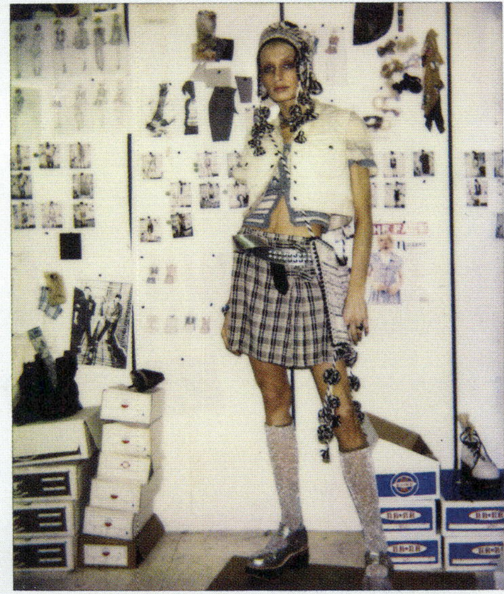

27. Lee
Cream denim fleece lined vest (open)
Blue Peruvian puff sleeve cardigan (top 4 buttoned, roll up sleeves)
Black/ cream plaid kilt

27. ACCESSORIES
- Pom pom hat (untied)
- ~~Peruvian purple and cream bag (wear across chest over right shoulder)~~
- Dog collar
- Silver studded belt
- Bracelet (wear on right wrist)
- Silver glitter knee-hi
- Silver Maryjane with wood platform (size 7)

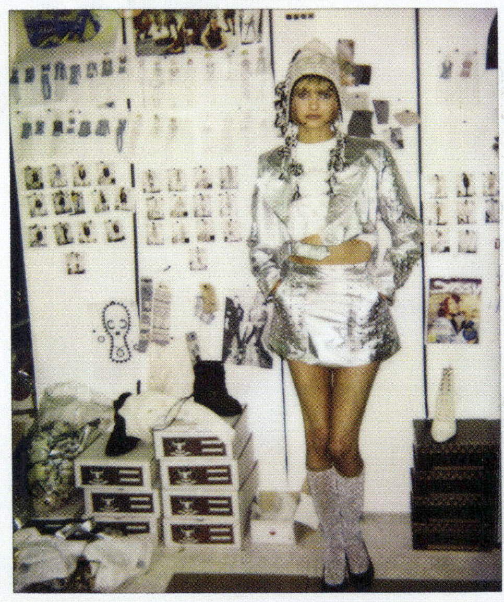

28. Linda
Silver studded leather crop biker jacket (open)
Dolly Head mini tee
Silver studded leather mini skirt

28. ACCESSORIES
- Peruvian Pom Pom Hat (untied)
- Silver glitter knee hi (from look #1)
- Silver pointed pump (size 6)

Dresser card, Stella Tennant, Spring 1994
Dresser card, Honor Fraser, Spring 1994
Dresser card, Lee Watson, Spring 1994
Dresser card, Linda Evangelista, Spring 1994

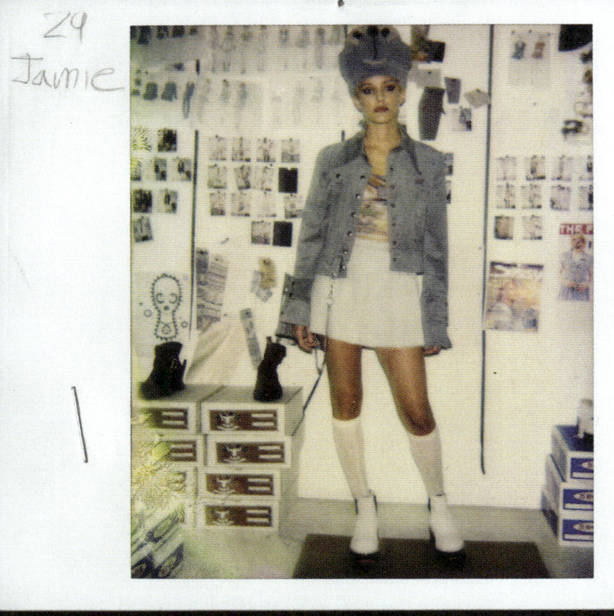

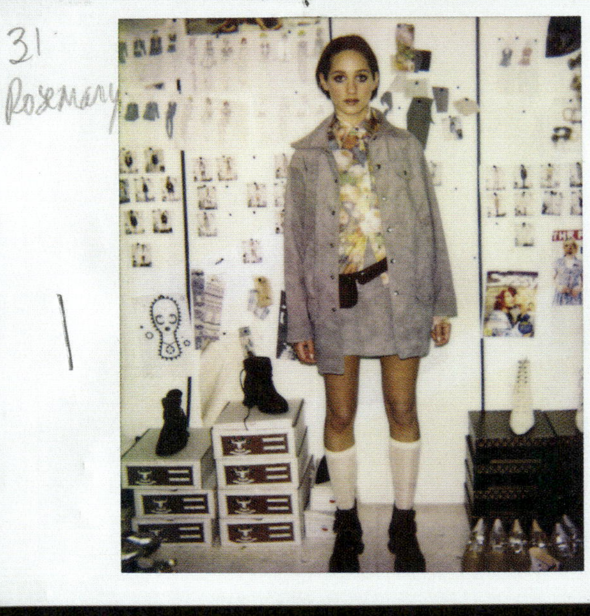

29. Jamie
Green ultrasuede battle jacket w/silver chain (coat open; cuffs open)
Photoprint l/s T-shirt
Green and cream stripe pleated seersucker mini

29. ***ACCESSORIES***
- ***Blue dog hat***
- ***Cream lace knee-hi***
- ***White suede lace up ankle boot with wood platform*** (size 7)

31. Rosemary
Purple ultrasuede jacket (open; cuffs open)
Photo print shirt (top 5 buttons closed)
Purple ultrasuede skirt

31. ***ACCESSORIES***
- ***Brown bag belt*** (bag center right)
- ***Cream lace knee hi***
- ***Brown suede boot w/buckle and white topstitching*** (size 9)

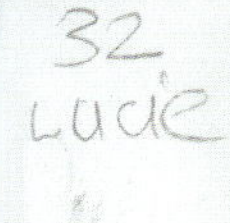

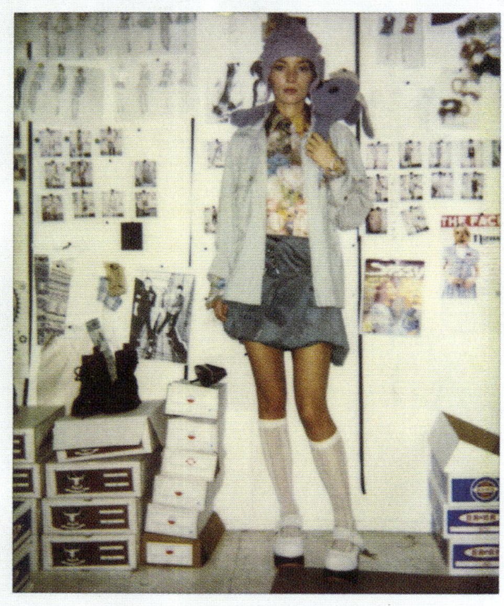

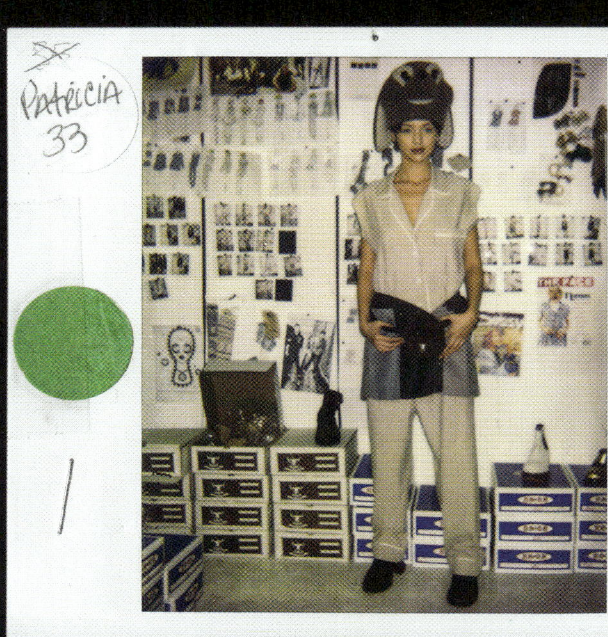

32. Lucie
Green and cream seersucker zip jacket (open)
Photo print shirt (closed; cuffs pulled down)
Green ultrasuede kilt w/suede bag

32. ***ACCESSORIES***
- ***Lavender popcorn knit cap with flaps*** (untied)
- ***Lavender puppy knapsack*** (stuffed; over left shoulder - hold with left hand)
- ***Cream lace knee-hi***
- ***White suede Maryjane with wood platform*** (size 7; needs shoe pad)

33. Patricia
Maroon and cream seersucker sleeveless pajamas (on top close all buttons)
Ultrasuede multi-color swing snap front mini skirt (over pants; top 2 snaps open)

33. ***ACCESSORIES***
- Stuffed ***dog hat***
- ***Brown suede bag belt*** (wear slung low; bag in front center)
- ***Creme lace knee-hi***
- ***Brown suede top stitch boot with buckle*** (size 7)

Dresser card, Jaime Rishar, Spring 1994
Dresser card, Rosemary Ferguson, Spring 1994
Dresser card, Lucie de la Falaise, Spring 1994
Dresser card, Patricia Hartmann, Spring 1994

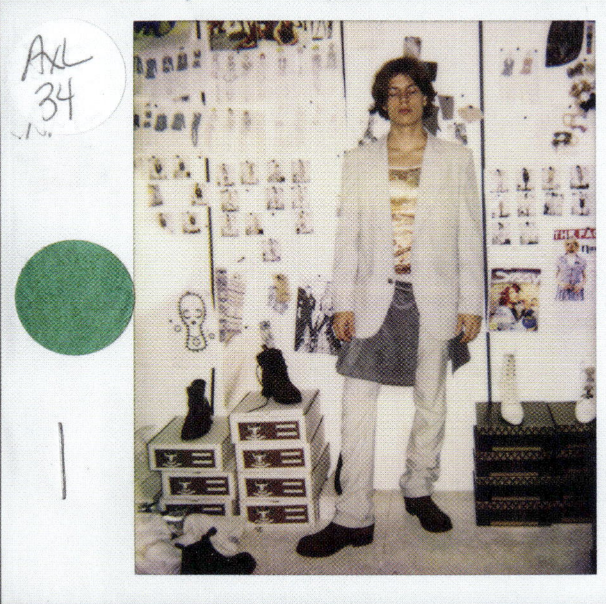

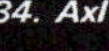

34. Axl
Blue and cream seersucker suit (open)
Photo print l/s shirt (out)
Blue ultrasuede kilt (open; pin top buckle w/lg. safety pin)

34. <u>ACCESSORIES</u>
. ***Brown suede pull on boot*** (size 10½)

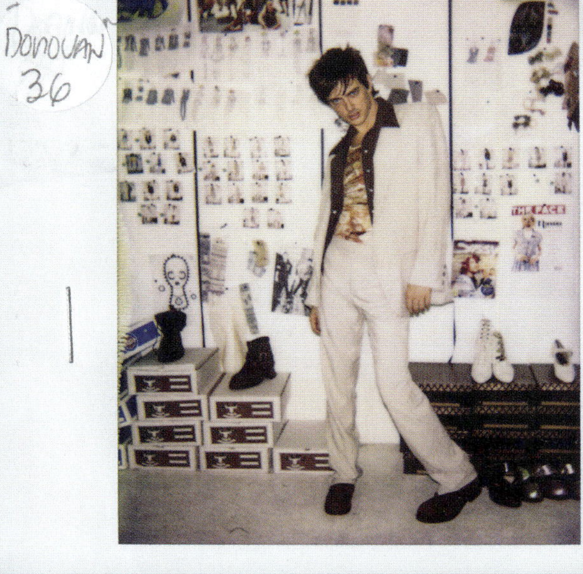

36. Donovan
Brown and cream seersucker suit (jacket open; take off on runway)
Brown ultrasuede vest (closed; collar out)
Photo print l/s tee shirt (out)

36. <u>ACCESSORIES</u>
. ***Brown suede pull-on*** (size 10)

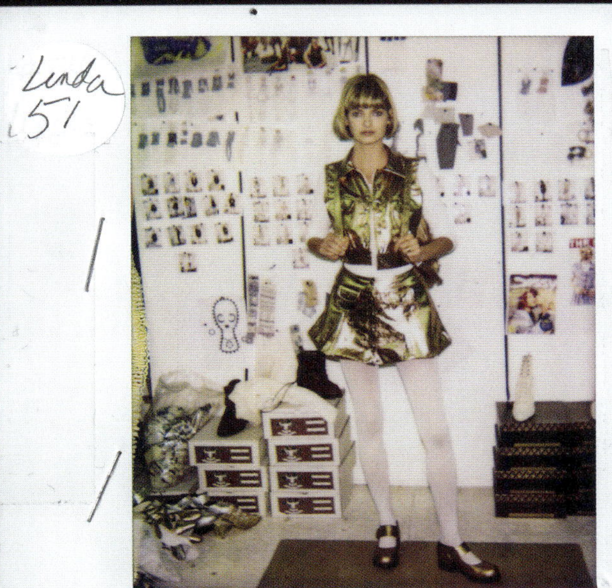

51. Linda
Copper leather vest (open)
(White leotard) (push sleeves up to elbow)
Copper leather snap front mini skirt (closed)

51. <u>ACCESSORIES</u>
. ***Copper leather knapsack*** (on back)
. ***White opaque tights*** (roll down waistband, below skirt)
. ***Copper Maryjane shoe*** (Size 7)

52. Eve
Blue leather wide lapel trench (open)
(White leotard)
Blue leather short skirt (closed)

52. <u>ACCESSORIES</u>
. ***Blue leather knapsack*** (stuffed)
. ***White opaque tights*** (roll down waistband below skirt)
. ***Blue Maryjane shoe*** (size 8)

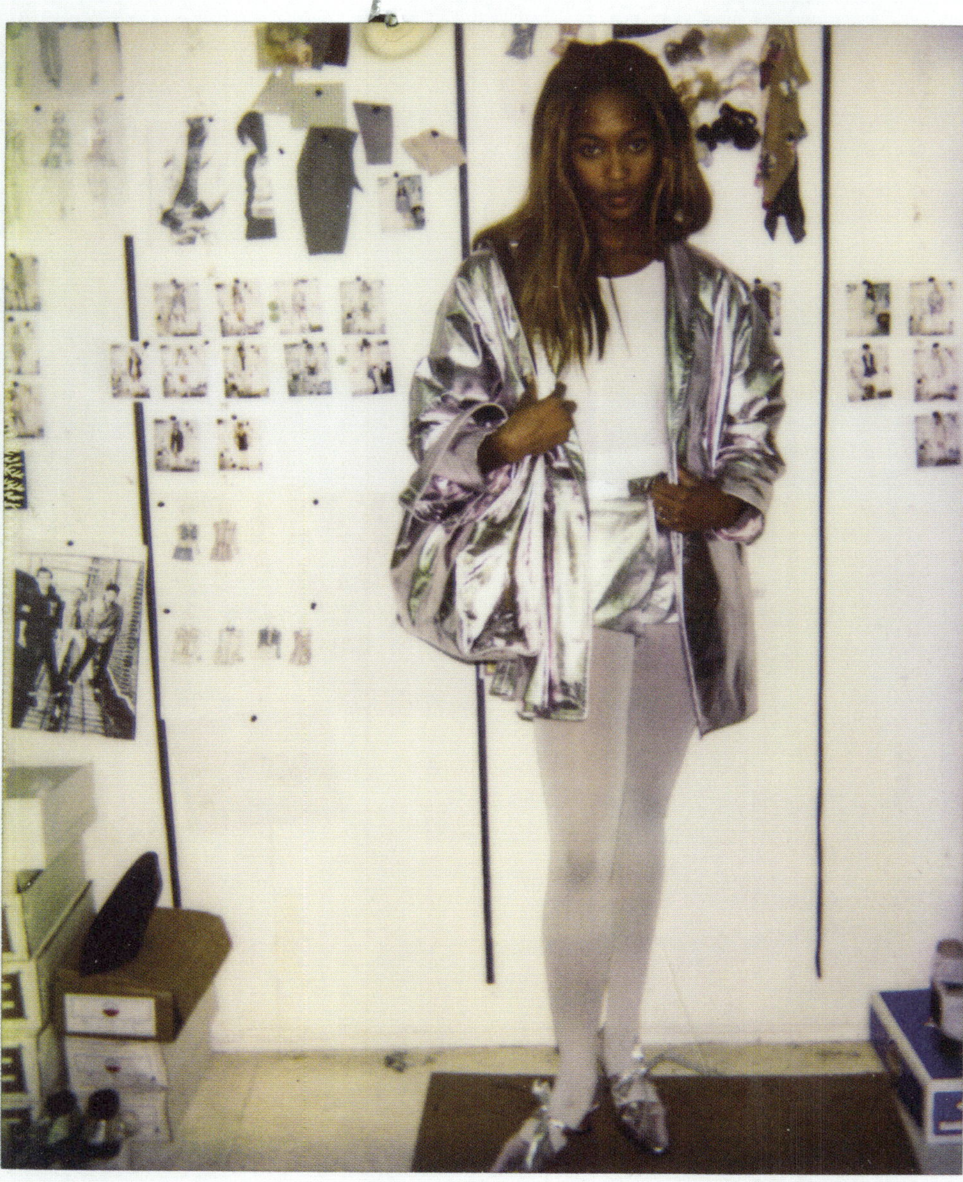

53. Naomi
Pink A-line leather coat (open)
(White leotard)
Pink leather hot pant

53. ACCESSORIES
- ***Pink leather shoulder bag*** (on right shoulder)
- ***White opaque tights*** (roll down waistband; below shorts)
- ***Pink pointed pumps w/bow tie*** (size 40)

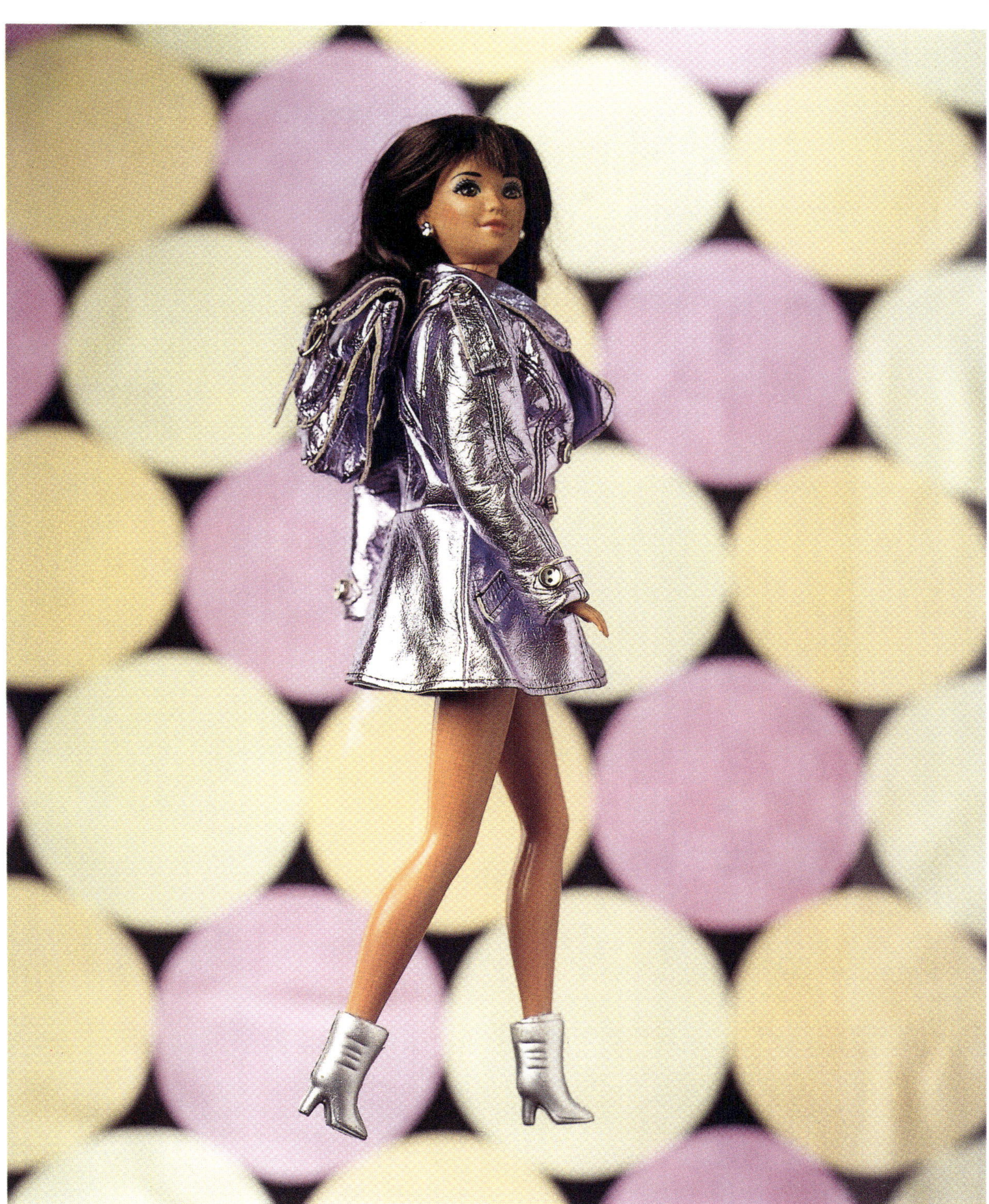

Photo: Dean Alexander, Photo Associates, Inc.

Boot Up

ANNA SUI
Doll and fabric
21 x 3 x 29

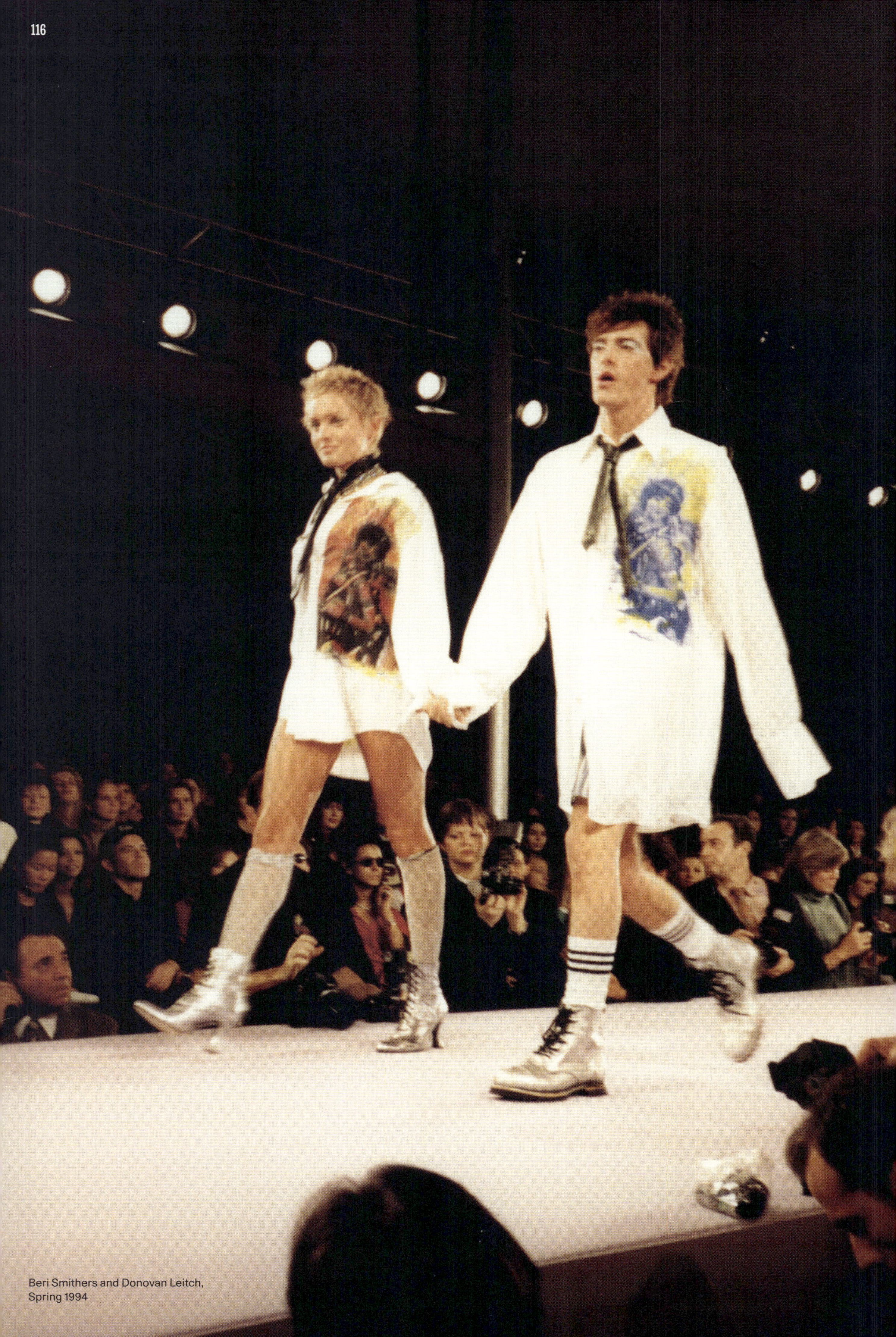

Beri Smithers and Donovan Leitch,
Spring 1994

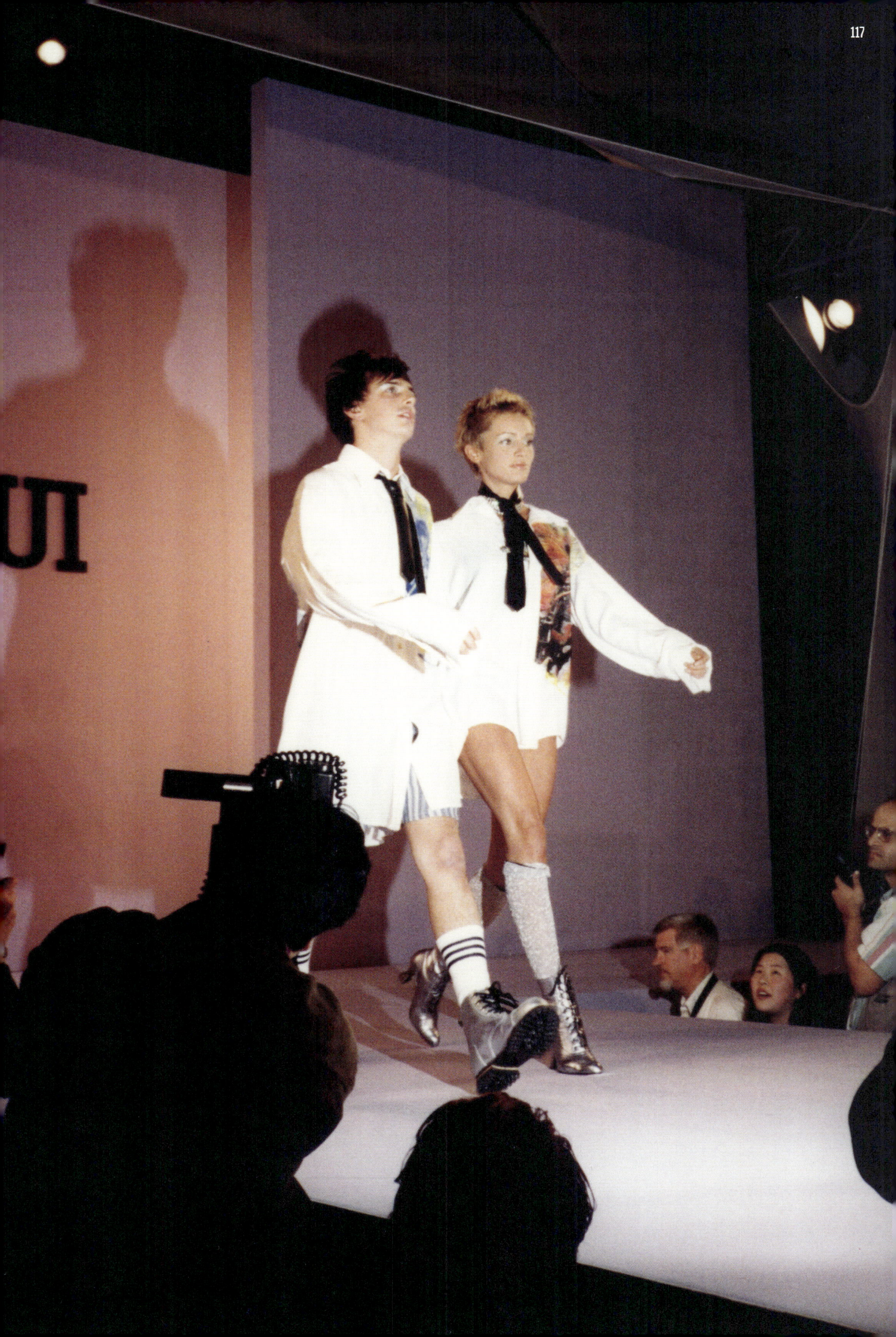

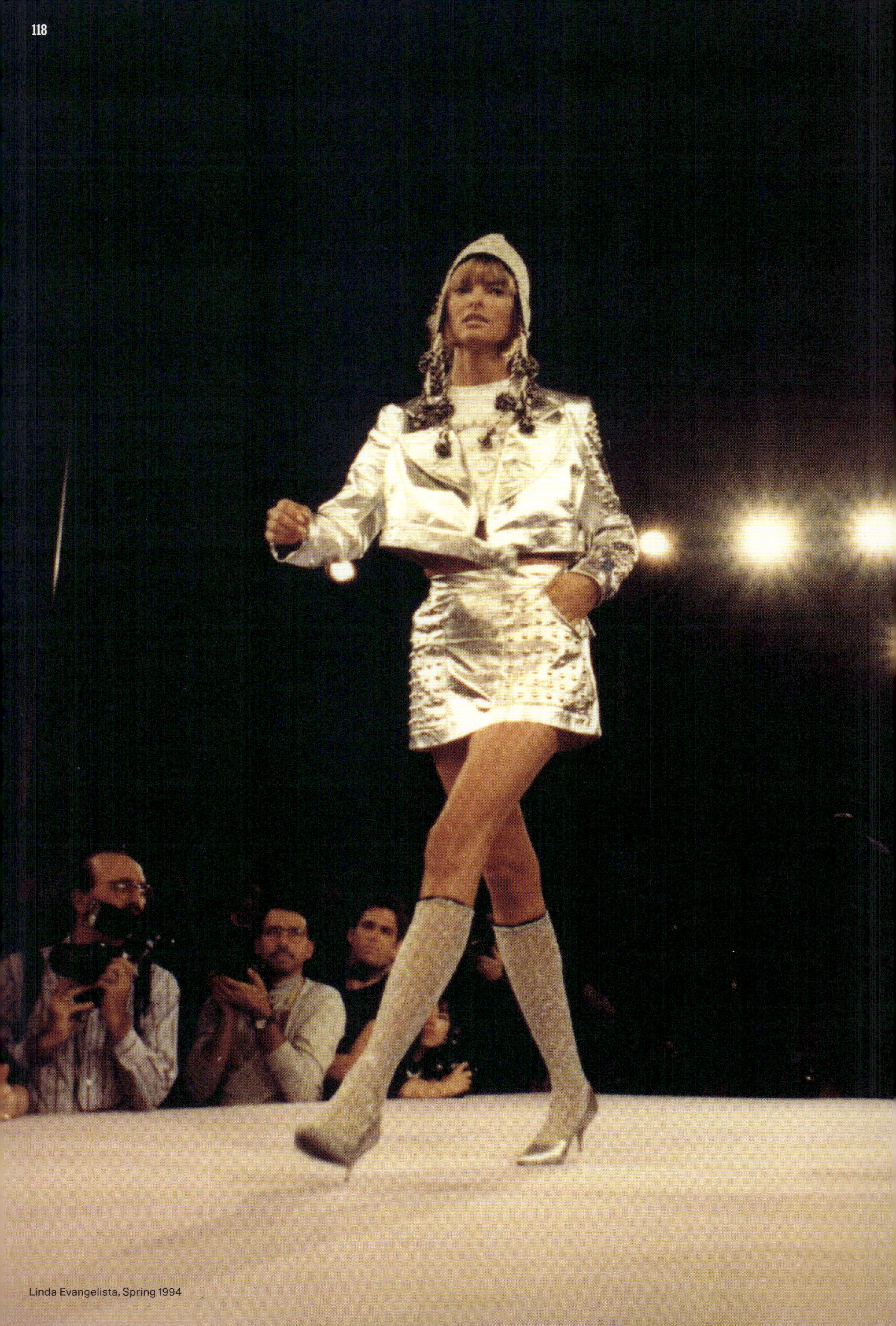

Linda Evangelista, Spring 1994

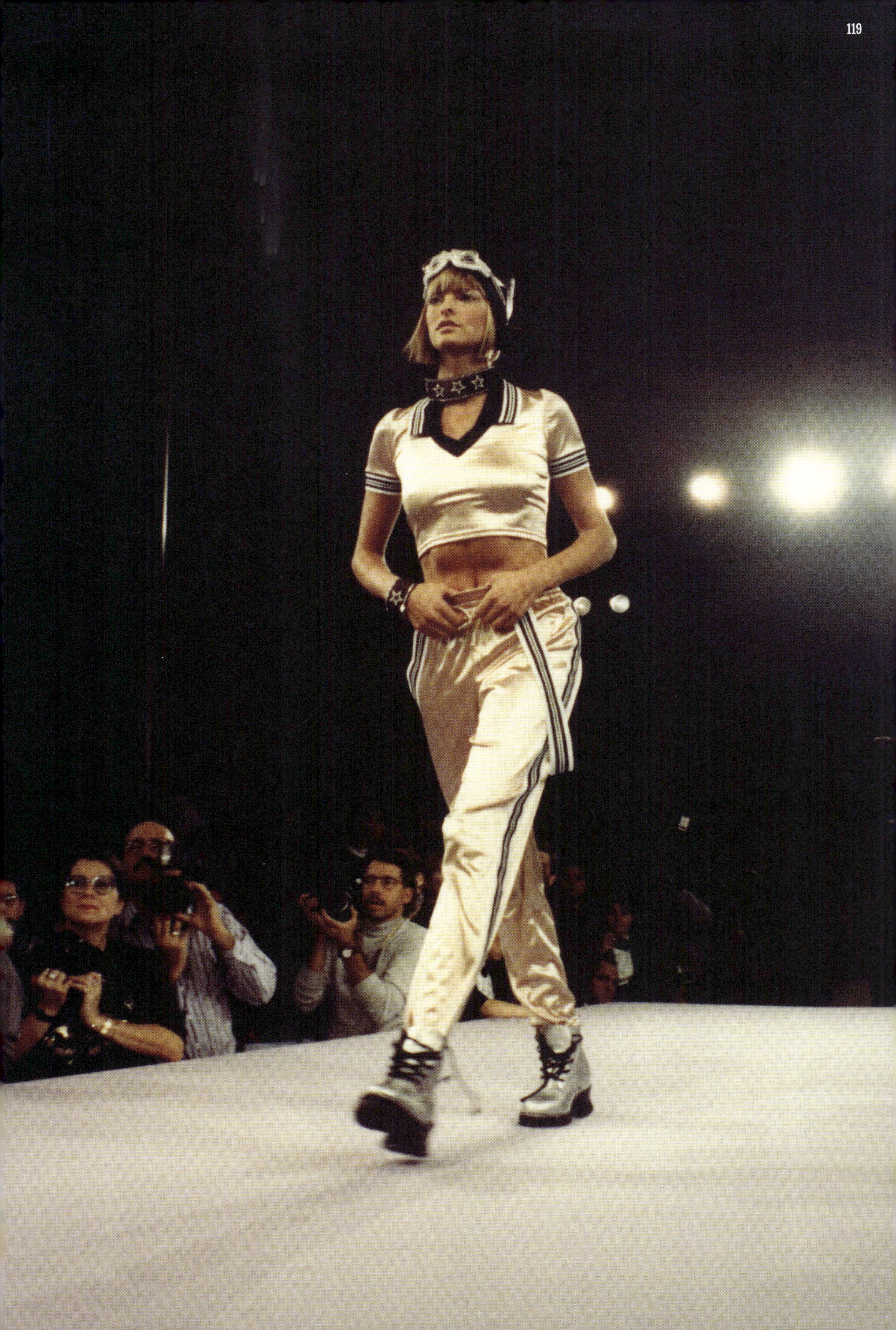

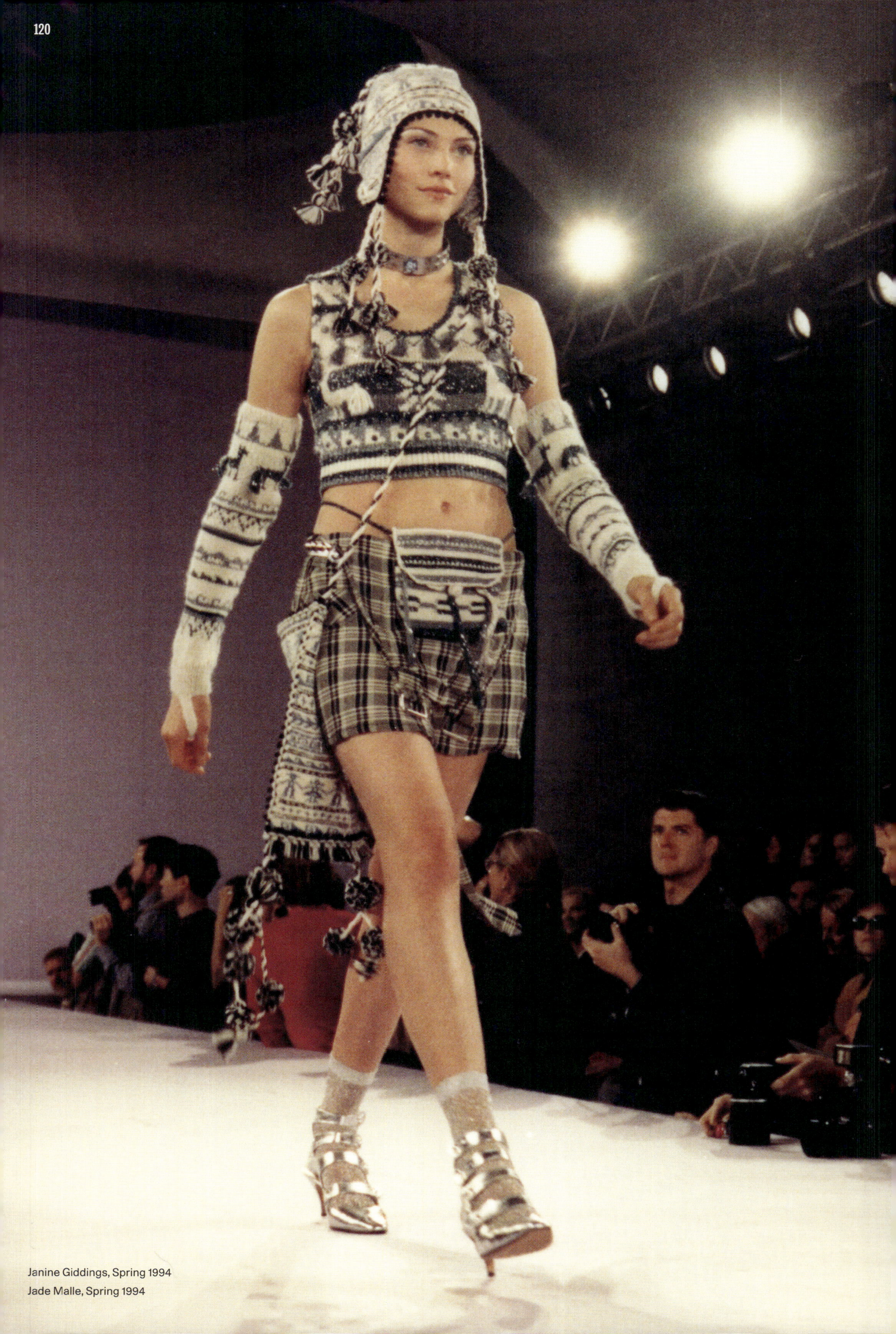

Janine Giddings, Spring 1994
Jade Malle, Spring 1994

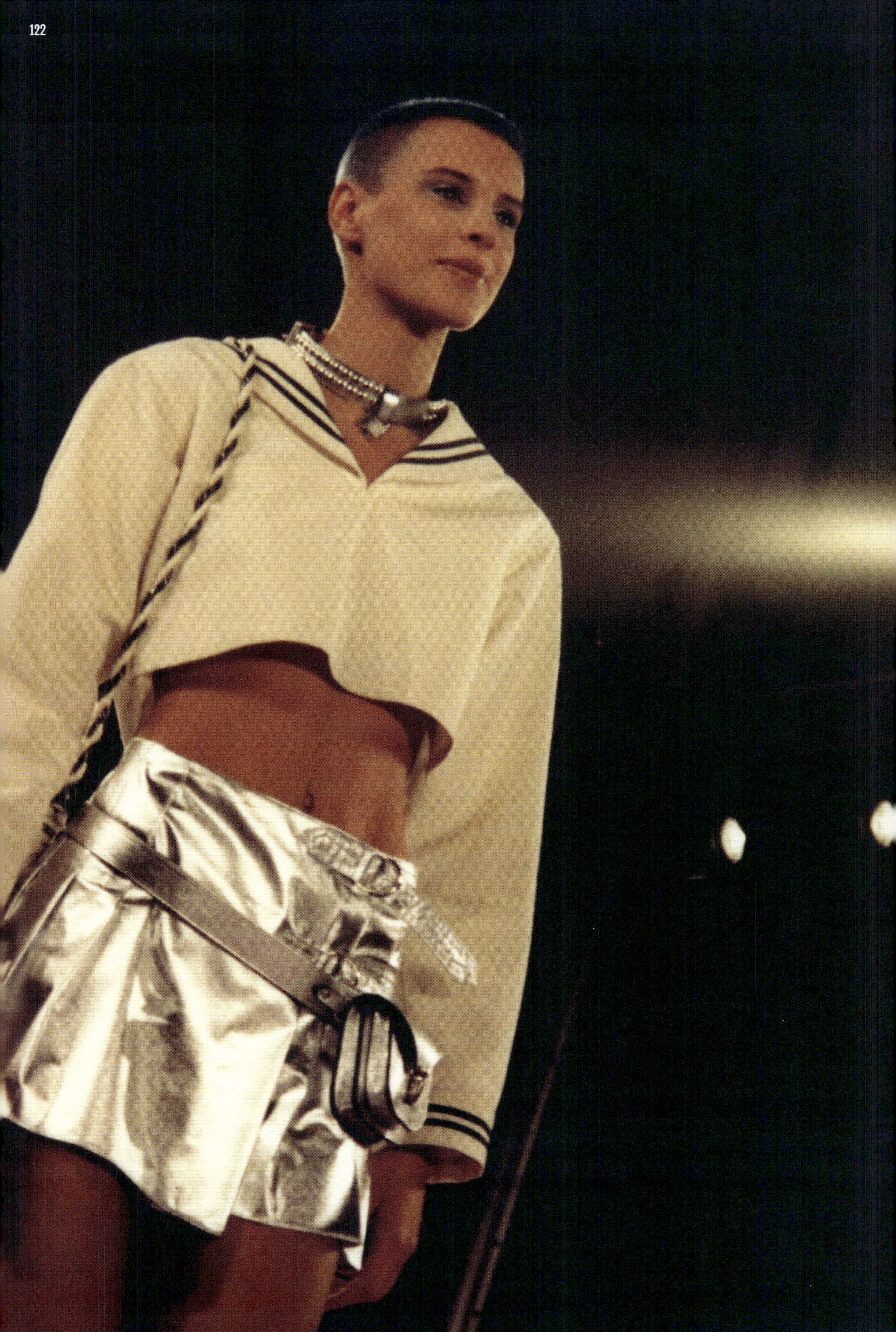

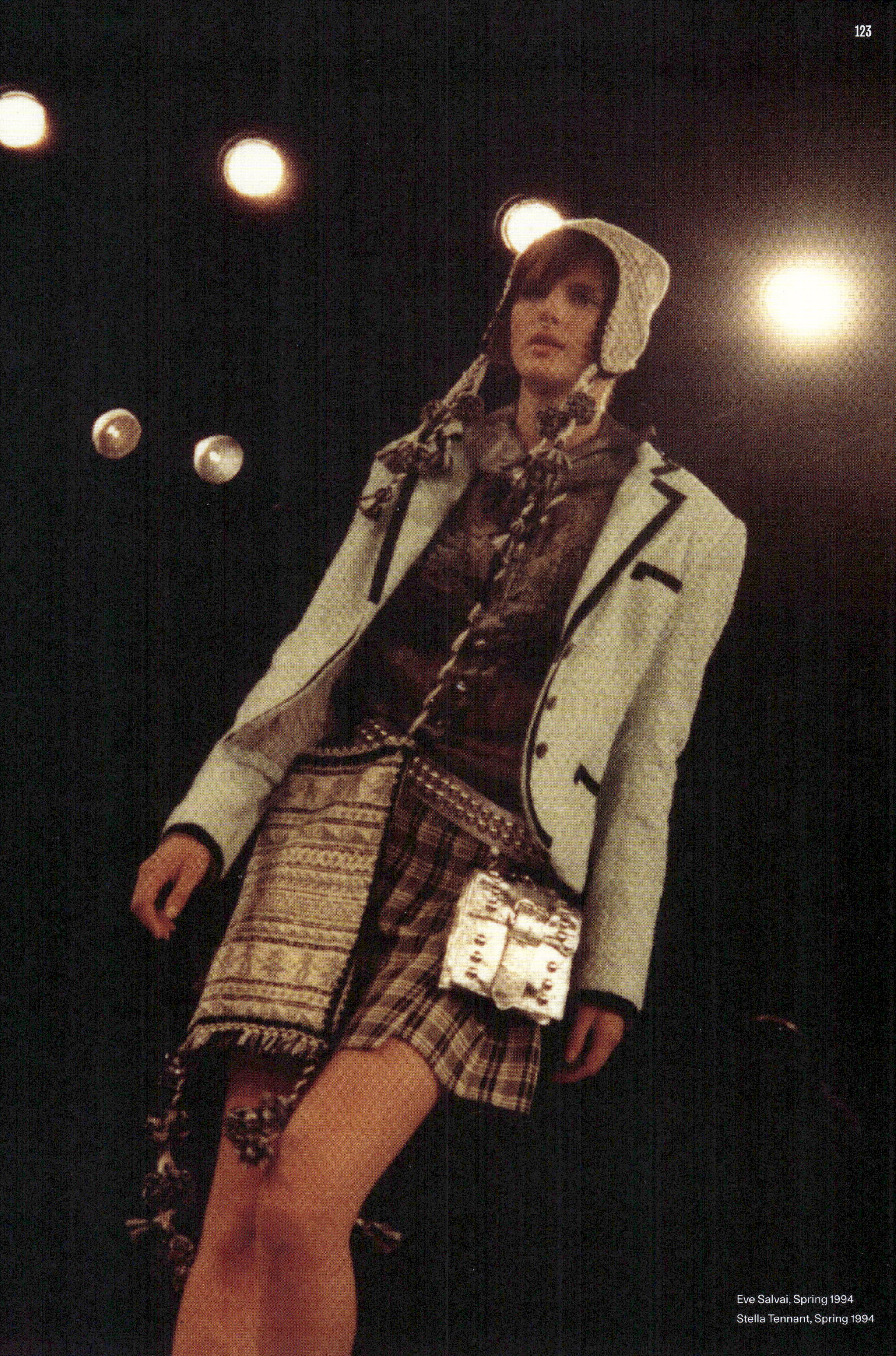

Eve Salvai, Spring 1994
Stella Tennant, Spring 1994

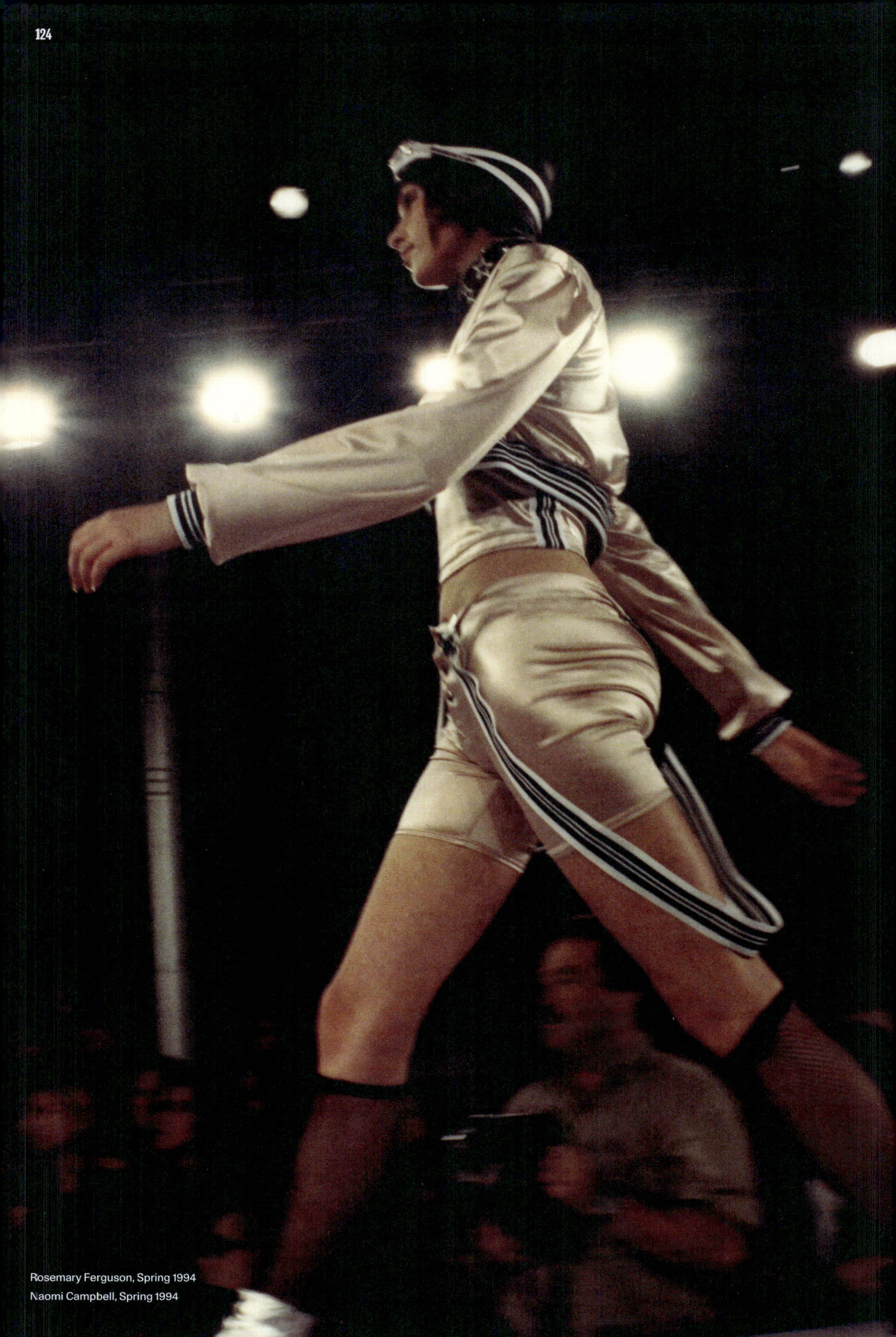

Rosemary Ferguson, Spring 1994
Naomi Campbell, Spring 1994

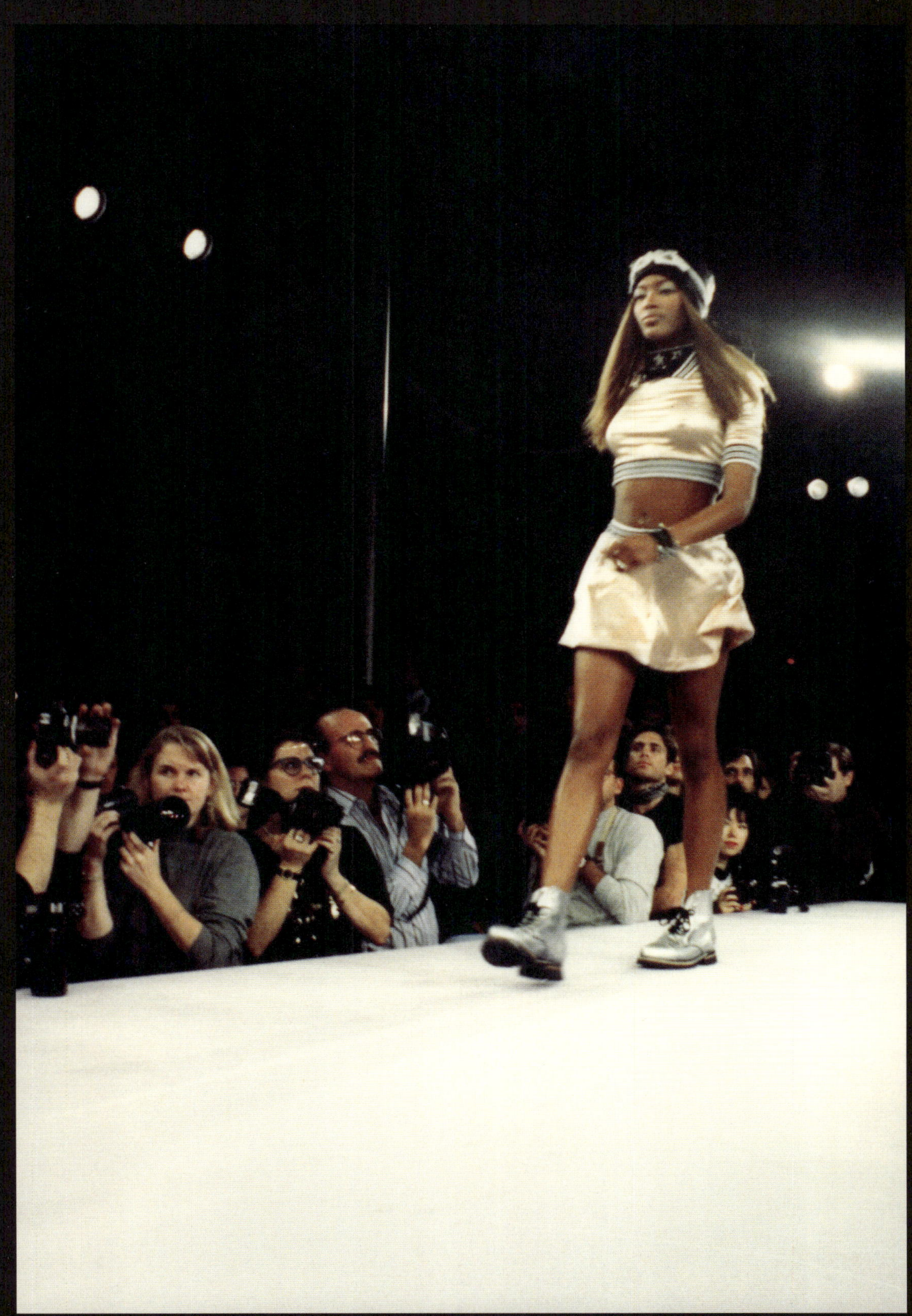

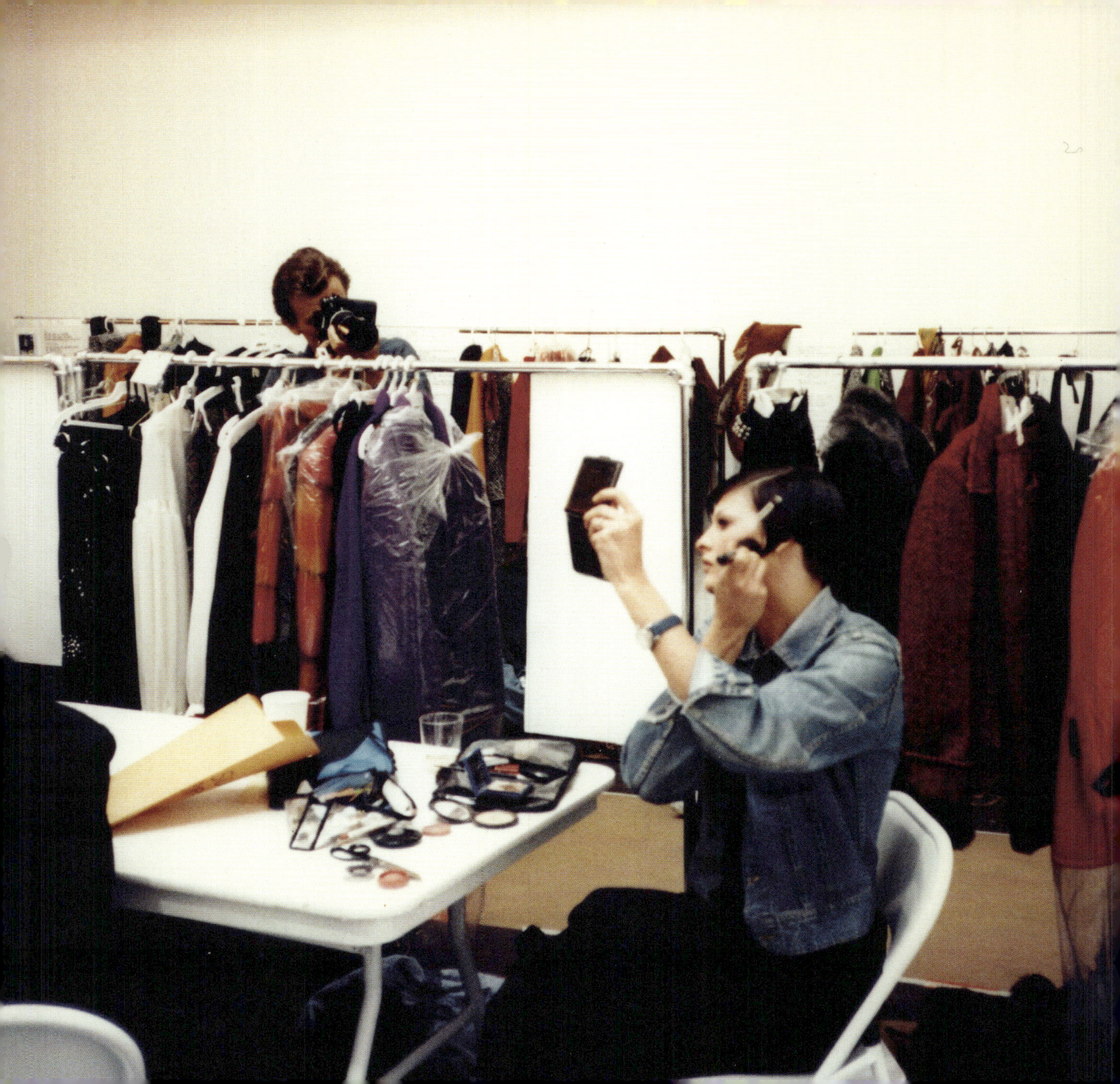

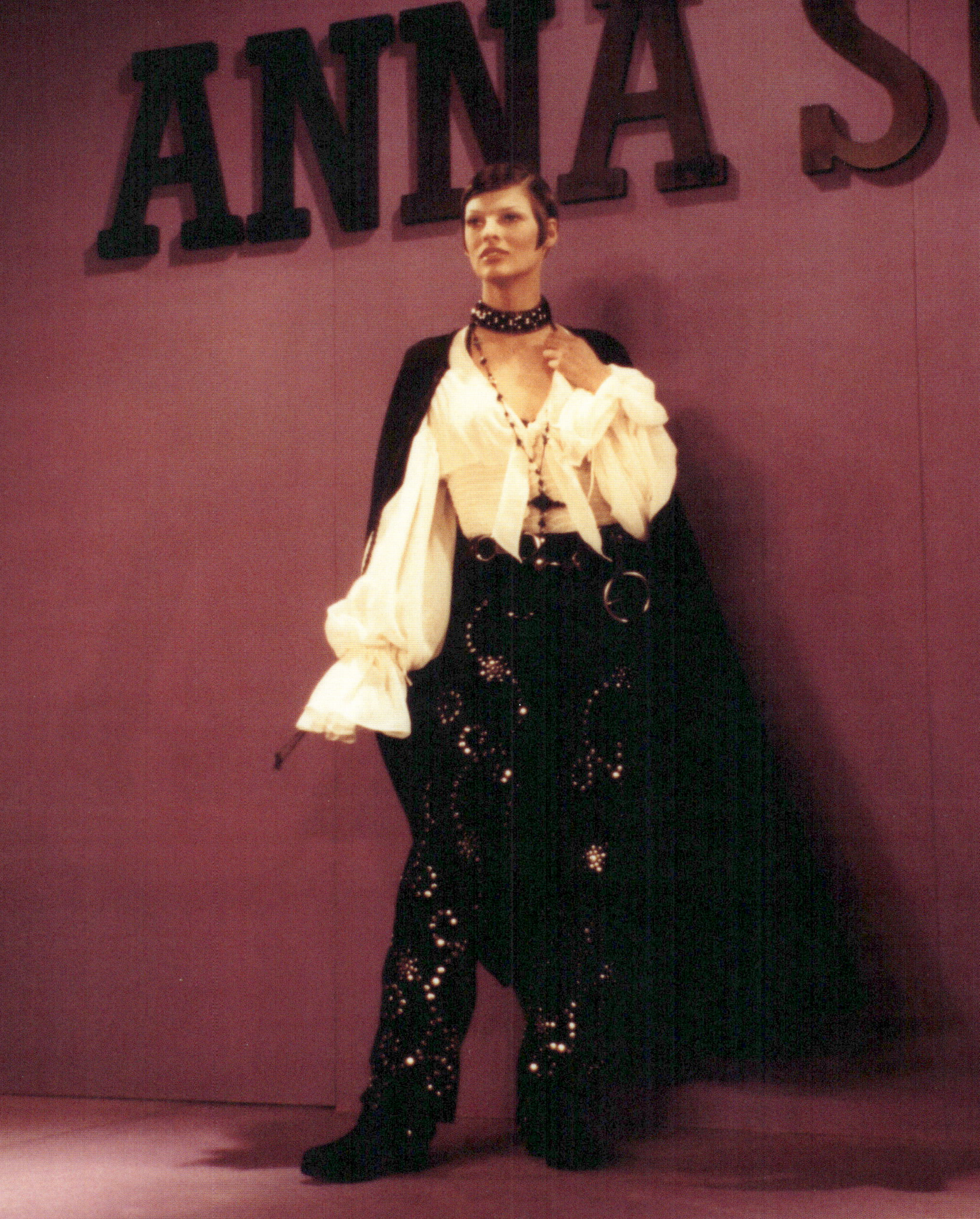
ANNA SU

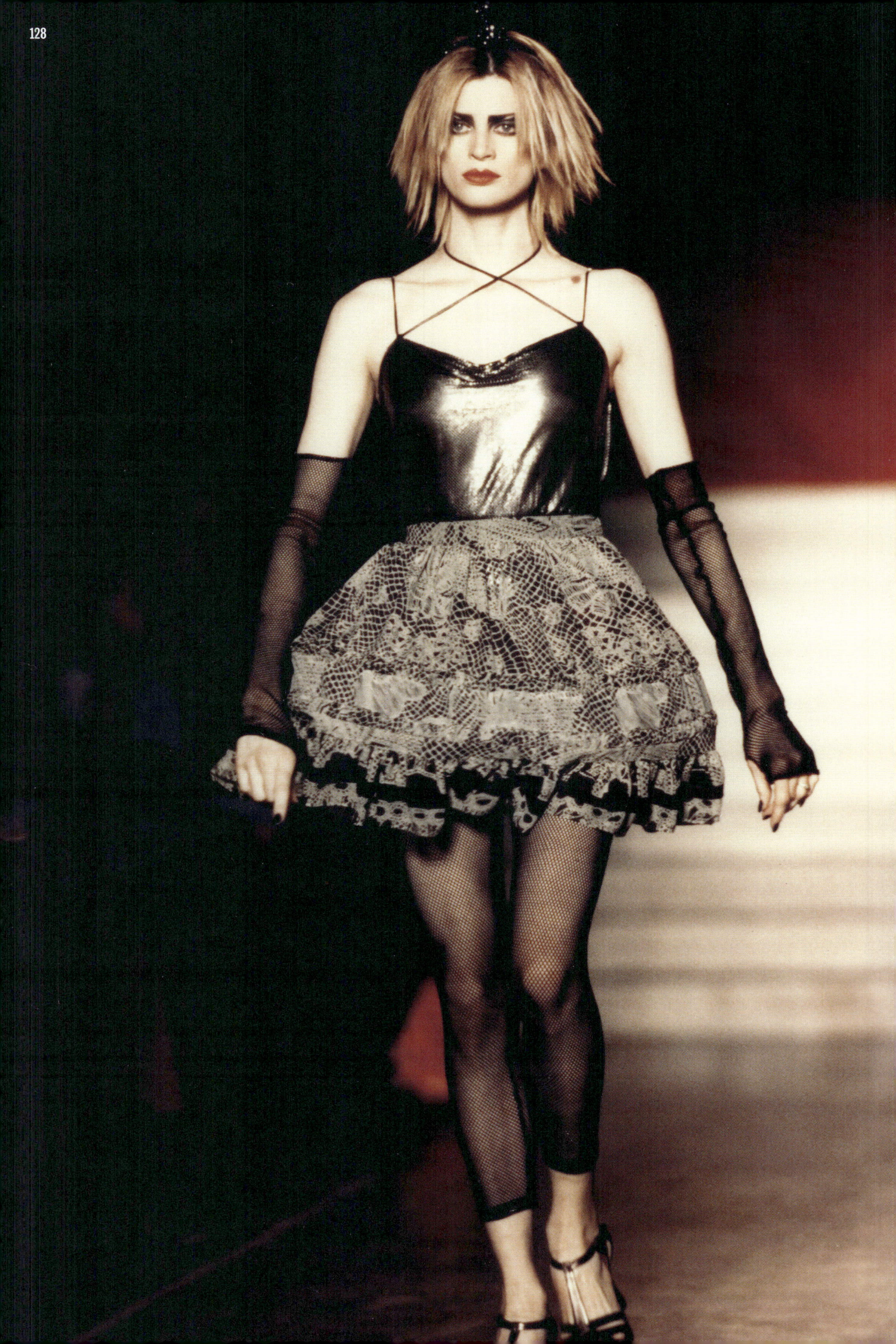

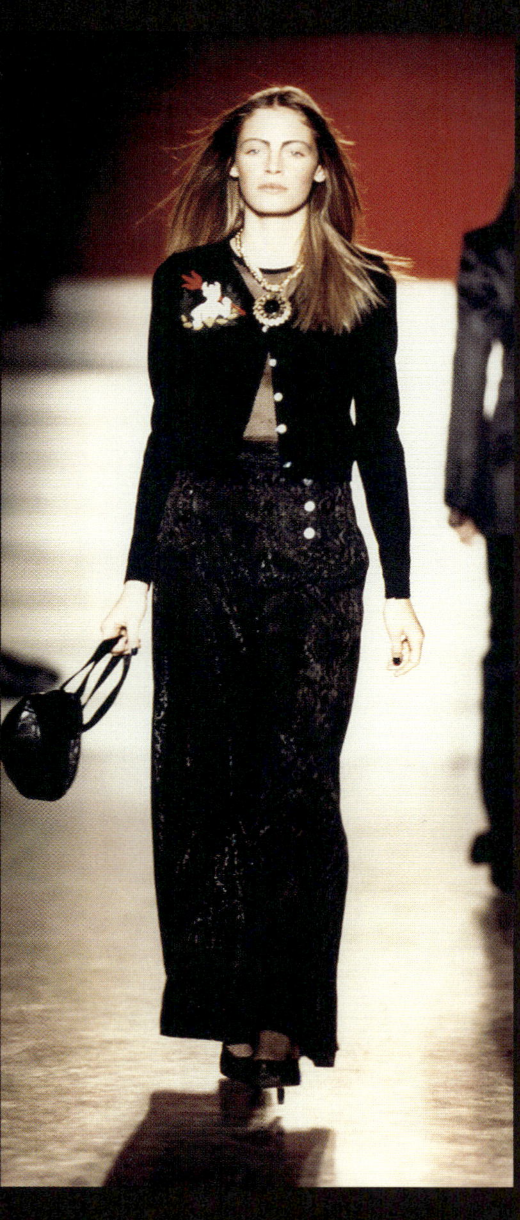

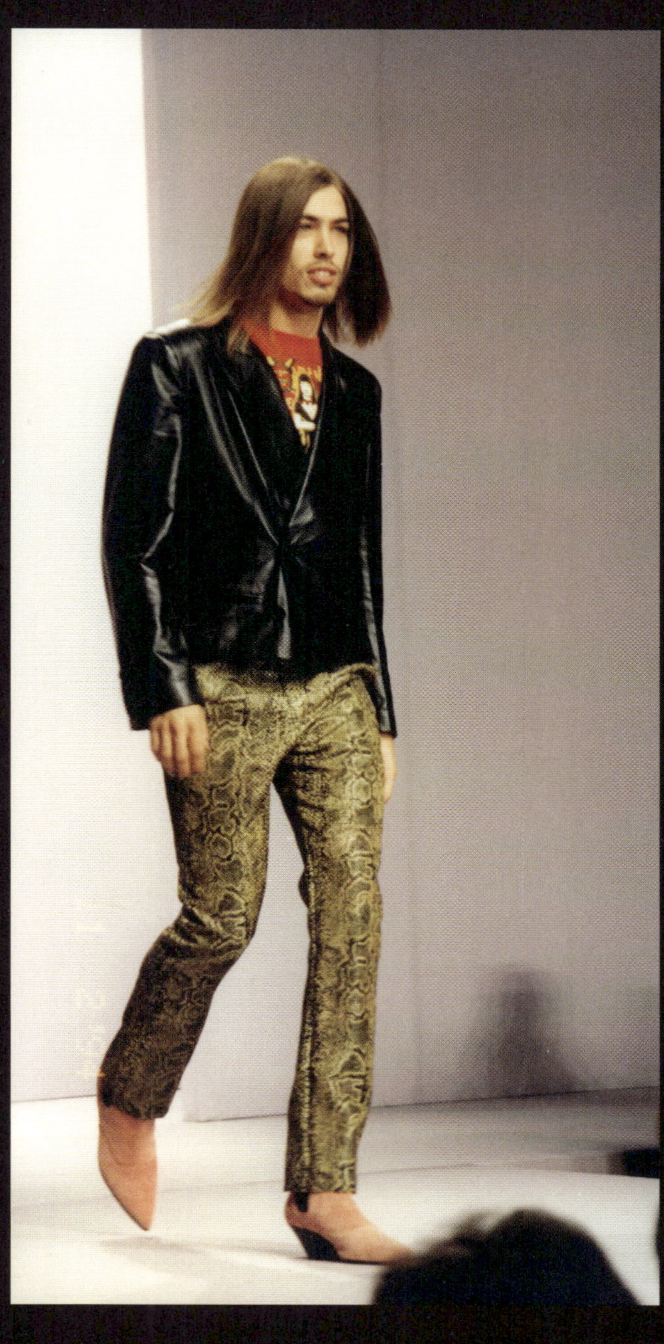

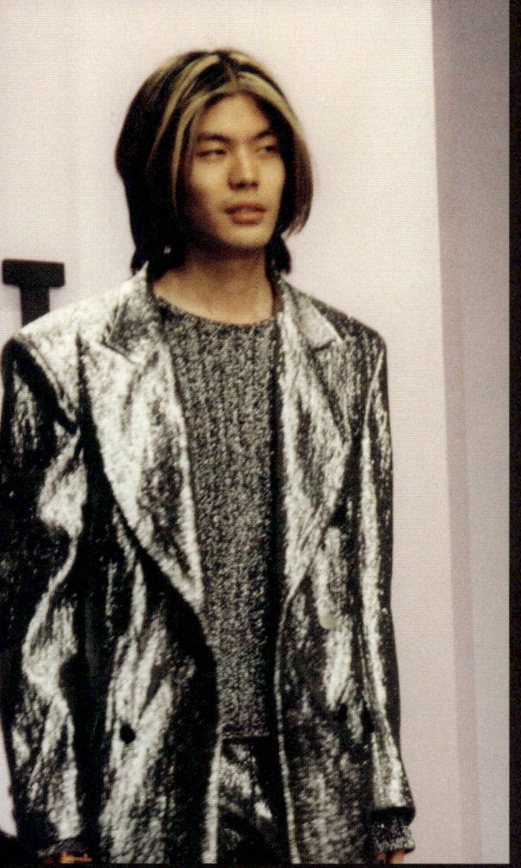

Kristen McMenamy, Fall 1997
Tanga Moreau, Fall 1997
Mike Campbell, Spring 1995
James Iha, Spring 1995

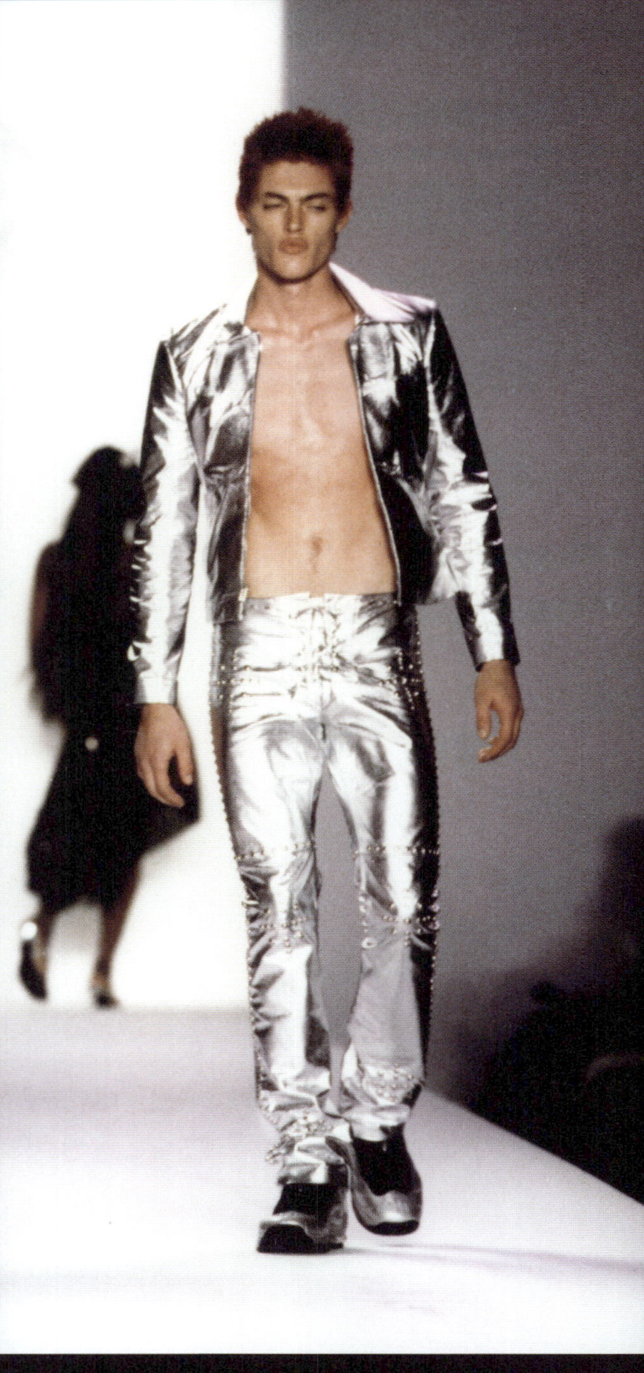

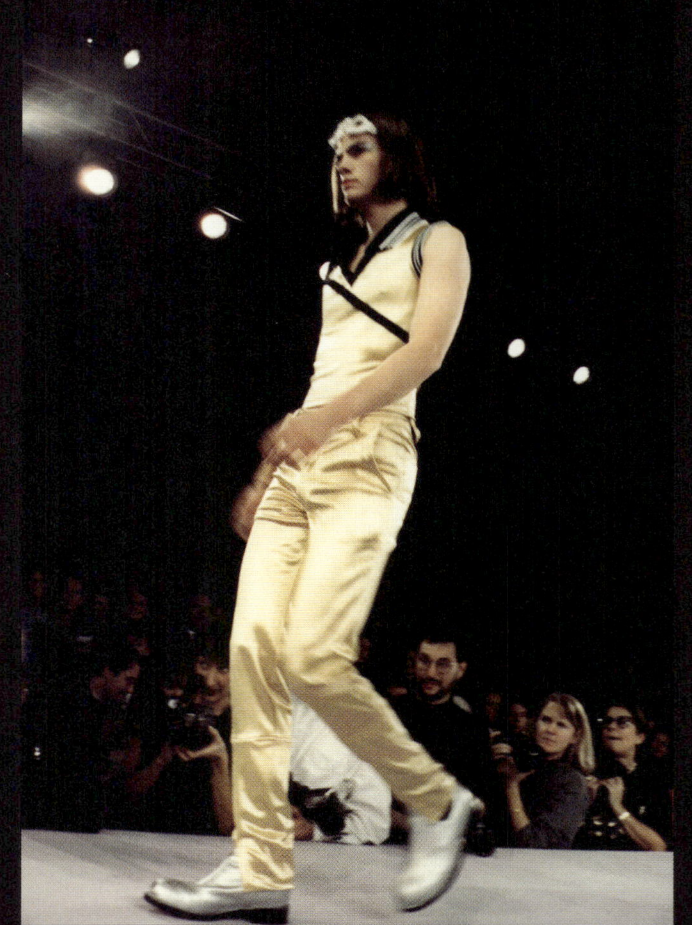

Joel McMillan, Spring 1999 (top)
Justin Scott, Spring 1994
Eve Savai, Spring 1994

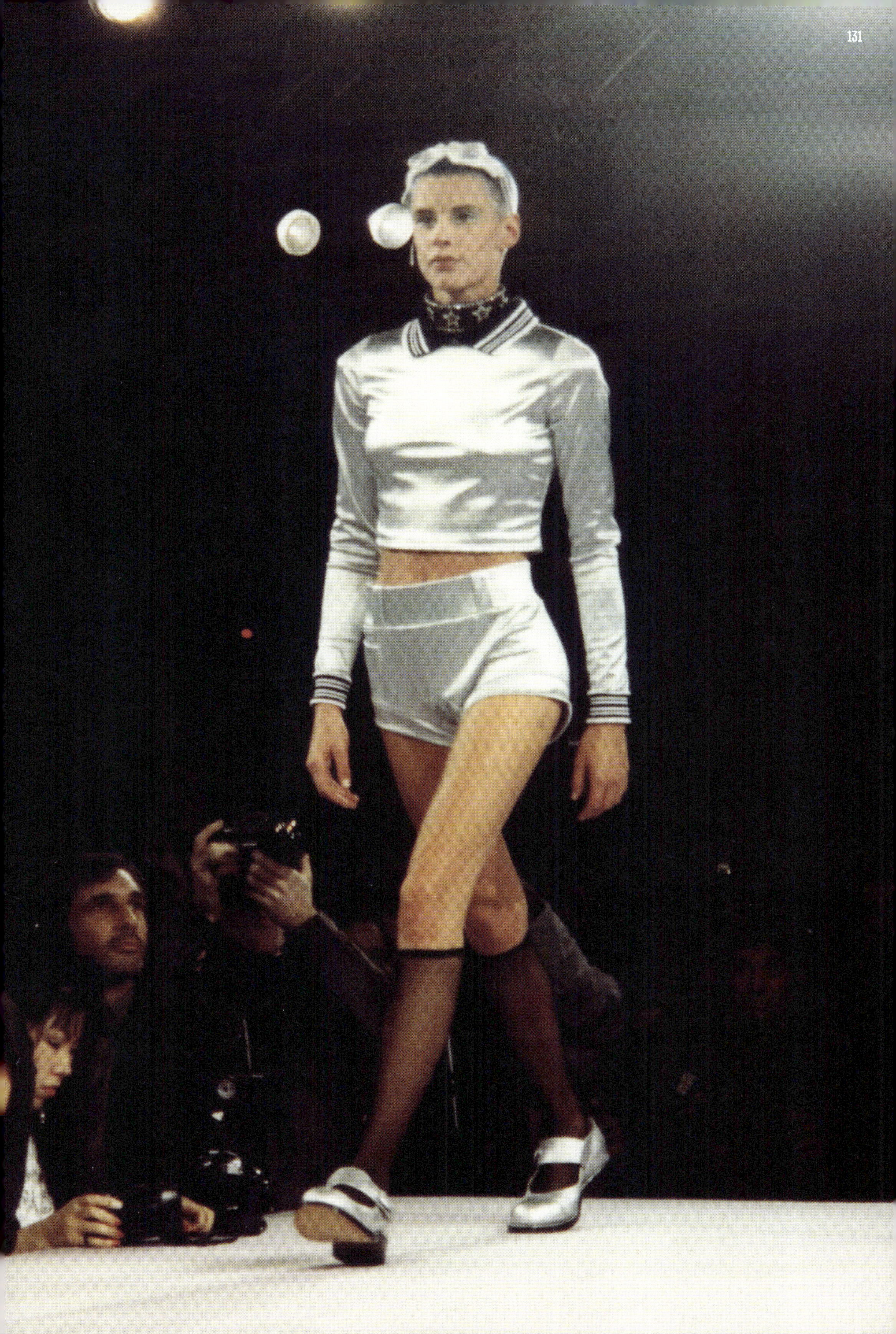

Helena Christensen and Mike Campbell, Spring 1995

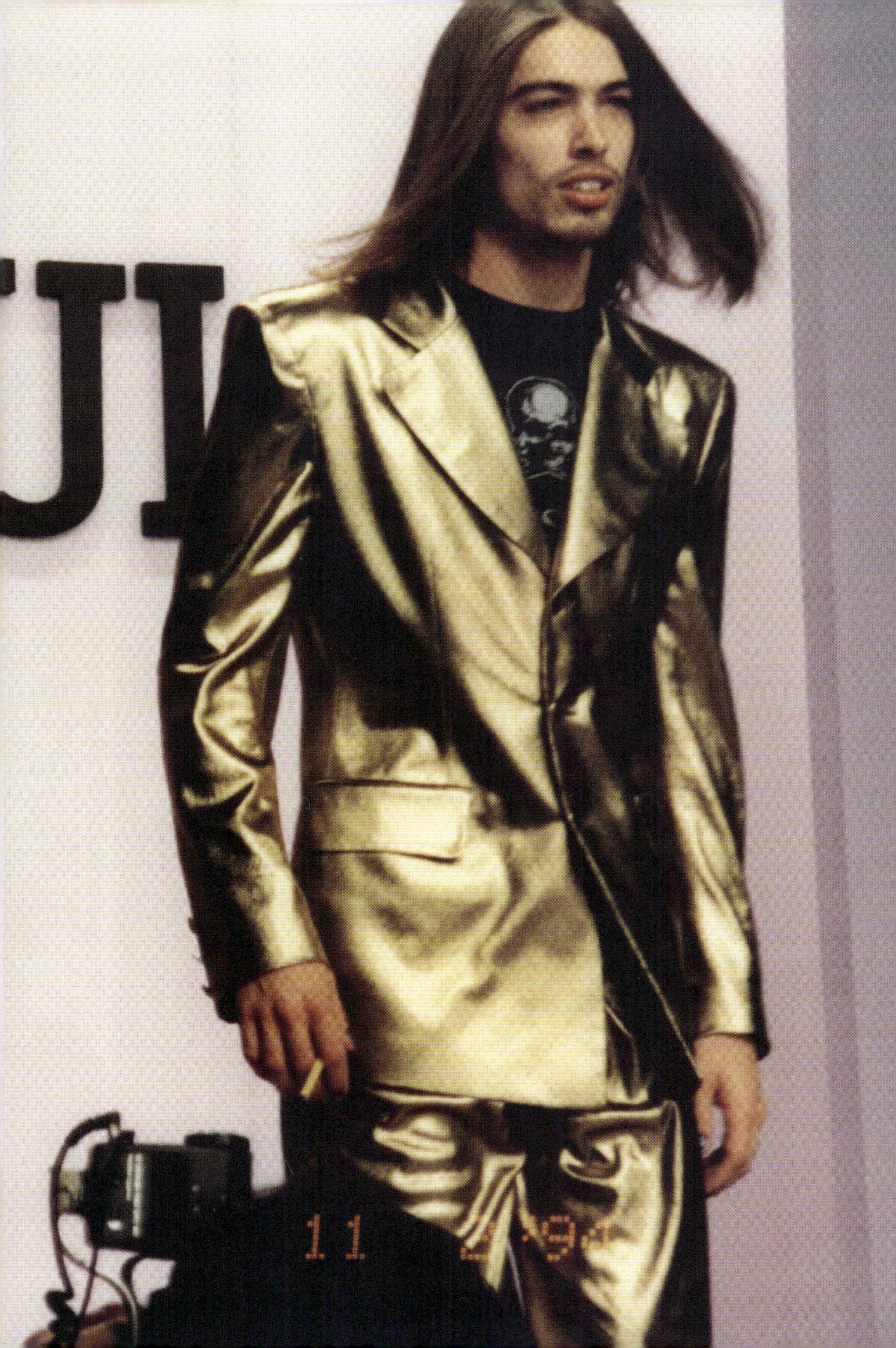

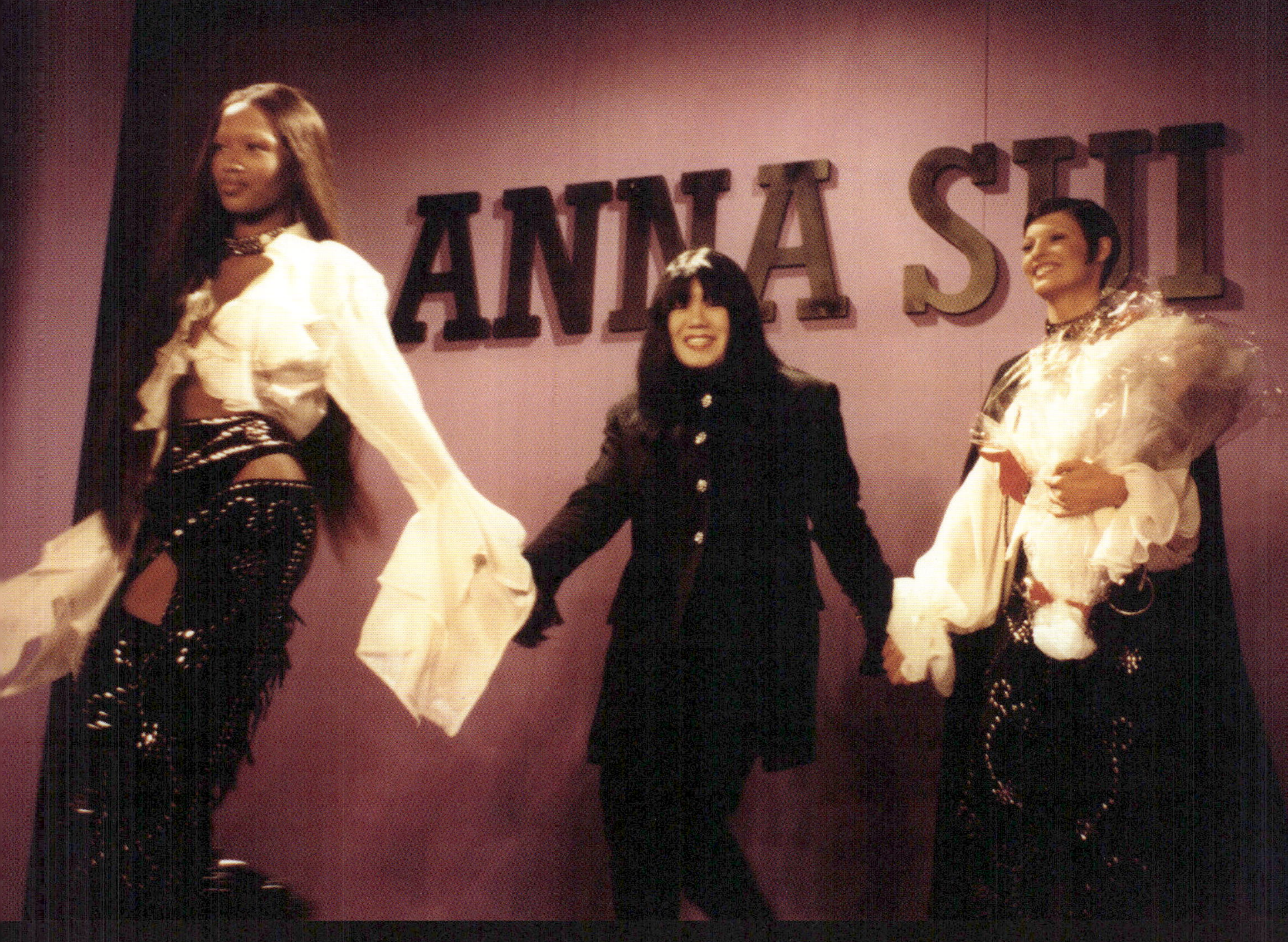

Naomi Campbell, Anna Sui, and Linda Evangelista in show finale, Fall 1992

Naomi Campbell, Fall 1992

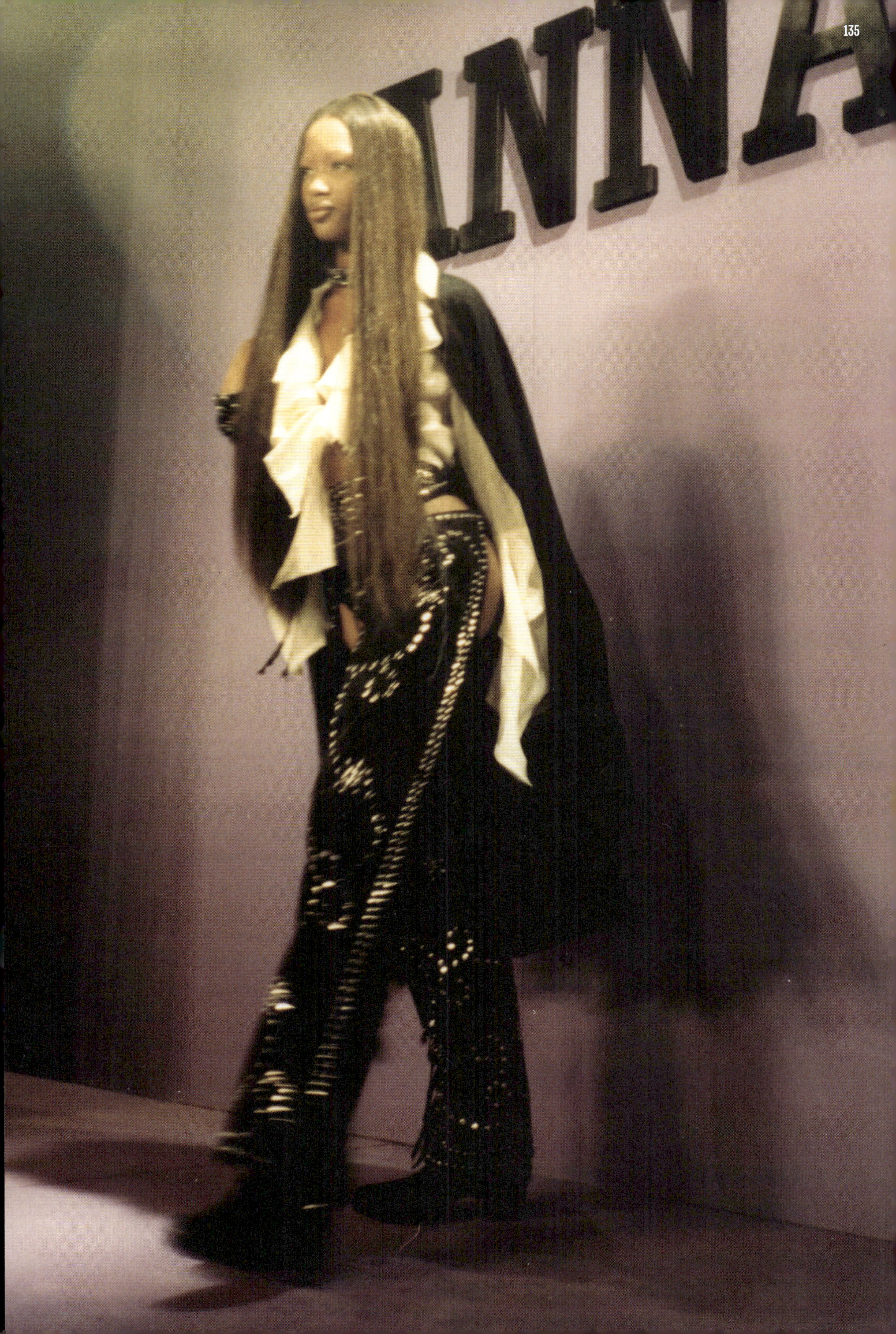
INNA

PREPPY

"Forget fashion's seamy side and step into the world of Geek Chic—a golly, gee-whiz kind of place. Here, wholesomeness rules and straight arrows don't have to play second fiddle to their hip downtown counterparts. 'The whole thing is very California' was how Sui described the collection, with elements of jazz, surfers and beatniks, 'all thrown together the way a kid in the suburbs would interpret it.'" *WWD*, November 3, 1995

ANNA SUI

I was trying to do preppy, but tongue-in-cheek, a "country club" collection coinciding with the Wes Anderson world, which was a geek chic thing that was starting to happen in the '90s. In the Spring/Summer 96 collection, I used khaki and madras. I did the Hush Puppy shoes, but in pastel colors, and had the models carry lunch boxes, and wear fun country club clothes. It was a bit ironic and subversive, the same way the baby doll dress was during the grunge period. One of my influences was *The Preppy Handbook* that came out in 1980. One of my favorite magazines, *Mademoiselle*, had a "Back to School" issue where everyone was wearing preppy fashion. Very *Love Story*: kilts, fleece jackets, beanies, and knee socks. You see that over and over again—it's one of my favorite looks. But, of course, there is always a twist. I loved the brands Ladybug and Villager. They were my favorites before I discovered rock music and hippie style.

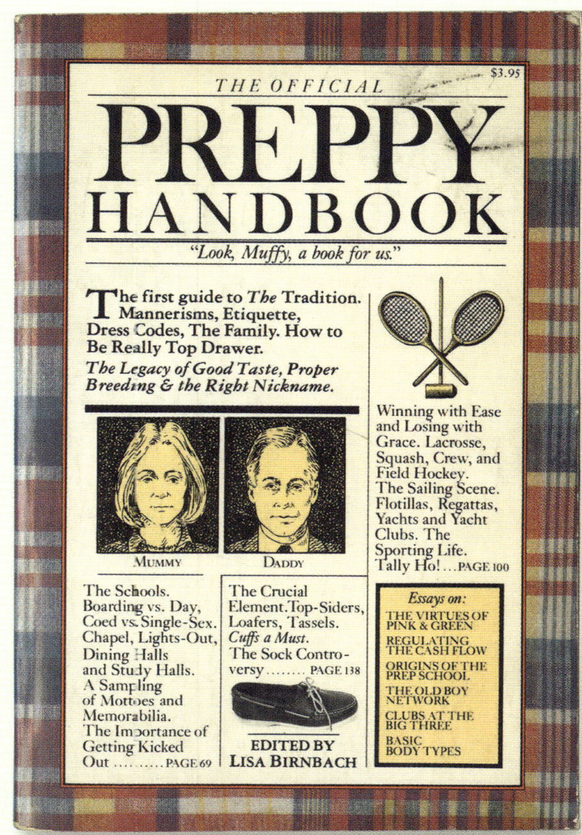

Forget fashion's seamy side and step into the world of Geek Chic — a golly, gee-whiz kind of place. Here, wholesomeness rules and straight-arrows don't have to play second fiddle to their hip downtown counterparts. "The whole thing is very California" was how Sui described the collection, with elements of jazz, surfers and beatniks, "all thrown together the way a kid in the suburbs would interpret it."

And Anna's urban customer is going to fall for it hook, line and sinker. Sui's fantasy kids hail from upbeat, optimistic stock — fresh-scrubbed Harvard hopefuls, after-school beach bums and aspiring beatniks. And they're all inventing their own take on cool, in a Liberty print-Hush Puppies sort of way. They mix flowers and plaids, clash colors and tote bright plastic lunchboxes. They like their skirts short but sweet and go wild in plaid bermudas with pastel fake leather. But madras is their real fashion passion; they just can't get enough of it, in jackets, pants, dresses— even bikinis. When situations call for a more grown-up dress code, they slip into little shifts — short, crisp and uncomplicated.

And very smart. You have to hand it to Sui — she can have tons of fun, make everybody feel great, and do it with clothes that are unpretentious and wearable. How neat is that?

WWD
November 3, 1995

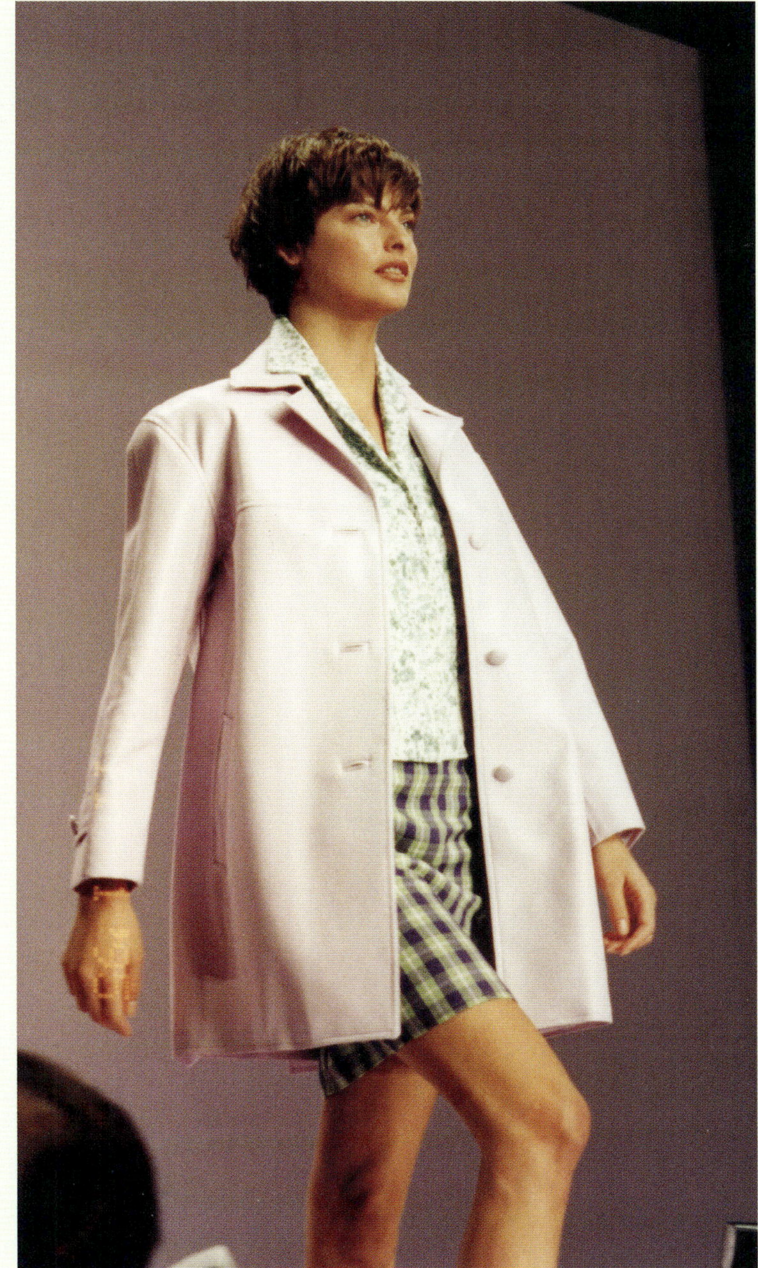

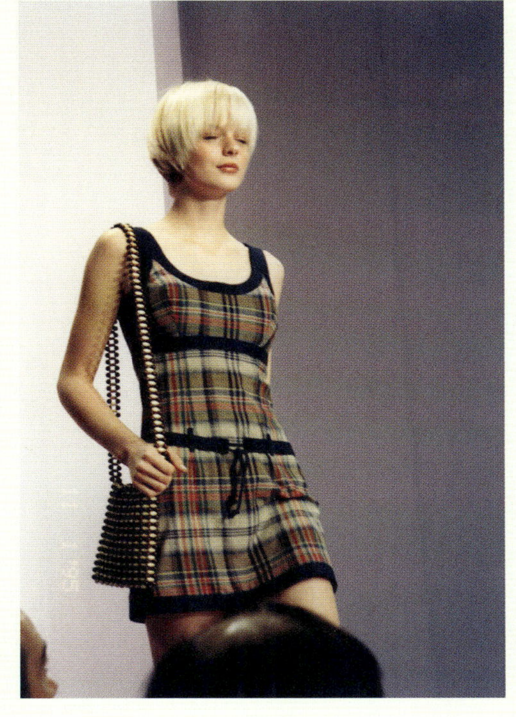

Cover of *The Official Preppy Handbook* by Lisa Birnbach, editor, 1980 (Workman Publishing Co., Inc.)

Linda Evangelista, Spring 1996

Farrah Summerford, Spring 1996

STEFF YOTKA

Preppy is a fashion identity so associated with white elitism and privilege that I think the only way to make it cool is for someone who doesn't come from that culture to reinterpret it. And I think that's what Anna does so well with all her different references. When she did looks that felt a little preppy, she always countered it with something that still feels very subcultural or very quirky—it's never like pure country club preppy. As someone who grew up in the '90s, seeing that kind of complexity in fashion felt really inspiring because they were unlike the fashion shows that were happening in that era from huge luxury brands that felt very authoritarian and presented a very polished version of a woman. If you look across Anna's shows, there's s a little bit of everybody—she was doing street casting or celebrity casting way before that became the norm in fashion. She's dipping into all these different references where if you're preppy, you're still punky. It all came together in this way that feels really aspirational if you want to just look like a slightly better and cooler version of yourself. She's not really selling you an unattainable dream that's so far out of reach. She's selling you a version of the coolest girl you already know and that you can maybe become with your own twist.

SOFIA COPPOLA

I always loved her preppy collection, and I was into it because it always had a twist to it. And it appealed to me because I'm so not preppy. So it was fun to play with that; we all kind of like the idea of country club and this world that we're not a part of so there was something punk about it. I just always thought that was cool, and Anna is playful and has a punk spirit about her.

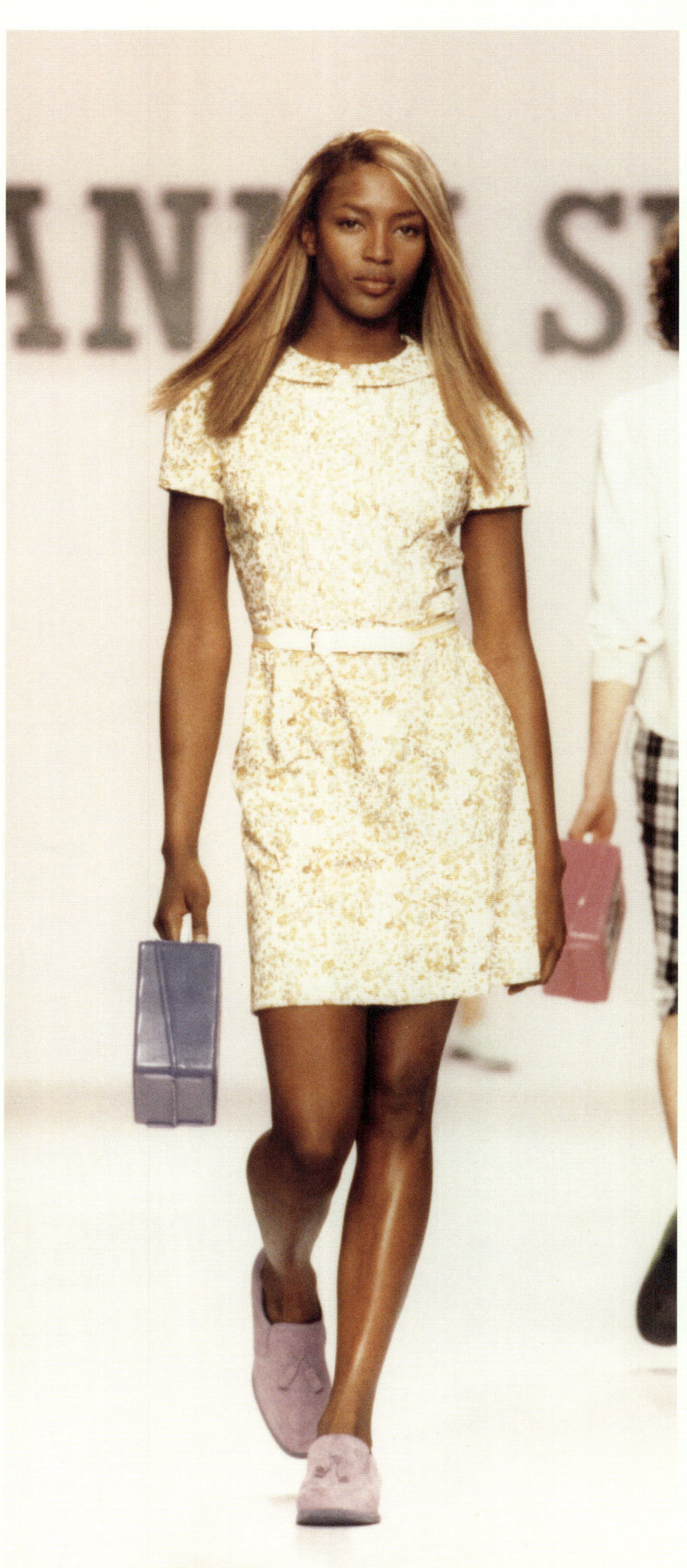

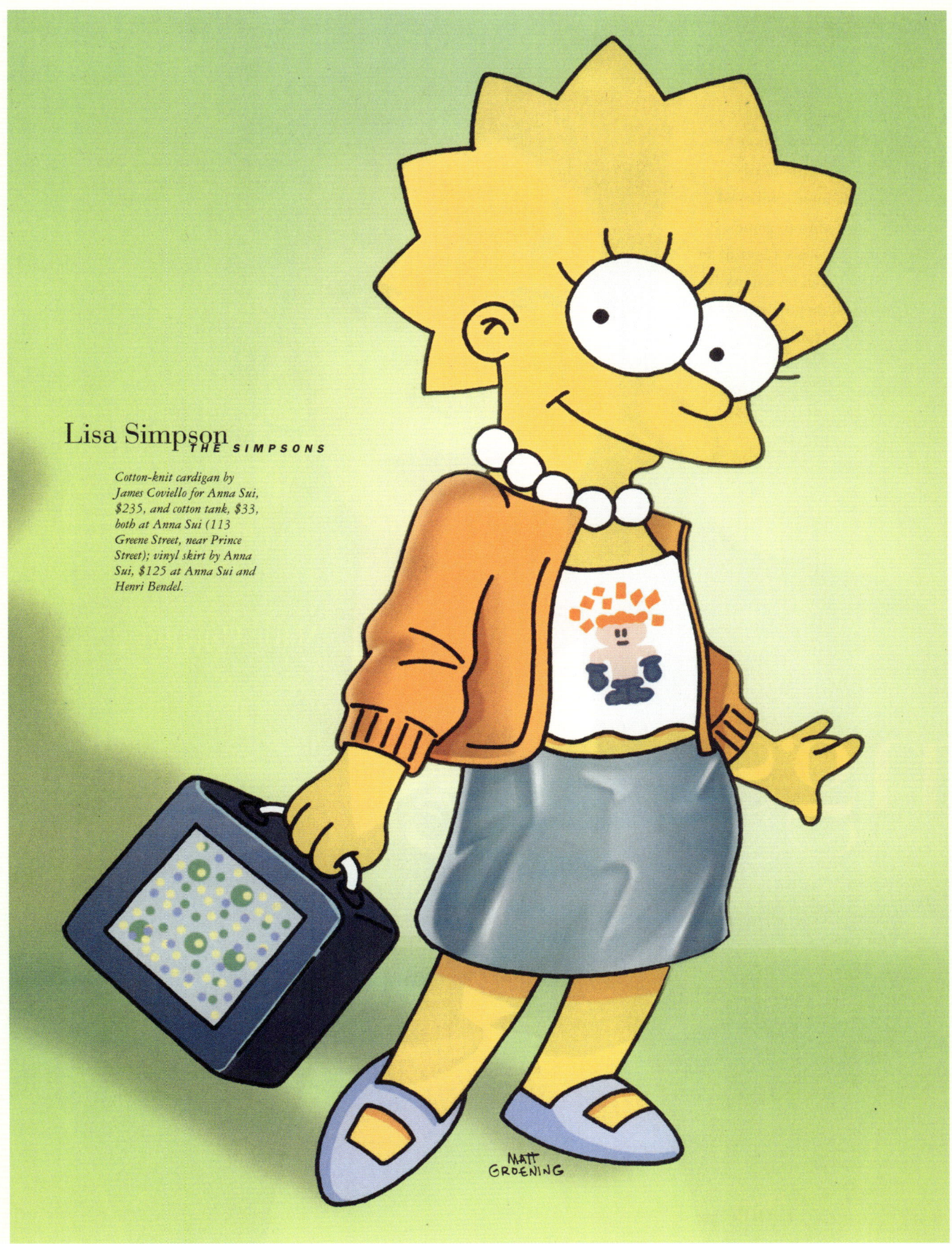

Naomi Campbell, Spring 1996

Lisa Simpson dressed in Anna Sui, Matt Groening for *New York Magazine*, February 26, 1996

"For Hush Puppies—the classic American brushed-suede shoes with the lightweight crepe sole the Tipping Point came somewhere between late 1994 and early 1995. The brand had been all but dead until that point....At a fashion shoot, two Hush Puppies executives ran into a stylist from New York who told them that the classic Hush Puppies had suddenly become hip in the clubs and bars of downtown Manhattan....By the fall of 1995 things began to happen in a rush. First the designer John Bartlett called. Then another Manhattan designer, Anna Sui, called wanting shoes for her show as well. In 1995, the company sold 430,000 pairs of the classic Hush Puppies, and the next year it sold four times that....How did that happen? Those first few kids, whoever they were, weren't deliberately trying to promote Hush Puppies. They were wearing them precisely because no one else would wear them. Then the fad spread to two fashion designers who used the shoes to peddle something else—haute couture....No one was trying to make Hush Puppies a trend. Yet somehow that's exactly what happened. The shoes passed a certain point in popularity, and they tipped."

Excerpt from

The Tipping Point: How Little Things Can Make a Big Difference

by Malcom Gladwell

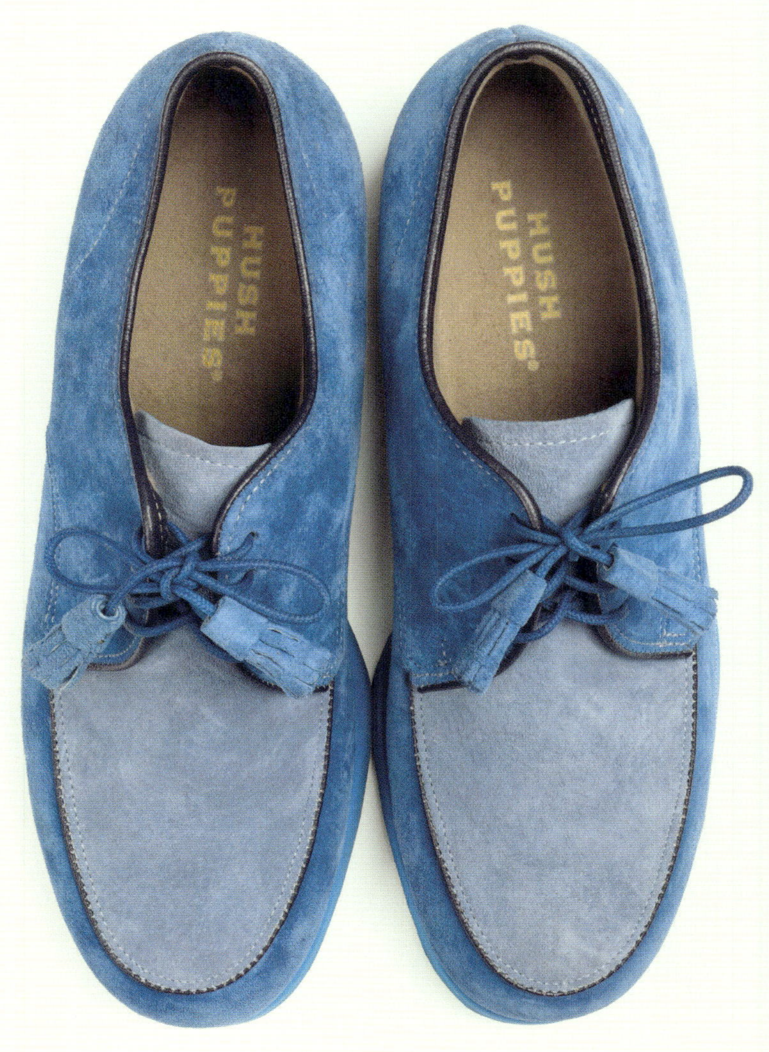

"No one was trying to make Hush Puppies a trend. Yet somehow that's exactly what happened."

Malcolm Gladwell, *The Tipping Point: How Little Things Can Make a Big Difference*, 2000, Little Brown & Co.

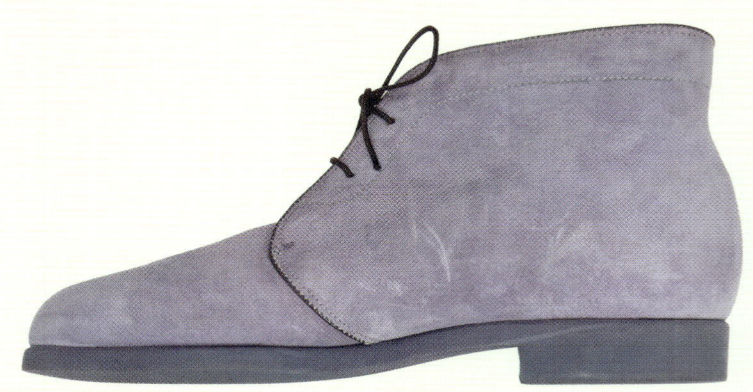

Anna Sui for Hush Puppies, 1996

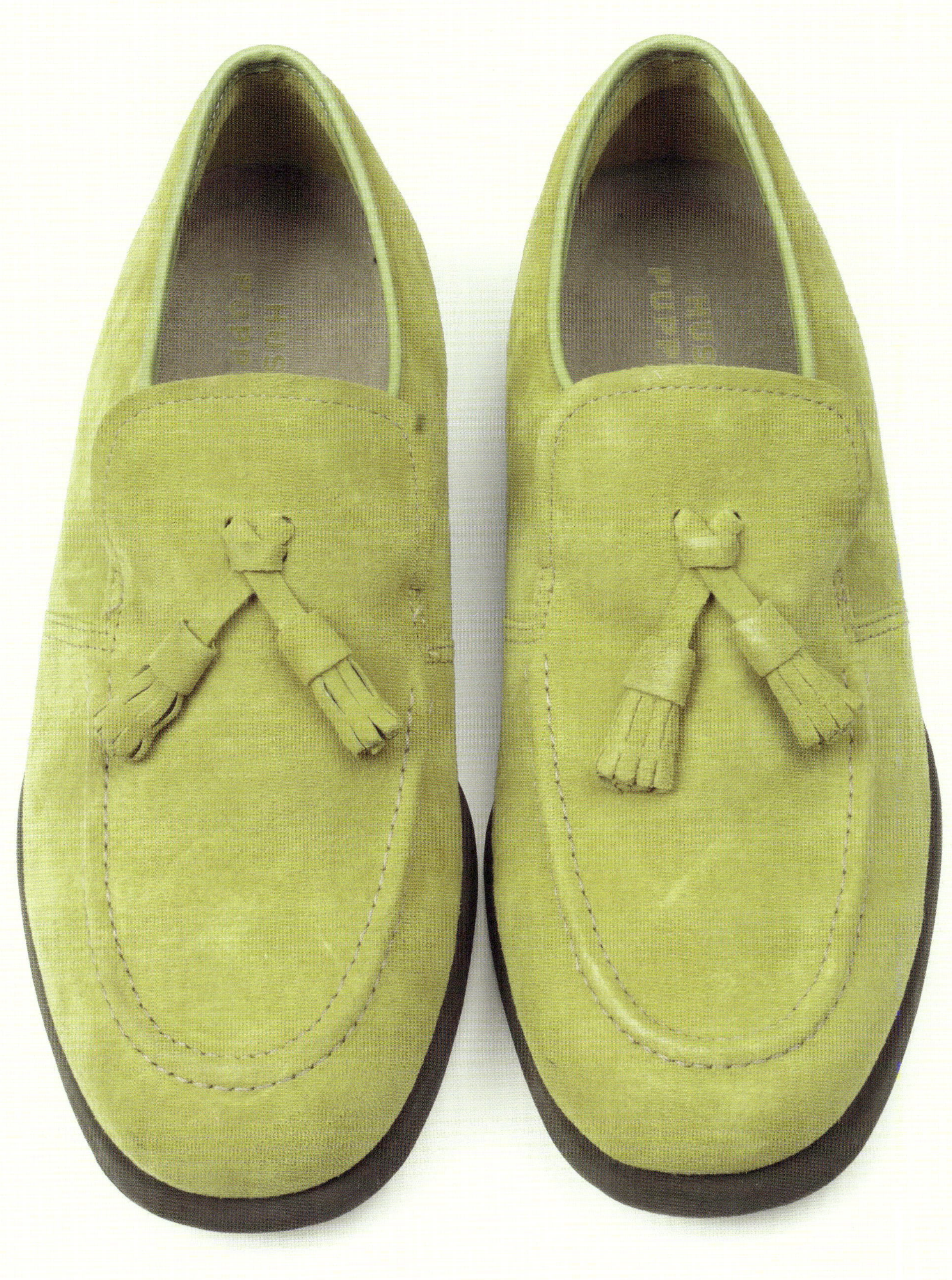

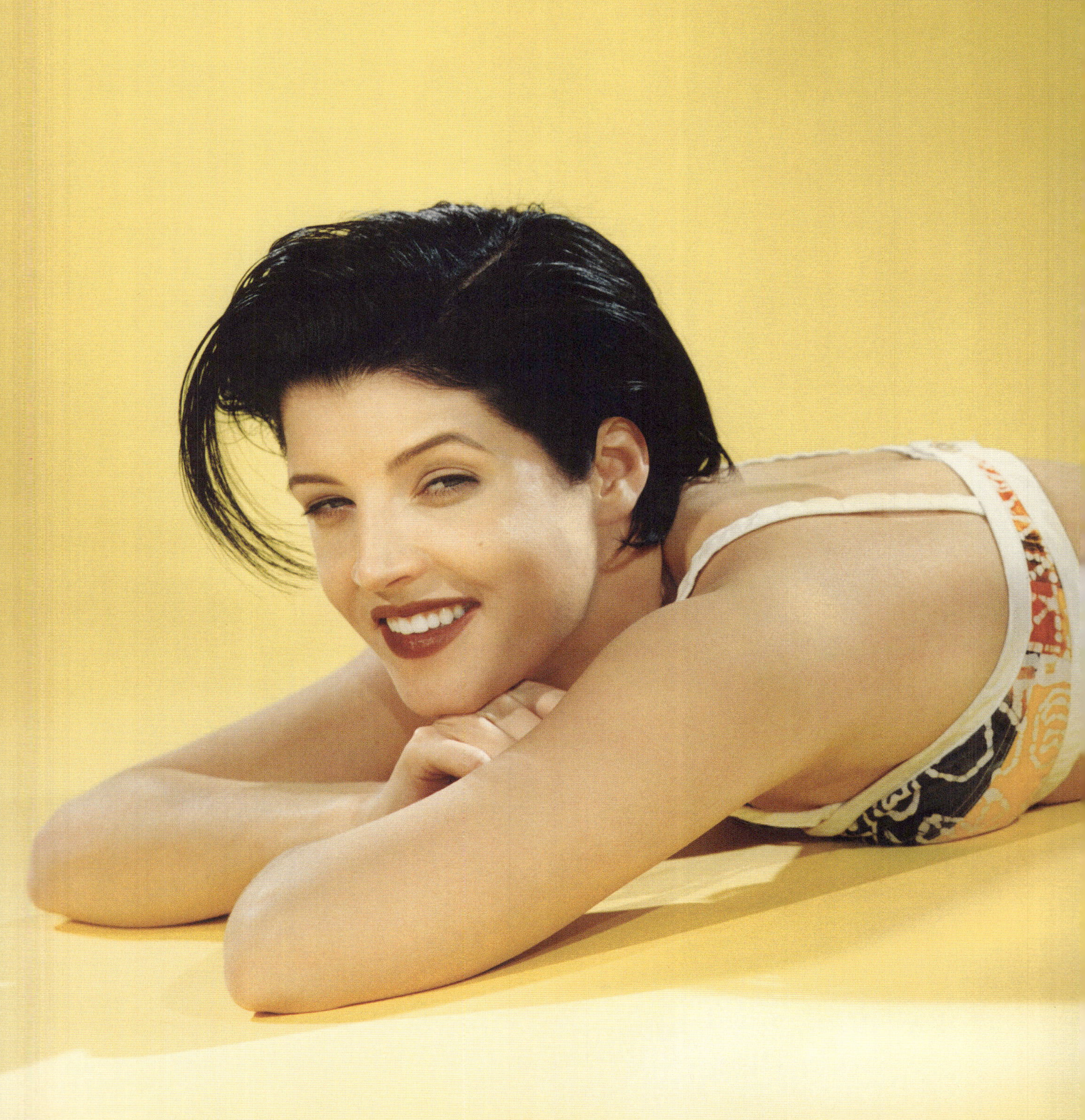

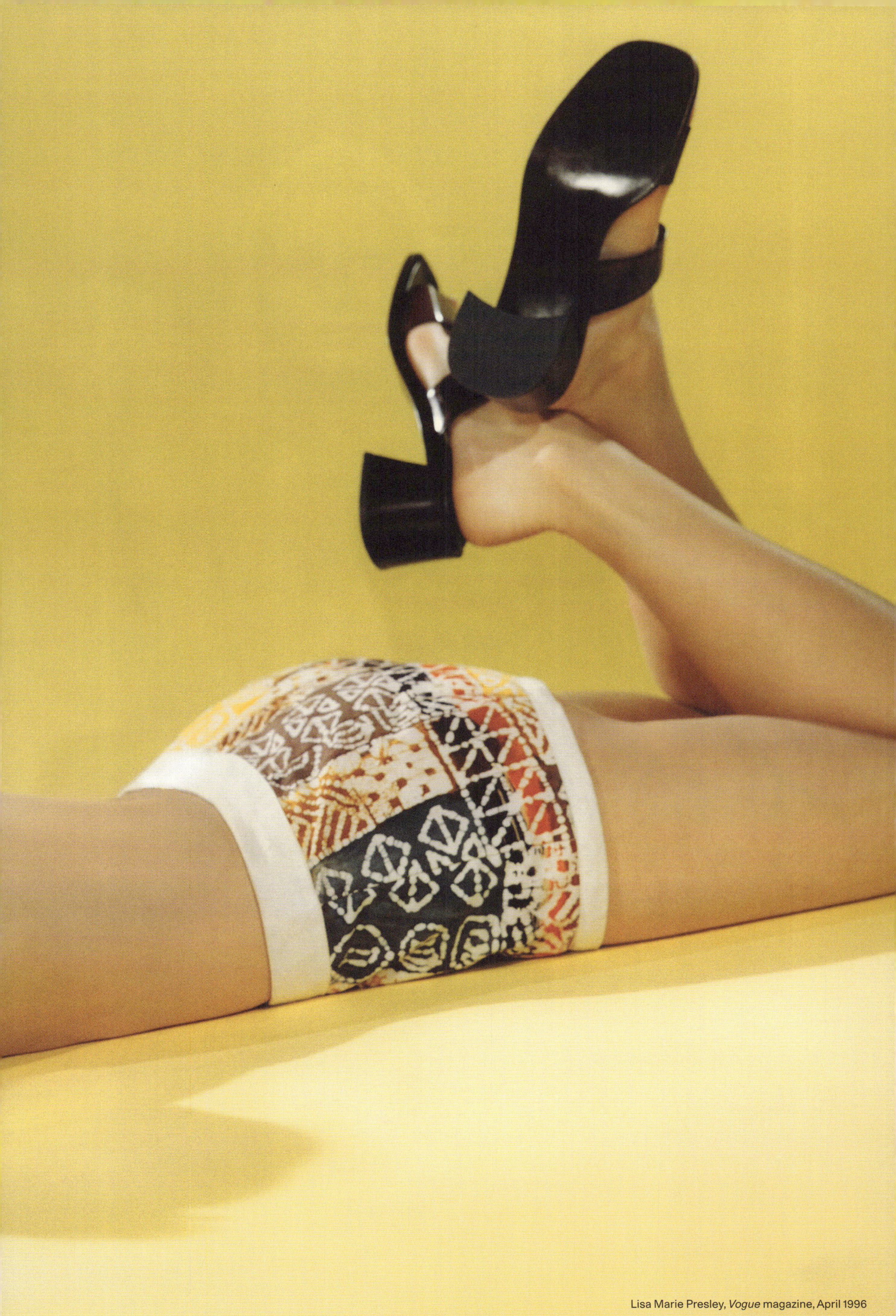

Lisa Marie Presley, *Vogue* magazine, April 1996

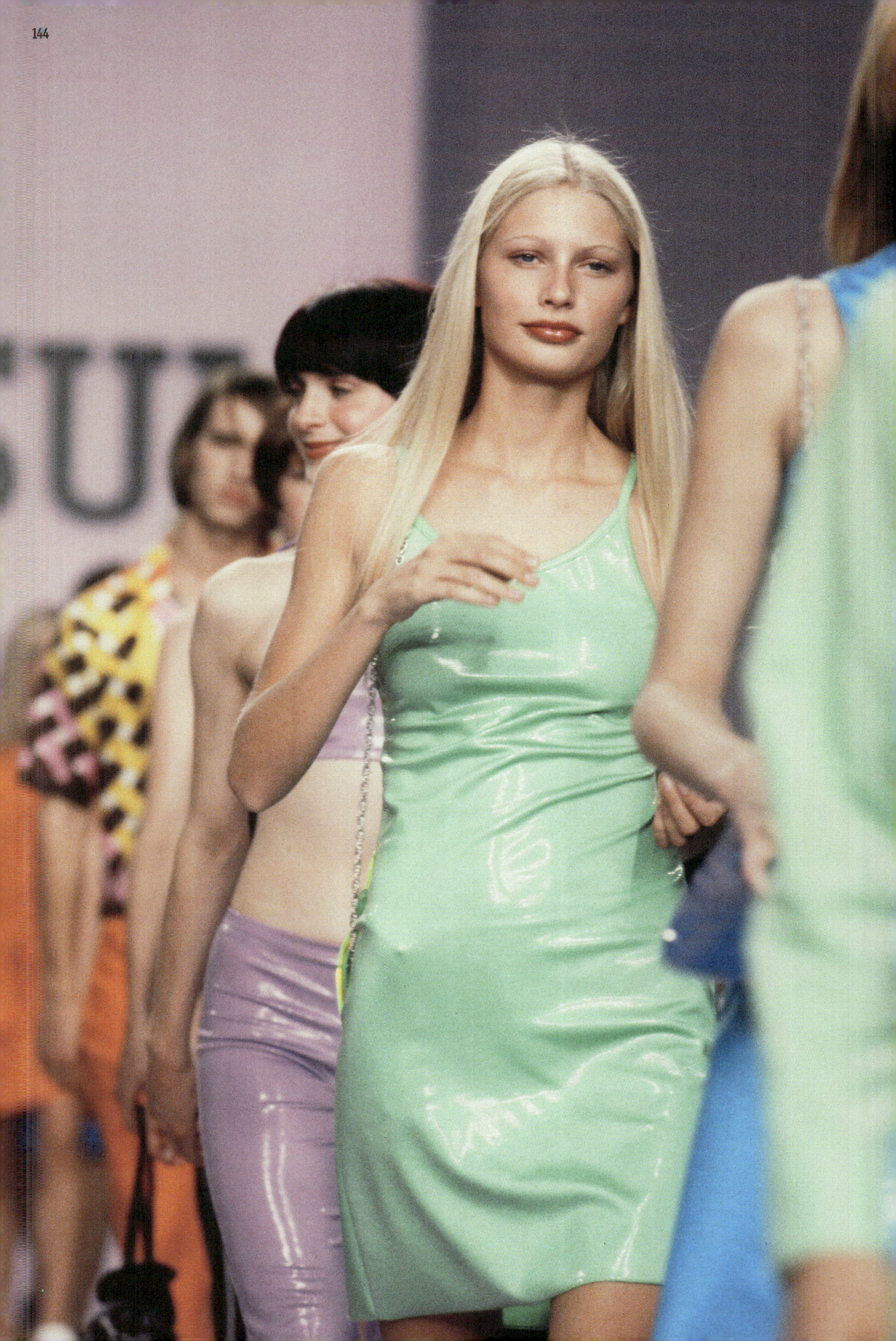

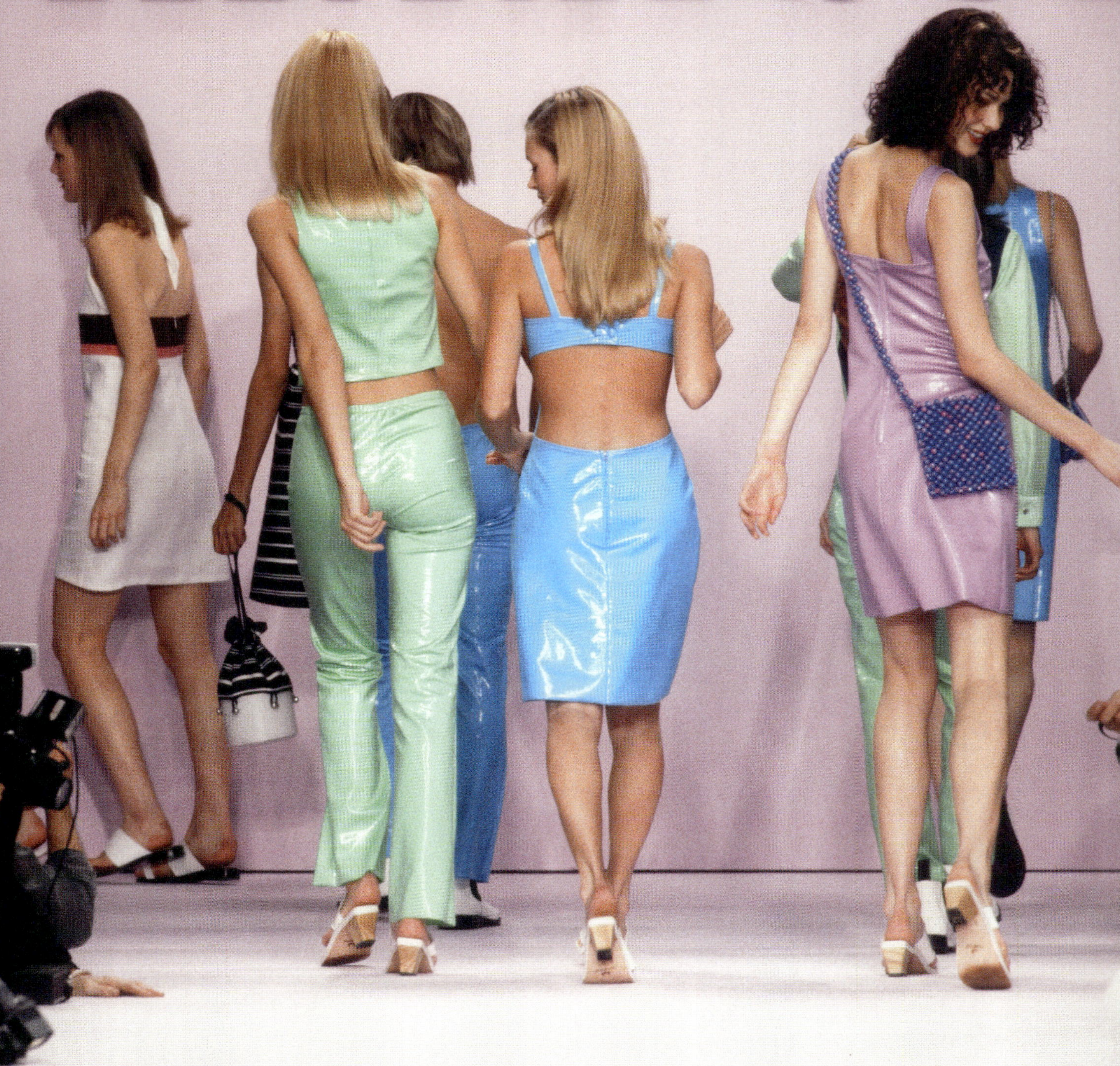

Stella Tennant, Kirsty Hume; Spring 1996

(from left to right): Guinevere Van Seenus,
Amber Valetta, Kate Moss,
Shalom Harlow; Spring 1996

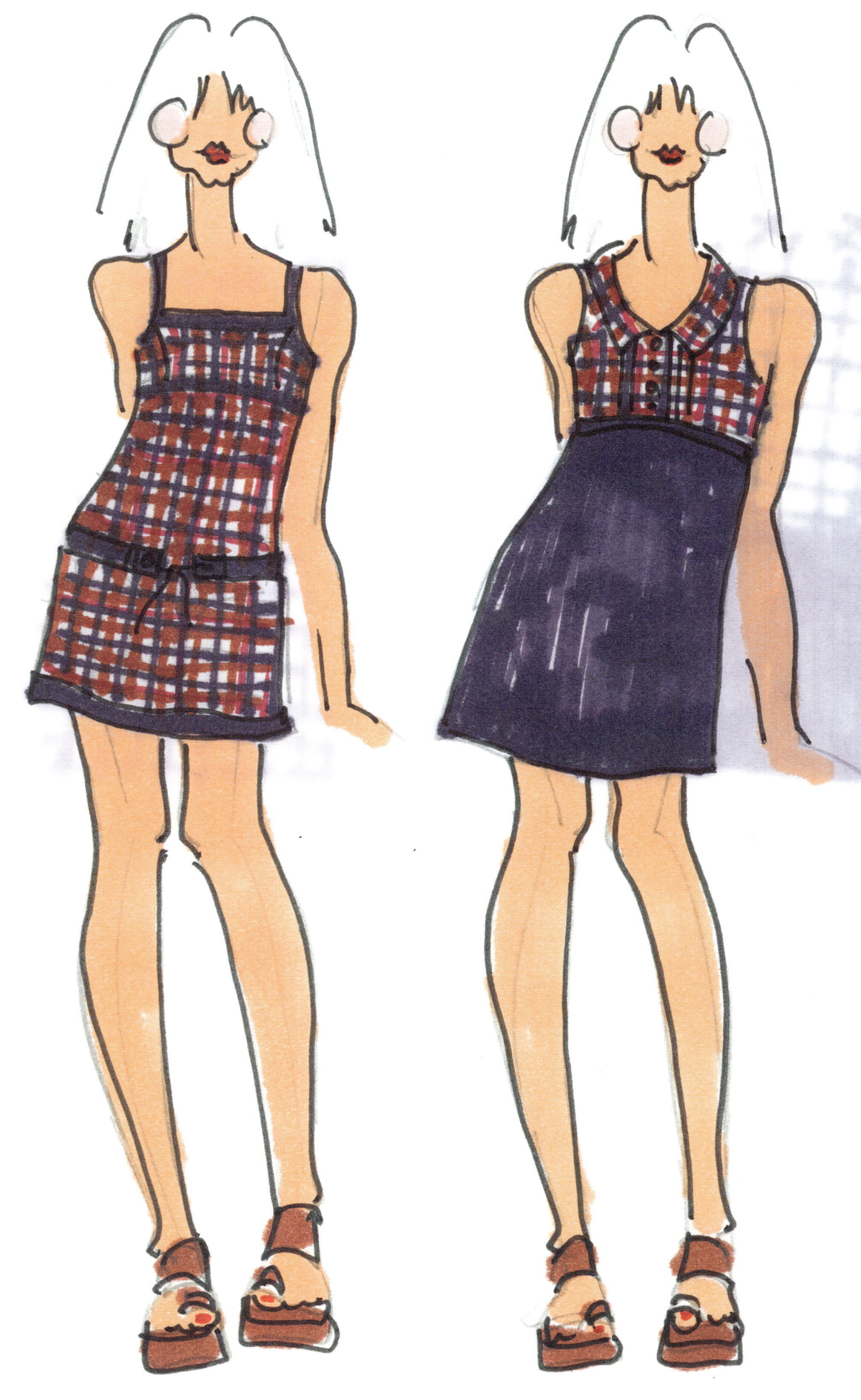

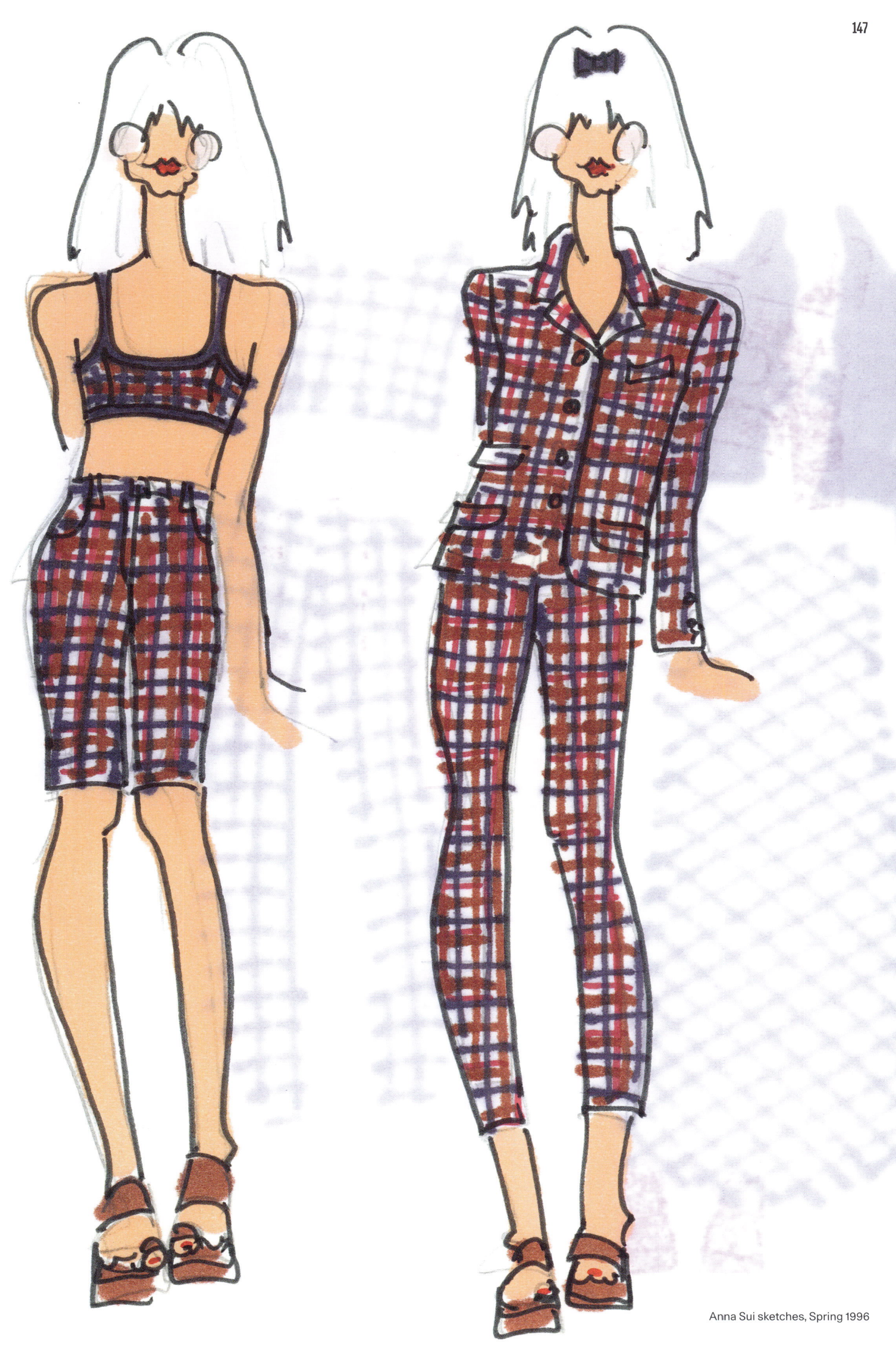

Anna Sui sketches, Spring 1996

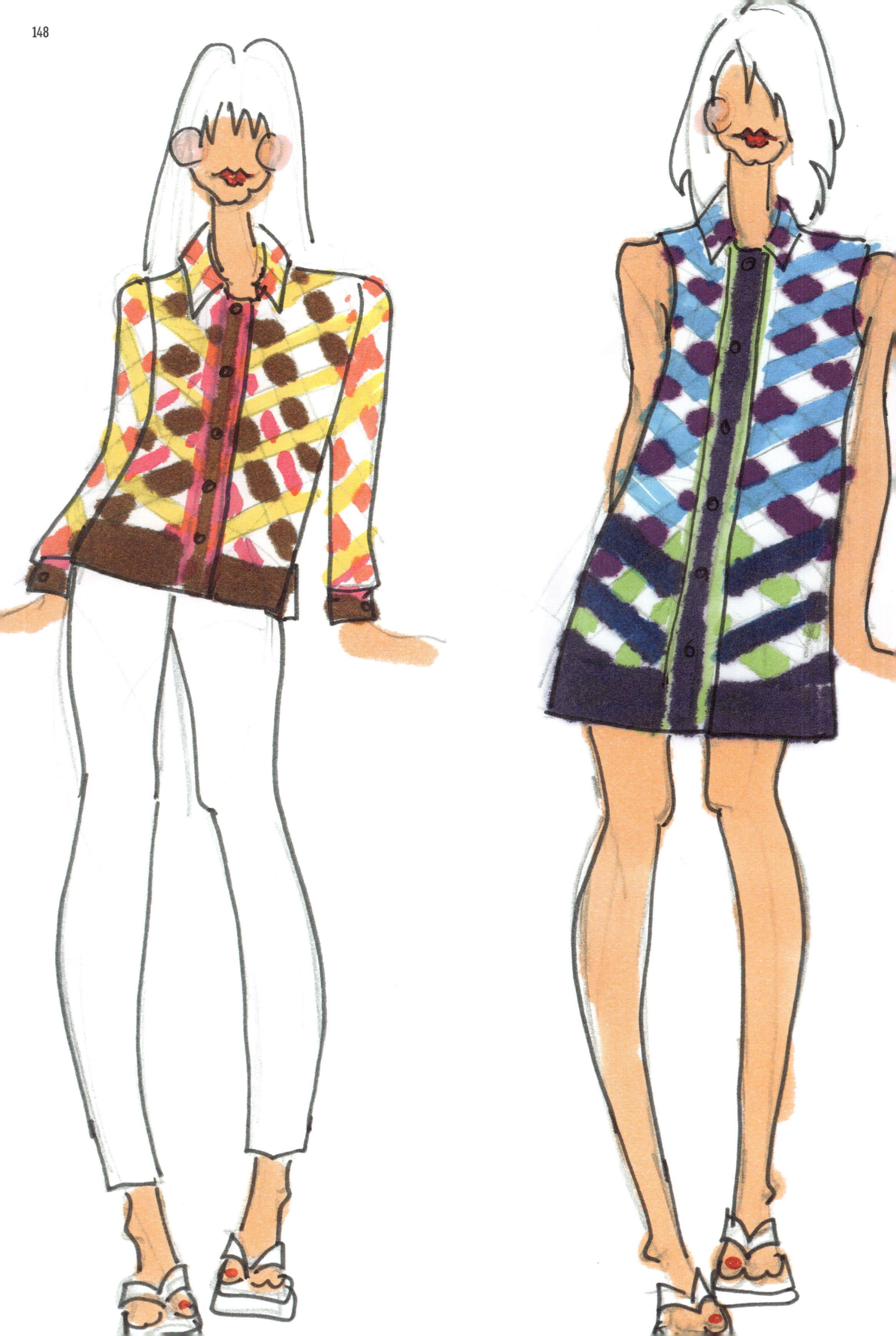

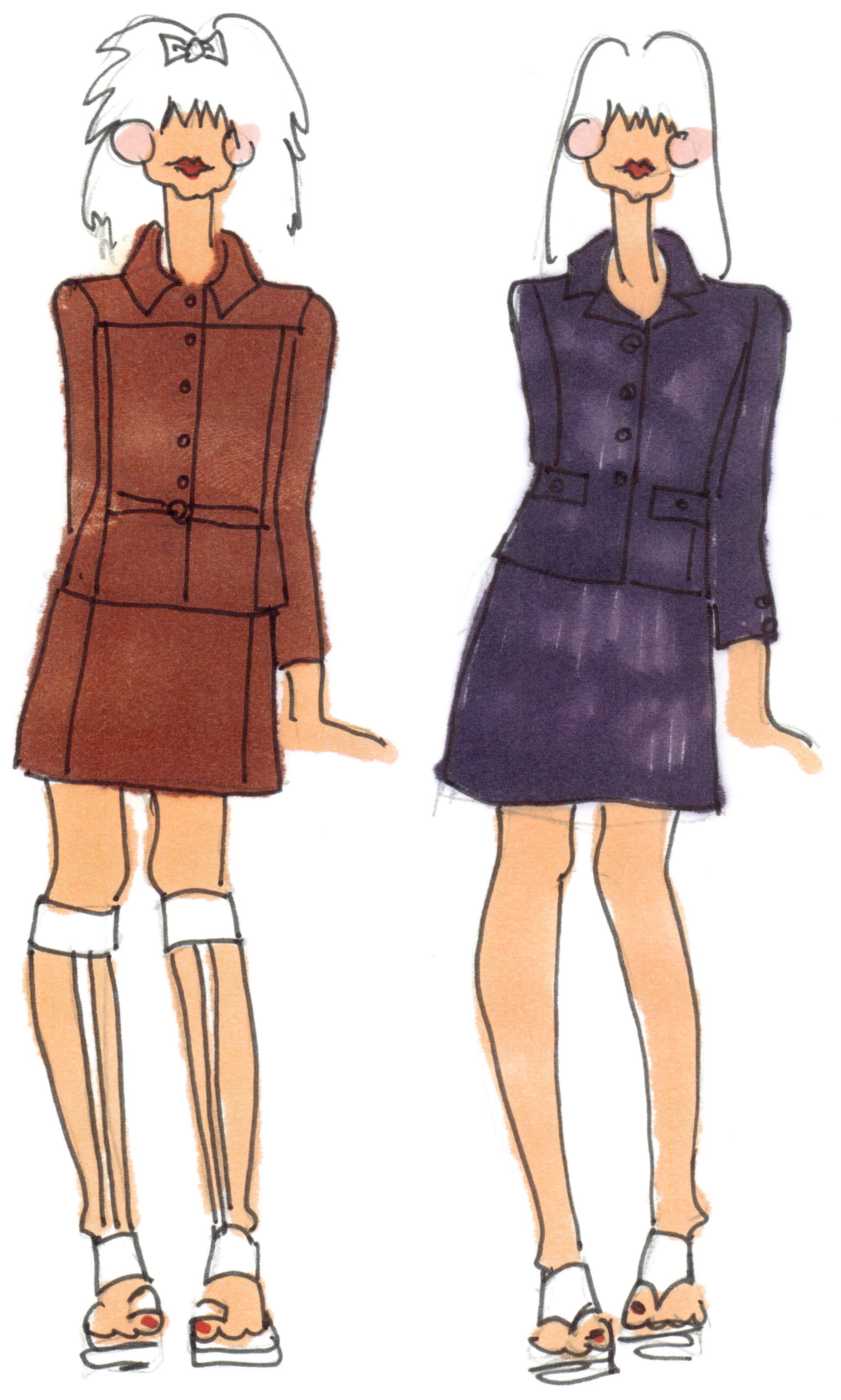

Anna Sui sketches, Spring 1996

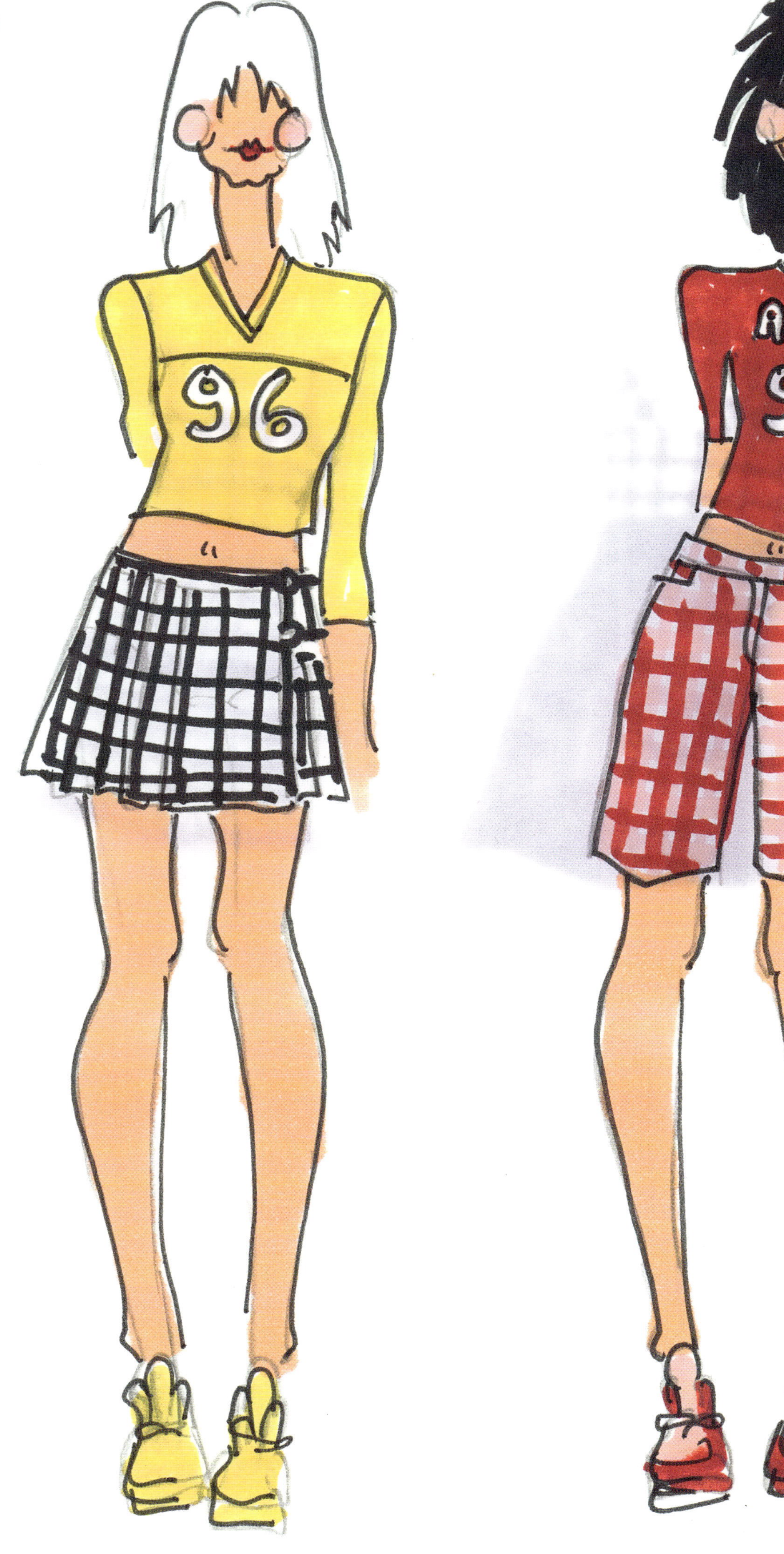
96
ANNA SUI
96

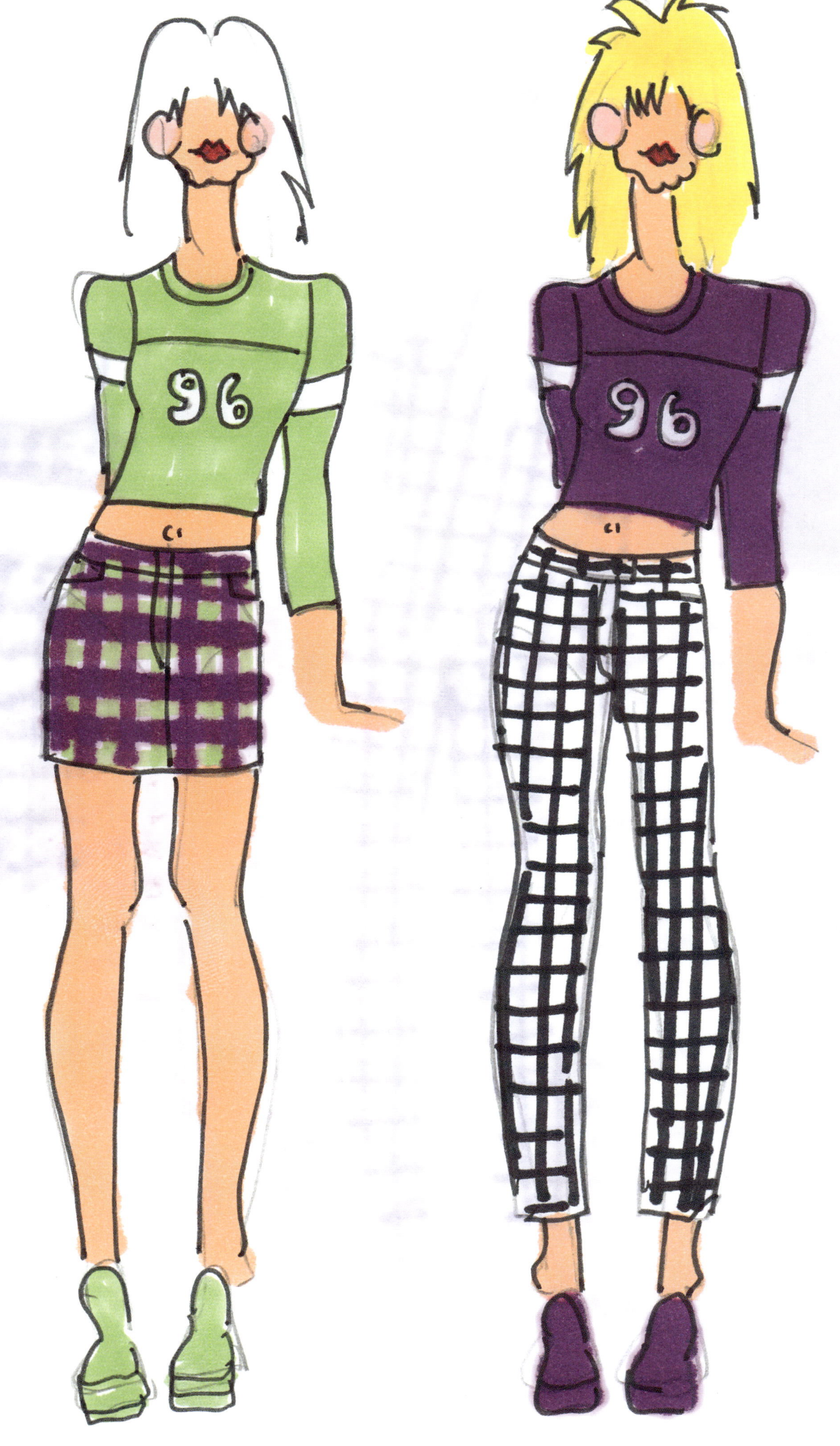

Anna Sui sketches, Spring 1996

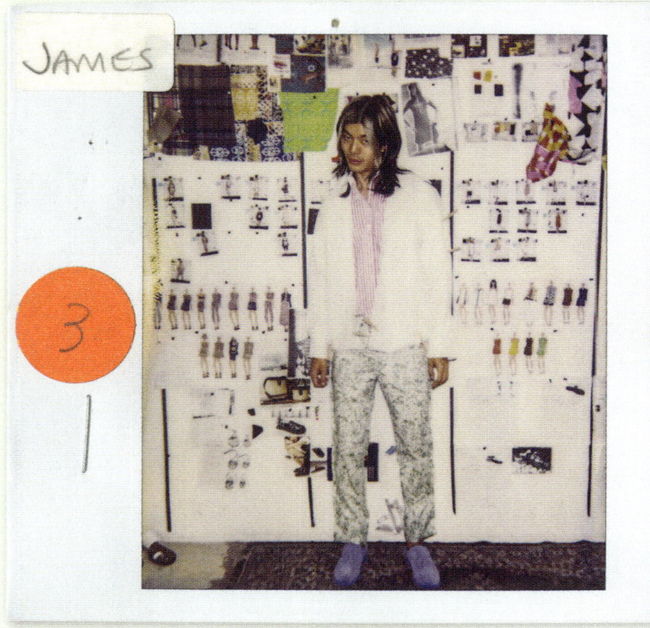

3. JAMES IHA
   . **White vinyl jacket** (jacket open)
   . **Pink + white stripe shirt** (wear out; top btn. open)
   . **Green print pant**

3. ACCESSORIES
   . **Blue hush puppies**

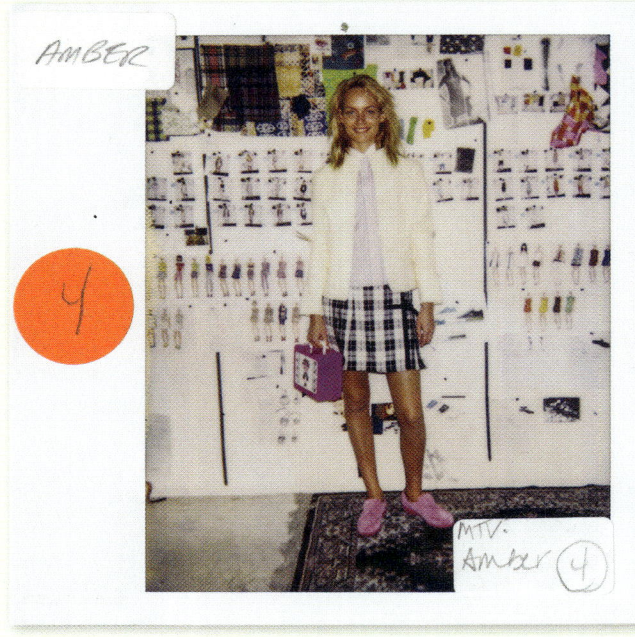

4. AMBER
   . **Yellow vinyl jacket** (wear open)
   . **Purple + white stripe shirt** (wear out; top 3 btns. open; keep collar inside of jkt.)
   . **Black + white plaid skirt**

4. ACCESSORIES
   . **Pink lunch box**
   . **Pink hush puppies**

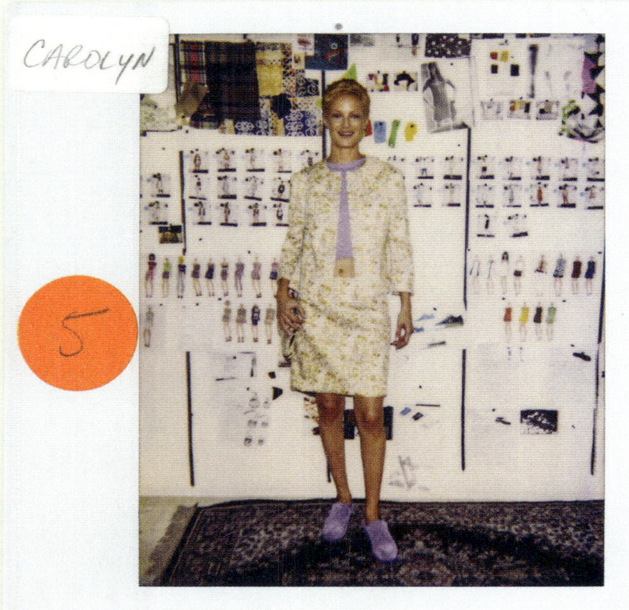

5. CAROLYN
   . **Yellow print jacket** (wear jkt. open)
   . **Purple sweater**
   . **Yellow print skirt**

5. ACCESSORIES
   . **Yellow print double handbag** (top bag facing outside)
   . **Purple hush puppies**

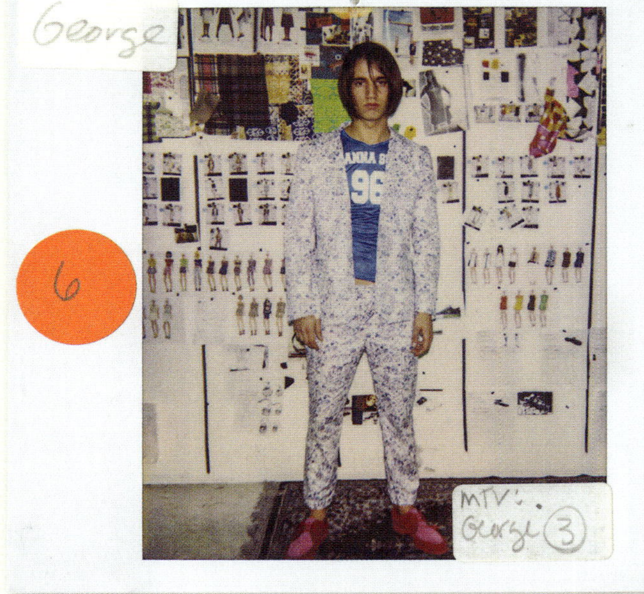

6. GEORGE
   . **Blue print jacket** (wear jkt. open)
   . **Blue football jersey**
   . **Blue print pant**

6. ACCESSORIES
   . **Pink 2 tone hush puppies**

Dresser card, James Iha, Spring 1996
Dresser card, Amber Valetta, Spring 1996
Dresser card, Carolyn Murphy, Spring 1996
Dresser card, George Clements, Spring 1996

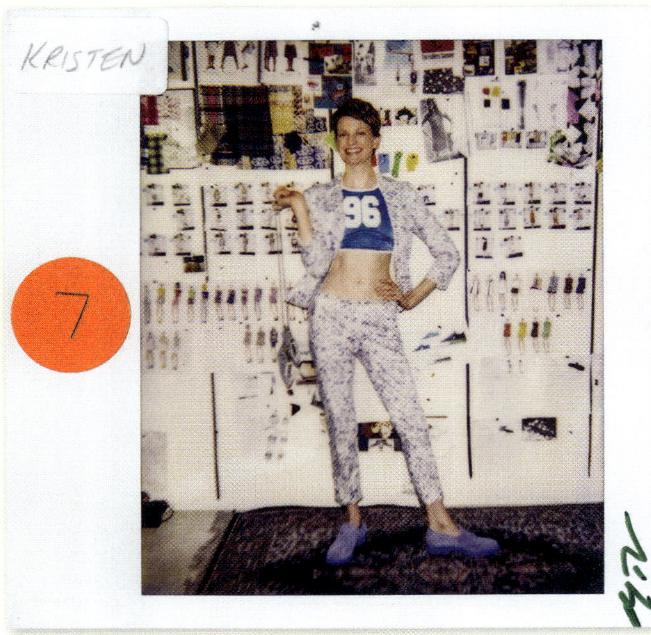

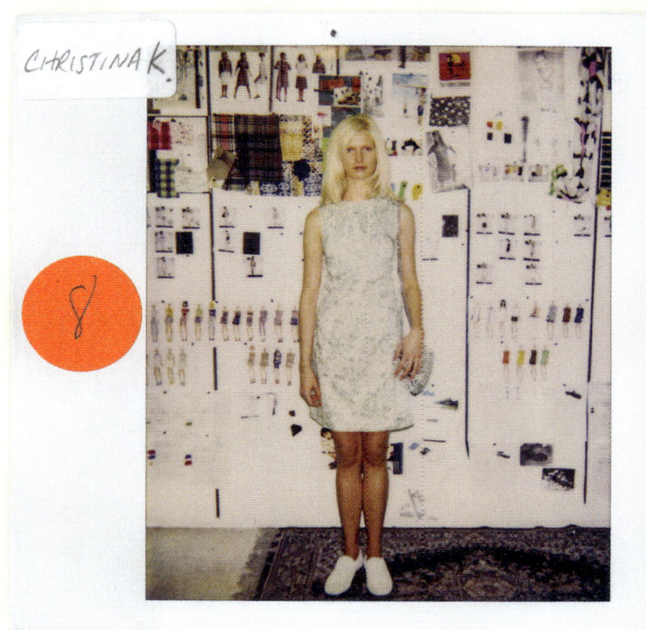

7. KRISTEN McMENAMY
- . **Blue print jacket** (wear open; take off on runway)
- . **Blue halter top** (tie in bow at back of neck & back)
- . **Blue print pant**

7. ACCESSORIES
- . **Blue print double handbag**(top bag on outside)
- . **Blue hush puppies**

8. CHRISTINA KRUSE
- . **Green print dress**

8. ACCESSORIES
- . **Green print double handbag** (make sure top bag is on outside)
- . **Green hush puppies**

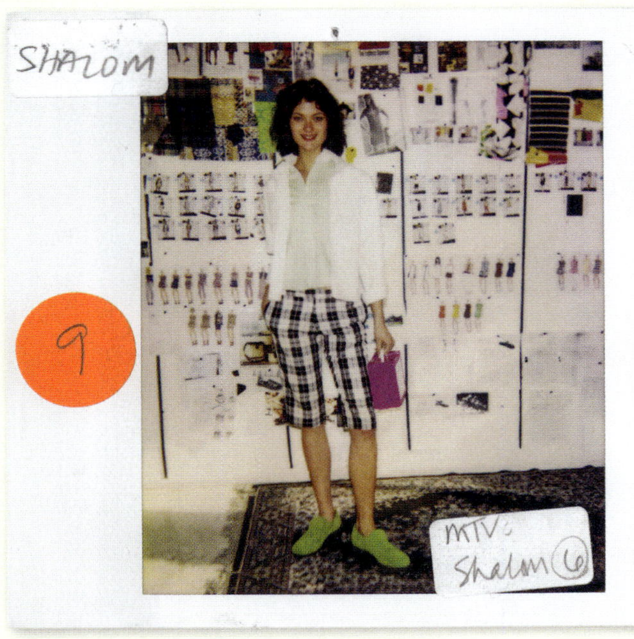

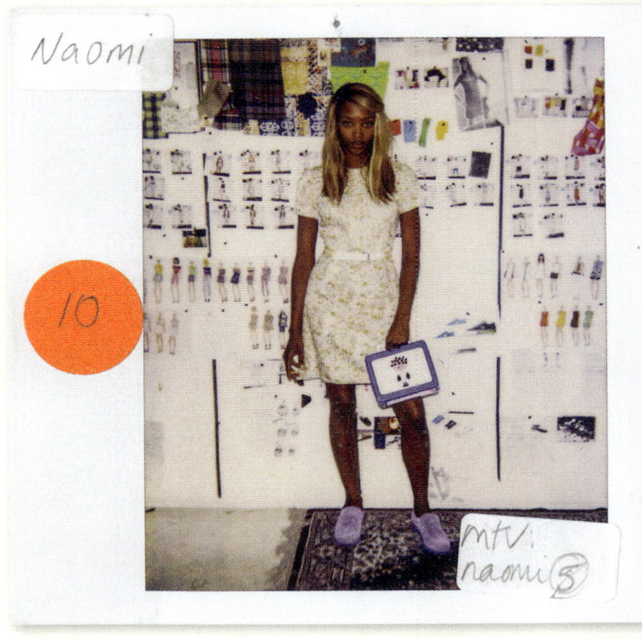

9. SHALOM
- . **White vinyl jacket** (wear open)
- . **Green + white stripe shirt** (wear out; top 3 buttons open)
- . **Black + white plaid bermudas**

9. ACCESSORIES
- . **Pink lunchbox**
- . **Lime green hush puppies**

10. NAOMI
- . **Yellow print dress**

10. ACCESSORIES
- . **Yellow and white belt**
- . **Purple lunch box**
- . **Purple hush puppies**

Dresser card, Kristen McMenamy, Spring 1996

Dresser card, Christina Kruse, Spring 1996

Dresser card, Shalom Harlow, Spring 1996

Dresser card, Naomi Campbell, Spring 1996

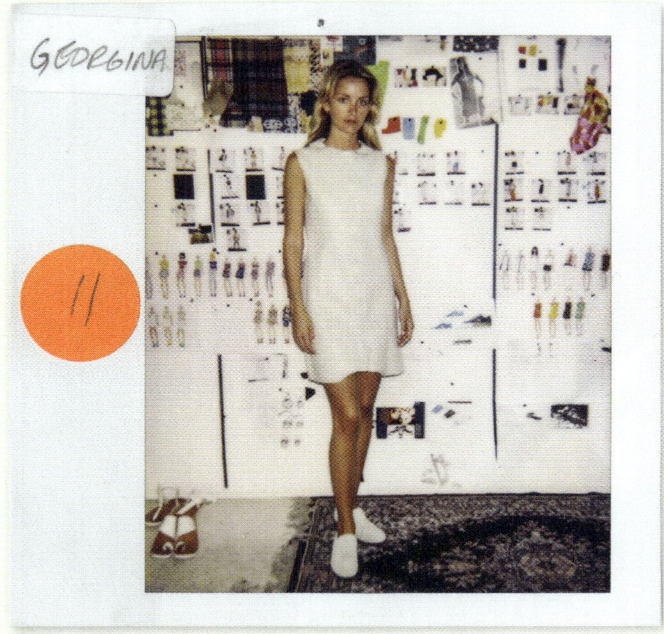

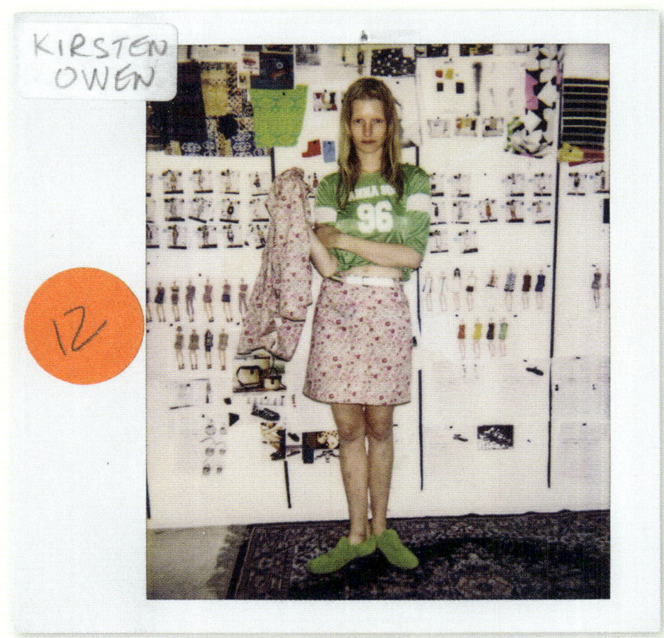

11. GEORGINA
 . Green vinyl dress

11. ACCESSORIES
 . Green hush puppies

12. KIRSTEN OWEN
 . **Pink print jacket** (open; take off on runway)
 . **Green football jersey**
 . **Pink print skirt**

12. ACCESSORIES
 . **Green/white stripe belt**
 . **Lime green hush puppies**

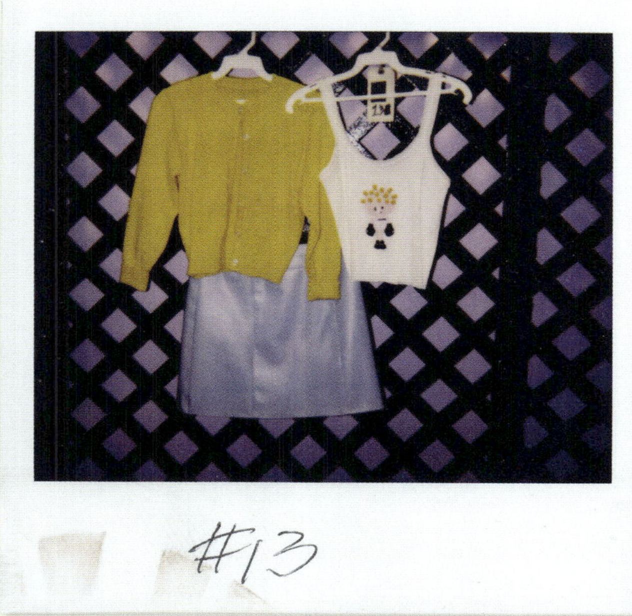

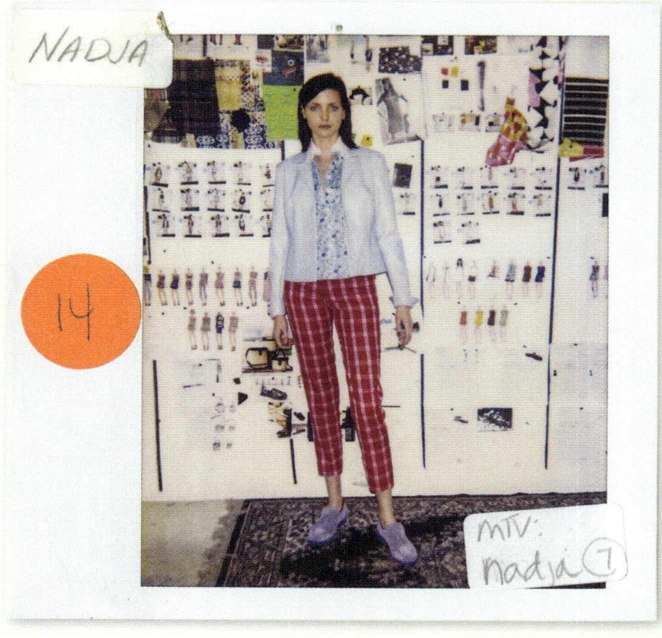

13. KYLIE
Yellow Sweater
White tank top
Blue Vinyl skirt

14. NADJA
 . **Blue vinyl jacket** (open; cuffs folded up one time)
 . **Blue print shirt** (wear top out; top 4 btns. open)
 . **Red + pink plaid pant**

14. ACCESSORIES
 . **Purple hush puppies**

Dresser card, Georgina Grenville, Spring 1996
Dresser card, Kristin Owen, Spring 1996
Dresser card, Kylie Bay, Spring 1996
Dresser card, Nadja Auermann, Spring 1996

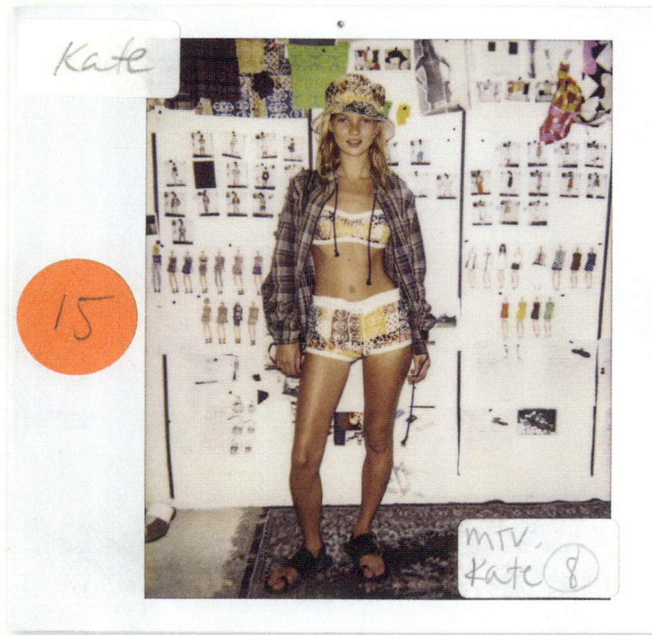

15. KATE
. **Brown madras jacket** (wear open; do not take off on runway)
. **Batik bathingsuit** (2 pc.)

15. ACCESSORIES
. **Brown leather single buckle bracelet** (wear on left wrist)
. **Brown plaid knapsack**
. **Brown sandal**

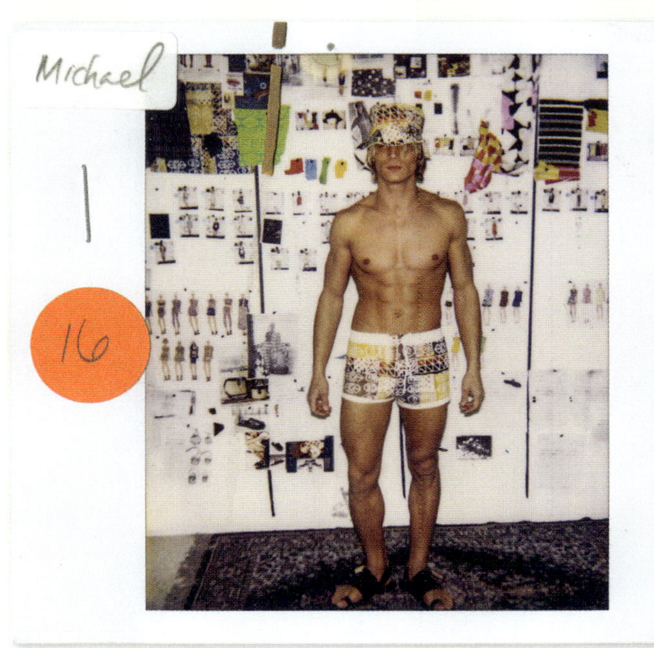

16. MICHAEL
. **Batik bathingsuit** (tie drawstring in knot + let strings hang)

16. ACCESSORIES
. **Batik hat**
. **Brown sandal** (w's sz.9)

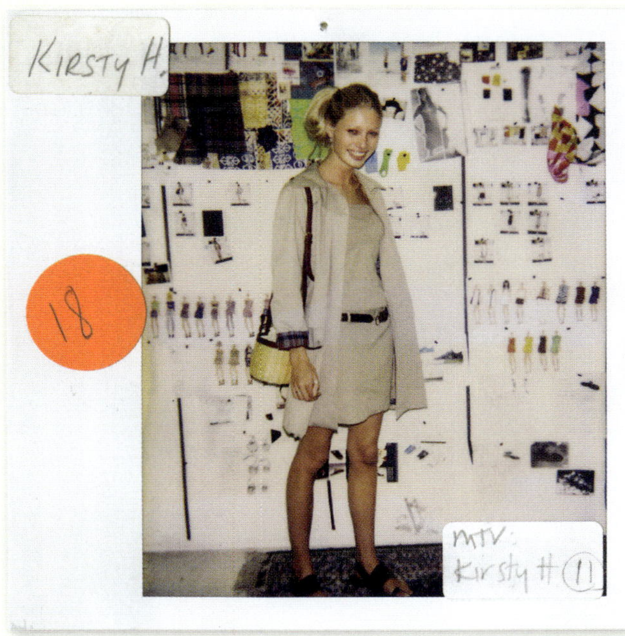

18. KIRSTY HUME
. **Khaki coat** (open)
. **Khaki dress**

18. ACCESSORIES
. **Brown leather tab belt** (on dress)
. **Straw fishing bag**
. **Brown flat sandal**

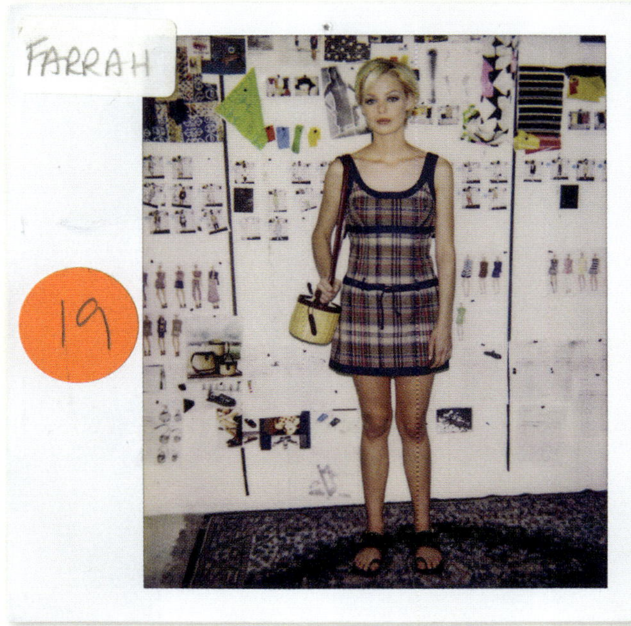

19. FARRAH
. **Blue madras bathingsuit dress** (tie drawstrings in ½ knot and let strings hang)

19. ACCESSORIES
. **Wood bead handbag**
. **Brown flat sandal**

Dresser card, Kate Moss, Spring 1996
Dresser card, Michael Loomis, Spring 1996
Dresser card, Kristy Hume, Spring 1996
Dresser card, Farrah Summerford, Spring 1996

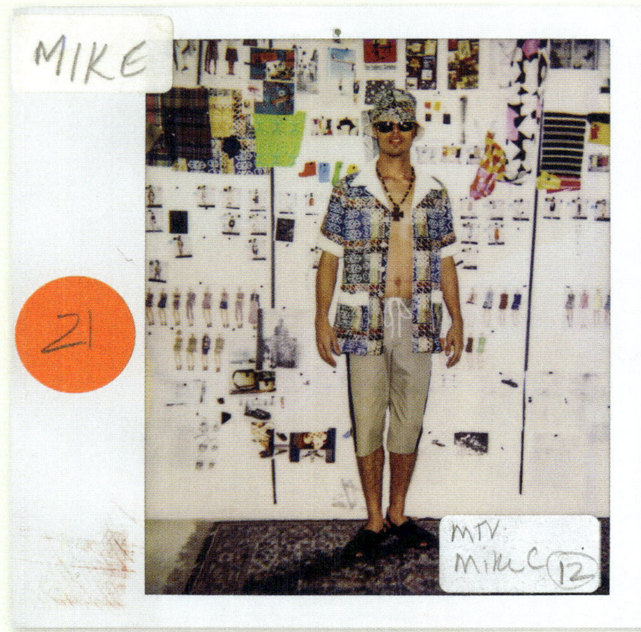

21. MIKE CAMPBELL
 . **Batik cabana shirt** (wear open)
 . **Khaki jams**

21. ACCESSORIES
 . **Batik hat**
 . **Bead cross**
 . **Black fly sunglasses**
 . **Brown mule**

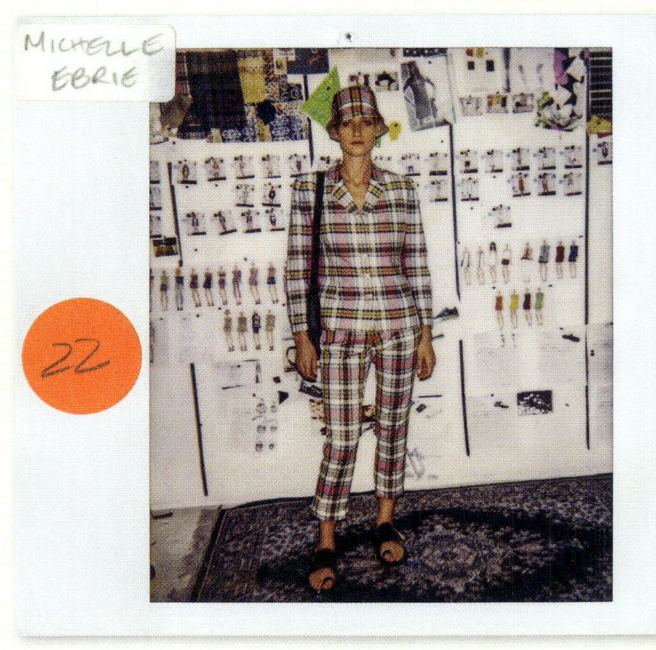

22. MICHELLE EABRY
 . **Pink madras jacket** (button all btns.)
 . **Pink madras pant**

22. ACCESSORIES
 . **Pink madras hat**
 . **Straw fishing bag**
 . **Brown flat sandal**

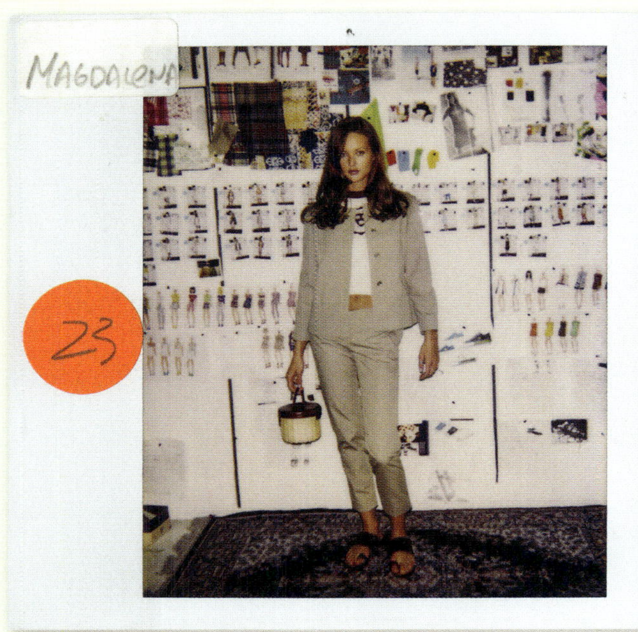

23. MAGDALENA
 . **Khaki jacket** (open)
 . **T-shirt** (do not tuck in)
 . **Khaki pant**

23. ACCESSORIES
 . **Straw fishing bag**
 . **Brown sandal**

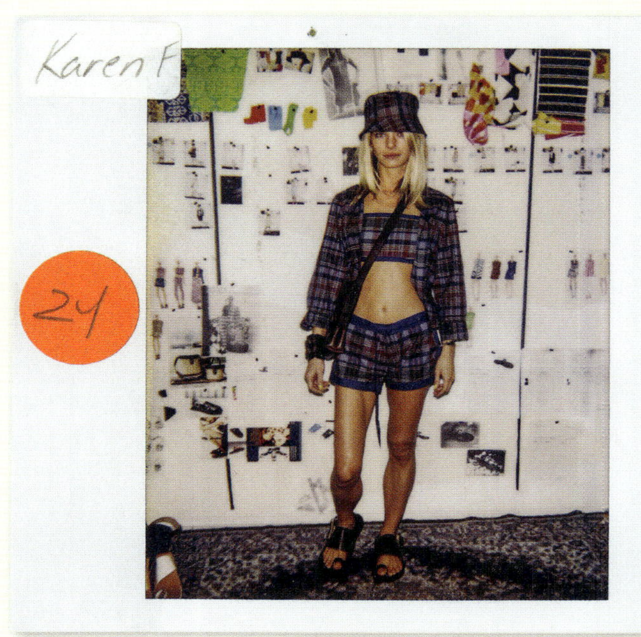

24. KAREN F.
 . **Blue madras shirt** (wear open; leave cuffs open)
 . **Blue madras bathingsuit** (2 pc.)

24. ACCESSORIES
 . **Blue madras hat**
 . **Brown leather bracelet** (double buckle on right wrist)
 . **Brown leather bag** (wear across chest; over shirt))
 . **Brown flat sandal**

Dresser card, Mike Campbell, Spring 1996
Dresser card, Michelle Eabry, Spring 1996
Dresser card, Magdalena Frackowiak, Spring 1996
Dresser card, Karen Ferrari, Spring 1996

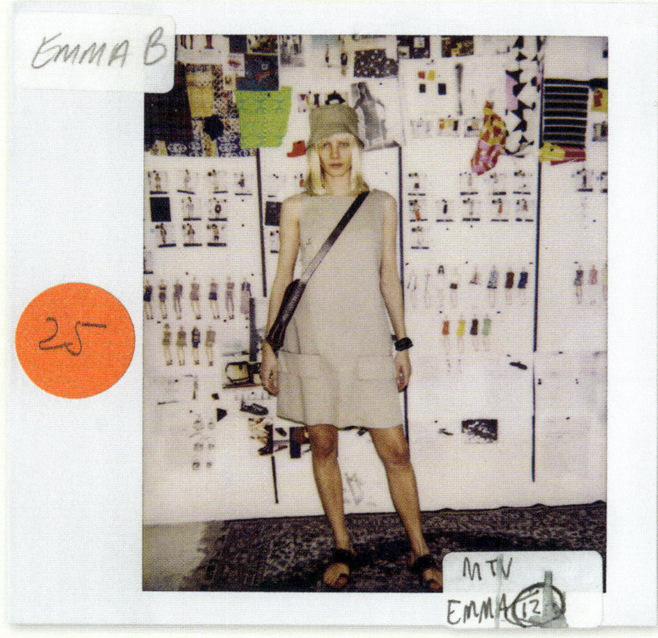

25. EMMA
. Khaki dress

25. ACCESSORIES
. Khaki hat
. Brown leather single buckle bracelet (on left wrist)
. Brown leather handbag
. Brown flat sandal

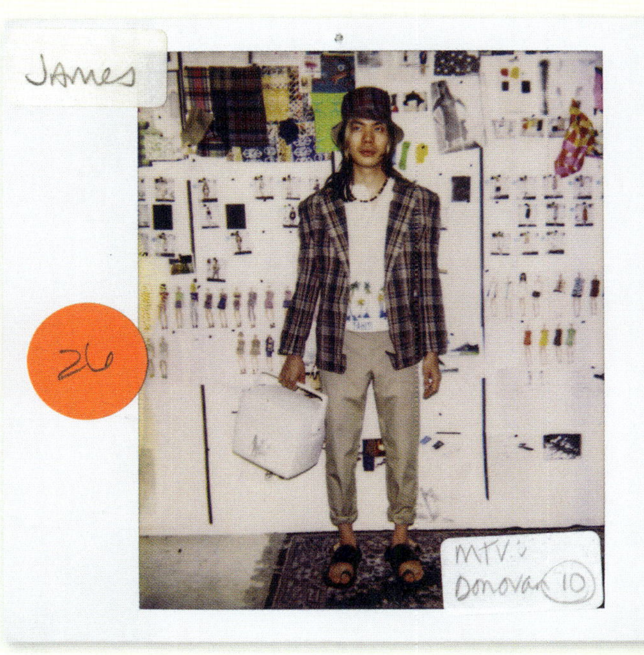

26. JAMES IHA
. Brown madras jacket (leave jkt. open)
. Ivory tahiti t-shirt (wear out; do not button btns.)
. Khaki pant (roll pant legs, 1 or 2x as per polaroid)

26. ACCESSORIES
. Blue plaid hat
. Brown beads (Hook on last ring for tightest length)
. White cooler
. Brown leather sandal (sz w10)

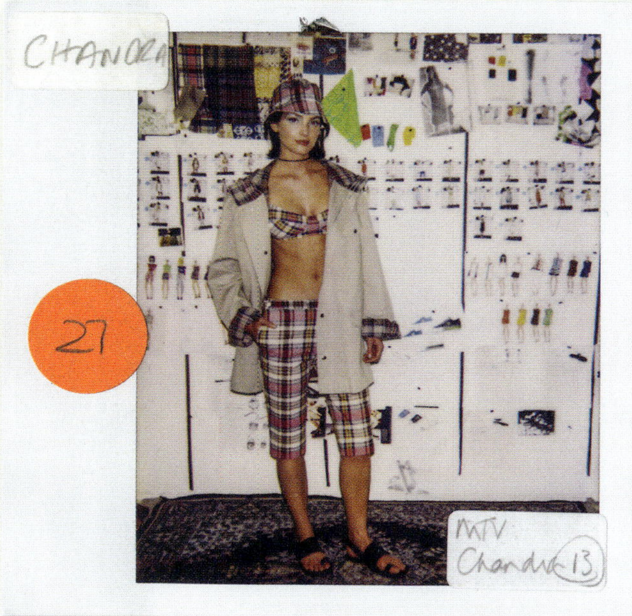

27. CHANDRA
. Khaki parka (wear open; take off on runway)
. Pink madras bathingsuit top
. Pink madras bermudas

27. ACCESSORIES
. Pink madras hat
. Brown leather single buckle bracelet (wear on left wrist)
. Brown leather cord choker (tie in bow at back of neck)
. Brown sandal

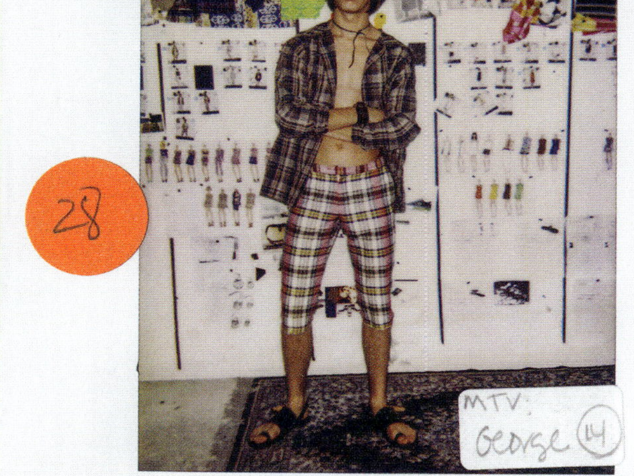

28. GEORGE
. Brown madras jacket (wear open)
. Pink madras bermudas

28. ACCESSORIES
. Brown leather cord choker (tie in knot + place as per polaroid)
. Brown leather single buckle bracelet (wear on right wrist)
. Brown sandal (w's sz. 9)

Dresser card, Emma Balfour, Spring 1996
Dresser card, James Iha, Spring 1996
Dresser card, Chandra North, Spring 1996
Dresser card, George Clements, Spring 1996

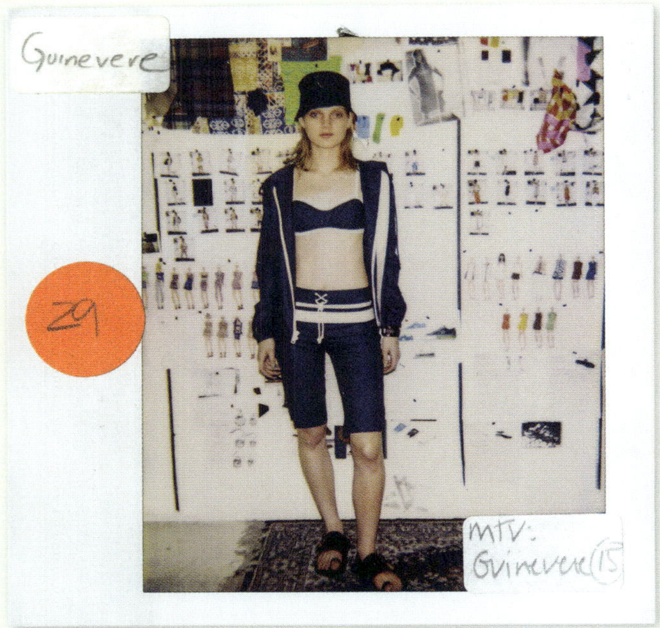

29. GUINEVERE
- . **Navy + white jacket** (jacket open)
- . **Navy + white bathingsuit top**
- . **Navy + white jams**

29. ACCESSORIES
- . **Navy hat**
- . **Brown leather single strap bracelet** (on left wrist)
- . **Brown flat sandal** (sz. 9)

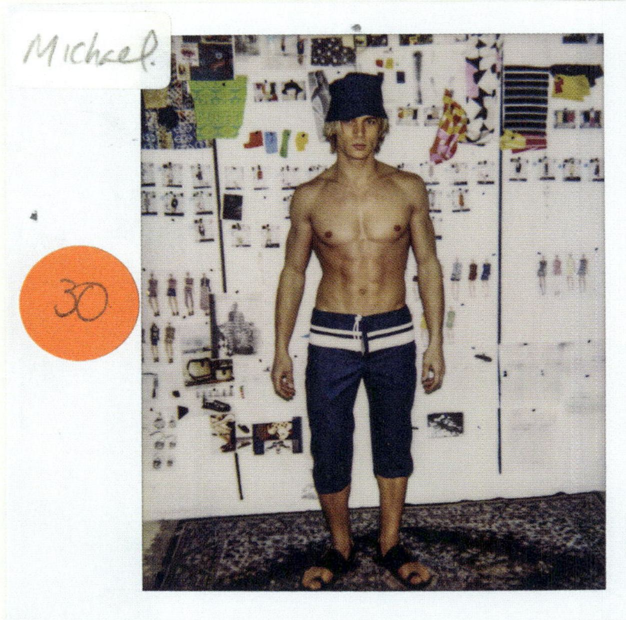

30. MICHAEL
- . **Navy + white jams** (place on hips 4" below belly button; tie drawstring ends in knot + let hang)

30. ACCESSORIES
- . **Navy hat**
- . **Brown sandals**(w's sz. 9; from last look #16)

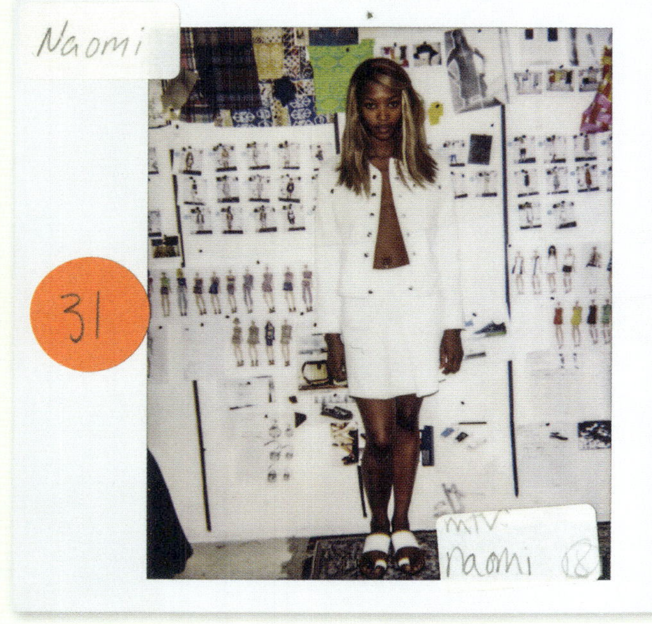

31. NAOMI
- . **White denim jacket** (wear open - nothing underneath)
- . **White denim skirt**

31. ACCESSORIES
- . **Silver chain w/charm**
- . **White flat sandal**

32. LINDA
- . **Orange shirtdress** (top 3 btns. open)

32. ACCESSORIES
- . **Silver chain w/charm**
- . **White wedge sandal** (sz. 9) (use for next look)

Dresser card, Guinevere Van Seenus, Spring 1996
Dresser card, Michael Loomis, Spring 1996
Dresser card, Naomi Campbell, Spring 1996
Dresser card, Linda Evangelista, Spring 1996

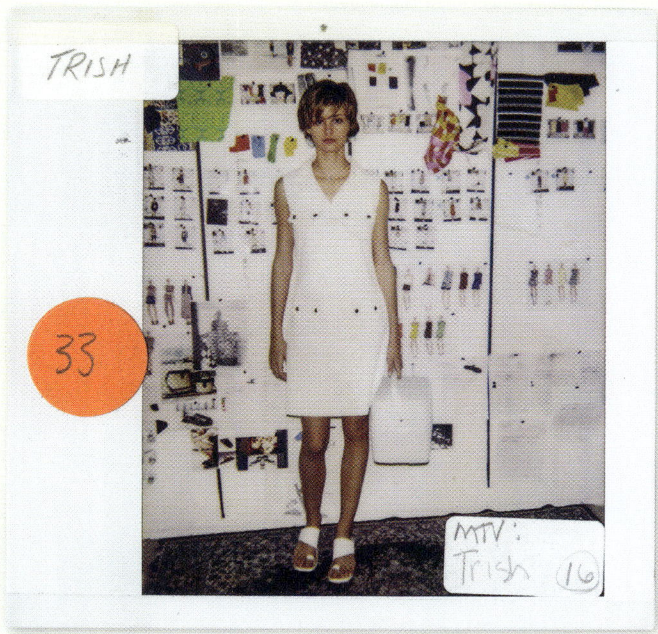

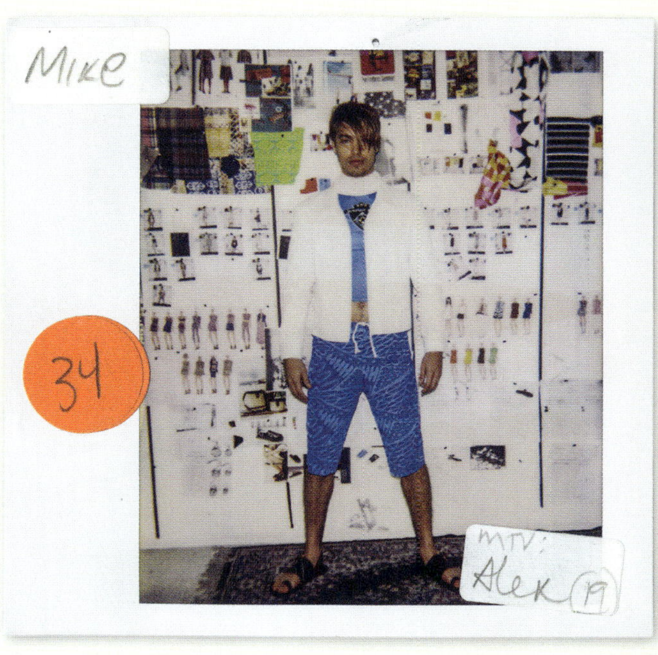

33. TRISH
White denim dress

33. ACCESSORIES
. **Silver chain w/charm** (from last outfit #2)
. **White wedge sandal**

34. MIKE CAMPBELL
. **White denim jacket** (open; do not take off on runway)
. **Blue surfer tee**
. **Blue jams**

34. ACCESSORIES
. **Brown sandal** (w's sz. 10)

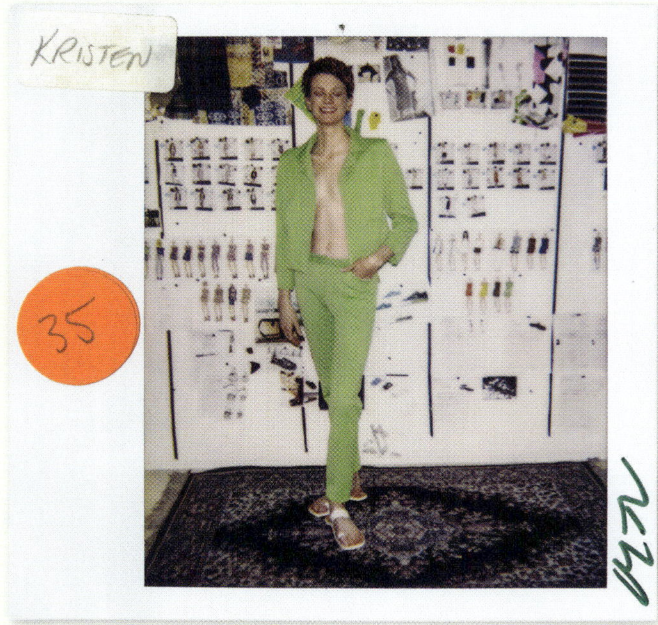

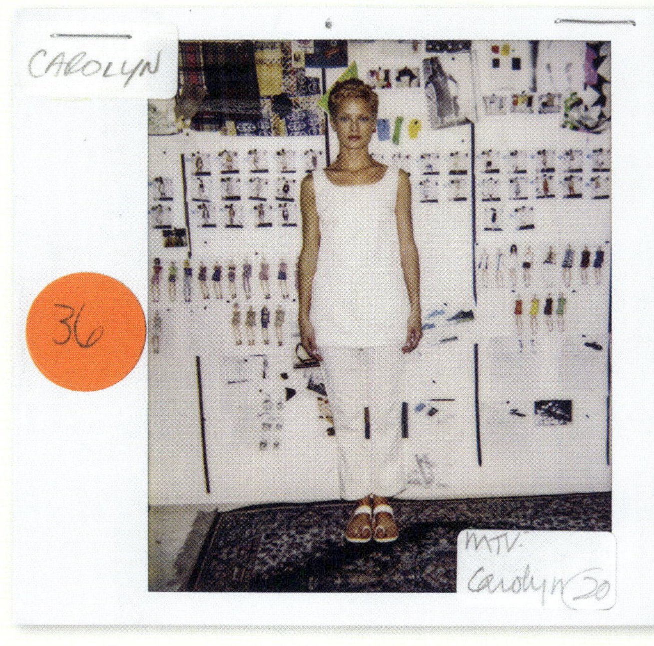

35. KRISTEN McMENAMY
. **Green jacket** (wear open; nothing underneath)
. **Green pant**

35. ACCESSORIES
. **Silver chain w/charm**
. **White sandal**

36. CAROLYN
. **White denim tunic** (wear out over pants)
. **White denim pants**

36. ACCESSORIES
. **Silver chain w/charm**
. **White sandal**

Dresser card, Trish Goff, Spring 1996
Dresser card, Mike Campbell, Spring 1996
Dresser card, Kristen McMenamy, Spring 1996
Dresser card, Carolyn Murphy, Spring 1996

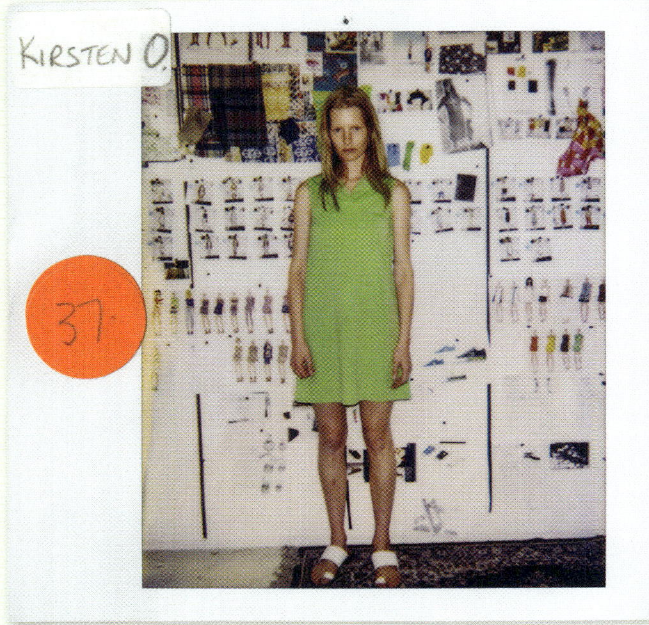

37. **KIRSTEN OWEN**
. **Green dress**

37. ACCESSORIES
. **Silver chain w/charm**
. **White flat sandal**

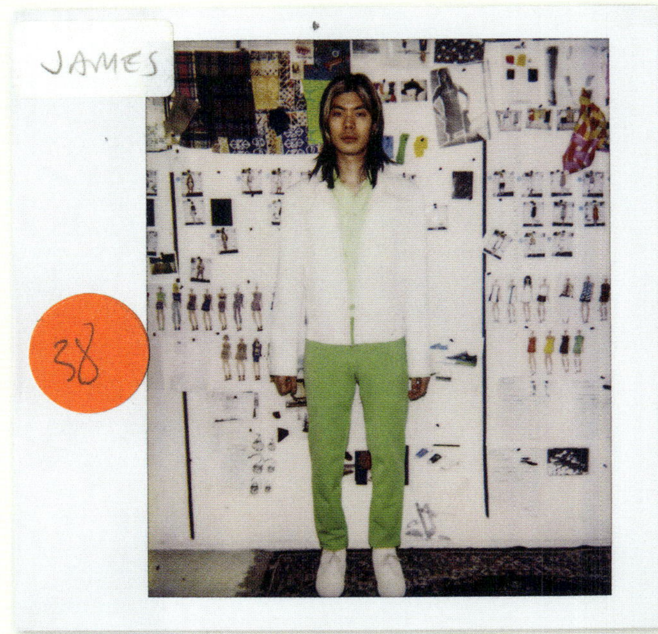

38. **JAMES IHA**
. **White denim jacket** (keep open) DO NOT TAKE OFF
. **Green shirt** (tuck in; top 2 btns. open) (use again in look #63)
. **Green pant**

38. ACCESSORIES
. **White boots** (use again in look #63)

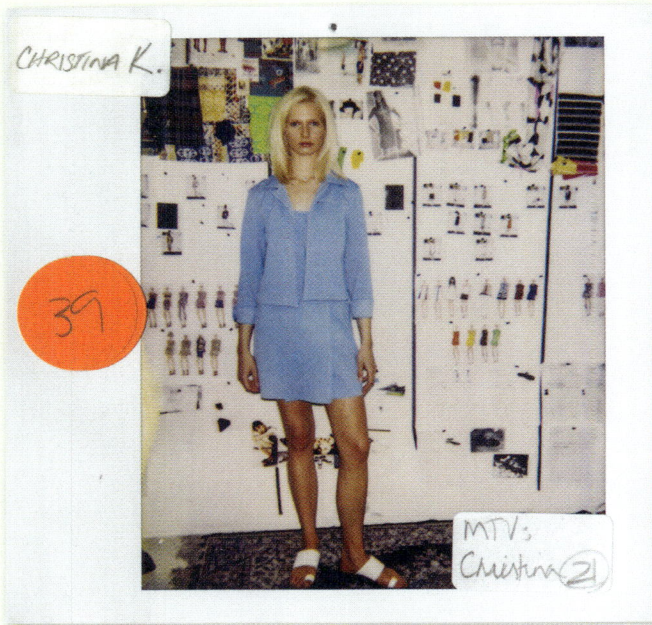

39. **CHRISTINA KRUSE**
. **Blue jacket** (open; take off on runway)
. **Blue dress**

39. ACCESSORIES
. **Silver chain w/charm**
. **White flat sandal**

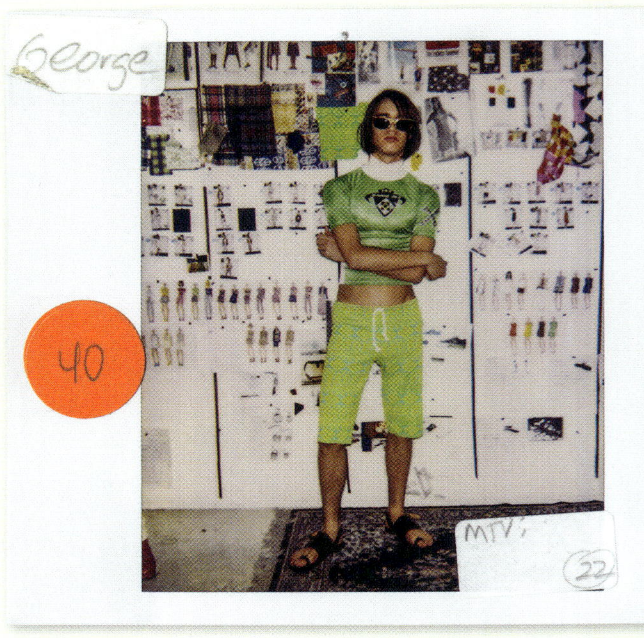

40. **GEORGE**
. **Green surfer tee**
. **Green jams** (tie drawstrings in knot; refer to polaroid; show muscles in waist; wear on hips; make sure pant waist is straight across; drawstring should be at top of waistband)

40. ACCESSORIES
. **Sunglasses**
. **Brown sandal** (use from last look #28)

Dresser card, Kristen Owen, Spring 1996
Dresser card, James Iha, Spring 1996
Dresser card, Christina Kruse, Spring 1996
Dresser card, George Clements, Spring 1996

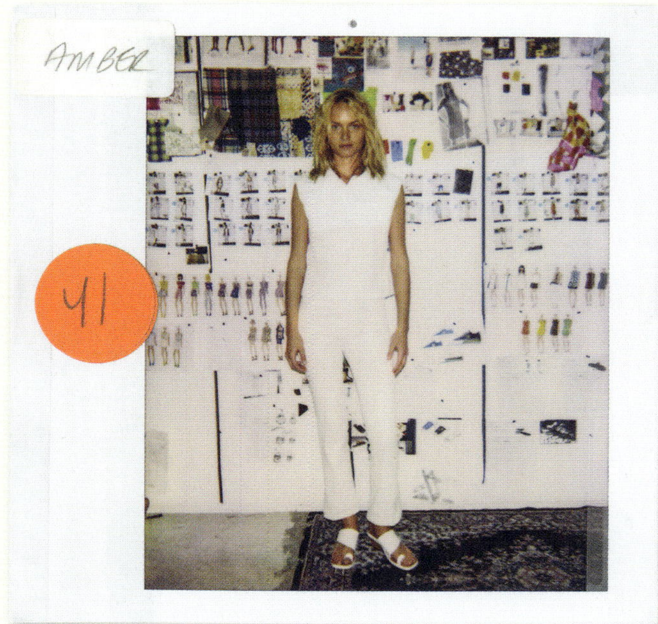

41. AMBER
. **White denim vest** (button 3rd snap only)
. **White denim pant**

<u>41.</u> <u>ACCESSORIES</u>
. **Silver chain w/charm**
. **White wedge sandal** (use again in look #66)

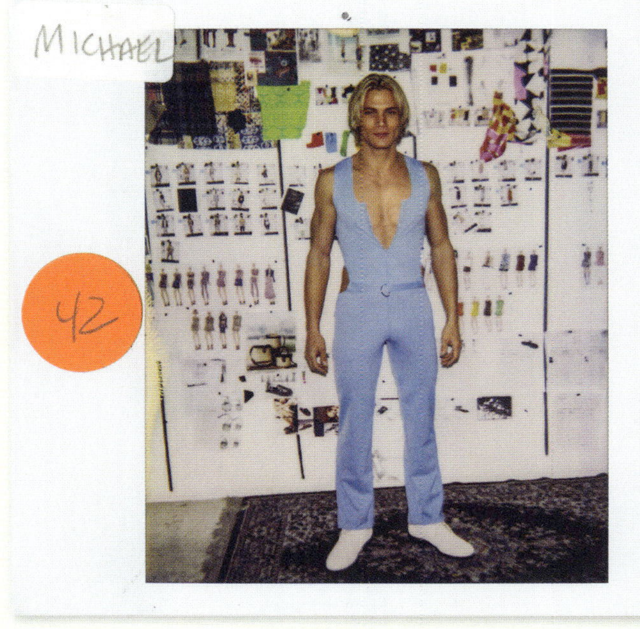

42. MICHAEL
. **Blue jumpsuit**

<u>42.</u> <u>ACCESSORIES</u>
. **White boots**

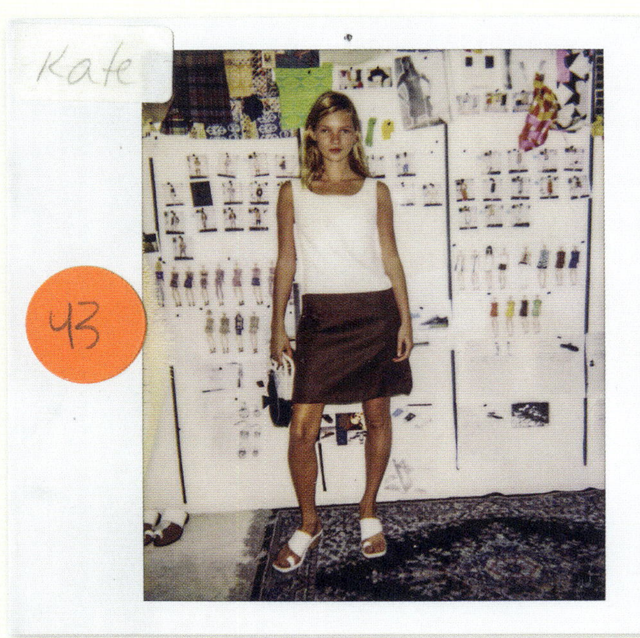

43. KATE
. **Brown + white dress**

<u>43.</u> <u>ACCESSORIES</u>
. **Brown + white bermuda bag**
. **White wedge sandal** (use again in look #59)

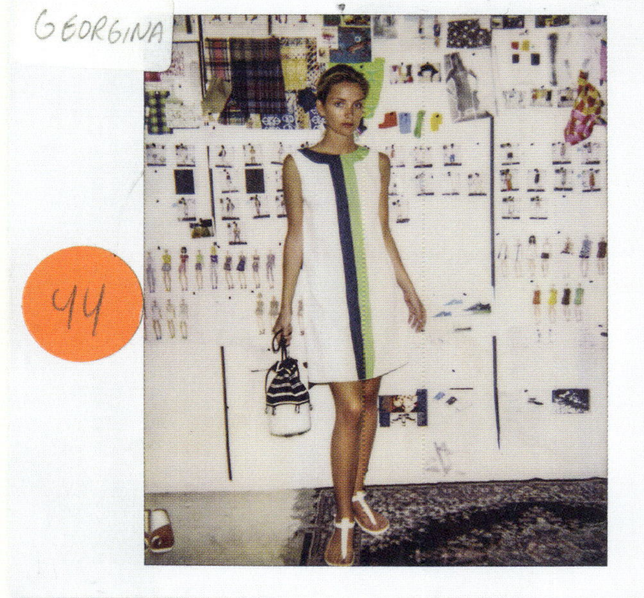

44. GEORGINA
. **White/green/navy dress**

<u>44.</u> <u>ACCESSORIES</u>
. **White/green/navy scarf** (tie around ponytail - see Garren)
. **White/navy bucket bag**
. **White thong sandal** (strap should lie straight down middle of foot) (sz. 10)

Dresser card, Amber Valetta, Spring 19
Dresser card, Micheal Loomis, Spring 1996
Dresser card, Kate Moss, Spring 1996
Dresser card, Georgina Grenville, Spring 1996

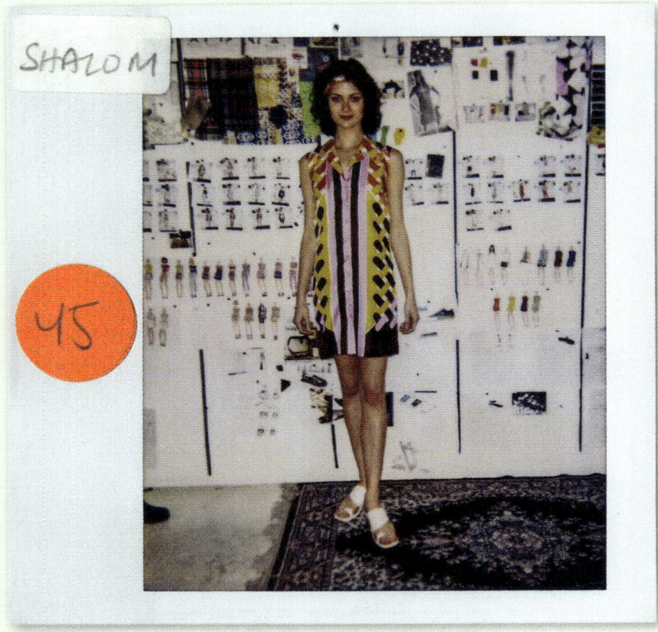

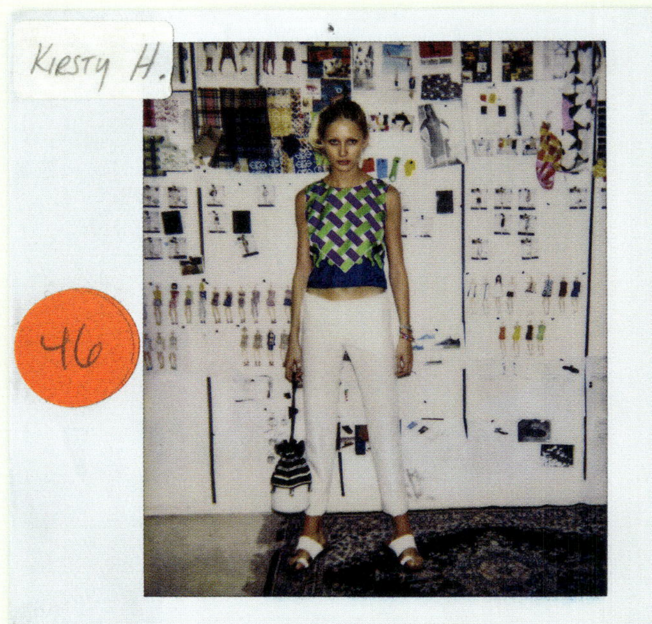

45. SHALOM
. Brown/orange/pink print dress

45. ACCESSORIES
. Yellow/orange/pink/brown scarf (see Garren)
. White wedge sandal (use again in look #64)

46. KIRSTY
. Navy/purple/green print shell
. White pant

46. ACCESSORIES
. White/navy bucket bag
. White flat sandal

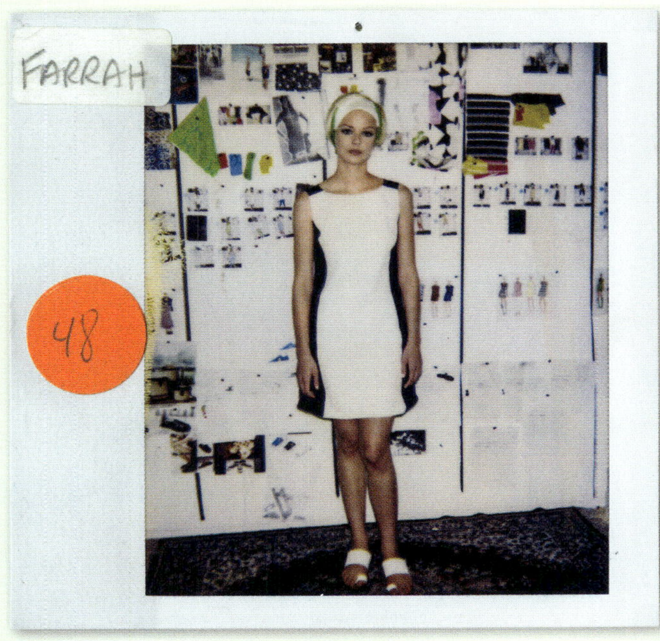

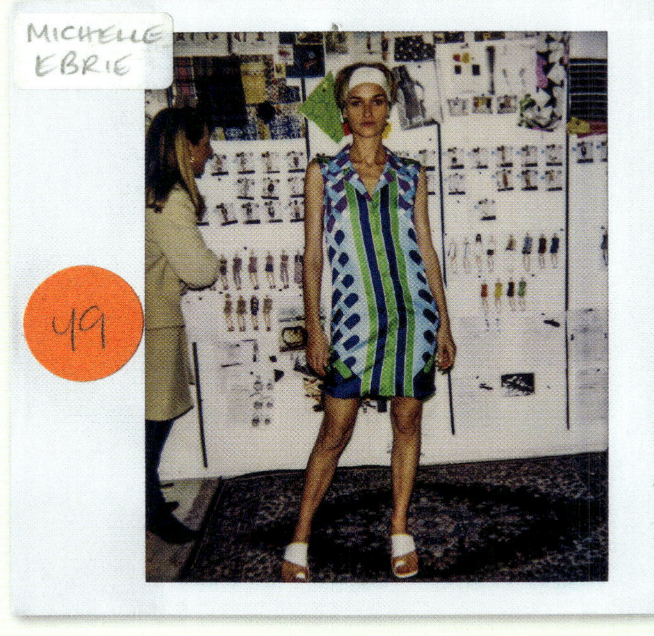

48. FARRAH
. Navy + white dress

48. ACCESSORIES
. Navy/white/green scarf (see Garren)
. White flat sandal

49. MICHELLE EABRY
. Navy/purple/green print dress (button all btns.)

49. ACCESSORIES
. Blue/green/navy scarf (see Garren)
. White wedge sandal

Dresser card, Shalom Harlow, Spring 1996
Dresser card, Kirsty Hume, Spring 1996
Dresser card, Farrah Summerford, Spring 1996
Dresser card, Michele Eabry, Spring 1996

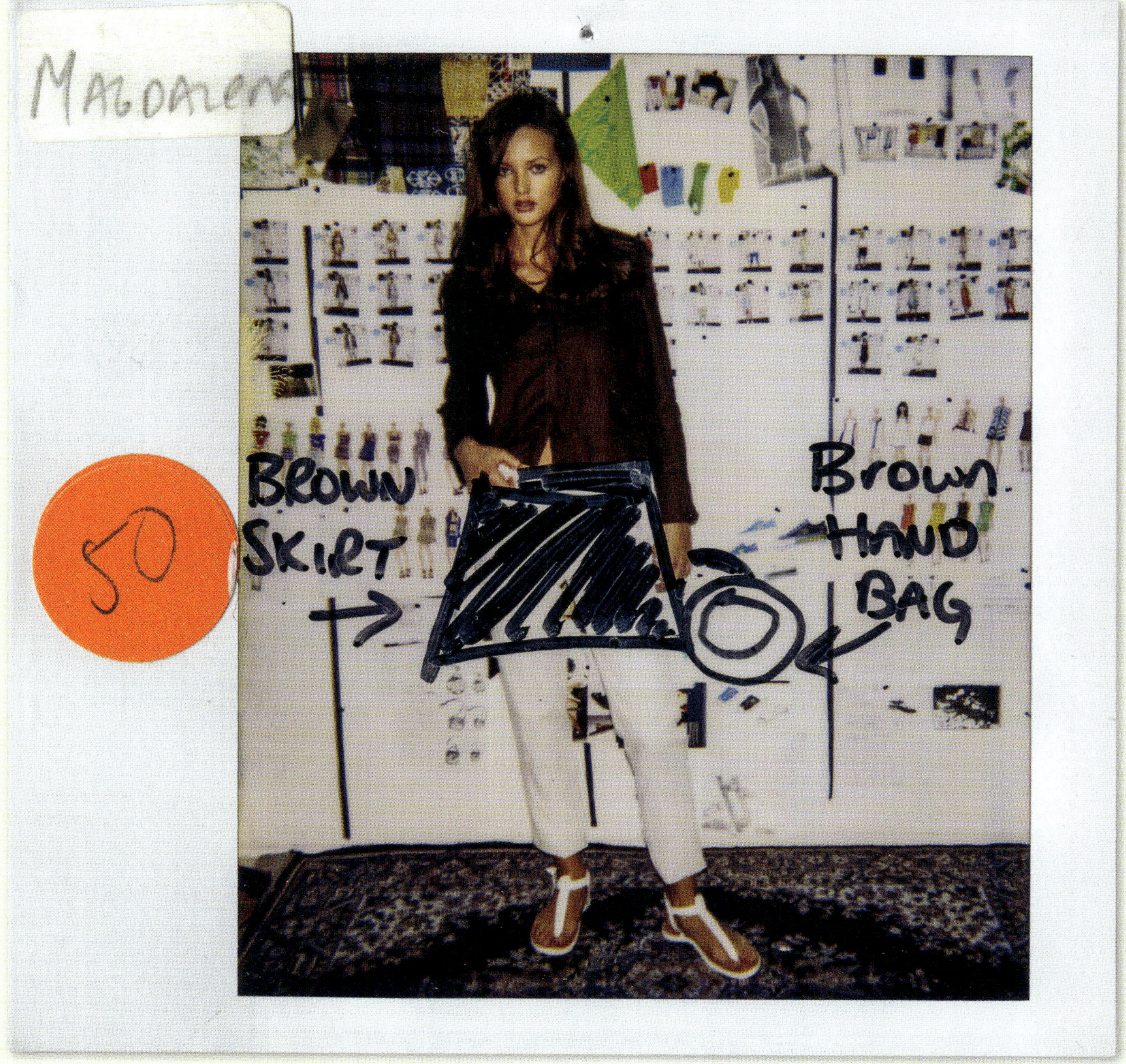

50. MAGDALENA
. **Brown jacket** (top 2 buttons done; the rest open)
. **Brown skirt**

50. ACCESSORIES
. **Brown bermuda bag**
. **White thong sandal**

Dresser card, Magdalena Frackowiak, Spring 1996

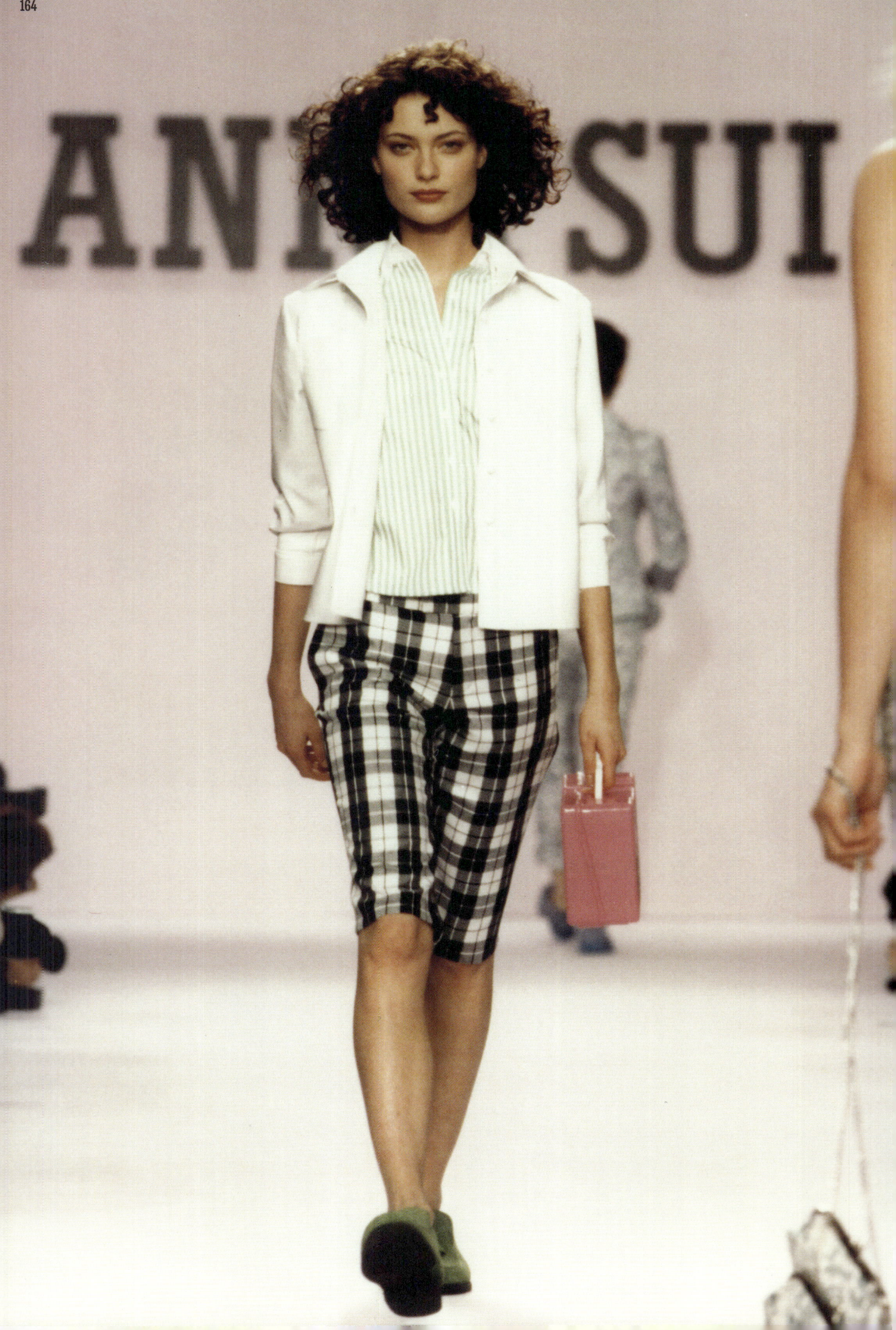

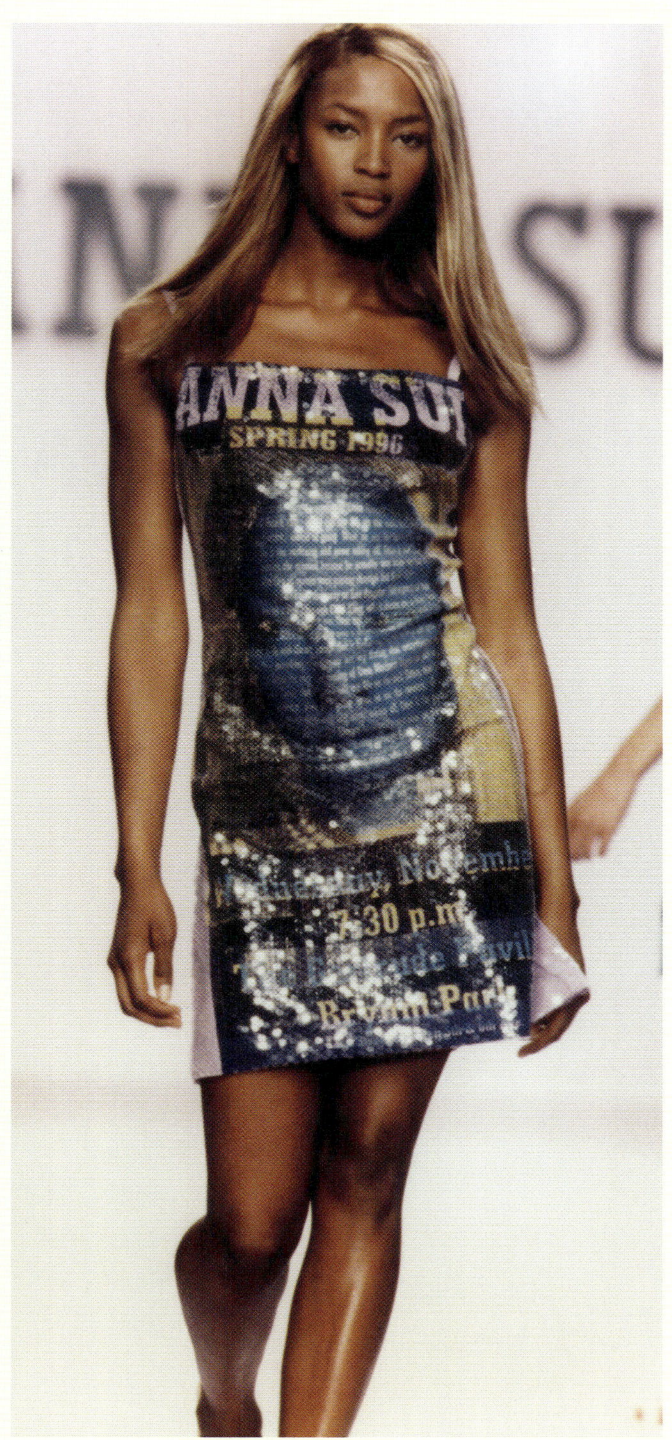

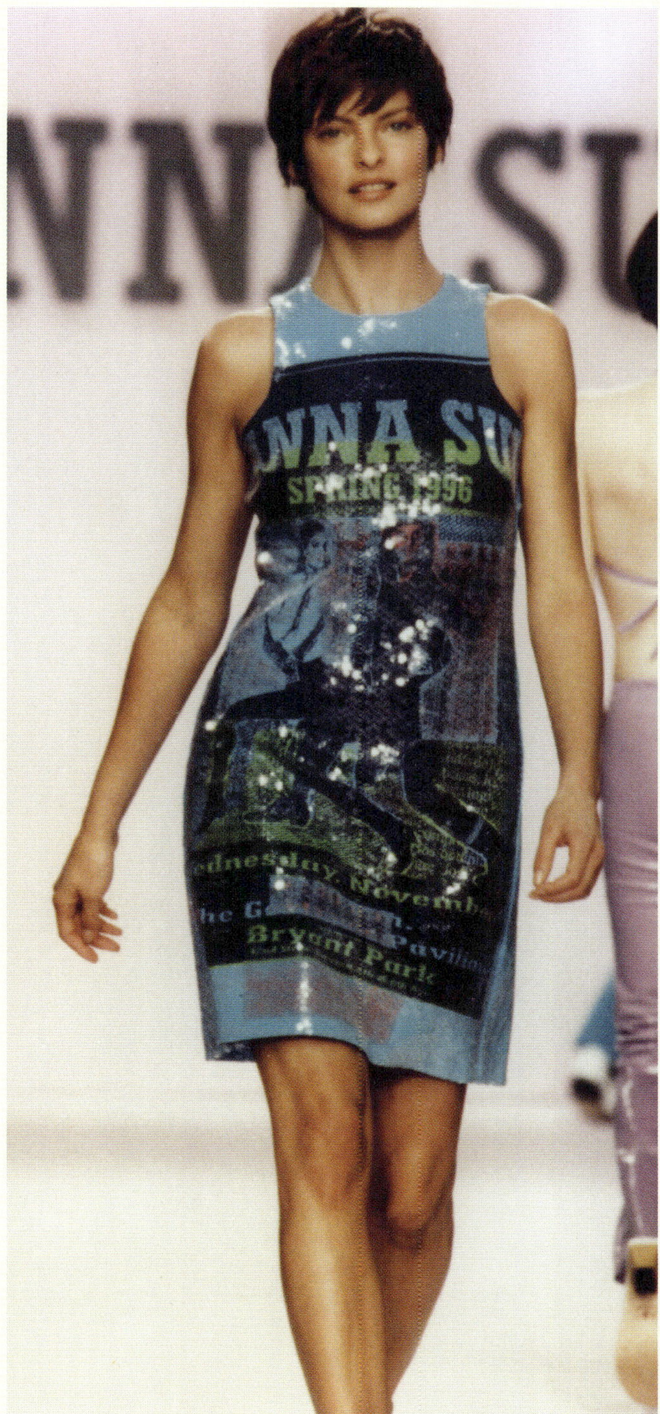

Shalom Harlow, Spring 1996

Naomi Campbell, closing look, Spring 1996

Linda Evangelista, closing look, Spring 1996

These dresses were printed with Steven Meisel photographs and covered in sequins.

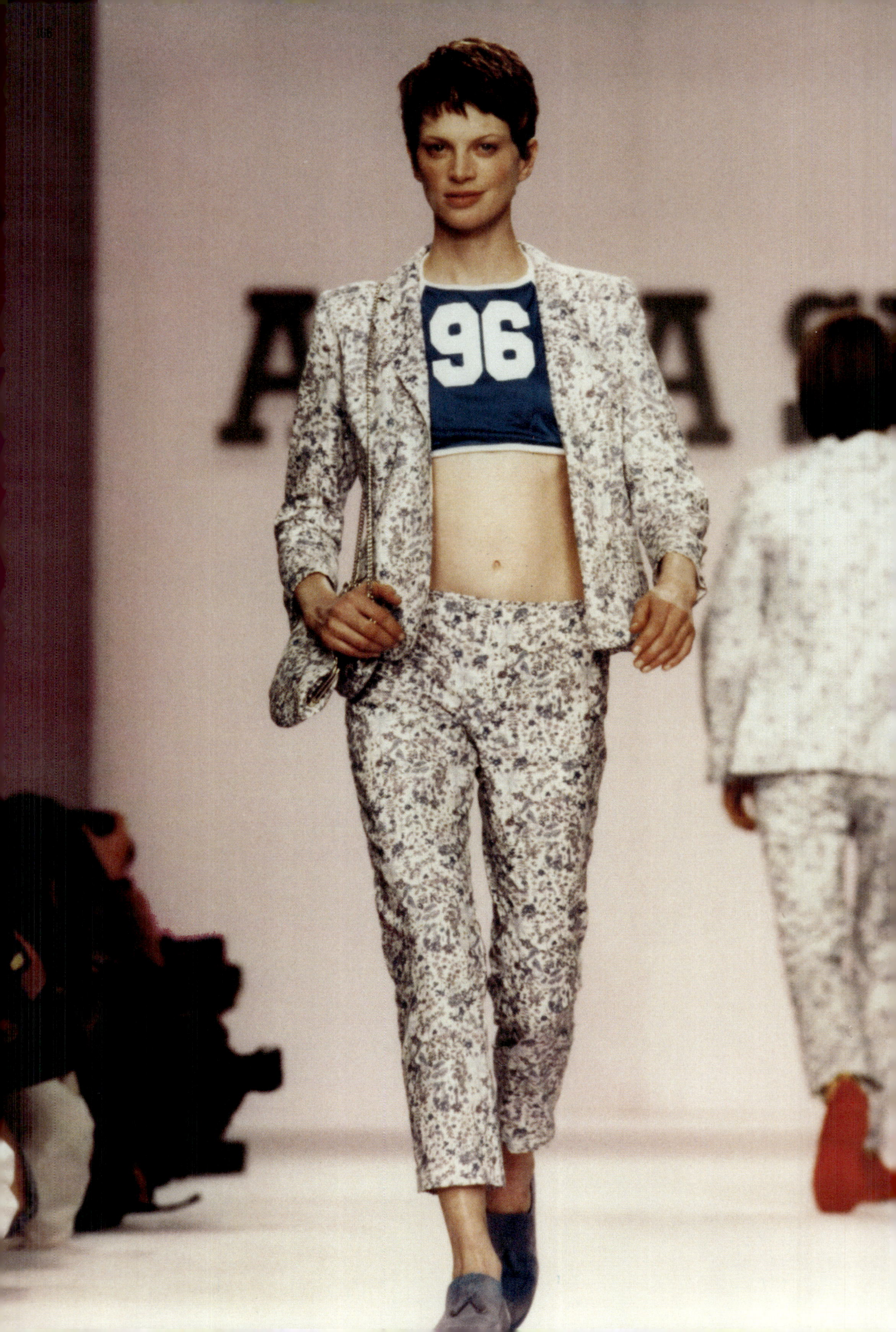
96

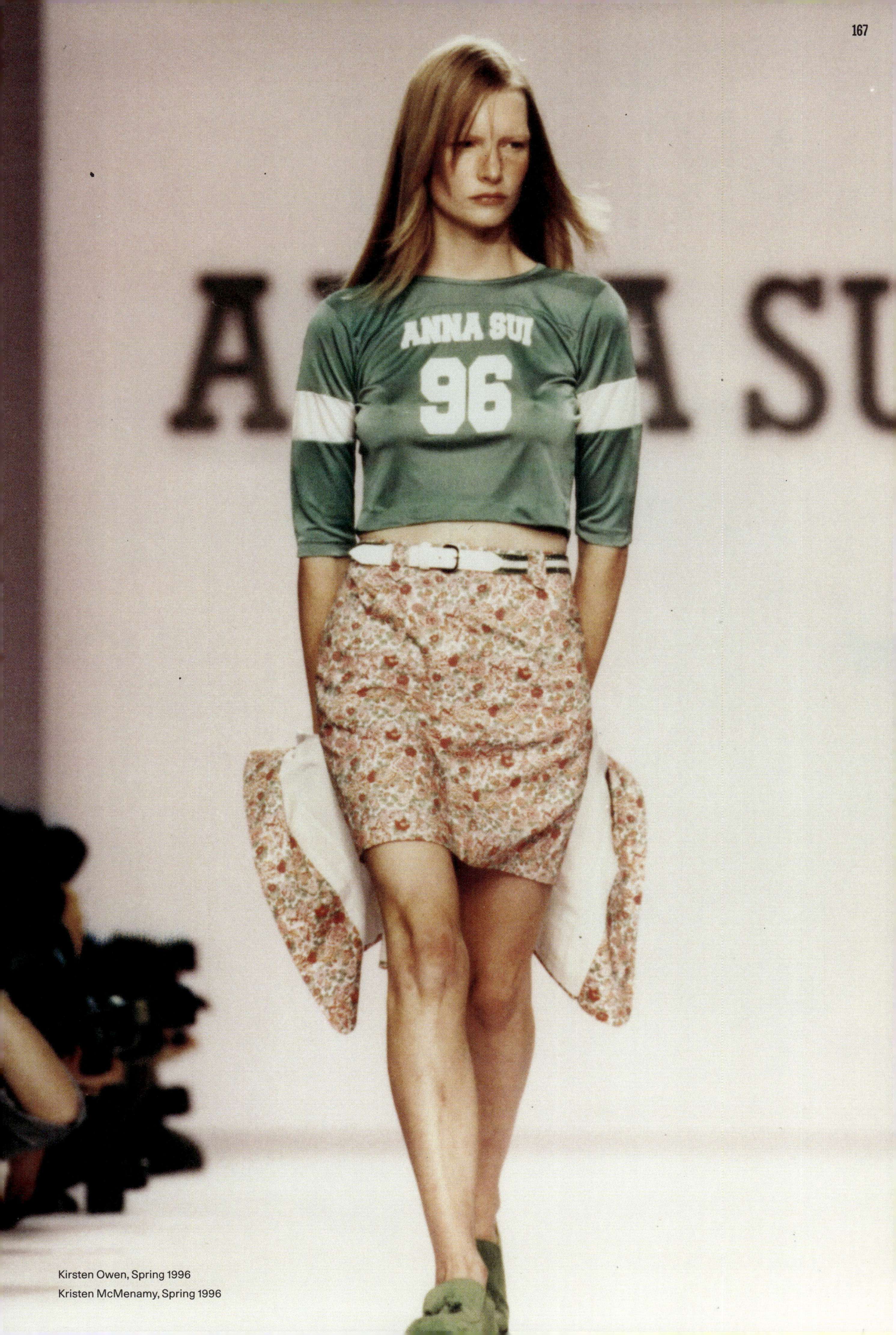

Kirsten Owen, Spring 1996
Kristen McMenamy, Spring 1996

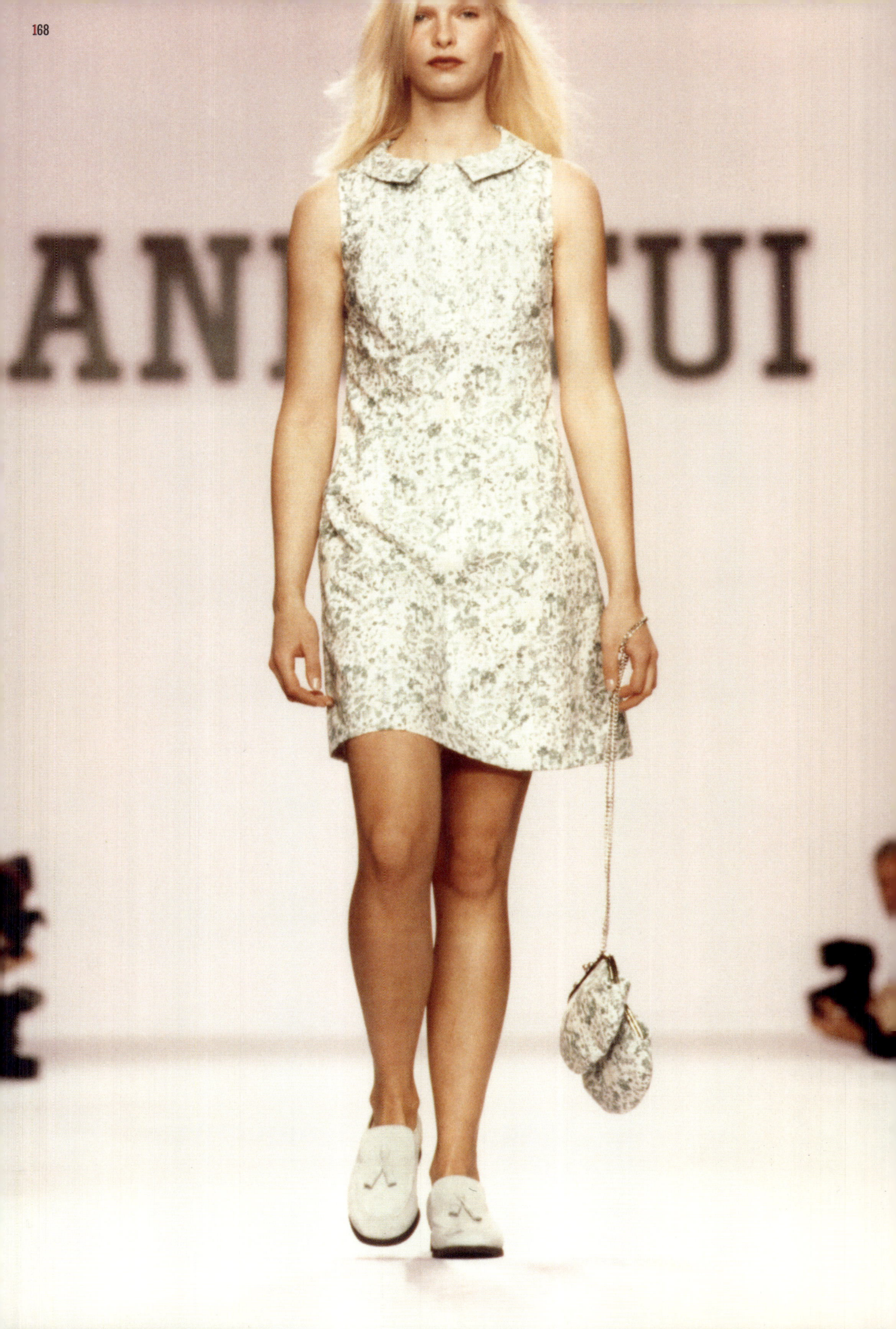

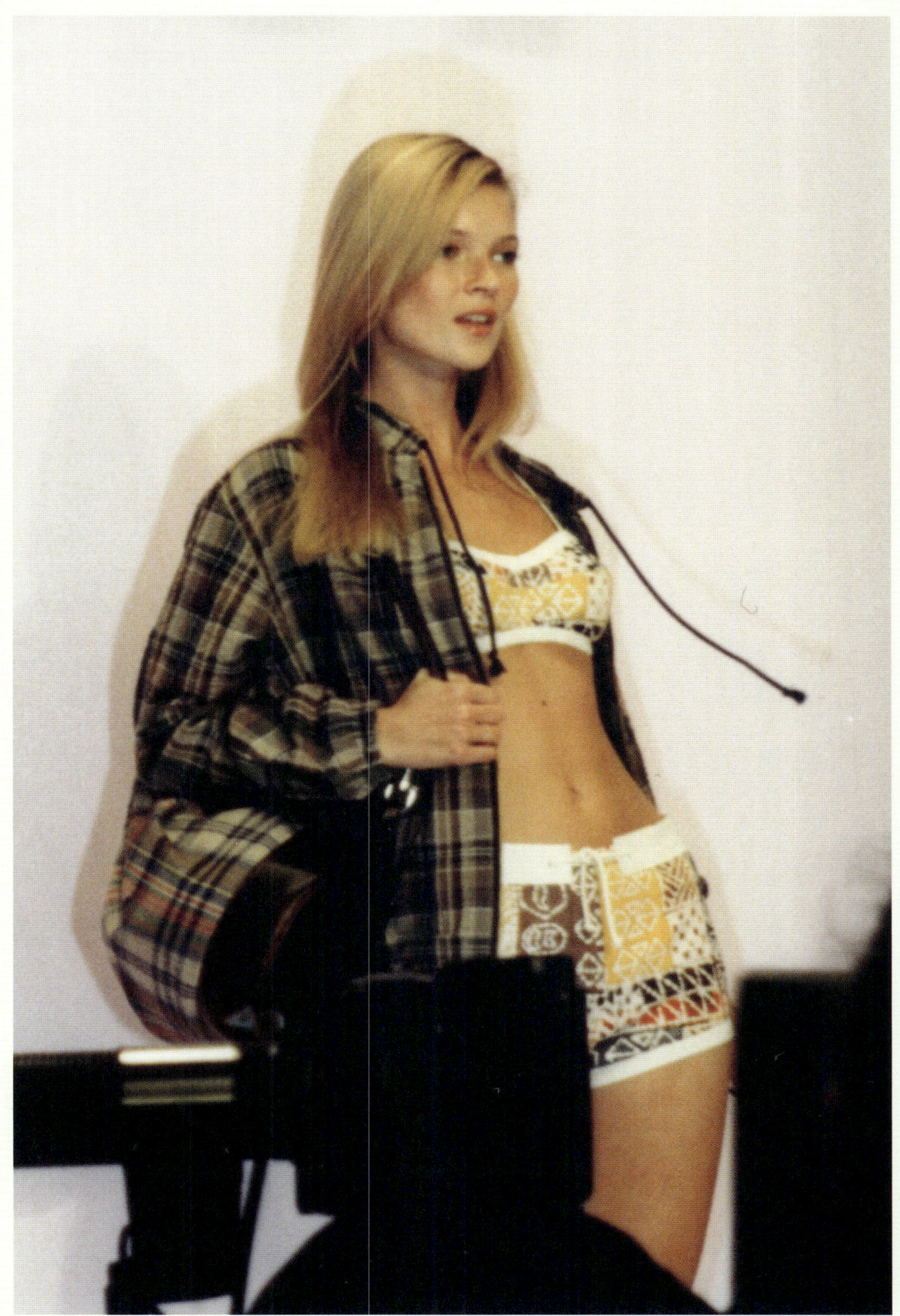

Kristina Kruse, Spring 1996
Kate Moss, Spring 1996

VINTAGE

"I like using nostalgic elements and adding things to bring them into this decade. What I love is to capture an old feeling and have it still look good."

The New York Times, December 1, 1991

ANNA SUI

It was kind of uncommon, especially growing up in middle-class suburbia, to wear secondhand clothes. I read about Barbra Streisand or Laura Nyro doing it. I heard about it, and knew it was a concept. I just thought it was cooler than going to the department store and buying something.

Even when I was in high school, I would see pictures of Paloma Picasso dressed in '40s dresses, and you could see that it was clearly influencing all the British designers, and Yves Saint Laurent did a scandalous collection that was inspired by fashion from the 1940s.

(On January 29, 1971, Yves Saint Laurent presented his "Libération" or "Quarante" collection inspired by 1940s wartime fashion. The couturier was inspired by Paloma Picasso, who dressed in flea market finds. The short dresses, platform shoes, padded shoulders, and heavy makeup evoking Paris during the Occupation caused a scandal. The collection, which was severely criticized by the press, gave full sway to the retro trend that quickly ended up conquering popular fashion).

Our generation, which didn't go through that, found it great and exciting. Because back then you could buy vintage pieces from the '40s and they were in great shape.

During that period, Detroit was very wealthy. When you went to a second-hand store, there was just so much you could buy. There was one thrift shop that I went to that whatever you could stuff into a paper bag from the supermarket, you could get for $5. And I would get like forty suits and coats with embroidery and beading and dresses that were sequined. It was a treasure trove, little hats, fur chubbies, platform shoes, you could find all that, because it was only thirty years between World War II to the '70s. To me, it was the coolest way to dress, all the Warhol movies, all the stars dressed that way, everybody was trying to look like movie stars

Shalom Harlow,
Vogue (Italy) magazine, July 1993

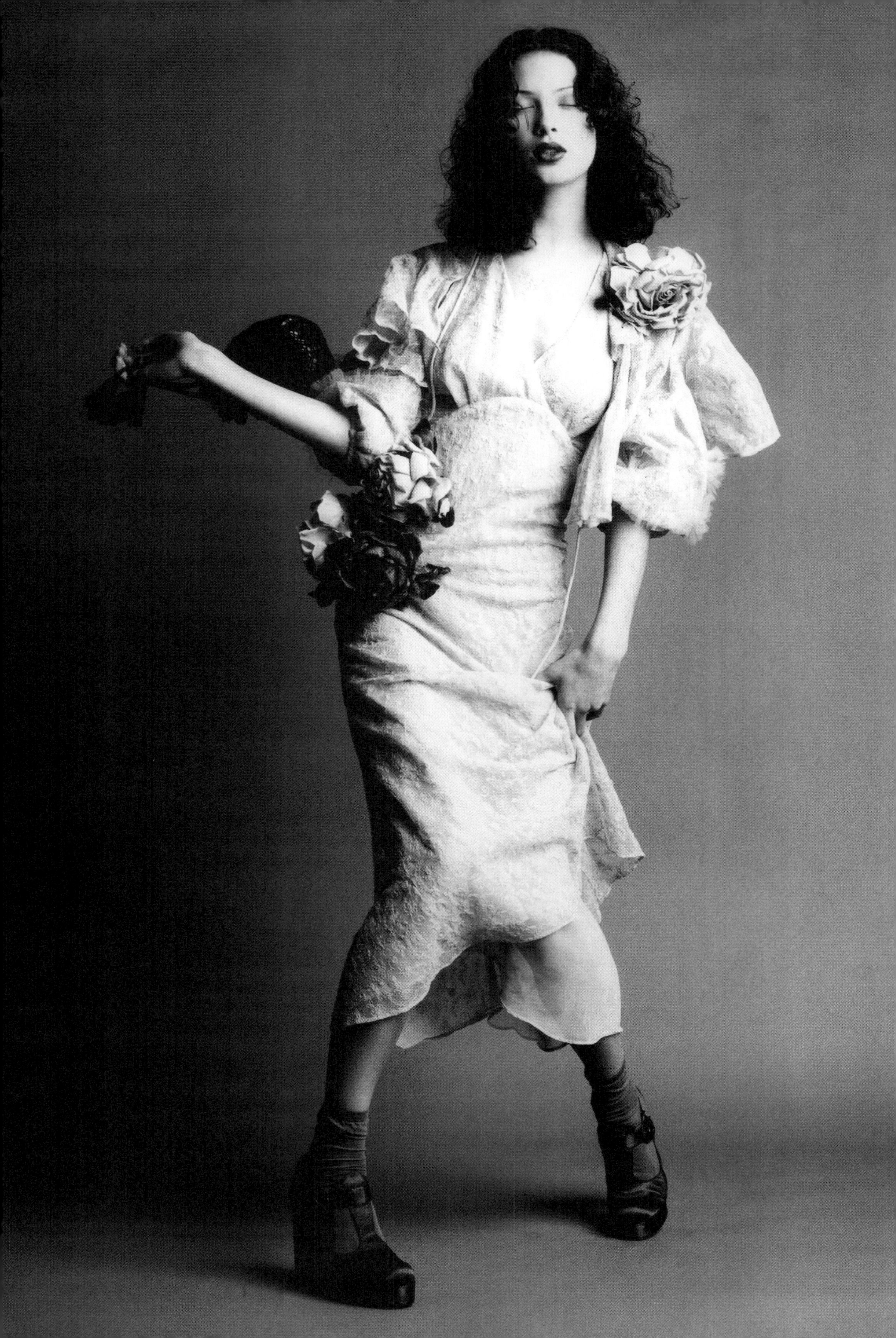

at that point. I loved all the jewelry, and you could see clearly how things were handmade from back when things weren't all manufactured—the handicrafts were still so prevalent. I loved all that. So that's kind of what made me love vintage and going to vintage stores and flea markets.

It wasn't really a concept to wear secondhand clothes at that point. And I think everyone that had these secondhand stores was just thrilled that kids were coming in and buying these things and mixing it with jeans and T-shirts. The '40s is one of my favorite periods, and you can see that over and over again in my collections where there's a vintage look but it's mixed with more contemporary clothes.

When we were doing fittings, the models were always asking where do you go vintage shopping, where is there a good flea market? Especially if they were new to town or new to the concept, particularly coming from a middle-class background, wearing secondhand clothing was really novel. And there was not a proliferation of secondhand stores like there are today, but I always managed to find them. And when I was in high school, I was already doing that, but not many people were wearing secondhand clothes at that point.

I think that there's always a touch of that flea market element in my collections. There's always a touch of that vintage element. No matter what time period or inspiration I'm using, I still like the handicraft aspect. There's still appliqué. There's still some sort of embroidery. There're still vintage details. Even when I did my preppy collection, it was still vintage preppy. I can't help myself with that. And as much as I want to modernize it, I still always look back to the things that I love.

Everyone has a chimera, which is a quest for the unattainable. And I think that that's what this whole thing is about—is that I saw glimpses of it, I didn't know what it was, but I knew I liked it. So, through my whole life and career, a lot of that discovery is a lot of the elements that I put into my collection. Again, I was lucky enough to be able to travel to Europe and start discovering those things, finding them in flea markets, finding them in secondhand stores, or actually meeting people from that period. And they would tell me about who their influences were, where they were getting their vintage—about shopping on Portobello Road, all that information is kind of like my chimera. I always think like, I've almost got it. I've almost got it, you know? I think that's really what my whole MO is, that's what's behind it all.

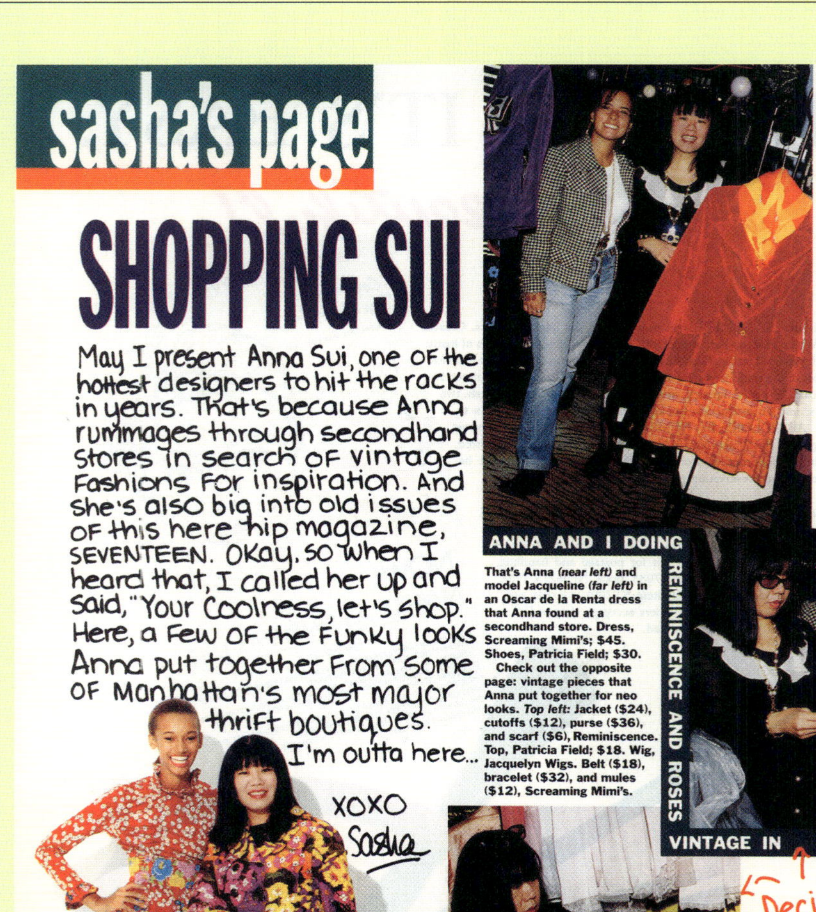
sasha's page

SHOPPING SUI

May I present Anna Sui, one of the hottest designers to hit the racks in years. That's because Anna rummages through secondhand stores in search of vintage fashions for inspiration. And she's also big into old issues of this here hip magazine, SEVENTEEN. Okay, so when I heard that, I called her up and said, "Your Coolness, let's shop." Here, a few of the funky looks Anna put together from some of Manhattan's most major thrift boutiques. I'm outta here... XOXO Sasha

ANNA AND I DOING REMINISCENCE AND ROSES VINTAGE IN NYC

That's Anna *(near left)* and model Jacqueline *(far left)* in an Oscar de la Renta dress that Anna found at a secondhand store. Dress, Screaming Mimi's; $45. Shoes, Patricia Field; $30.

Check out the opposite page: vintage pieces that Anna put together for neo looks. *Top left:* Jacket ($24), cutoffs ($12), purse ($36), and scarf ($6), Reminiscence. Top, Patricia Field; $18. Wig, Jacquelyn Wigs. Belt ($18), bracelet ($32), and mules ($12), Screaming Mimi's.

MARC JACOBS

Anna is a huge lover of fashion and there are perhaps periods in fashion that she prefers or that she has a real connection to. She's always loved finding vintage pieces. It was so different then to what it is now. New York was filled with vintage clothing stores. Some of them were super cool and you'd always be able to find some kind of treasure in them. And now vintage doesn't exist the way it used to be. And in the East Village, you could find places. I remember going vintage shopping with her and I bought this opera costume that was all black velvet with tons of frilly stuff coming out of the sleeves [see p. 24]. And then I remember trips with Anna in London where we were all starving and Anna would be like, no, no, we have to keep shopping because everybody's gonna close in two hours. And she just loved vintage shopping, and she was very inspired by these vintage finds. I know Saint Laurent did a collection that was very controversial. It was his most controversial collection. And it was very much based on the models of the '70s period and the kind of 1940s clothes they were finding in thrift shops. So like some of the coolest, most stylish models back in the '70s were all dressed in all these vintage clothes that they used to find at the Paris flea markets or in the London vintage stores. That's just one of those periods that Anna loves. It's always had this cool girl vibe, that a cool girl mixes vintage clothes with whatever that she's got—that's style.

LINDA EVANGELISTA

Anna was always very inspired by vintage. Every designer looks to either

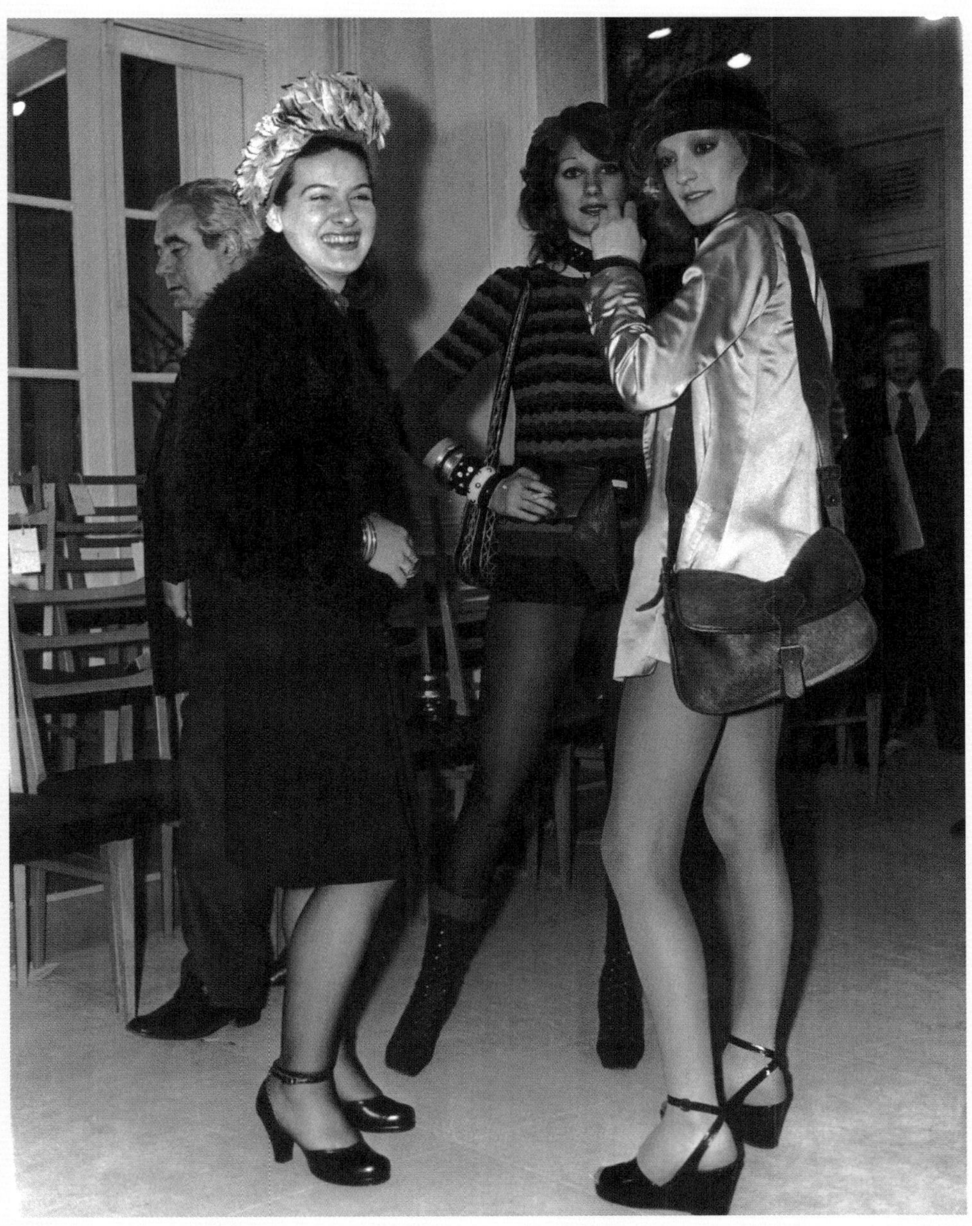

culture or the past for inspiration. I remember being in Rome with Anna [see p. 28] for Valentino's thirtieth anniversary. And it was the first big gala I had ever been to. I went with Anna and Steven Meisel, and we had the most wonderful weekend. I remember going to the Valentino archives with them to choose some outfits for the events happening that weekend. And instead of choosing all the recent pieces he designed, like everyone else, we went in and grabbed things from the '50s and '60s. I was a redhead for a very brief moment, and that's where I debuted it. We chose a green suit, and a pink evening gown. the gala was incredible—all those Italian women with their real jewels. Anna played a big part in helping to dress me. It was so much fun. She's always inspired by retro, but takes it to today and puts her flair into it and makes it her own.

SOFIA COPPOLA

I always loved fashion since I was a really little kid and the people that my parents were friends with were very fashionable. There was this one, Monique Montgomery, who was the wife of a film producer who, in the late '70s, would wear '40s dresses and Bakelite jewelry. And I always remember that as a little kid. There's a side of Anna that that relates to that. I've always loved the way that the '40s were done in the '70s and I think she does it so well. There's something always glamorous about that. The Saint Laurent collection in the 1970s was such a scandal, and I loved movies that were set in the '30s and the '70s—the concept of fashion is that it is always about the idea of something evolving and changing so often. In the '90s I was in my early 20s, and it was an exciting time to be a young person out in the world buying your own clothes for the first time. We wore a lot of thrift store clothes, and I really felt like Anna and Marc were making clothes that I was excited about, that felt like for me and not how it felt when the clothes were for unrealistic unattainable images of women. It was much more casual in a way that was relatable. Anna's clothes were always inventive, creative, and beautiful. She's very feminine and you felt like she loves and understands women. She drew on a lot of references that you hadn't seen in clothes before but came from vintage and antiques, and different bands and eras and music scenes—and put together in a way that just hadn't been done before. She just has a real point of view which was exciting and unique. And it was fun to see her world. She loves beauty and always has a kind of a sparkle and magic to it.

Sasha Charnin's page, *Seventeen* magazine, January 1992

Paloma Picasso, Marisa Berenson, and Loulou de la Falaise at the Yves Saint Laurent collection, January 1971

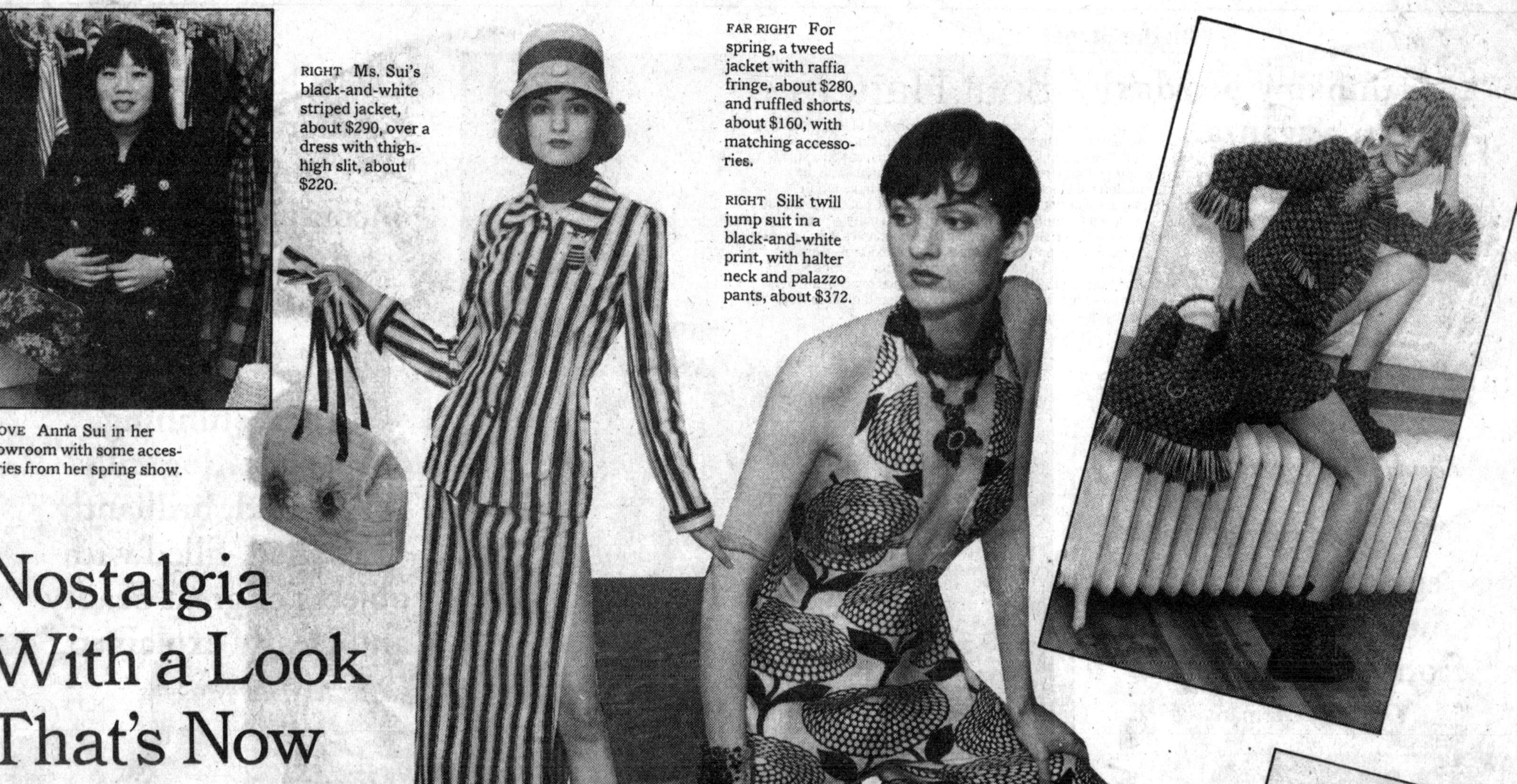

ABOVE Anna Sui in her showroom with some accessories from her spring show.

RIGHT Ms. Sui's black-and-white striped jacket, about $290, over a dress with thigh-high slit, about $220.

FAR RIGHT For spring, a tweed jacket with raffia fringe, about $280, and ruffled shorts, about $160, with matching accessories.

RIGHT Silk twill jump suit in a black-and-white print, with halter neck and palazzo pants, about $372.

Nostalgia With a Look That's Now

Anna Sui's inspiration may come from a Balenciaga suit in an old magazine, from a Barbie doll's traveling costume, from a photograph of Lady Diana Cooper working in her garden or from a length of vintage fabric. Then her imagination soars.

The Balenciaga suit ends up with raffia fringe and ruffled shorts. Barbie's straw hat and cork-soled sandals become accessories for striped denim sportswear, along with Lady Diana's gardening gloves and a mammoth bumblebee pin. The vintage fabric, a bold print from the 1960's, leads to a revival of palazzo pants.

"I like using nostalgic elements and adding things to bring them into this decade," the designer said. "What I love is to capture an old feeling and have it still look good."

Youth and Wit

Although Ms. Sui has been running her own business for 11 years, interpreting the latest fashions for the junior market, she made a breakthrough in April with her first formal show, at which some of the world's top models cavorted in her youthful clothes and witty accessories. Fashion magazines featured her clothes; department stores put them in the windows. Her spring show last month was equally successful.

"Doing fashion shows has taken me to another level," Ms. Sui said, sitting in her New York showroom surrounded by samples of her spring clothing and accessories. "Last year I did $1.75 million. This year I'm doing much better than that. The way the economy is now, I'm getting a lot of attention because of my prices."

She keeps prices down by using less expensive fabrics like denim and piqué and by having the clothes made in New York, where she can keep tabs on the factories and correct mistakes before they become costly.

Her fall collection sold out quickly at Bloomingdale's, said Kalman Ruttenstein, the store's vice president for fashion direction, who put her black chiffon dresses in the window with

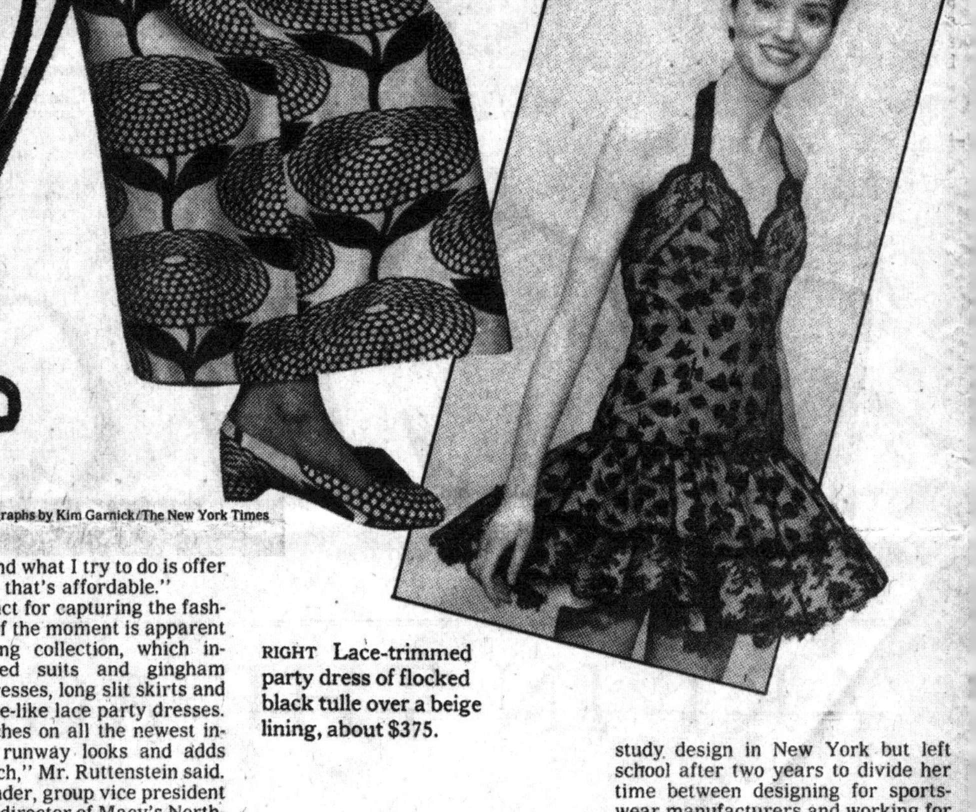

Photographs by Kim Garnick/The New York Times

ABOVE Yellow-and-black gingham dress with quilted skirt, about $250, worn over a black tulle petticoat.

RIGHT Lace-trimmed party dress of flocked black tulle over a beige lining, about $375.

Harley-Davidson motorcycles in November. "She probably offers more fashion for the price than anyone else at that price range," Mr. Ruttenstein said, "and the customer responded."

While most of the new generation of designers is selling jackets for $400 or $500, sometimes much more, Ms. Sui's jackets are $200 to $300. "Part of the fun of my clothing is that it's not so precious," she said. "You can enjoy yourself wearing them because you don't have to worry about damaging a $2,000 jacket. What's fun about fashion to me is that it's always changing, and what I try to do is offer a new thing that's affordable."

Her instinct for capturing the fashion feeling of the moment is apparent in the spring collection, which includes tweed suits and gingham baby-doll dresses, long slit skirts and lacy, lingerie-like lace party dresses.

"She touches on all the newest international runway looks and adds her own touch," Mr. Ruttenstein said.

Bruce Binder, group vice president and fashion director of Macy's Northeast, plans to move Anna Sui's clothes from the junior department to New Signatures with the work of other hot young designers. "She has tremendous creativity, but she's willing to work with a store and make changes for us," he said. "Her accessories are such fun we'll be housing them together with her clothes."

Accessories are one way she puts her signature on her styles. Tweeds, gingham checks and 1960's prints are shown with matching hats, bags and shoes. The hats are made for her by James Coviello, the bags by Jill Stuart. Eric Beamon makes beaded jewelry, which Ms. Sui describes as part hippie and part David Webb, in colors to go with the clothes.

"I love accessories and working with accessory designers," Ms. Sui said. "I collect jewelry and bags and hats, even though I never wear hats."

Her knack for putting together a total look comes from the years she spent as a stylist for the fashion photographer Steven Meisel, who has been a friend since their days as students at the Parsons School of Design. She left her native Detroit to study design in New York but left school after two years to divide her time between designing for sportswear manufacturers and working for Mr. Meisel. As his stylist she met star models like Linda Evangelista, Christy Turlington and Naomi Campbell, who helped to attract other models for her shows.

"Last November I took time off and did styling with Madonna and Lady Miss Kier," she said. "For many years I couldn't decide between styling and designing. It's kind of a youthful fantasy that you can do everything, but you have to learn the business you're in. Basically, the most important thing, I've learned, is to ship the clothes on time with good quality."

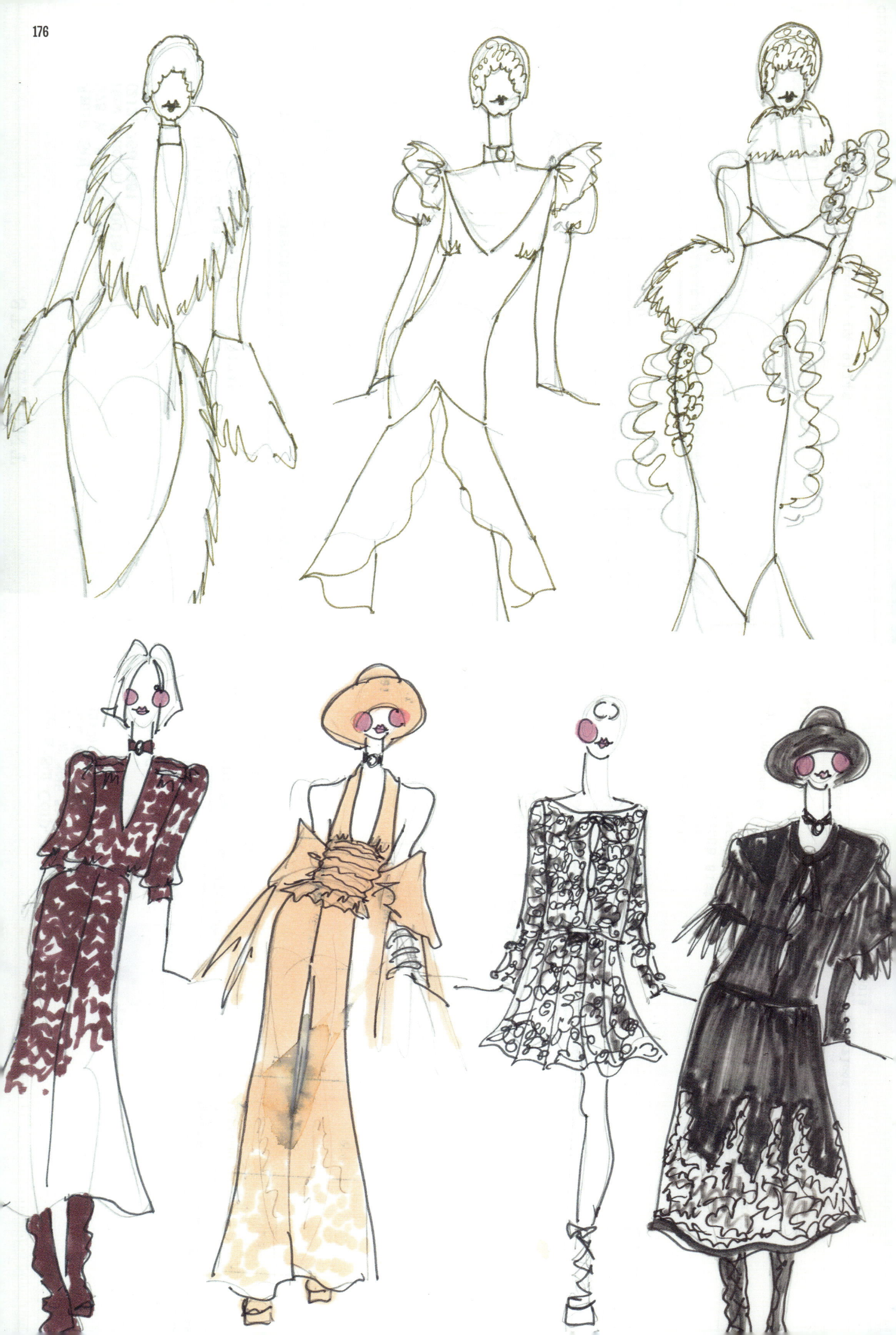

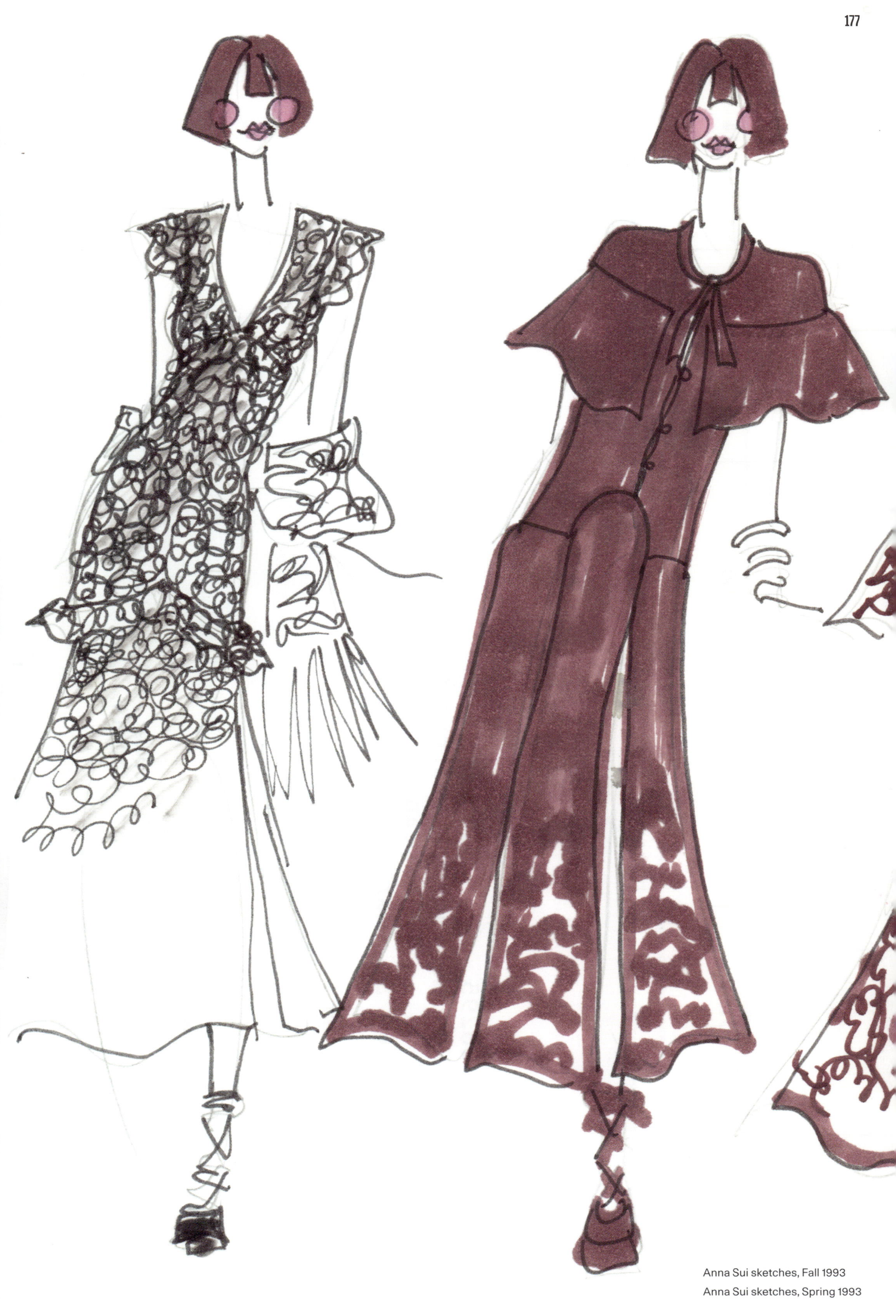

Anna Sui sketches, Fall 1993
Anna Sui sketches, Spring 1993

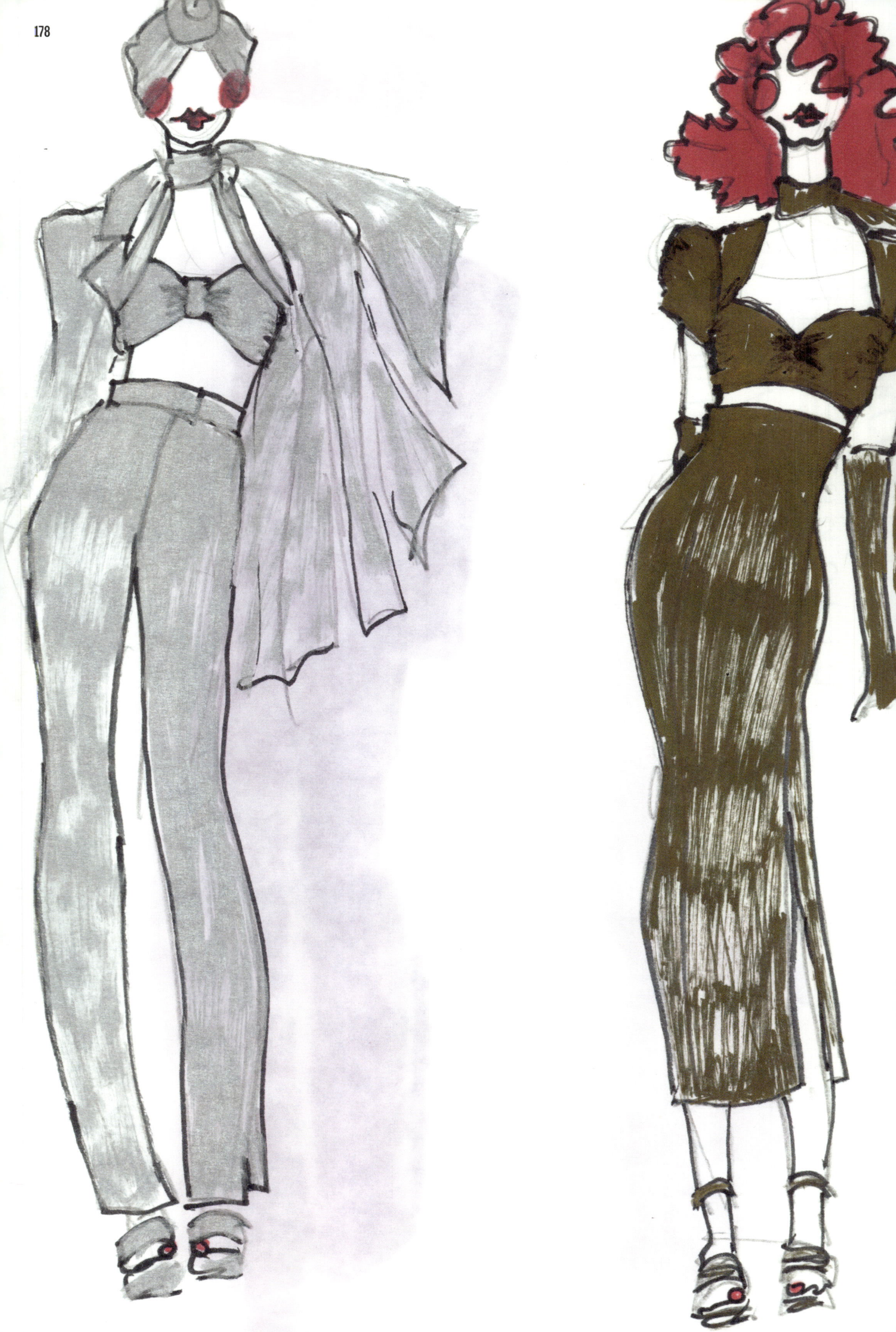

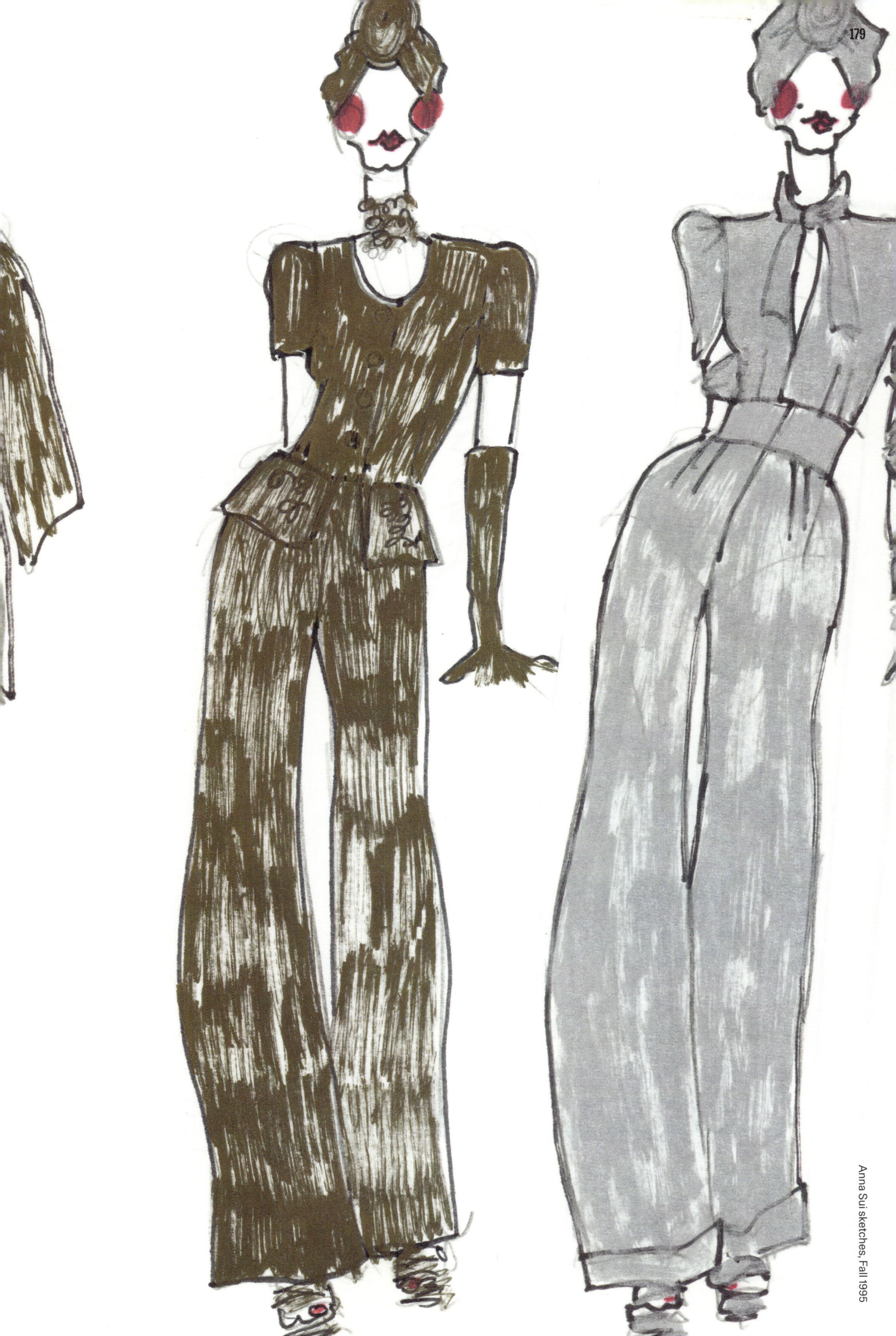

Anna Sui sketches, Fall 1995

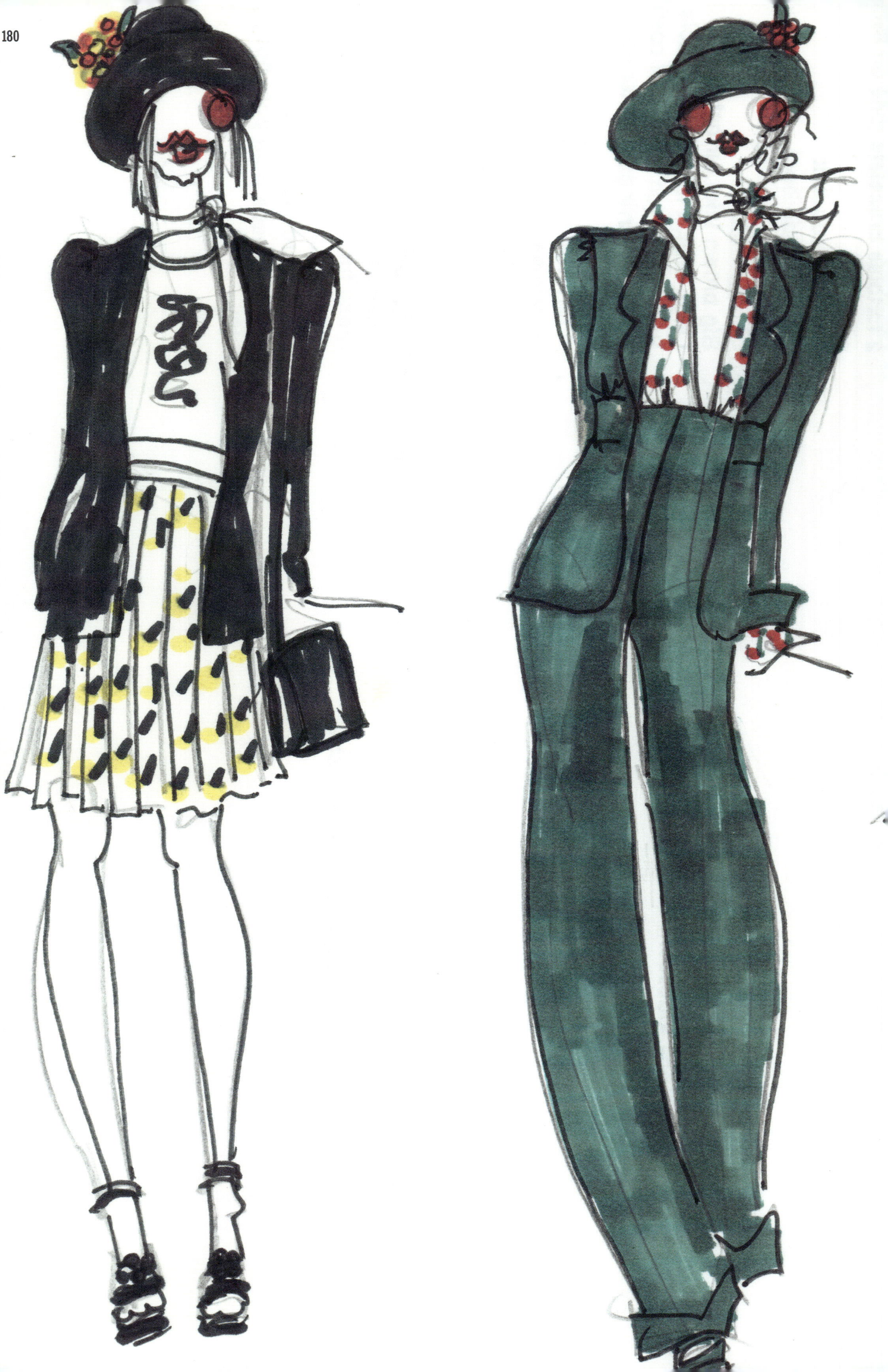

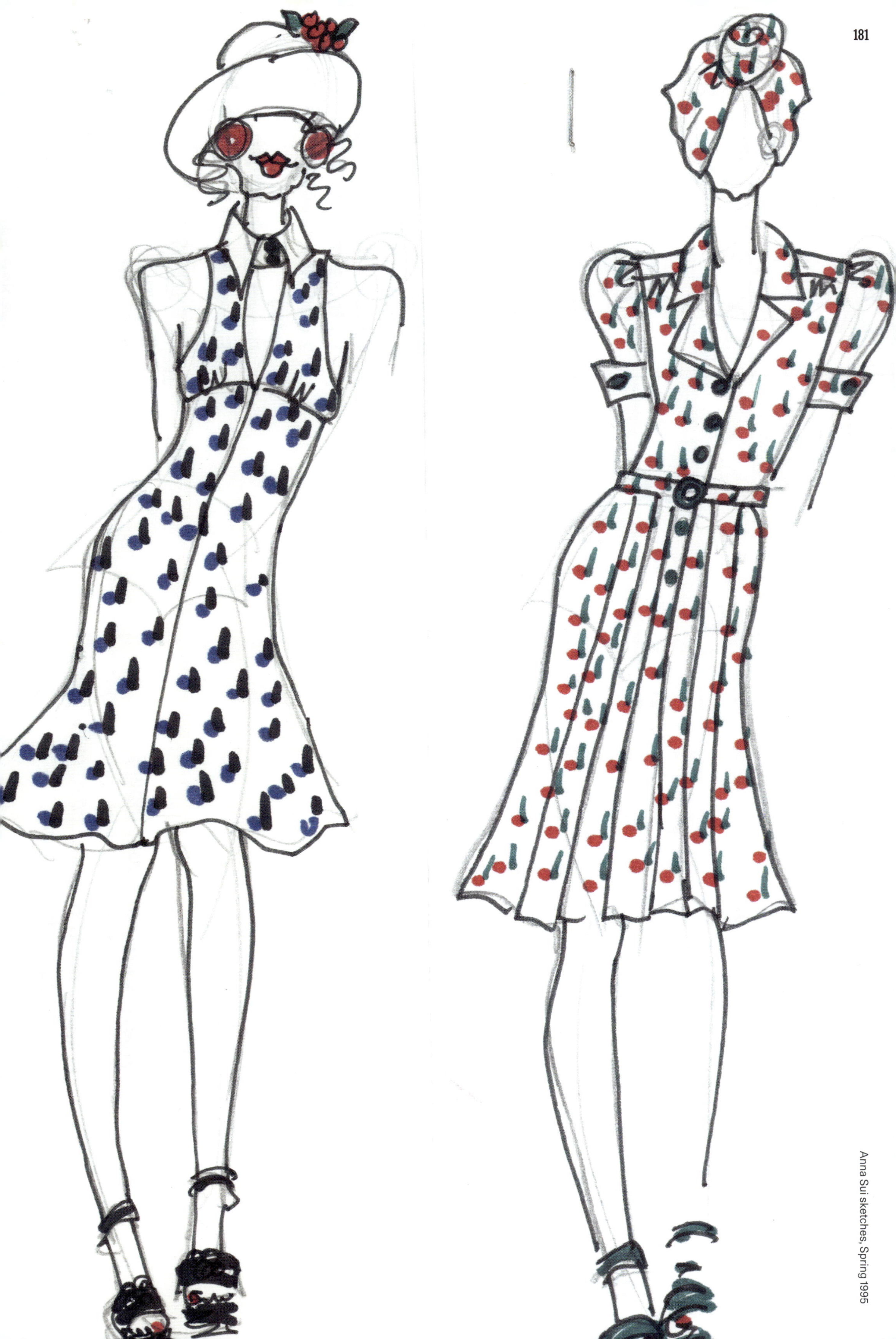

Anna Sui sketches, Spring 1995

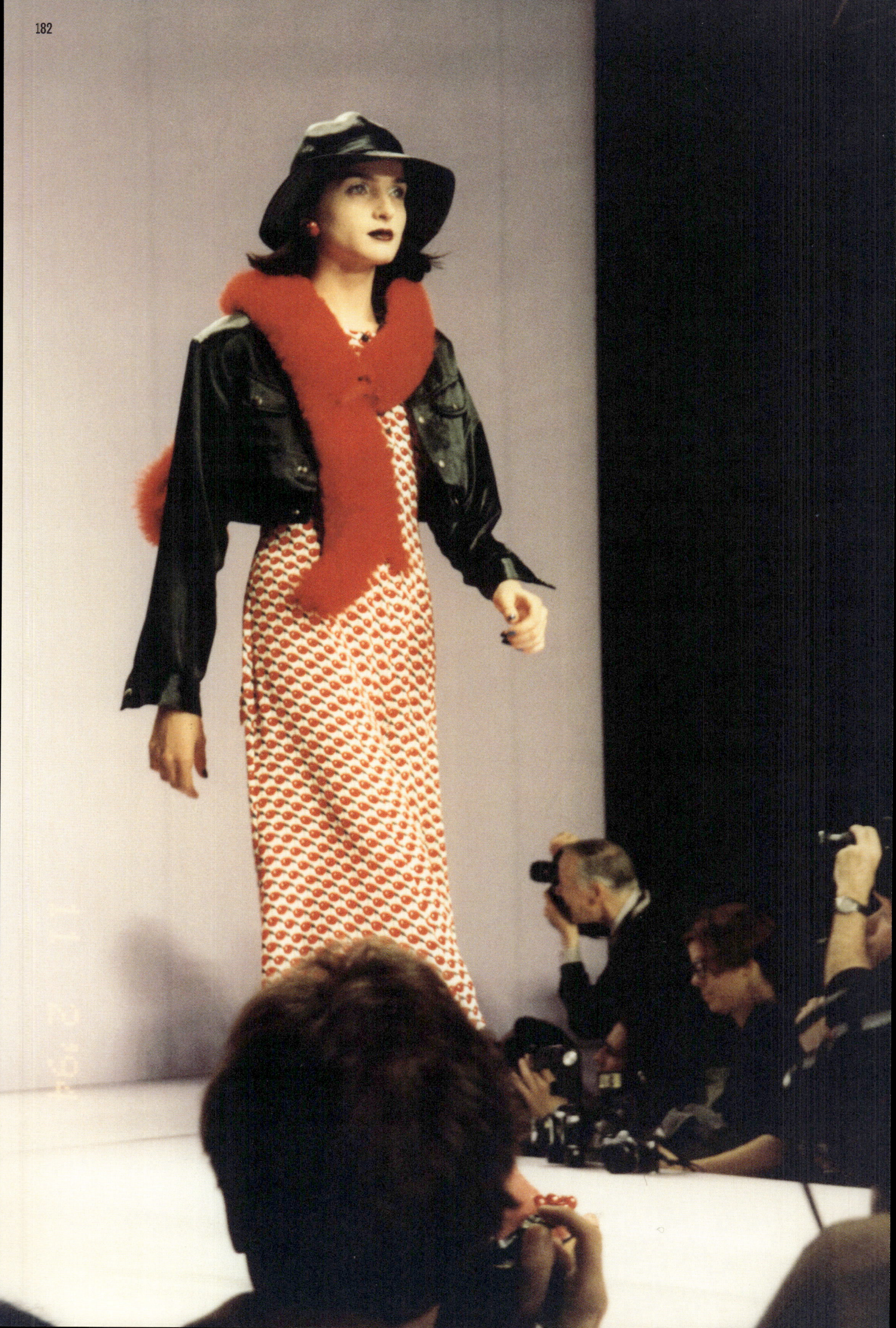

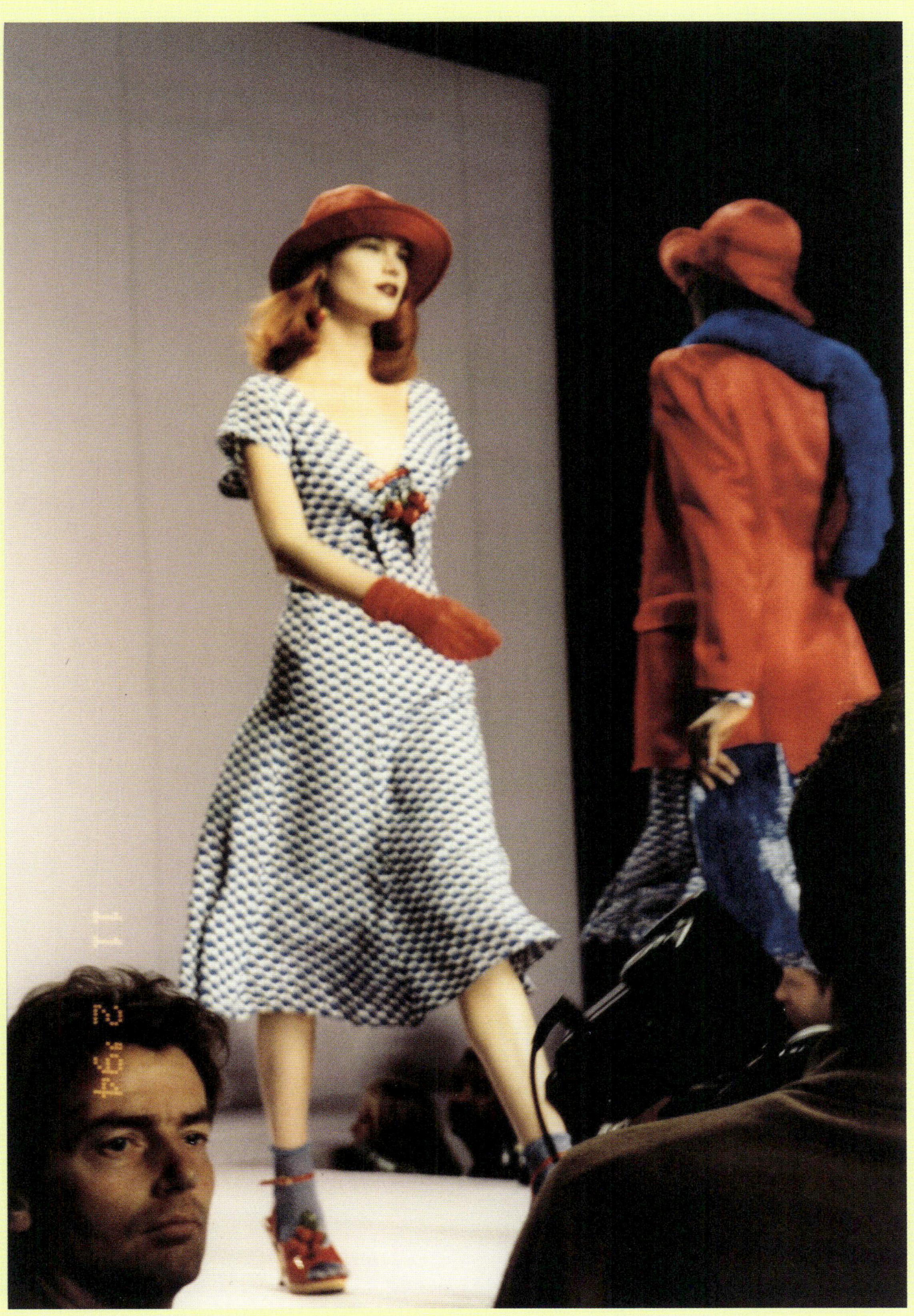

Michelle Hicks, Spring 1995
Meghan Douglas, Spring 1995

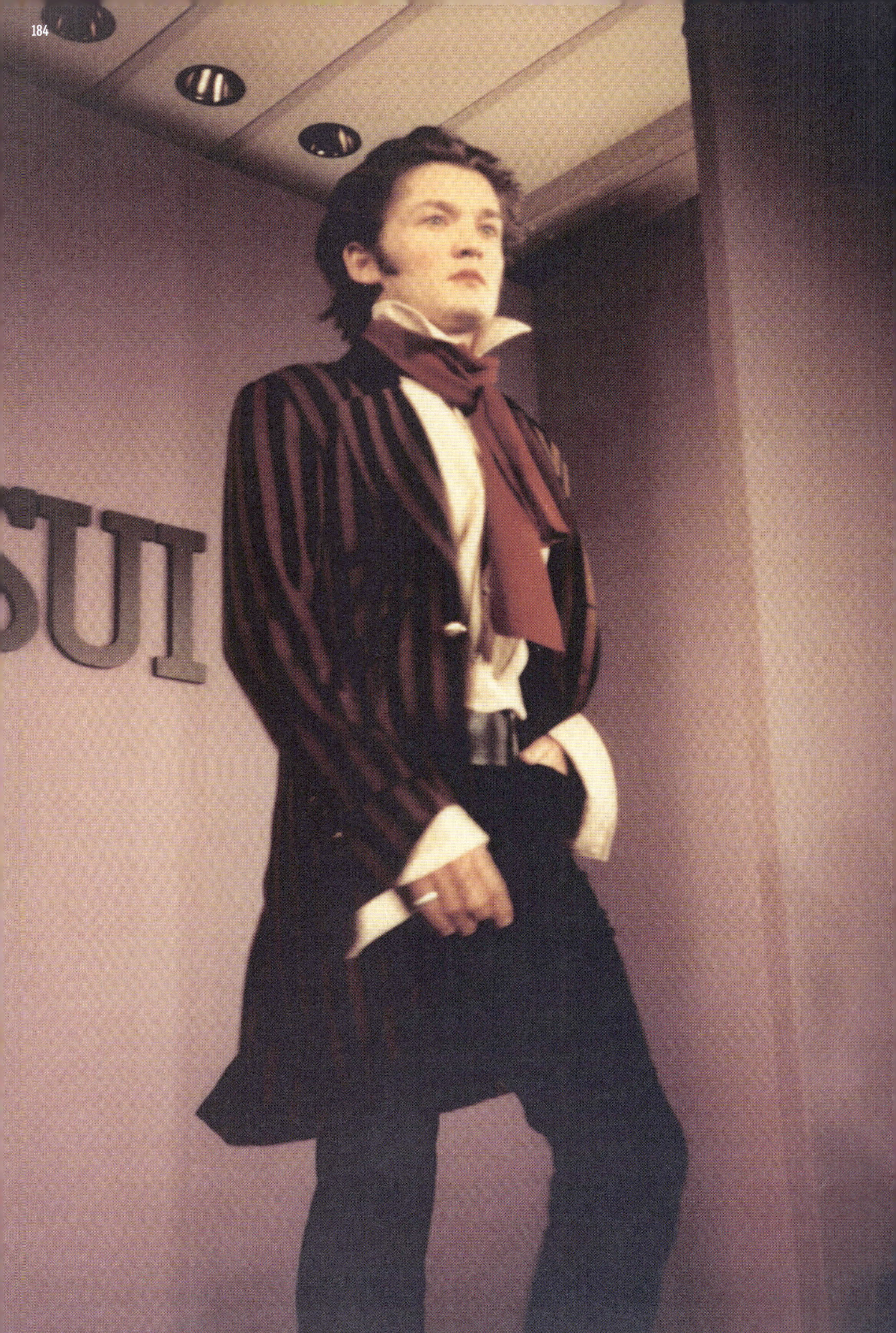
SUI

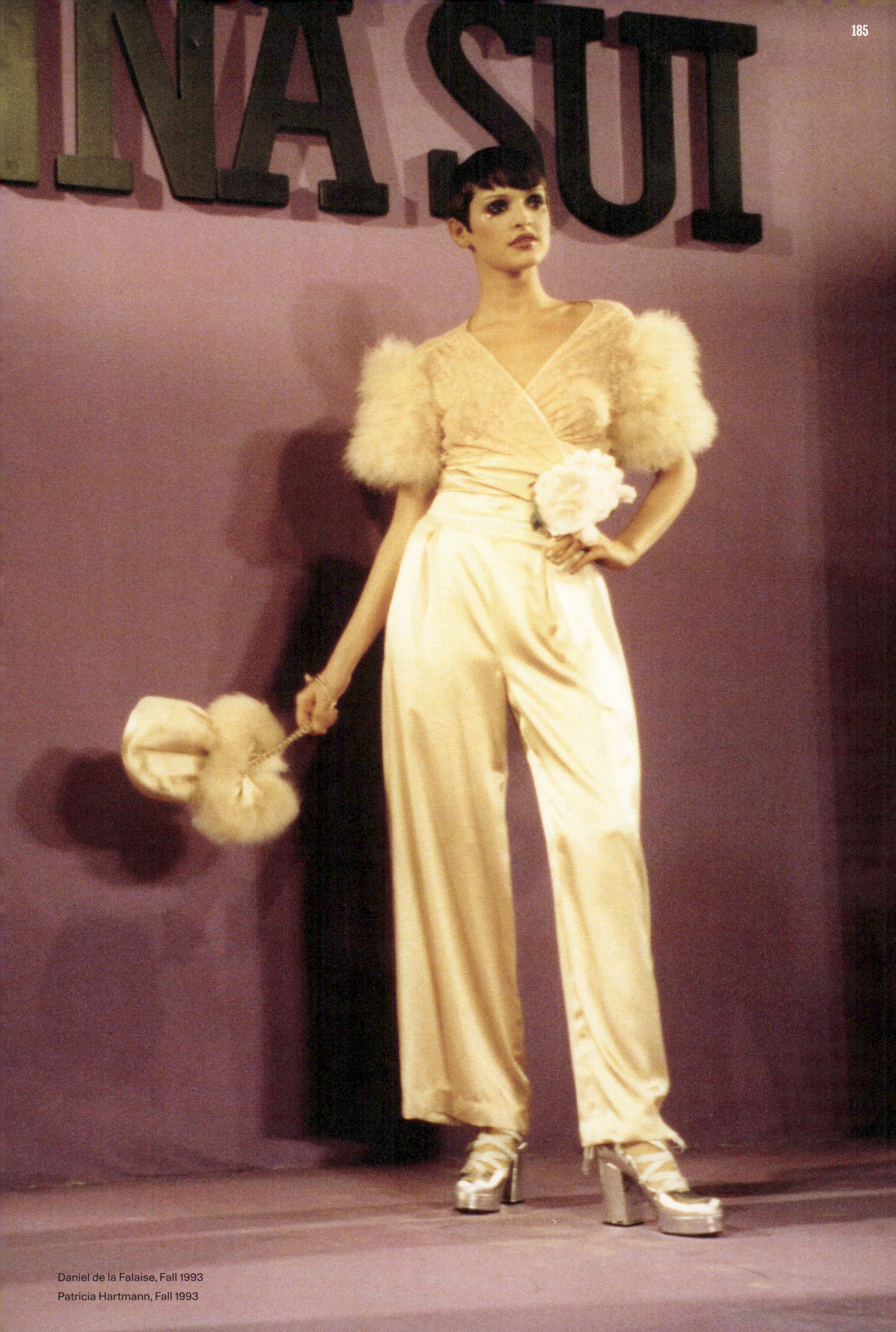

Daniel de la Falaise, Fall 1993
Patricia Hartmann, Fall 1993

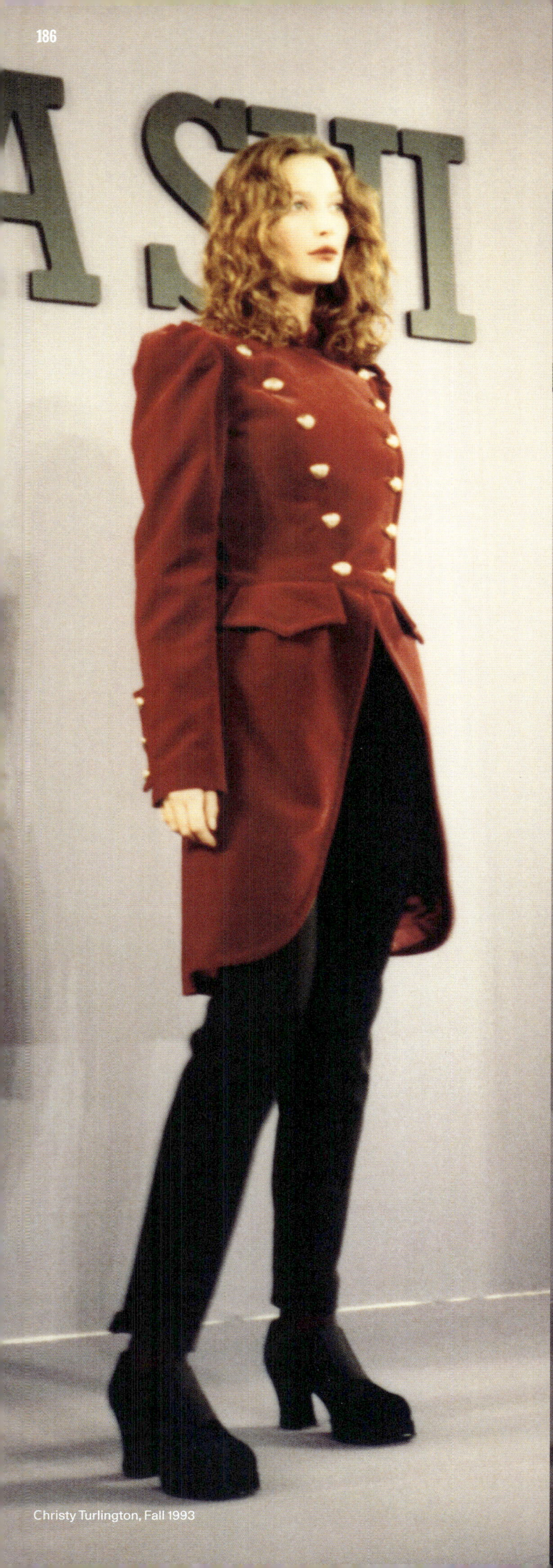

Christy Turlington, Fall 1993

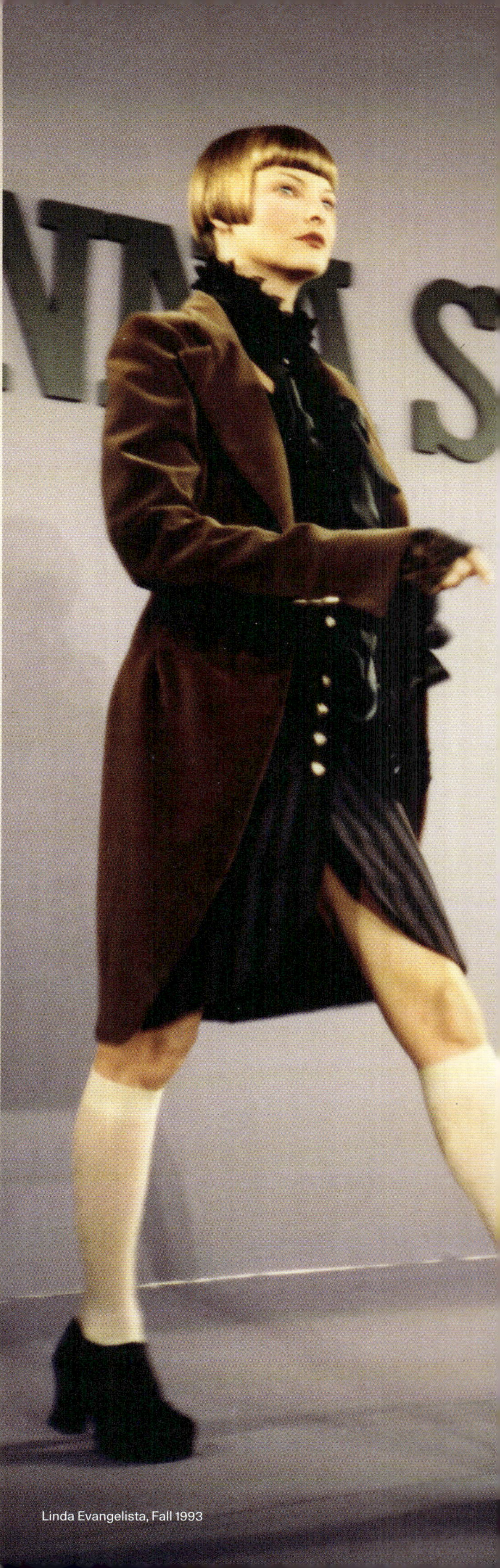

Linda Evangelista, Fall 1993

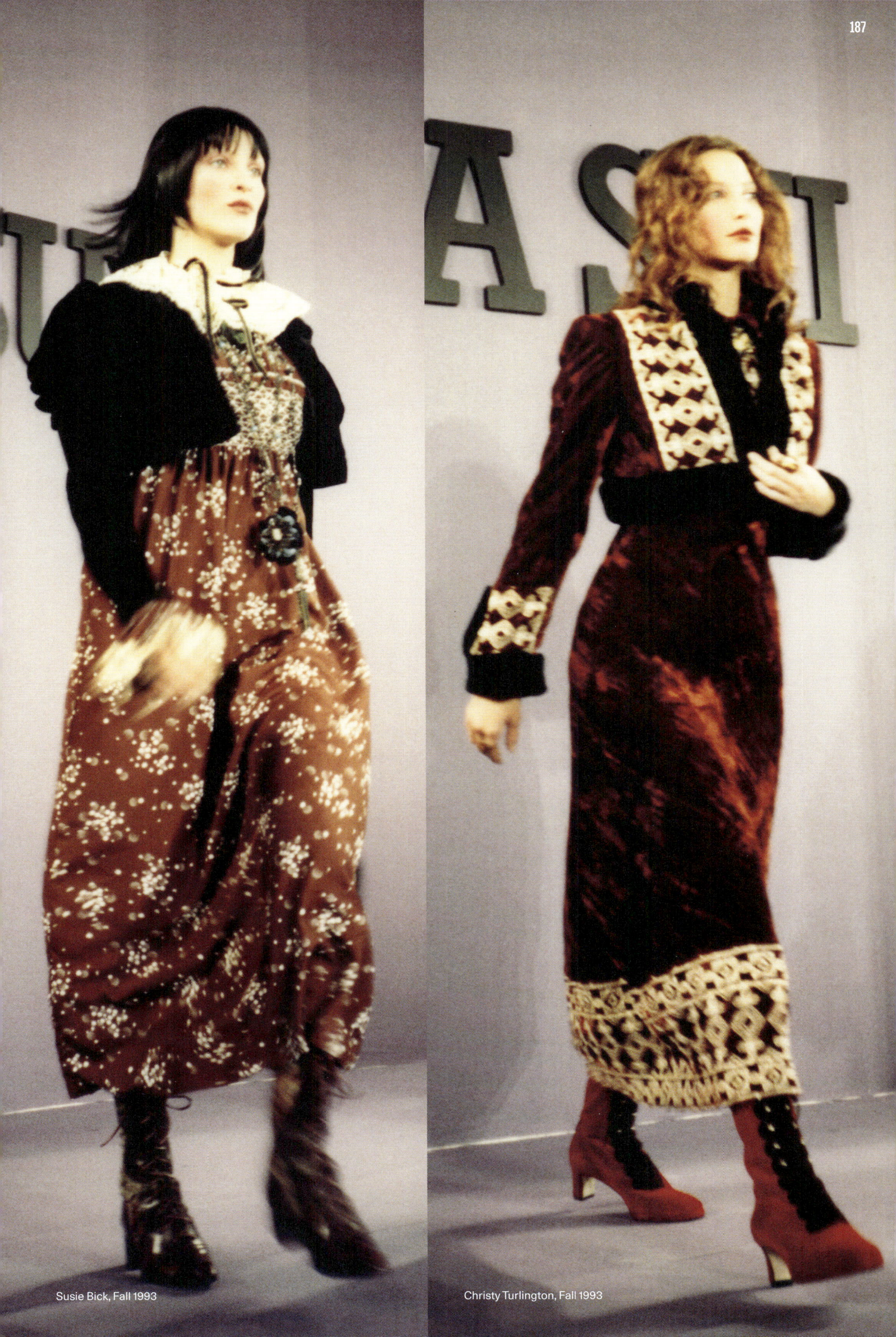

Susie Bick, Fall 1993

Christy Turlington, Fall 1993

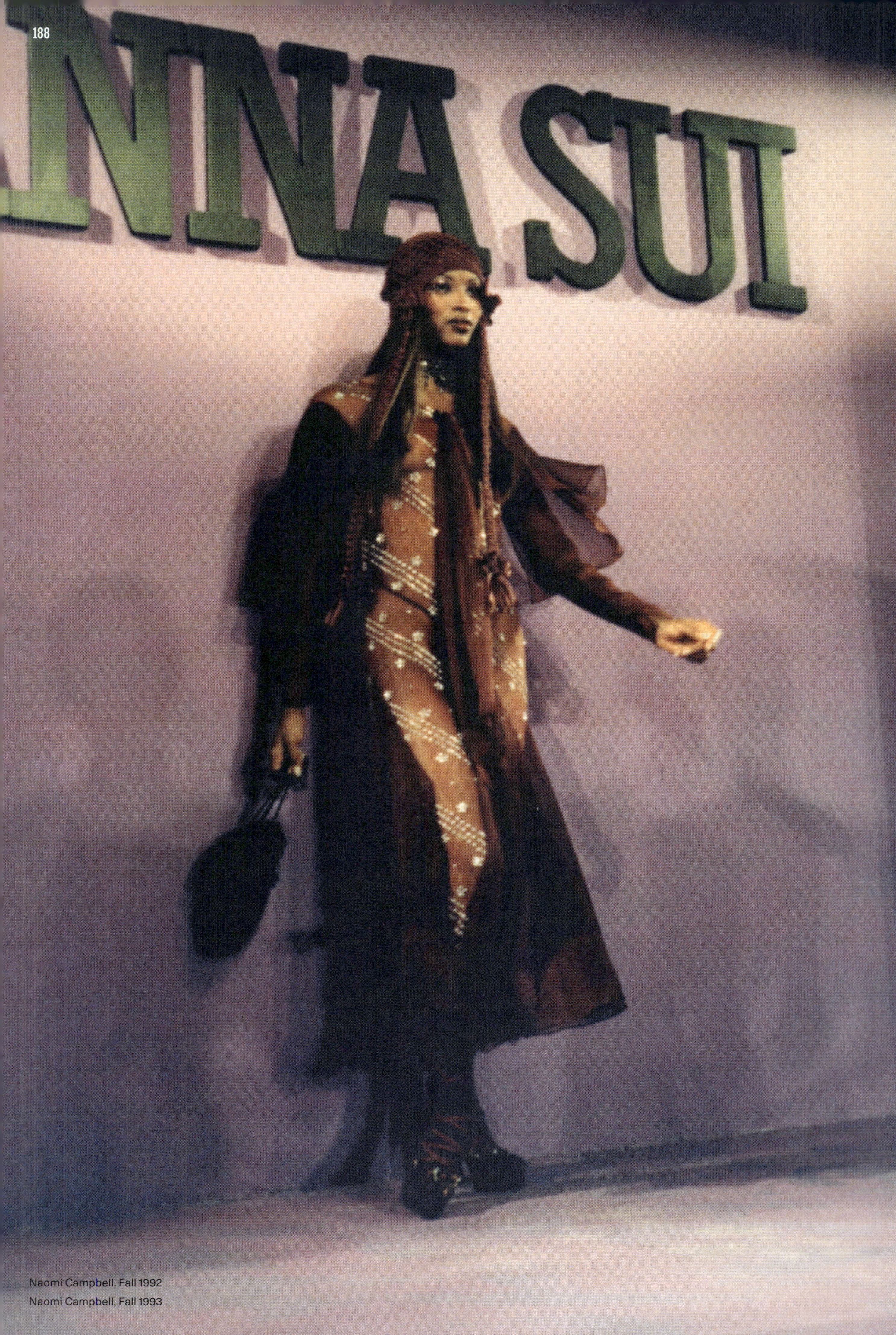

Naomi Campbell, Fall 1992
Naomi Campbell, Fall 1993

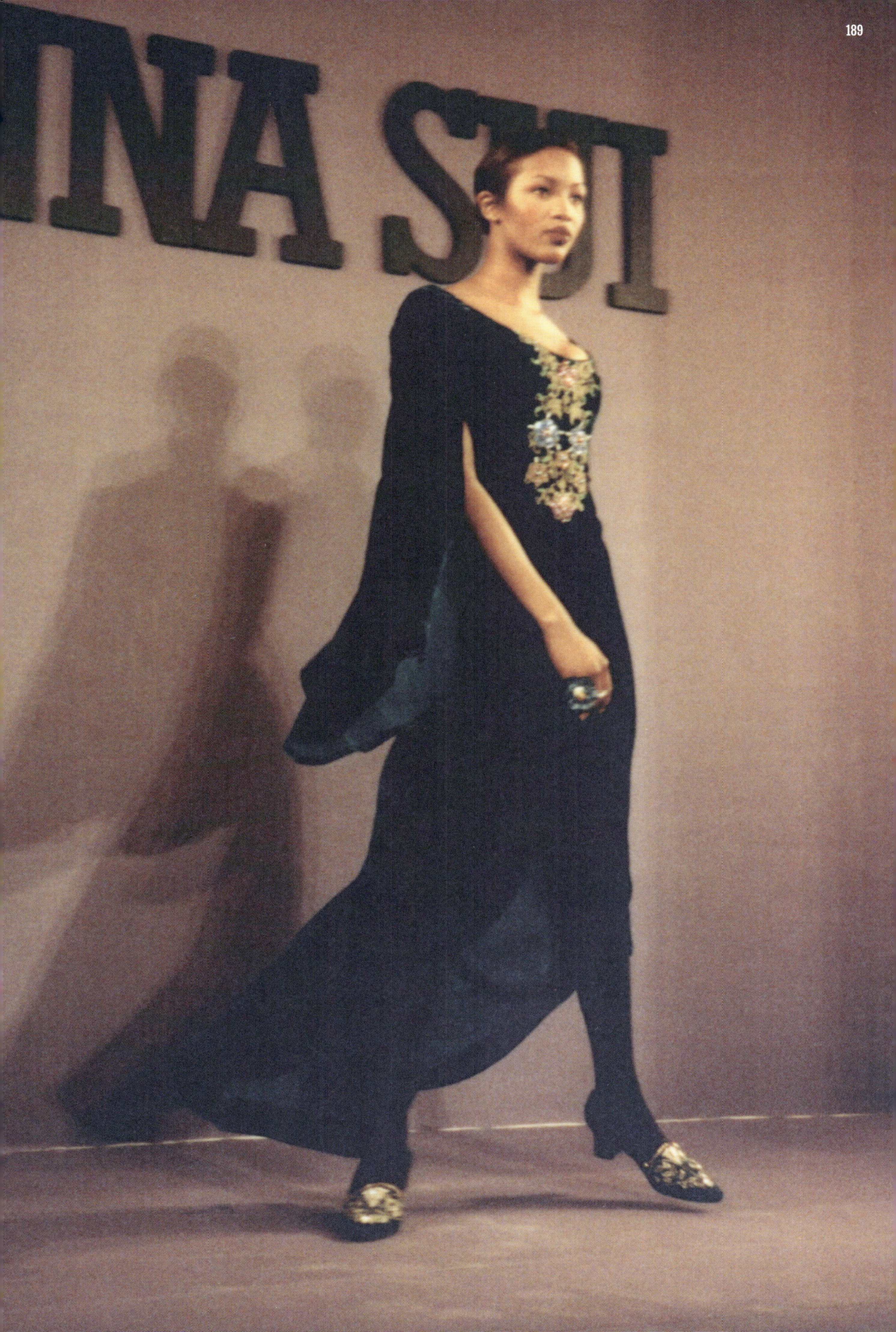

THE FIRST RUNWAY SHOW (1991) – ANNA SUI

Growing up, I was directly influenced by what I saw in *Seventeen* magazine. I remember there were British issues of *Seventeen* where they would go to England and shoot pictures on Carnaby Street, and some of the English designers like Mary Quant were represented. That was my first love—that style and fashion. And when I decided to do that first show, I thought it would be an homage to those things that I loved and that I spent hours looking at. The houndstooth, the peacoat, the kilts, the window panes, those were the most successful. And that eventually became the influence of the film *Clueless*, which was a couple years later. It started a whole different wave of a category for fashion. It wasn't teeny bopper anymore. And it wasn't designer, it was somewhere in between. I think that it resonated because so many of the models were wearing clothes on the runway that were more for their age and that they could relate to—rather than wearing mommy's clothes. That's what the press caught on to. Christy and Linda backstage at my next show wearing those fashions, where the season before they would have been wearing Chanel or Versace—they found clothes for their age group and it really started catching on and then of course it filtered down into the mass market.

"There was a multiple fashion collision Wednesday evening. It looked as if Sly and the Family Stone crashed into Coco Chanel and then got rear-ended by Christian Lacroix. The show, the first by Anna Sui, was a riot."

The New York Times, April 12, 1991

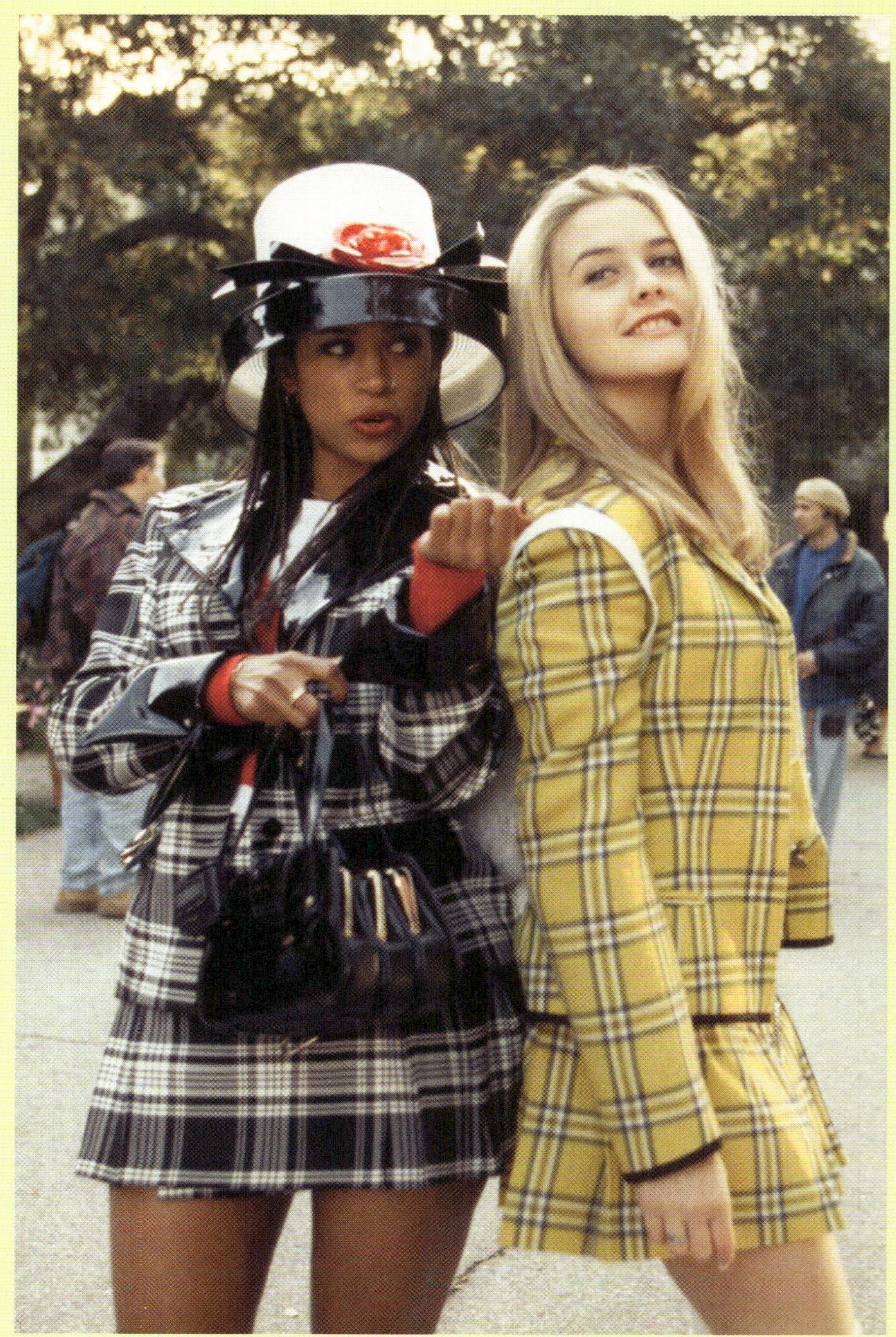

Alicia Silverstone and Stacey Dash, *Clueless* film still, 1995

Christy Turlington and Naomi Campbell wearing Fall 1991 collection with Tony Auerbach and Louis Chaban backstage, Fall 1992

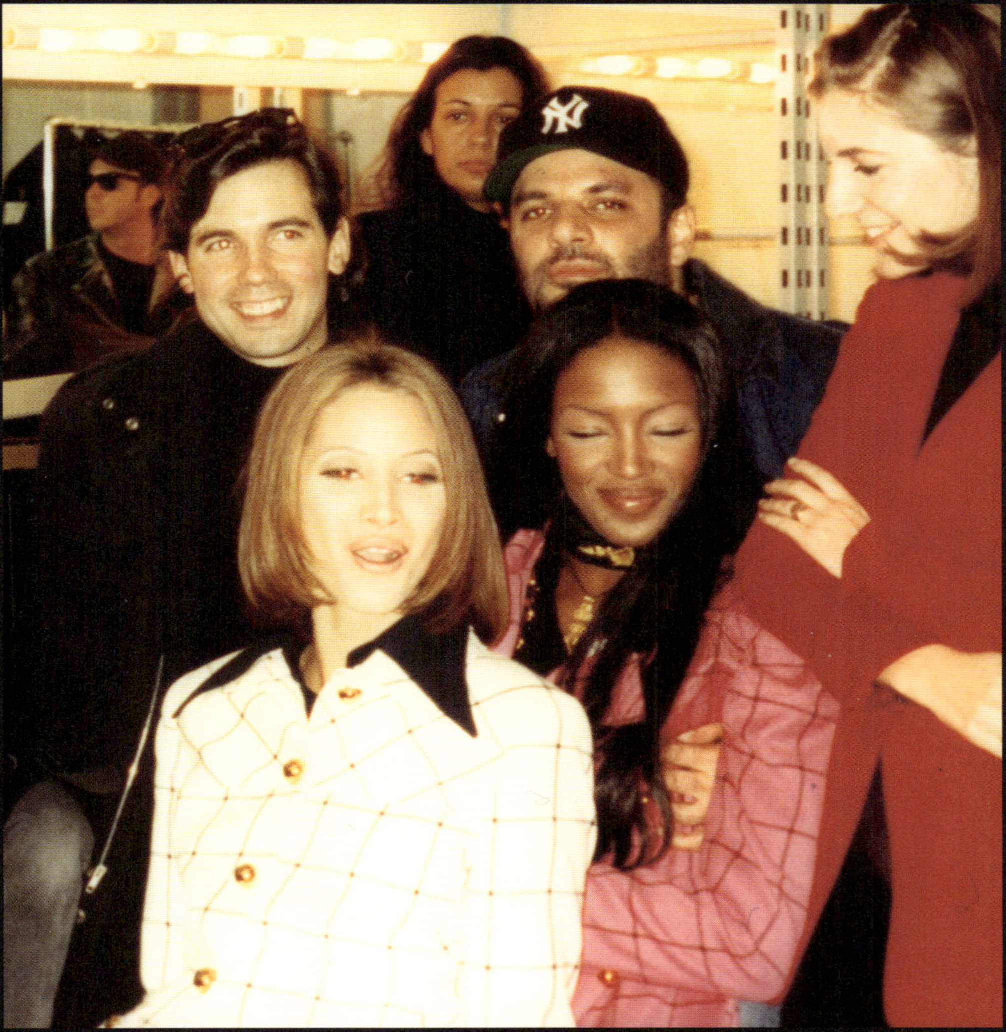

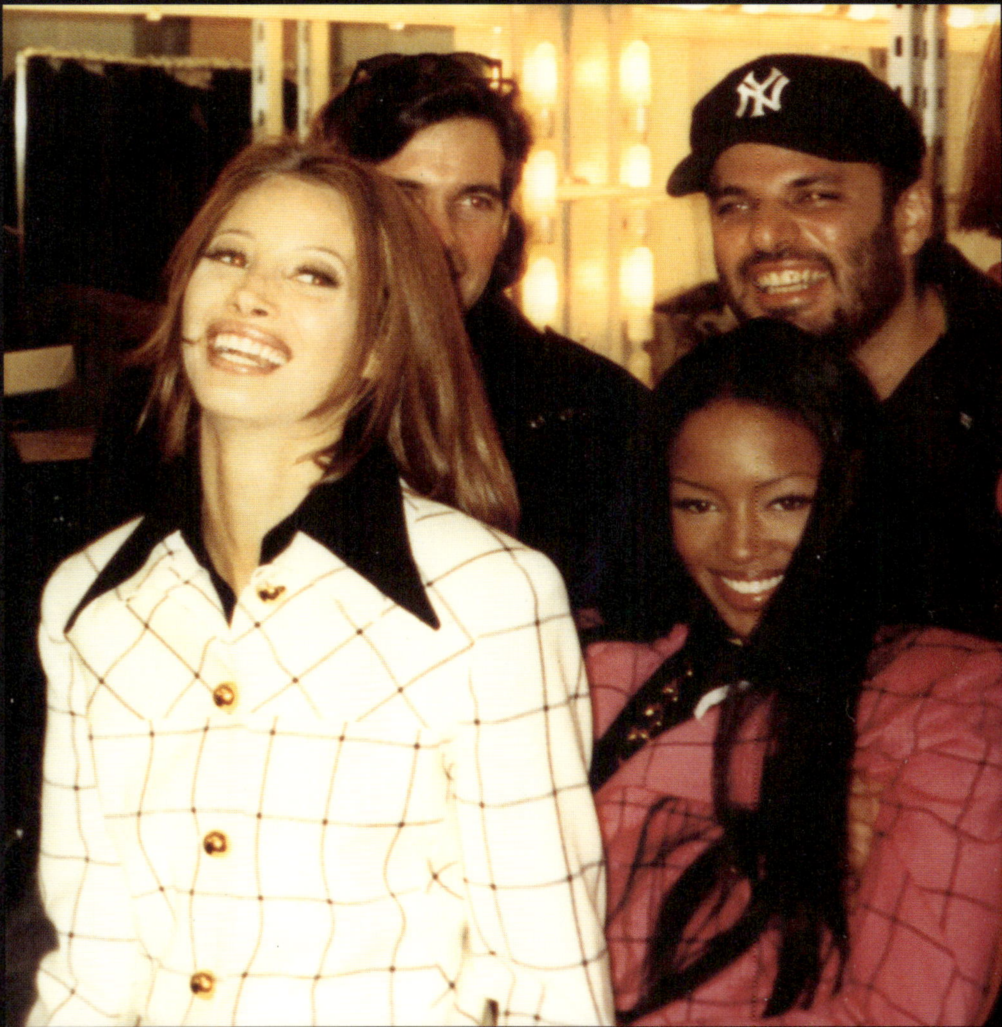

② Naomi.

Blk motorcycle jacket
orange blouse
Houndstooth pleated skirt

accessories

blk chain loafer	chain belt
blk knee socks	brooch
yellow vinyl cap	Ring
yellow vinyl glove.	bracelet.

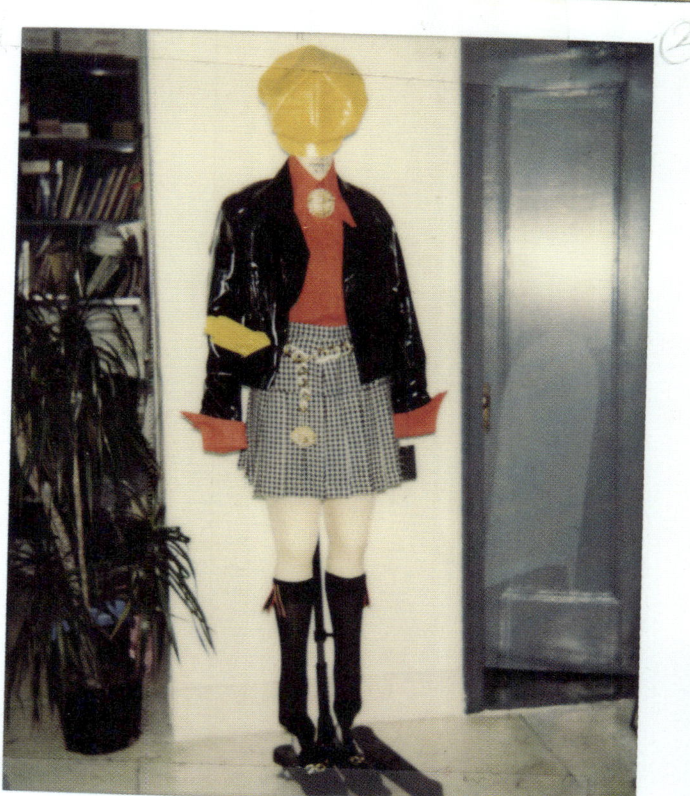

(5) Karen
Houndstooth peacoat
red poor boy turtleneck
black vinyl skirt

accessories
yellow tights
red vinyl cap
red vinyl gloves
houndstooth spats
blk belt

blk Beatle boot
cross medallion

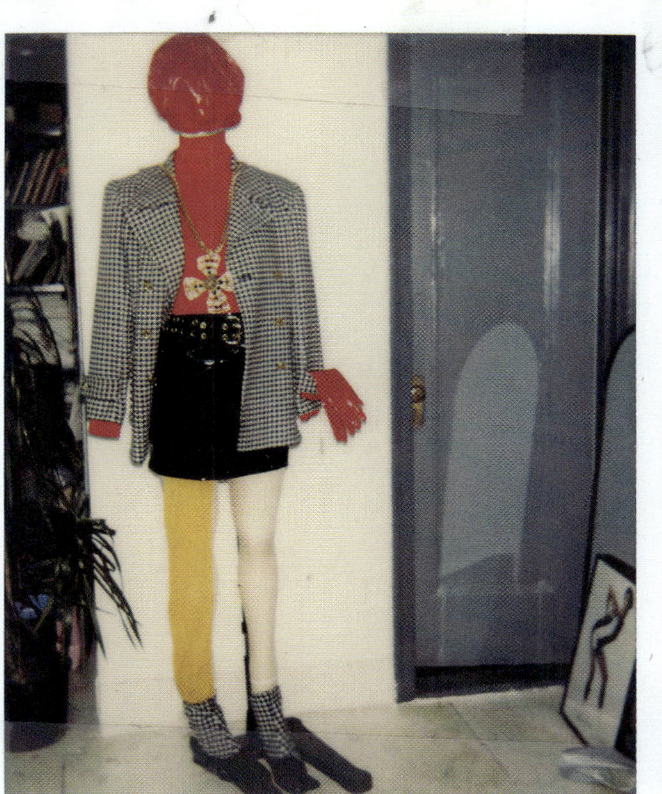

(8)

Yasmeen
Red vinyl jacket
black vinyl shorts.
Ivory blouse.

<u>accessories</u>
black vinyl belt medallion
black thigh high boots
black vinyl gloves
yellow tights.
blk vinyl cap

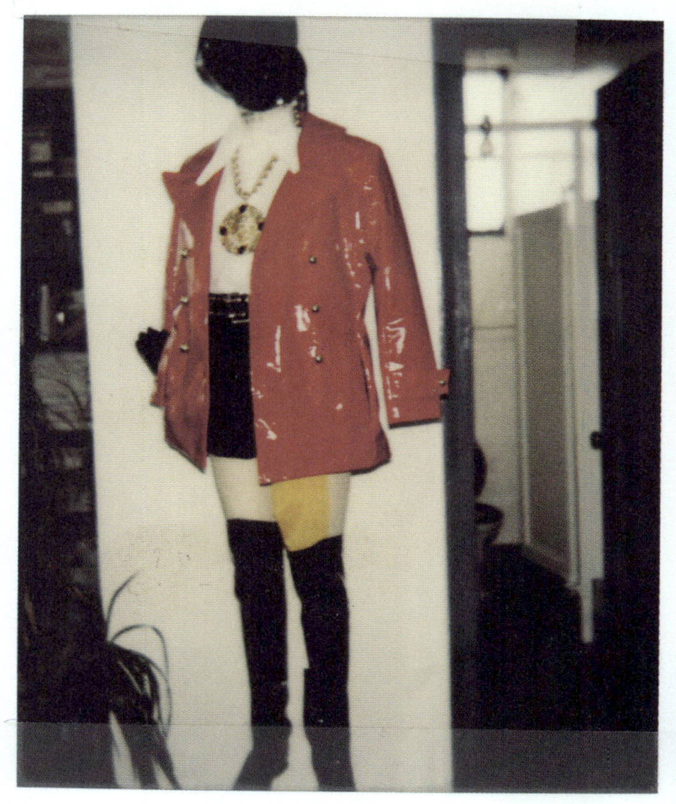

(9) Naomi:
Yellow windowpane jacket
yellow windowpane skirt
Red poorboy turtleneck.

accessories
yellow windowpane hat
yellow windowpane purse
yellow windowpane shoes
ivory ribbed tights.

watch
pin
black loafer

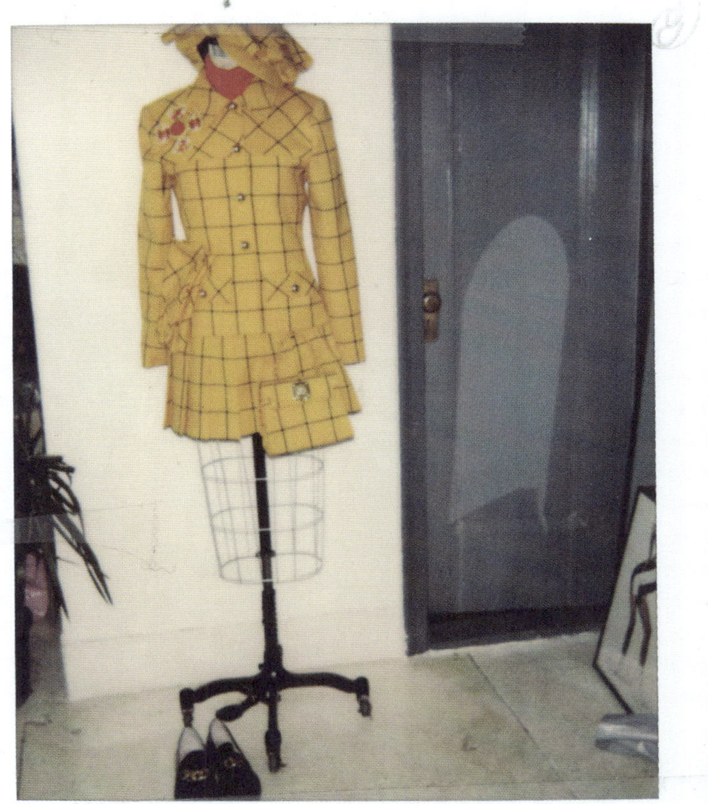

(11) Raven.
Pink windowpane peacoat
pink windowpane kilt
Ivory poorboy rib turtleneck

accessories

pink windowpane cap
pink windowpane gloves
pink windowpane purse
pink windowpane spats.
black Beatle boots.
cross medallion
ivory ribbed tights
Ribbon watch

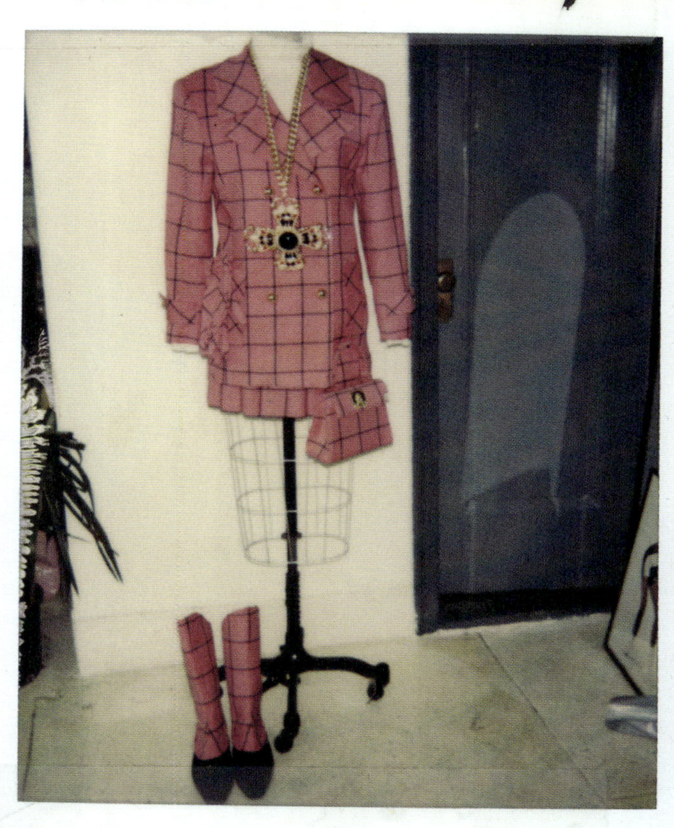

(2) Karen

Cream double breasted suit

accessories

gold + pearl bracelet

Cross necklace

gold purse

ivory shiny tights

ivory shoe

ivory gloves

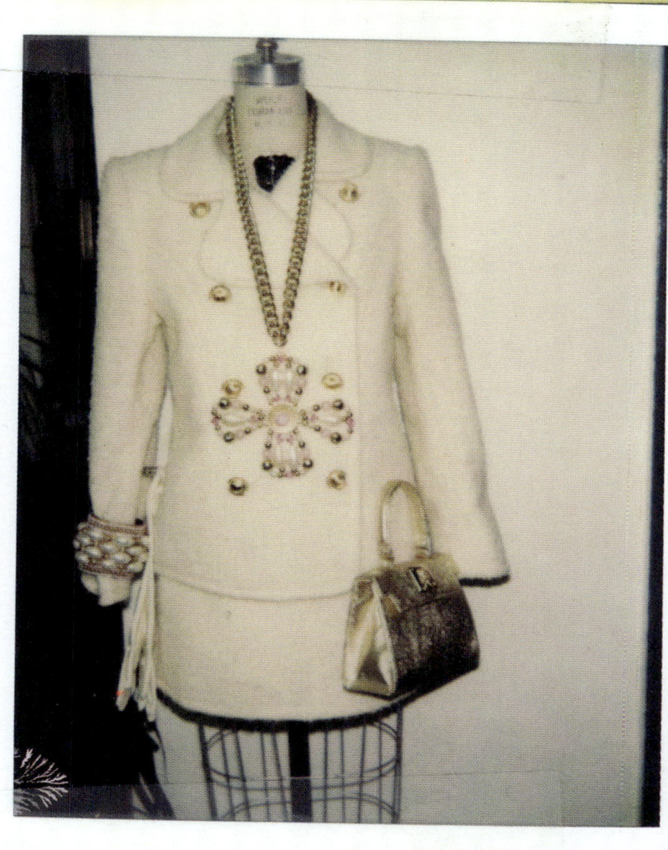

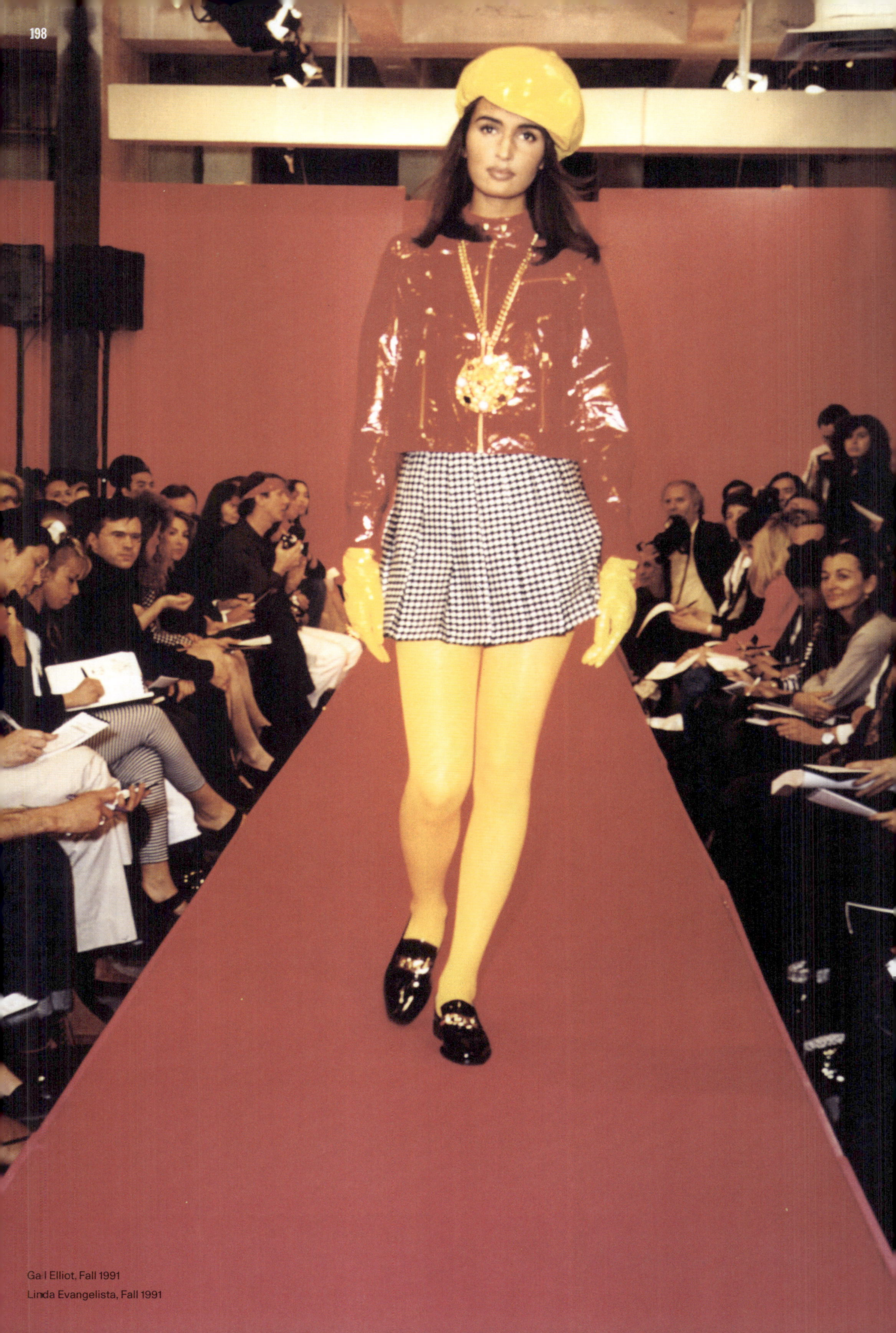

Gail Elliot, Fall 1991

Linda Evangelista, Fall 1991

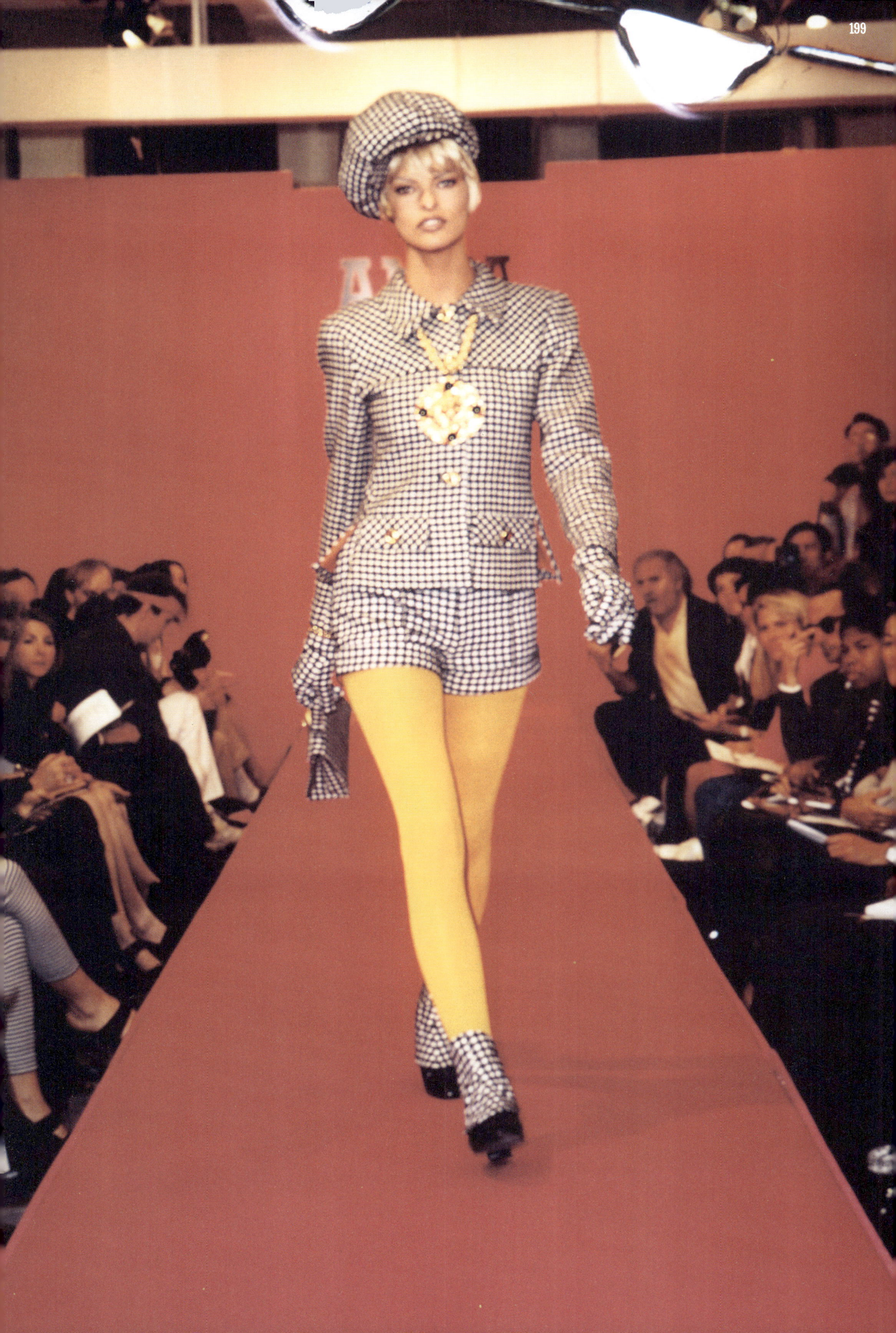

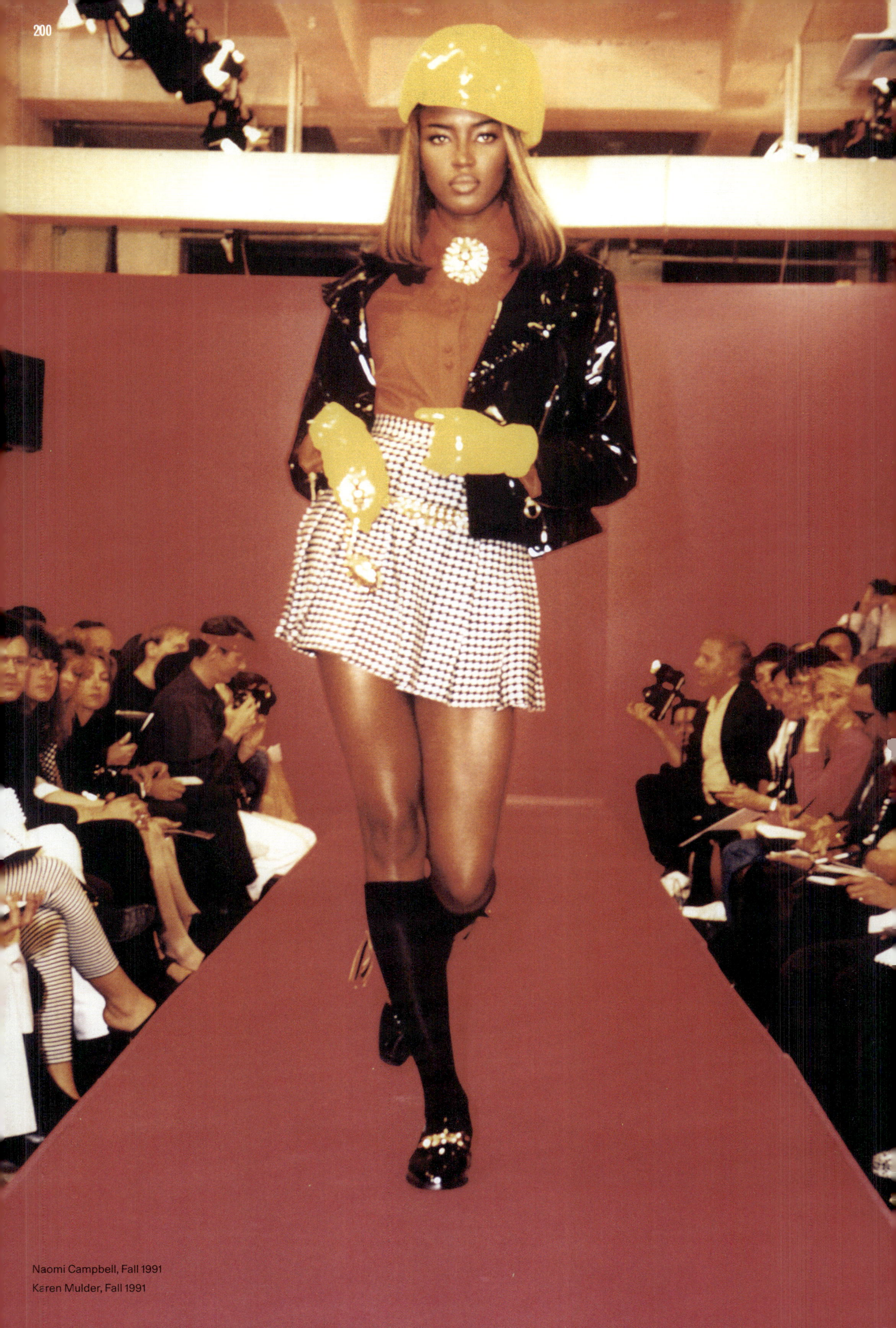

Naomi Campbell, Fall 1991
Karen Mulder, Fall 1991

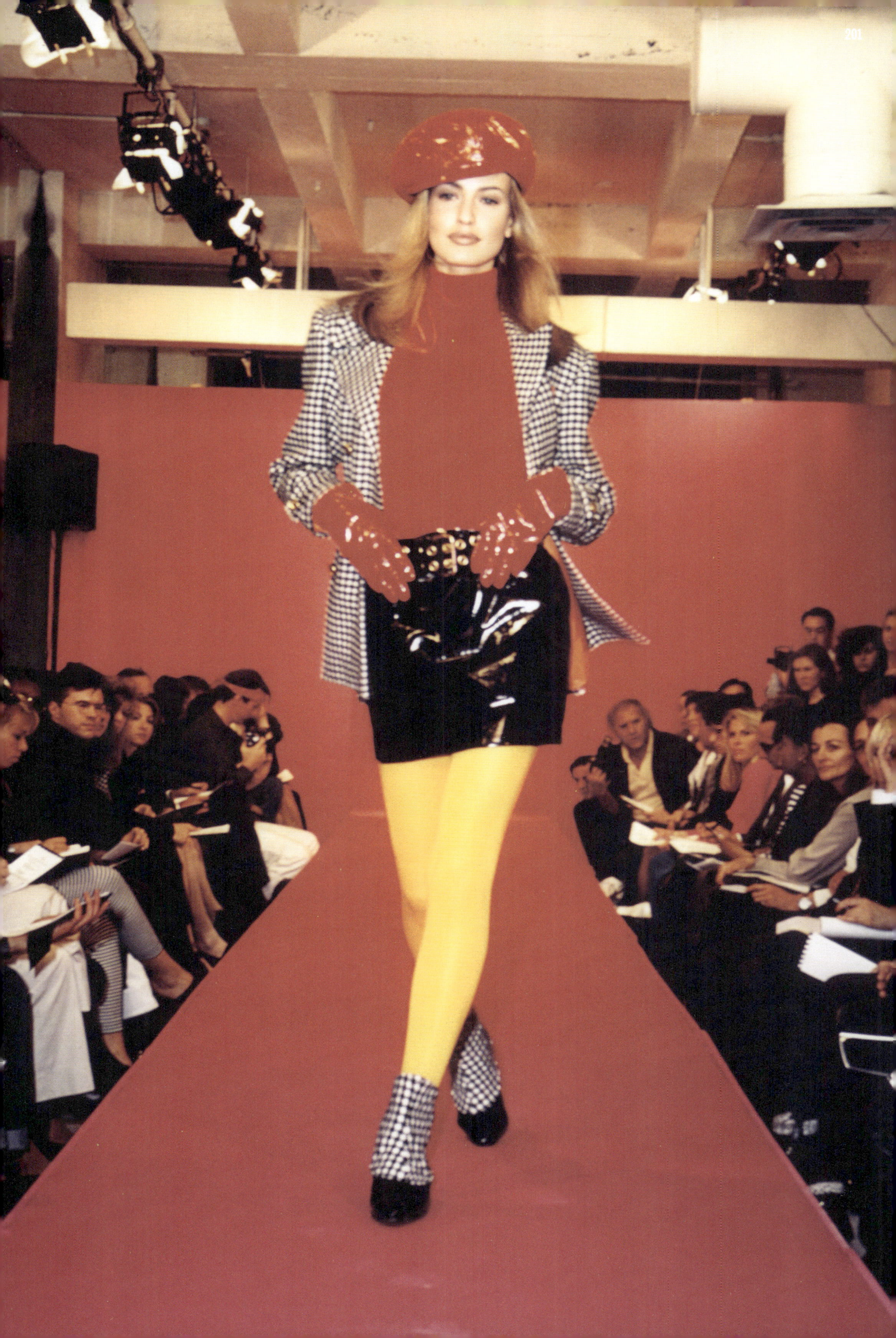

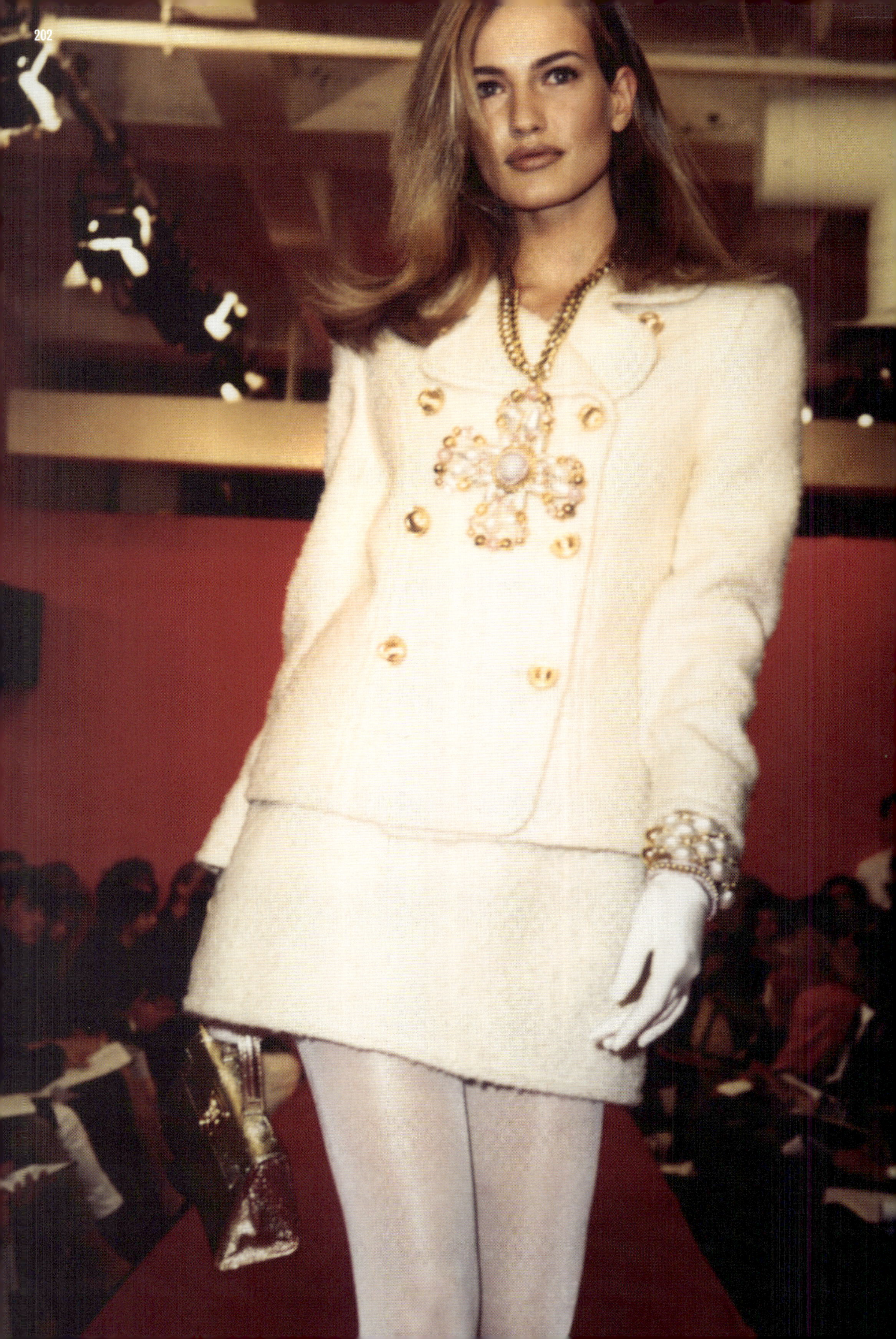

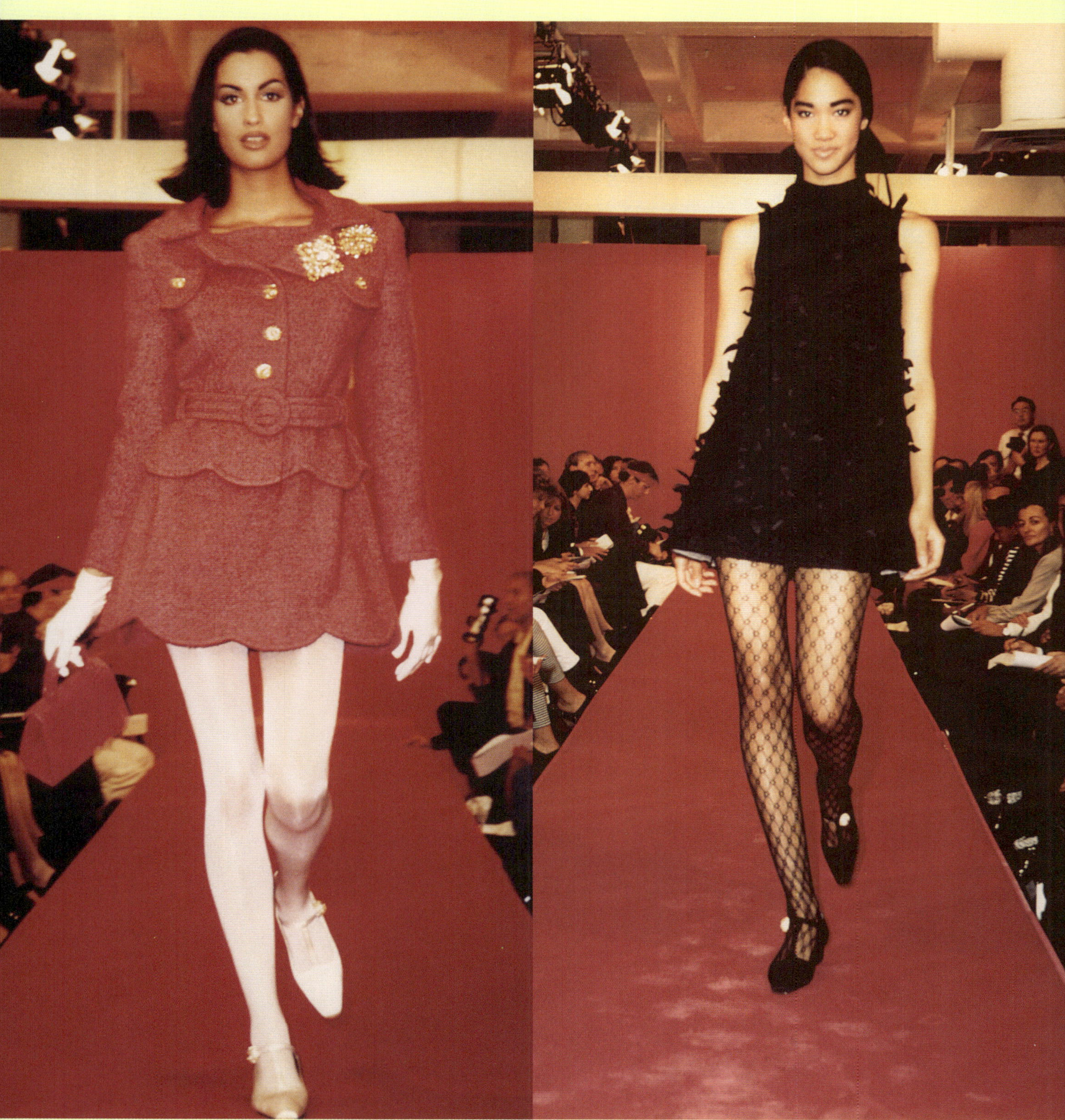

Karen Mulder, Fall 1991
Yasmeen Ghauri, Fall 1991
Kimora Lee Simmons, Fall 1991

THE FOLK COLLECTION – ANNA SUI

It was no secret that I loved the whole hippie and bohemian look. The alternative music of the '90s reminded me of that Bob Dylan moment when he went electric. And I started looking at pictures of that period and found out about the Newport Folk Festival and looking at what the women were wearing, like Mary Travers or Joan Baez. It was very Scandinavian. I realized that Joan Baez was wearing Marimekko and with her long hair parted in the middle. And a lot of the women were walking around carrying these big guitar cases. I thought, "okay, I want to do my runway like this." It just so happened I had just moved into my apartment building and my neighbor across the hall was Murray Lerner, who did the documentary on the Newport Folk Festival when Dylan went electric. He showed me the film footage and it was so stunning because it was stark black and white, shot mostly at night, dimly lit. Peter, Paul and Mary standing on a stark stage and the high contrast of the film was just breathtaking. He edited a shorter version for us and we projected it on the runway. I found this woman that did hand-cut sandals and she custom made sandals for us. At the same time Jordan Betten made these leather bags that were hand laced and I convinced him that he could make leather pants too. I showed him how to make a pattern for pants and he started making all these leather pants that were all hand laced. And then we did a mixture of shearling jackets with it. So it was that whole look that was a combination of Scandinavian but also left wing New England college student and with the triangle scarves and the long straightened hair. So we just had a lot of fun with it and I remember Amy Spindler, the *New York Times* fashion editor then, said that that was her absolute favorite collection. In that issue of *T, The New York Times Style Magazine* she wrote this whole story with my inspiration board and all my influences.

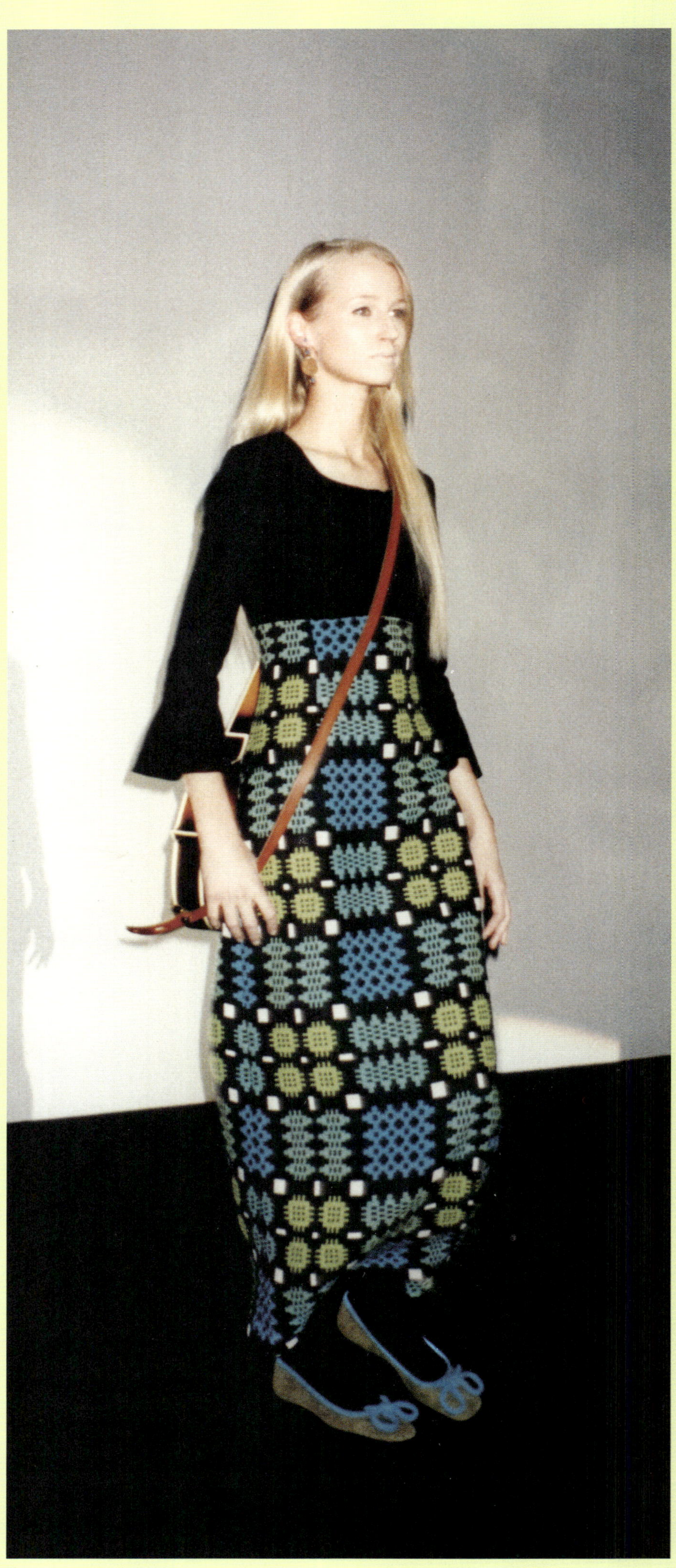

Esther De Jong, Fall 1999

Sunniva Stordahl Bjorklund, Fall 1999

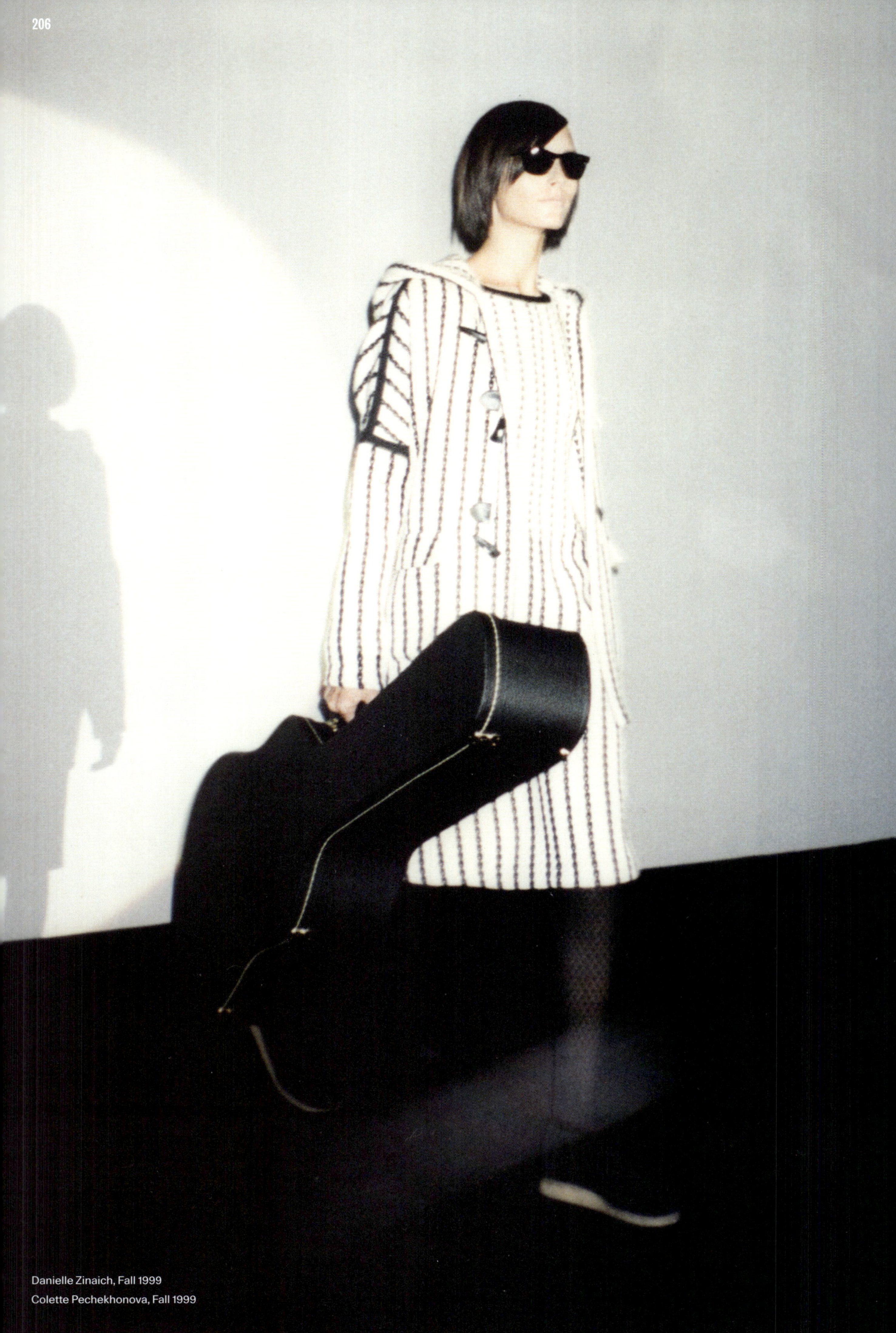

Danielle Zinaich, Fall 1999
Colette Pechekhonova, Fall 1999

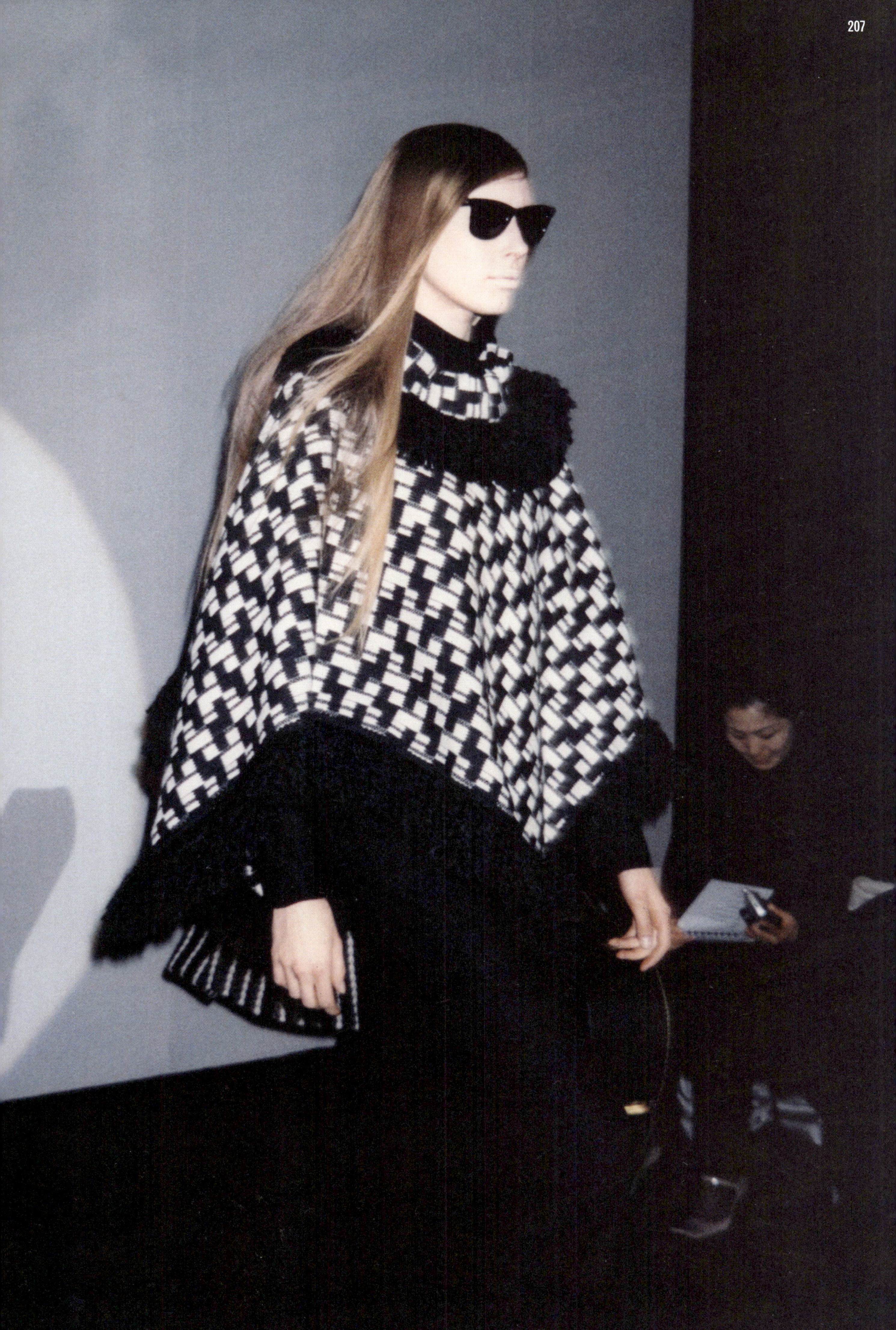

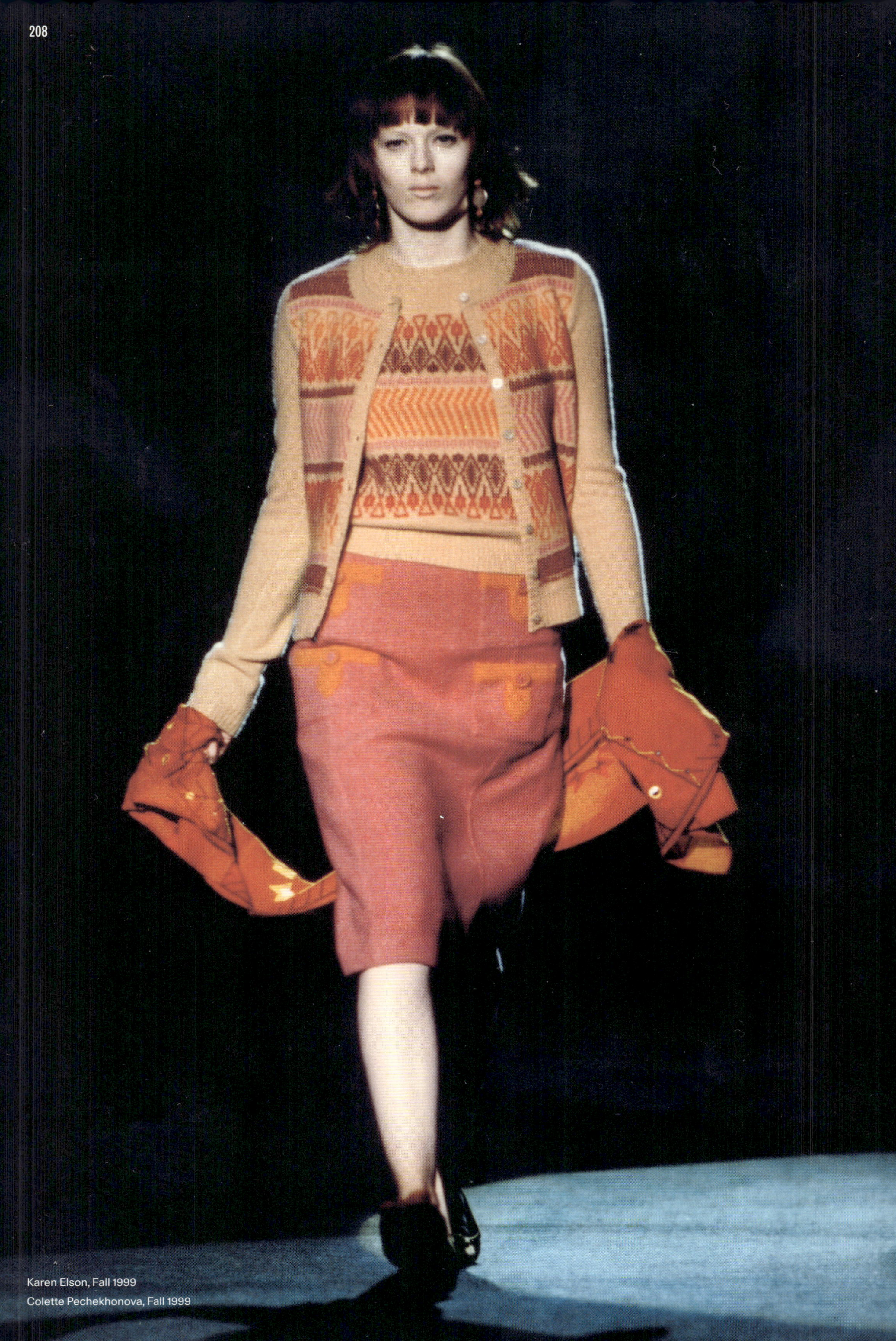

Karen Elson, Fall 1999
Colette Pechekhonova, Fall 1999

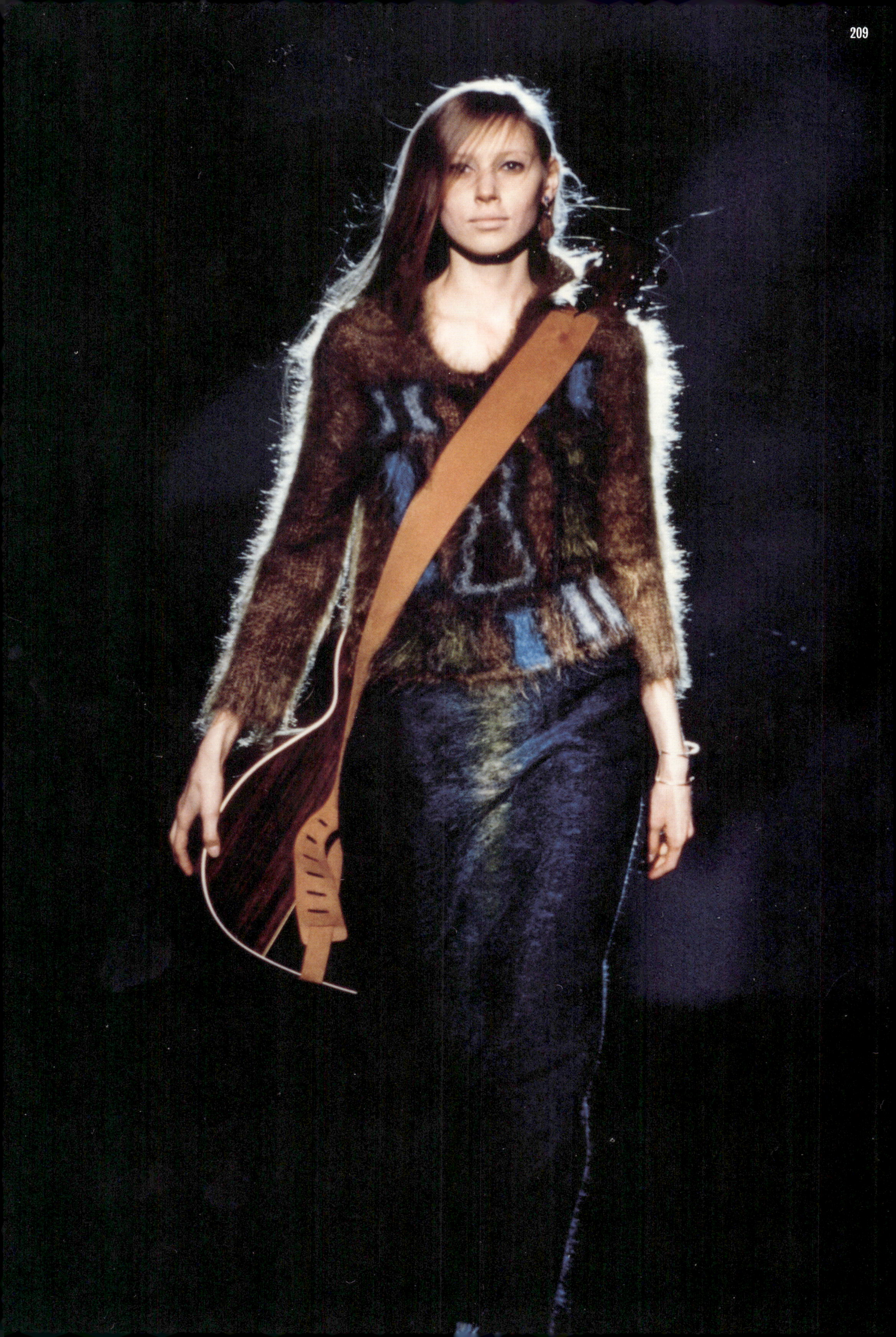

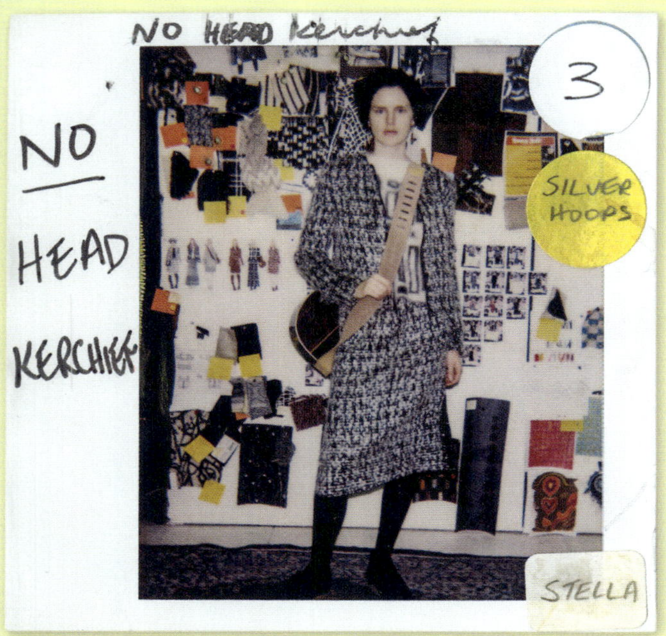

3. **STELLA**
- **Black and white mohair tweed jacket** (wear open)
- **White mohair intarsia sweater** (wear out)
- **Black and white mohair tweed skirt**

3. **ACCESSORIES**
- **Silver hoop earrings w/wood circle** (clip-ons)
- **Black diamond pattern tights**
- **Black shearling shoe**
- **Guitar** (strapped across left shoulder and chest)

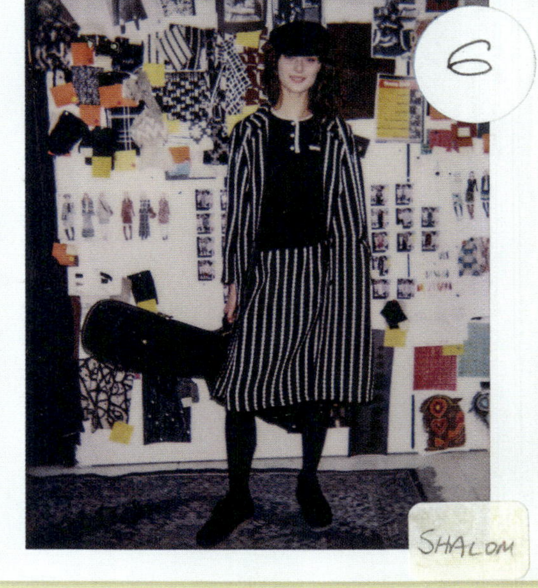

6. **SHALOM**
- **Black and white chain link wool jacket** (wear open)
- **Black thermal henley** (wear top out, button all buttons)
- **Black and white chain link wool skirt**

6. **ACCESSORIES**
- **Black cap**
- **Black diamond pattern tights**
- **Black shearling shoe**
- **Black guitar case**

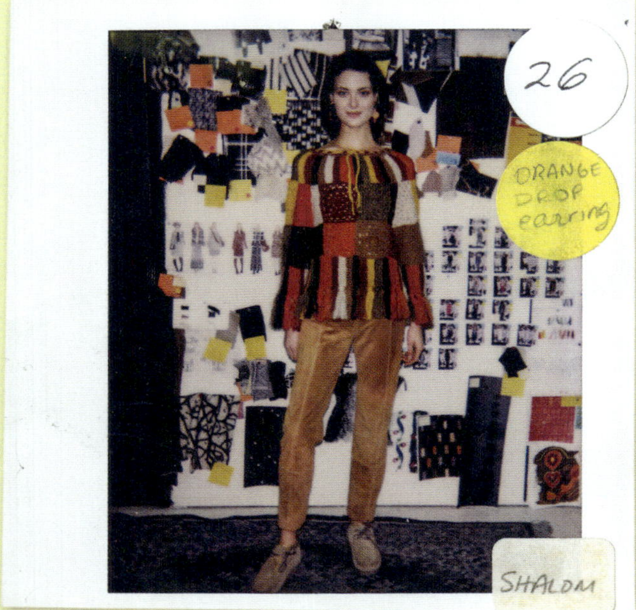

26. **SHALOM**
- **Mohair patchwork sweater** (tie laces in a knot at neck)
- **Camel suede pant**

26. **ACCESSORIES**
- **Orange and wood drop earrings**
- **Beige shearling shoe**

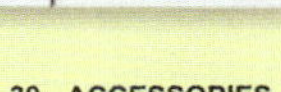

30. **COLETTE**
- **Brown mohair intarsia sweater** (pull neckline forward)
- **Blue mohair ombré long skirt**

30 **ACCESSORIES**
- **Turquoise and wood drop earrings**
- **Silver and blue cuff bracelet**
- **Sock**
- **Black applique boot**
- **Guitar** (strap goes on right shoulder and chest, guitar on back)

Dresser card, Stella Tennant, Fall 1999
Dresser card, Shalom Harlow, Fall 1999
Dresser card, Shalom Harlow, Fall 1999
Dresser card, Colette Pechekhonova, Fall 1999

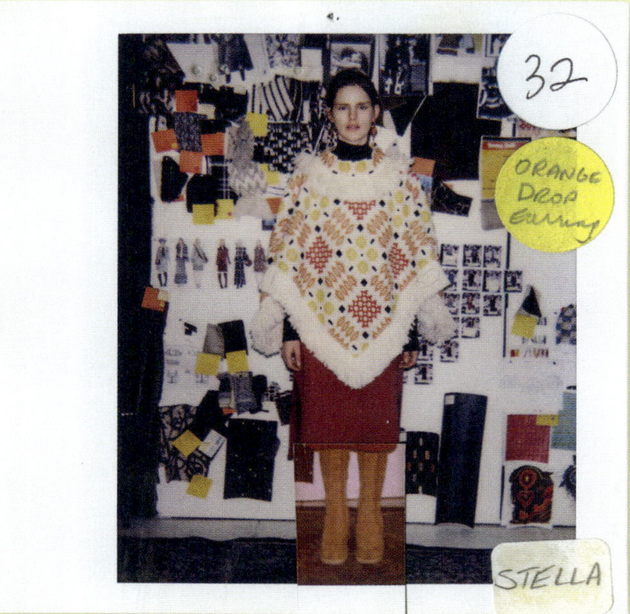

32. STELLA
- Orange and white waffle weave poncho
- Black turtleneck
- Pink tweedy fleece skirt

32 ACCESSORIES
- Orange wood circle drop earrings
- Black diamond pattern tights (keep on from look #3)
- Camel shearling boot

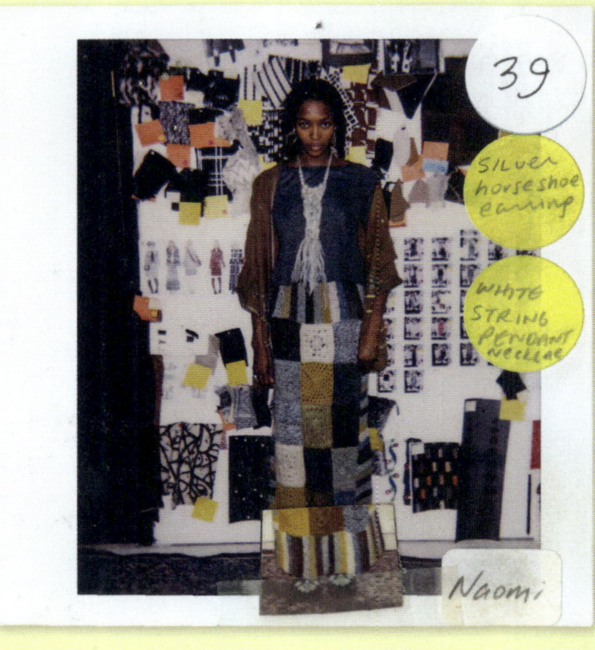

39. NAOMI
- Blue mohair thermal top
- Mohair patchwork long skirt

39. ACCESSORIES
- Silver wishbone earrings
- Olive embroidered and mirrored shawl
- Lt. blue string and pebbles pendant necklace
- Black applique flat

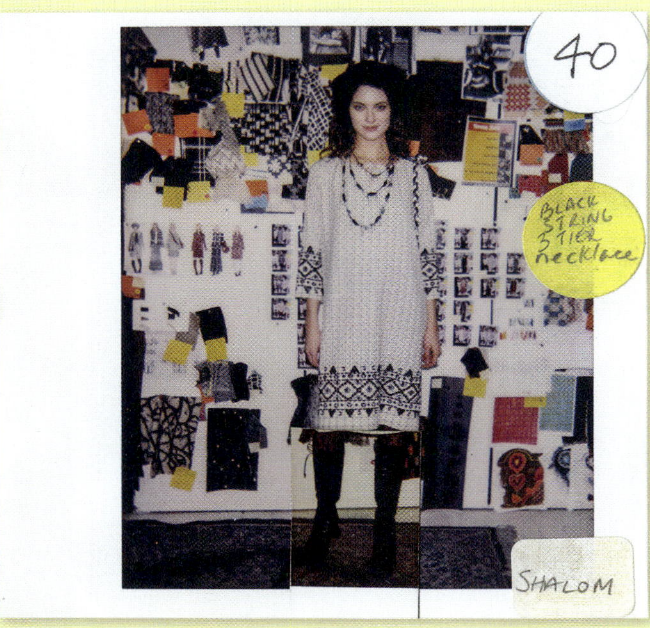

40. SHALOM
- **White sequin windowpane dress** (tie straps at neck in knot)

40. ACCESSORIES
- Black crochet headkerchief
- Black string and rhinestone multistrand pendant necklace
- Black fleur de lis tights
- Ivory sequin shoulderbag
- Black velvet and satin boot

49. RUFUS
- **White shearling** (wear open)
- **Black thermal henley**
- **White wide wale corduroy jean** (from last look #27)

ACCESSORIES

49.
- **Socks** (from last look #27)
- **Black boot** (2 rubber bands on each boot at calf for narrow fit under pant--use again in next look)

Dresser card, Stella Tennant, Fall 1999
Dresser card, Naomi Campbell, Fall 1999
Dresser card, Shalom Harlow, Fall 1999
Dresser card, Rufus Wainwright, Fall 1999

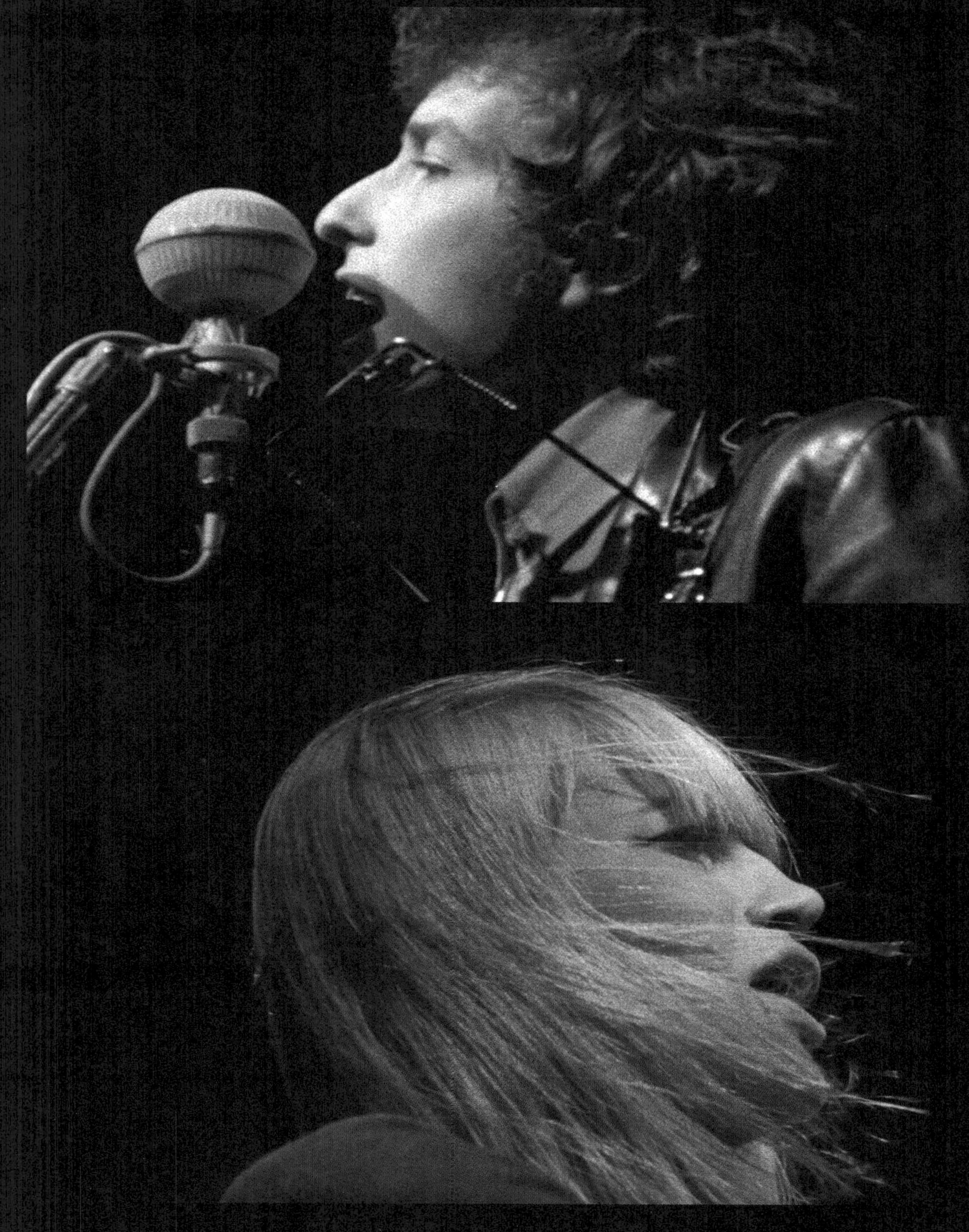

Bob Dylan, still from the Murray Lerner film, *Festival!*, 1967

Mary Travers of Peter, Paul and Mary, still from the Murray Lerner film, *Festival!*, 1967

Joan Baez and Bob Dylan, New York City, 1960s

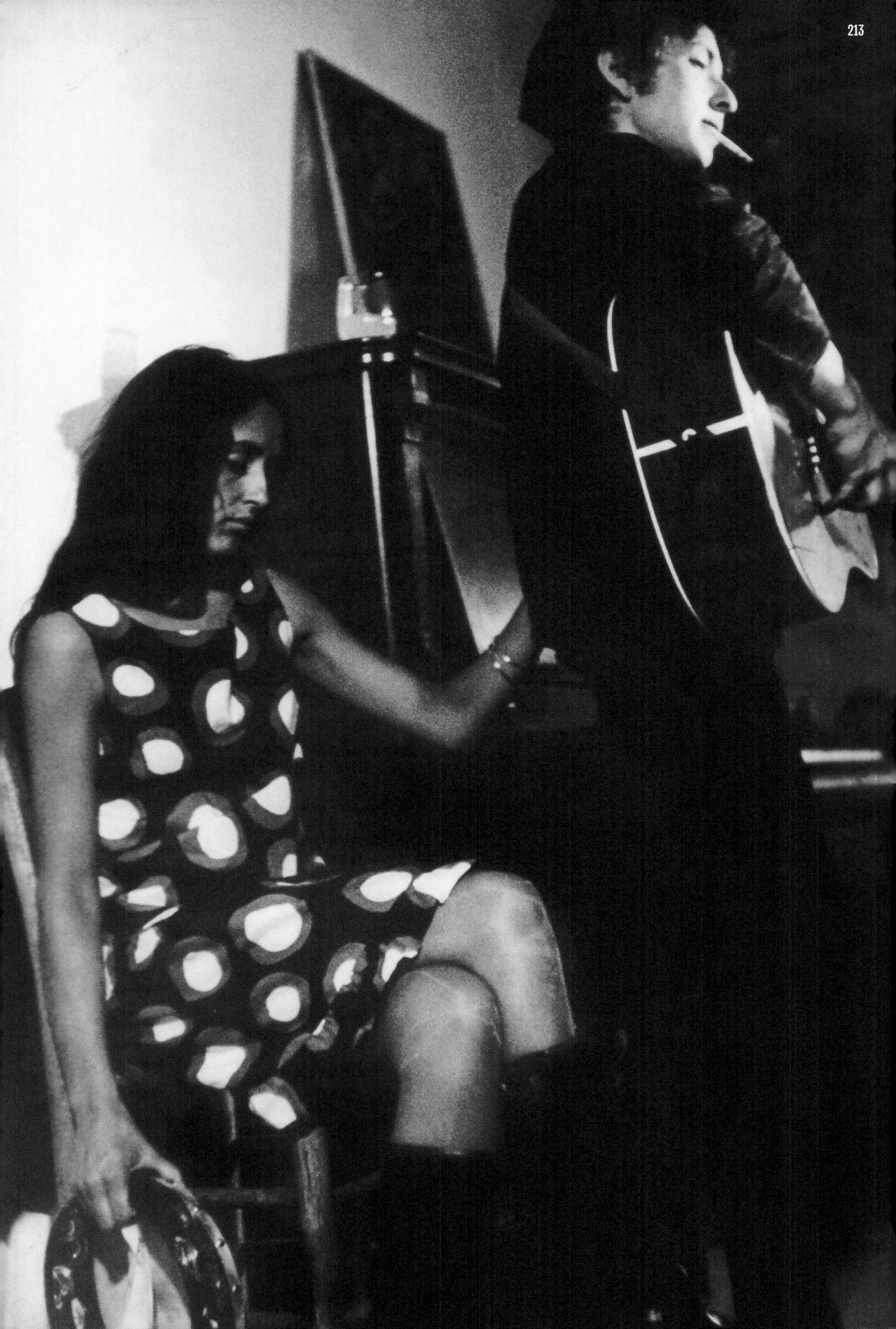

BIOGRAPHIES

ANNA SUI

Anna Sui is one of New York's most beloved and accomplished fashion designers, known for creating contemporary original clothing inspired by copious amounts of research into vintage styles and cultural arcana. Sui joined New York's creative cultural underground in the 1970s, forging important relationships in the worlds of fashion, photography, art, music, and design.

A first-generation Chinese American, Sui came of age in a suburb of Detroit. Hers is a classic American success story which she describes in her own terms: "You have to focus on your dreams, even if they go beyond common sense. How could this young girl from the suburbs of Detroit become a success in New York? It was always that dream." Sui was part of a generation of fashion designers who remade American style in the 1990s. She rejected 1980s power dressing, with its corporate suits and big shoulder pads, in favor of a more relaxed silhouette that reflected the values of youth culture.

Since her premiere runway show in 1991, Sui has produced over sixty collections, and she remains at the helm of her independent brand. Her label has grown to include accessories, cosmetics, and fragrance, and she operates boutiques in the United States and Asia. A passionate advocate for New York City's Garment District, she has located her business and produced her fashion lines in the city for over forty years.

CHRISTY TURLINGTON BURNS

Christy Turlington Burns is the founder and president of Every Mother Counts. Burns's work in maternal health began after she experienced a childbirth-related complication in 2003—an experience that inspired her to direct and produce the documentary feature film *No Woman, No Cry*, about the challenges women face throughout pregnancy and childbirth around the world. Under her leadership, Every Mother Counts has invested over $42 million to support awareness raising, community-led solutions, and advocacy for systems change. Before founding EMC, Burns received international acclaim as a model representing the world's biggest fashion and beauty brands which she leveraged to become a health and wellness advocate. She has published two books: *Living Yoga: Creating A Life Practice* (2002), and edited, with Amy Schumer, *Arrival Stories: Women Share Their Experiences of Becoming Mothers* (2022). In 2023, she served as an executive producer for the Apple TV documentary series *The Super Models*. Burns has won awards and accolades, including the Distinguished Alumni Award from New York University, being named one of *Time*'s 100 Most Influential People and *Glamour Magazine's* Woman of the Year. Burns graduated Cum Laude from New York University's Gallatin School of Independent Studies and studied Public Health at Columbia University's Mailman School of Public Health. She has completed ten marathons on behalf of Team EMC and lives in New York City.

SOFIA COPPOLA

Sofia Coppola has made eight films, including *The Virgin Suicides* (1999); *Lost in Translation* (2003), for which she won an Academy Award for Best Screenplay; *Marie Antoinette* (2006); *Somewhere* (2010); *The Bling Ring* (2013); *The Beguiled* (2017), with which she made history as only the second woman to win Best Director prize at the Cannes Film Festival; *On the Rocks* (2020), and *Priscilla* (2023), which garnered Cailee Spaeny the Best Actress prize at the Venice Film Festival. In addition to her film career, Coppola directed a production of Giuseppe Verdi's classic opera *La Traviata* at the Rome Opera House with fashion designer Valentino Garavani and production designer Nathan Crowley. In 2023, Mack Books published her book *SOFIA COPPOLA ARCHIVE*, which is currently in its fifth reprinting.

LINDA EVANGELISTA

A lifelong love of fashion led Linda Evangelista to pursue a career as a model. With scores of collaborations with legendary photographers and designers, Evangelista captured the zeitgeist of the 1990s and became instrumental in birthing the term "supermodel" and, in the process, became one of the most influential models of all time. Throughout her storied career, Evangelista has inspired generations of creatives, used her celebrity to champion marginalized communities, and raised funds and awareness for HIV/AIDS and breast cancer, among other worthy causes.

ILEEN GALLAGHER

Ileen Gallagher is the founder of ISG Productions, which specializes in creative development, management, and production of cultural, entertainment, and educational experiences that inspire and inform. Her arts-related projects include *Jean-Michel Basquiat: King Pleasure*; *Art and Ideals: John F. Kennedy* at the Kennedy Center; the Clive Davis Gallery at New York University; *Unzipped and Exhibitionism: The Rolling Stones*; the Walt Disney Family Museum; the 50th Anniversary of Monterey Pop Festival; *Charles Ives* at the American Academy of Arts and Letters; the Harley Davidson Museum; and *Rock Style* at the Metropolitan Museum of Art. Prior to starting her own firm, she was the Director of Exhibitions at the Rock and Roll Hall of Fame and Museum and has held staff positions at the Library of Congress, Ringling Museum of Art, the Queens Museum of Art, and the DeYoung Museum, and for over fifteen years taught exhibition planning and design in the graduate museum studies program at NYU.

MARC JACOBS

Marc Jacobs was born in New York City in 1963. After graduating from the High School of Art and Design in 1981, he entered Parson's School of Design. As a design student there, Jacobs was the recipient of some of the school's highest honors, including Design Student of the Year. In 1984 Jacobs designed his first collection with the Marc Jacobs label. The following year, Jacobs received the distinct honor of being the youngest designer ever to be awarded the fashion industry's highest tribute: the CFDA Perry Ellis Award for New Fashion Talent. In 1997, Jacobs became the first creative director for Louis Vuitton, introducing ready-to-wear and accessories to the prestigious luggage house. Over the next sixteen years, his runway collections, shows, and campaigns, along with historic artist collaborations, helped shape the global fashion landscape.

With stores across the globe, Marc Jacobs International now includes ready-to-wear and accessories, a children's line called Little Marc Jacobs, multiple award-winning fragrances, the bookstore Bookmarc, Marc Jacobs Beauty, and most recently Heaven by Marc Jacobs.

His company continues to be committed to giving back to the communities where it has stores and beyond. They have been involved with over a hundred charities worldwide and the ongoing support of many of these charitable projects—as well as new collaborations—continues to be a top priority.

STEFF YOTKA

Steff Yotka is the Global Editorial Director of *i-D*. As an editor and fashion critic in New York, her work has appearedin *Vogue*, *i-D*, *Harper's Bazaar*, and *Business of Fashion*, among other publications. She's a lifelong fan of Anna Sui who had her childhood bedroom painted the exact same shade of purple as Sui's Greene Street store, who crashed Sui's shows in the early 2000s, and who reviewed Sui's collections for *Vogue Runway* from 2017 to 2022.

ACKNOWLEDGMENTS

A special thanks to my dad Paul Sui and brother Eddy Sui for documenting the runway shows through their own eyes.

Ileen Gallagher
Isabel Venero
Abbott Miller
Steven Meisel
Ruk Richards
Kevin Hatt
Raoul Gatchalian
Thomas Lau
Satoshi Saikusa
Spur magazine
Ellen Von Unwerth
Jesse Frohman
Roxanne Lowit
Vanessa Salle
Ken Regan Camera 5
Suzanne Regan
Murray Lerner
Noah Lerner
Laura Wills
Michael Economy
Joan Bedor
Linda Evangelista
Christy Turlington
Sofia Coppola
Marc Jacobs
Steff Yotka
Weatherly Giblin

Thank you to all the amazing friends and models that appear on these pages. Thanks to all the Anna Sui team members and contributors who made these shows happen.

First published in the
United States of America in 2025 by
Rizzoli Electa, A Division of
Rizzoli International Publications, Inc.
49 West 27th Street
New York, NY 10001
www.rizzoliusa.com

Publisher: Charles Miers
Editor: Isabel Venero
Production Manager: Maria Pia Gramaglia
Designer: Abbott Miller, Daniel Varillas, Pentagram

2025 2026 2027 2028 / 10 9 8 7 6 5 4 3 2 1

ISBN: 978-0-8478-4059-5
Library of Congress Control Number on file

Printed in Hong Kong

The authorized representative in the EU for product safety and compliance is Mondadori Libri S.p.A., via Gian Battista Vico 42, Milan, Italy, 20123, www.mondadori.it

Jacket front: Zoe Cassavettes, Roman Coppola, and Sofia Coppola wearing Anna Sui Fall 1994, *Interview* magazine. Photo by Ellen von Unwerth / Trunk
Jacket back: Anna Sui in her studio in 1994. Photo by Jesse Frohman

Photo Credits

Portfolio of backstage photos by Kevin Hatt, pages 2–11.

12: Ellen von Unwerth / Trunk; 17 (top): Stephen Sweet/Shutterstock; 17 (bottom): Ken Regan / Camera 5; 19 (bottom): Patrick McMullan/Patrick McMullan via Getty Images; 24–25: Ted Dayton; 27 (bottom): Jean-Luce Huré/Bridgeman Images; 35: Satoshi Saikusa; 7 (top): Kim Garnick/*The New York Times*; 58–59: Bill Cunningham/*The New York Times*; 60: Rob Watkins/Alamy Stock Photo; 61: MediaMedium/Alamy Stock Photo; 63, 64: Steven Meisel; 66 (top): United Archives GmbH/Alamy Stock Photo; 66 (bottom): ABC/Courtesy Everett Collection; 67 (top): Universal Pictures/ Alamy Stock Photo; 85: Steven Meisel; 86: Allstar Picture Library Limited/ Alamy Stock Photo; 90: Roxanne Lowitt; 97: Satoshi Saikusa; 98: Marc Hom; 99 (top): Satoshi Saikusa; 99 (bottom): Kevin Mazur/WireImage; 102–03: Corina Lecca/*The New York Times* (top left); Steve Sands/Outline (bottom left); Peter Mountain/Miramax Films (right); 115: Dean Alexander, Photo Associates, Inc.; 139: Illustration by Peter Alexander. THE SIMPSONS' © and ™ 1990 20th Television. All rights reserved; 142–43: Steven Meisel; 171: Steven Meisel; 173: Getty; 174–75: Kim Garnick/*The New York Times*; 190: Paramount/Courtesy Everett Collection; 213: Dick Waterman

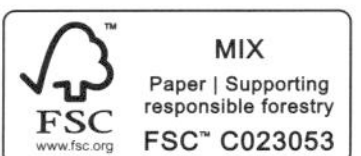